WORKS ISSUED BY
THE HAKLUYT SOCIETY

———

THE HAKLUYT HANDBOOK
VOLUME I

SECOND SERIES
NO. 144

ISSUED FOR 1974

Serenissimæ et potentissimæ Principi
Divæ Elizabethæ Angliæ Franciæ
et Hibernæ Reginæ fidei ortho-
doxæ propugnatrici &c.

Annus iam agitur tertius (Serenissima Regina) ex quo in Collegio vestro ædis Christi Oxoniæ unanimi multorum consensu electus censorio muneri (quod vocant) præfuerim id-est, ut Politicorum Aristotelis libros prælectionibus meis illustrarem, et disputationes politi-cas censura et iudicio meo dirimerem. Consultissimum mihi tum videbatur Interpretes græcos, Latinos veteres Neotericos, politos barbaros, omnes peruoluere, et ANALYSIN in octo Politicorum Aristotelis libros contexere. Tandem aspirante cæptis meis diuina gratia, Opus istud varium multiplex muolutum ad exitus diu optatos perduximus. Quod ipsum quon-am a vestra Maiestate quodammodo profectum esse videtur (cum et olim in Collegio Westmonasteriensi, et postea in florentissima æde Christi Oxoniæ per multos iam annos alumnus vester fuerim, et nunc a Domino Edwardo Staffordio viro ornatissimo et fidelissimo vestro, ad Regem Gallorum Legato in locum Ministri sim accersitus) Serenissimæ Maiestati vestræ opti-mo iure deberi agnosco, vestroque fausto nomini consecratum esse cupio. Et sane huius argumen-ti opera nulli inter omnes Christianos Principes iustius quam vestræ Maiestati conserrari debet, cuius in republica administranda prudentiam et fœlicitatem plusquam humanam, non modo om-nes circum uicini Reges, respublicæ omnes admirantur, et obseruant, sed et Moscouitarum Turcarum Persarum potentissimi Monarchæ obstupefacti adorant. Quamobrem accipies Princeps nobilissime in præstantissimi philosophi præstantissimum opus hanc nostram Analysin natam illam quidem in umbris Academiæ, succesissius horis elucubratam, nequaquam perpolitam ut usu Aulico. Ut autem hanc Analysin non susciperem, non magis me multorum labores perutiles illi quidem et magna laude digni, utinam undequaque absoluti et perfecti, impedire et remorari debuerunt, quam diuinum illud Platonis ingenium et eloquentia pene incredibilis Aristotelem et alios a scriben-do deterruerunt. Multa quidem prædixerunt illi bene: sed et alius fortasse nonnulla ab ipsis prætermissa non male, uel quia posteriores cogitationes plerunque solent esse prudentiores, uel quia non ita difficile est inuentis addere. Ut autem aliis uel mihi aliquando quicquam in mentem ue-niat, cuius tua Maiestas non antea fuerat scientissima, ne sperari quidem ullo modo potuit. Tantú scripto hoc meo saltem beneuolo, si minus integro, iusque omnibus numeris absoluto, obsequium et ob-seruantiam meam testatam et consignatam esse volui. Deus optimus maximus Maiestatem ves-tram, præsidium et decus orbis immortale Ecclesiæ Reipublicæ, literis et literatis, diutissimæ incolu-mem ac sospitem conseruet. Ex æde Christi Oxoniæ, Calendis Septembris Aᵒ Domini 1583.

Maiestati vestræ

Deuotissimus subditus

Richardus Hakluyt
verbi Dei Minister.

Richard Hakluyt's autograph dedicatory letter to Queen Elizabeth, prefixed to his *Analysis* of Aristotle's *Politics*, dated 1 September 1583.

The Hakluyt Handbook

Edited by

D. B. QUINN

VOLUME I

THE HAKLUYT SOCIETY
LONDON
1974

© The Hakluyt Society 1974

Library of Congress Catalogue Card Number: 72–87176

ISBN 0 521 08694 9 vol. 1
0 521 20211 6 vol. 2
0 521 20212 4 set of two vols.

Printed in Great Britain
at the University Printing House, Cambridge
(Brooke Crutchley, University Printer)

Published by the Hakluyt Society
c/o The British Museum
London WCIB 3DG

To the memory of
Raleigh Ashlin Skelton

Contents

VOLUME I

PART ONE
A HAKLUYT PERSPECTIVE

PART TWO

HAKLUYT'S USE OF THE MATERIALS AVAILABLE TO HIM

PART THREE

FROM 1552 TO 1616

VOLUME II

PART FOUR

CONTENTS AND SOURCES OF THE THREE MAJOR WORKS
By A. M. and D. B. QUINN

PART FIVE

HAKLUYT'S BOOKS AND SOURCES

CONTENTS

Preface

The Hakluyt handbook is intended to assist students of the greatest English editor of travel narratives to find their way amongst his works and compilations and in the modern literature which has grown up around them. The Hakluyt Society has indeed, since its foundation in 1846, endeavoured to honour Richard Hakluyt the younger, 1552–1616, whose name it has borne and whose example it has attempted to follow, and has made a continuous effort to add to the knowledge of his life and achievements. Yet, though its publications are nearing the 300th volume, it has never provided any comprehensive guide to what he has done. The idea of the Hakluyt handbook developed originally in conversations between the late Dr R. A. Skelton, then honorary secretary of the Society, and Professor D. B. Quinn some years ago. The idea was taken up by the Council of the Hakluyt Society who set up a committee to work on the project. Besides the two persons mentioned, Dr E. S. de Beer, Mr G. R. Crone, Mr G. P. B. Naish, Dr Helen Wallis, Professor E. M. J. Campbell and Dr Terence Armstrong all contributed valuable advice and assistance, and there was gradually built up a plan and a body of contributors to carry it into effect. On Dr Skelton's retirement from the honorary secretaryship of the Society in 1966, Dr Armstrong identified himself closely with the project and has given much help in bringing it to a conclusion. Dr Skelton undertook to organize the bibliographical side of the project, as well as to contribute a section on maps. Unfortunately, he was diverted by other tasks and the bibliographical work had not proceeded far at the time of his death in December 1970 though his map contribution had been delivered. Professor Quinn, after an interval, was able to take up this task, but the long delays which members and contri butors have borne, though regrettable, were inevitable in the circumstances.

The handbook is intended to serve several distinct purposes. The first part is a conspectus of modern views on the significance of various aspects of Hakluyt's work. It is in part intended as a stimulus to further study in these and other fields associated with Hakluyt's activities. In this section the Society is fortunate to have dad the co-operation of Emeritus Professor George B. Parks, Queen's College, New York, the doyen of Hakluyt studies, Professors J. H. Parry and Francis M. Rogers, both of Harvard University, Mr G. R. Crone, Mr G. P. B. Naish, National Maritime Museum, Dr R. A. Skelton, Professor Quinn, University of Liverpool, Mr G. V. Scammell, Pembroke College, Cambridge, Professor N. E. Osselton, University of Leiden, Dr Helen Wallis, British Museum and Mr Colin R. Steele, Bodleian Library.

The second part of the volume is devoted to the first study so far made of the extent to which Hakluyt used fully and success-fully the materials available to him at the time, and how far he failed to exploit useful sources. For this we were able to recruit a team of regional specialists, Professor Donald Lach, University of Chicago, Professor Beckingham, Professor Quinn and Dr Terence Armstrong, Mr Michael Strachan, Mr W. E. D. Allen, Dr Helen Wallis, Dr K. R. Andrews, University of Hull, Dr P. E. H. Hair, University of Liverpool, Dr G. D. Ramsay, St Edmund Hall, Oxford, Mr J. S. G. Simmons, All Souls College.

Part III is a guide to the events of Hakluyt's life. Professor G. B. Parks wrote the standard life, *Richard Hakluyt and the English voyages*, as far back as 1928 and equipped it with a full chronology. It was reprinted with some addenda in 1961. The late Professor Eva G. R. Taylor added much of the documentation in her *Original writings and correspondence of the two Richard Hakluyts*, which the Society published in two volumes in 1935. The present chronology has been compiled by Professor Quinn largely from these sources, but incorporates new information which has sub-sequently become available and brings up to date earlier references. We are still far from having had the last word on Hakluyt's biography and it is to be hoped that in a second edition of this book, whenever that will be needed, research will disclose fresh information on aspects of his life and works, and will throw new light on his achievements and influence.

Parts IV and V, which occupy the second volume, are concerned with the books for which Hakluyt was in one way or another responsible. Details are given of the bibliographical problems and surviving copies of Hakluyt's major works. Professor Loren E. Pennington, Kansas State Teachers College, Emporia, Kansas, has written a valuable essay on the secondary Hakluyt literature. An attempt is also made to trace Hakluyt's sources in detail in his three major compilations. Much of the work which Dr Skelton had planned he was unable to complete, but it has been possible to build on foundations he had laid. Mr C. E. Armstrong, New York, has come to the help of the Society by an extensive revision for the handbook of work he had published on *Principal navigations* (1598–1600) in 1955. Professor Quinn and Mrs Alison Quinn have put together such existing data as there are, and have carried the bibliographical work forward in certain respects. It must be emphasized, however, that all the contributors to this section wish to stress that their work is exploratory, rather than definitive: it represents most of what is known, but by no means all that can be discovered. The reprinting of the list of works published by the Society will be useful for reference, even though it is bound by its nature rapidly to go out of date. We are indebted to Mr E. L. C. Mullins and the Royal Historical Society for help in its presentation.

It is inevitable that there should be a good deal of overlapping between the various parts of the book, but we believe that the surviving materials can best be seen in varying contexts and have not tried to impose a uniform pattern of treatment. The indexes, which we owe to Mrs Alison Quinn, bring out, we hope, the nature of the connections between them.

The Society has in the course of the writing and compilation of these volumes contracted many obligations to individuals and institutions all over the world. Our thanks, even where it has not been possible to be specific, are given with full appreciation of the goodwill and co-operation we have everywhere encountered.

April 1972   C. F. BECKINGHAM
President

Illustrations

VOLUME I

VOLUME II

Acknowledgements

The Hakluyt Society, Professor Quinn and the contributors to *The Hakluyt handbook* are grateful to the following for granting permission to reproduce material in their possession: to the trustees of the British Museum for the frontispiece and for illustrations 1 to 6, 9, 10, 13 to 15, 18 to 25, 28 to 32, 34, 35, 37 to 47, 49, 50, 52 to 54; to the Bodleian Library, Oxford, for illustrations 12 and 16; to the Provost and Fellows of King's College, Cambridge, for illustration 27; to the Honourable Society of the Inner Temple for illustration 17; to the Henry Huntington Library, San Marino, California, for illustrations 7 and 8; to the Virginia Historical Society for illustration 28; to the Manuscript Division, The New York Public Library, Astor, Lenox and Tilden Foundations, for illustration 11; and to the Rare Book Division, The New York Public Library, Astor, Lenox and Tilden Foundations, for illustrations 36, 48 and 51.

Usages and abbreviations

'u' and 'v', 'i' and 'j' have been retained in their contemporary usage except for citations of the titles of Hakluyt's *Divers voyages* (1582), *Principall navigations* (1589), and *Principal navigations* (1598–1600).

English books are published in London unless otherwise stated.

References to Hakluyt's works are to the original editions throughout. For convenience of reference a concordance of *Principal navigations* (1598–1600) with *Principal navigations* (1903–5) is given on pp. xxv–xxvi.

Arber, *Transcript*. Edward Arber, ed., *A transcript of the registers of the Company of Stationers of London, 1554–1640*, 5 vols. (1875–94)

Atkinson. G. Atkinson, *La littérature géographique française de la renaissance* (Paris, 1927). *Supplément* (1936)

B.M. British Museum (now Reference Division, British Library)

B.S.A. Bibliographical Society of America

DNB. *Dictionary of national biography*

DV. Richard Hakluyt, *Divers voyages touching the discoverie of America* (1582)

Lumley [with a number]. *The Lumley library. The catalogue of 1609*, edited by Sears Jayne and Francis R. Johnson (1956)

N.H.L. Naval Historical Library (formerly Admiralty Library)

N.R.S. Navy Records Society

O.E.D. Oxford English dictionary

Parks, *Hakluyt*. George Bruner Parks, *Richard Hakluyt and the English voyages* (New York, 1928; reissued with corrections 1961)

PN (1589). Richard Hakluyt, *Principall navigations* (1589)

PN (1598–1600 & 1599–1600). Richard Hakluyt, *Principal navigations* (1598–1600 and 1599–1600)

P.R.O. Public Record Office

Quinn, *Gilbert*. D. B. Quinn, ed., *The voyages and colonising enterprises of Sir Humphrey Gilbert*, 2 vols. (1940)

Quinn, *Richard Hakluyt editor*. D. B. Quinn, *Richard Hakluyt editor*, introductory to facsimiles of *Divers voyages* (1582) and *A shorte and briefe narration of the two navigations to Newe Fraunce* (1580), 2 vols. (Amsterdam, 1967)

Quinn, *Roanoke voyages*. D. B. Quinn, ed., *The Roanoke voyages, 1584–90*, 2 vols. (Cambridge, 1955)

Quinn and Cheshire, *Parmenius*. D. B. Quinn and N. M. Cheshire, *The new found land of Stephen Parmenius* (Toronto, 1972)

Quinn and Skelton, edd., *PN (1589)* (1965). D. B. Quinn and R. A. Skelton, edd., Richard Hakluyt, *Principall navigations (1589)*, 2 vols. (Cambridge, 1965)

S.T.C. *Short-title catalogue of English books, 1476–1640*, edd. A. W. Pollard and G. R. Redgrave (1926)

Taylor, *Hakluyts*. E. G. R. Taylor, ed., *The original writings and correspondence of the two Richard Hakluyts*, 2 vols. (1935)

Concordance between *Principal navigations* (3 vols. 1598–60) and
Principal navigations (12 vols. 1903–5)

I (1598)	I (1903)
The Epistle Dedicatorie	
Sig. *2–3v	pages xxxi–xxxviii
A preface to the Reader	
Sig. 4–**2v	pages xxxix–lix
Panegyrick verses	
Sig. **3–3v	pages lx–lxii
Pages 1–144	pages 1–355
	II (1903)
Pages 144–338	pages 1–487
	III (1903)
Pages 338–514	pages 1–482
	IV (1904)
Pages 515–619	pages 1–268

II (1599)	I (1903)
Epistle Dedicatorie	
Sig. *2–4v	pages lxiii–lxxiii
	IV (1904)
Part i, 1–72	pages 269–457
	V (1904)
Part i, 72–268	pages 1–512
	VI (1904)
Part i, 268–312	pages 1–118
	VI (1904)
Part ii, 1–155	pages 119–527
	VII (1904)
Part ii, 155–203	pages 1–132

III (1600)	I (1903)
Epistle Dedicatorie	
Sig. A2–3v	pages lxxiv–lxxx
	VII (1904)
Pages 1–128	pages 133–465

Concordance between *Principal navigations* (3 vols. 1598–60) and
Principal navigations (12 vols. 1903–5) (*cont.*)

PART ONE

A HAKLUYT PERSPECTIVE

1

Hakluyt's view of British history

J. H. PARRY

The Elizabethans wrote history as well as making it. The stately progression of the chronicles – Hall, Holinshed, Stow, Speed, Camden – is witness of the interest of sixteenth-century Englishmen in England's past. Chronicles, to be sure, are not history as a modern historian understands it. Most chroniclers were not concerned to investigate, establish or explain, but merely to record. In writing of their own times, they noted diligently those happenings which to them seemed interesting or strange. Marriages and accessions, battles and embassies, comets and monstrous births – nothing came amiss. In writing of the past, they took on trust the tales related by their predecessors, and so, in Aubrey's words, 'stitched up for us our English history', without much attempt to distinguish between the significant and the trivial, between the plausible and the unlikely.

This is not to say that the chroniclers lacked all sense of history. Camden, whose *Annales* is by far the best of its kind, certainly did not. Camden used the same conventional year-by-year form as his predecessors; like them he was miscellaneous in his choice of topics and sometimes – though apologetically – he made mention of monsters. On the other hand, he used, and often cited, documentary sources, and tried to set events in their proper perspective. In his pages we can trace the connecting threads of policy and purpose, cause and result; we can see chronicle approximating history. Nor can it be said that the Elizabethan chroniclers – least of all Camden – were wholly random and arbitrary in their choice of events to be recorded. There was a principle of selection: that of national patriotism. The chroniclers wrote not only to inform and amuse, but also to celebrate, to extol. The England of Elizabeth's later years was orderly and prosperous, internationally respected, fortunate in arms, especially by sea. Englishmen liked

3

to brag about English successes, with all the strident boastfulness of the newly arrived; but they felt also the anxieties of the newly arrived. They wanted reassurance that the glories of their own time were not mere sudden and temporary accidents of fortune. The chroniclers, dipping selectively into the past, provided a pedigree of glory. While Camden exhausted his ingenuity in eulogy of the Queen, Stow, Speed and the rest performed a complementary service. If Elizabeth cherished the Navy, they declared, so had her father done, in his day. If Englishmen rightly rejoiced in the defeat of the Armada, so should their bosoms swell with ancestral pride when they read of Agincourt.

Camden, representing the culmination of a long tradition of chronicle making, was Hakluyt's contemporary and friend. The two had in common an intense patriotism, loyalty to the Protestant establishment, scholarly inclinations, and a conservative cast of mind, which impelled them to associate present successes with past precedents. Presumably they shared a common attitude towards the history of their own country. On Hakluyt's part, however, this attitude was never made explicit. Unlike Camden, Hakluyt was not a writer of history. He was a geographer, a propagandist for overseas adventure, a collector and editor of first-hand narratives of travel. He handled his material with the care and judgement of a good historian, but made no attempt to compact it as continuous narrative, preferring to let his sources speak for themselves. His views on British history, or any history, have to be pieced together from his dedications and prefaces, and inferred from his choice of documents.

Hakluyt believed that the quickest and surest way to increase the power and wealth of England lay in overseas trade, especially in the East, and ('seeing we are so farre from want of people') in settlement, especially settlement in some part of America not occupied by Spain. One of his principal objects in ferreting out and publishing narratives of voyages, was to make available the best and latest information on trades and places which Englishmen might profitably exploit. He rightly thought that original accounts, published in full, would be more reliable than any abstract or compilation. The supply of useful information, however, was not his only object. There was an injustice to be put right. In France, wrote Hakluyt, dedicating the *Principall naviga-tions* to Walsingham in 1589, 'I both heard in speech, and read' in books other nations miraculously extolled for their discoueries and notable enterprises by sea, but the English of all others for their sluggish security, and continuall neglect of the like attempts especially in so long and happy a time of peace, either ignomin-iously reported, or exceedingly condemned.' Of the Englishmen of Hakluyt's own day, such criticism was patently unjust:

> in this most famous and peerlesse gouernement of her most excellent Maiesty, her subiects through the speciall assistance, and blessing of God, in searching the most opposite corners and quarters of the world, and to speake plainly, in compassing the vaste globe of the earth more then once, haue excelled all the nations and people of the earth. For . . . who euer heard of Englishmen at Goa before now ? what English shippes did heeretofore euer anker in the mighty riuer of Plate ? passe and repasse the vnpassable (in former opinion) straight of Magellan, range along the coast of Chili, Peru, and all the backside of Noua Hispania, further then any Christian euer passed. . . & last of al returne home most richly laden with the commodities of China, as the subiects of this now florishing monarchy haue done ?

So Hakluyt set out to publish, in orderly geographical and chronological sequence, 'the maritime record of our own men'.

Not merely, however, 'our own men' in his own time, but always, time out of mind. Repeatedly Hakluyt reflected the hankering of his contemporaries for continuity and ancient precedent. 'It can not be denied, but as in all former ages, they haue bene men full of actiuity, stirrers abroad, and searchers of the remote parts of the world.' Hakluyt tried valiantly to marshal evidence in support of this assertion, but with very limited success, at least for 'ages' before that of Henry VII and the Cabots. Mandeville's *Travels* bulks large in the *Principall navigations*. There is a note by John Dee on Nicholas of Lynn and his mysterious treatise on the Arctic, the *Inventio Fortunata*. Two apocryphal voyages of discovery are mentioned briefly: Macham's voyage to Madeira, and the twelfth-century discovery of America by Madoc ap Owain Gwynnedd. The rest is chiefly anecdotes about crusaders, or about kings – Arthur and Malgo, Edgar and Alfred

– who were said in one way or another to have encouraged maritime adventure. Hakluyt could not, of course, confine him⁄self here – as he almost always did in dealing with sixteenth⁄century travels – to *ipsissima verba*. Most of this early material came from medieval chronicles, either directly or through sixteenth⁄century compilers. What Hakluyt really thought about the historicity of Giraldus Cambrensis or Geoffrey of Monmouth is hard to say. He showed no obvious scepticism; he had nothing else to go on, and presumably he gave them the benefit of the doubt. He cited Madoc's alleged voyage, along with Cabot's real ones, in the 'Discourse of Western Planting', as precedent and justification for English activities in America. One would like to believe in Madoc. It may be noted in passing that Hakluyt rarely used the word British, and when he did, he meant either *ancient* British, or else English plus Welsh. He was a Herefordshire man, and the Welsh were close kin. Madoc, if not precisely an Englishman, was as good as one for Hakluyt. Not so the Irish. Their considerable early sea⁄going exploits are not mentioned. Ireland was a colony by conquest. In his dedication of the trans⁄lated Laudonnière, Hakluyt even likened Strongbow's Irish plantation to the settlements of the Portuguese captains⁄donatary in Brazil.

The *Principal navigations* of 1598–1600 is a much bigger book than that of 1589. Where the 'record of our own men' was deficient, Hakluyt supplemented it from the records of foreigners, and so produced a work much more complete, and more efficient for his practical purposes, than its predecessor. In subtle ways, also, the later version reveals changes in Hakluyt's feelings about his own country's history. The note of patriotism is still sounded in dedications and prefaces, but less stridently, as befitted an England stronger, more confident and more secure; though it is true that some accounts, such as that of Fenton's 'troublesome voyage', which reflect small credit on English leadership, are drastically cut. The antiquity and continuity of English maritime tradition are still emphasized; indeed the medieval sources, collected with Camden's help, are much increased in number; but they are more critically selected. Mandeville's *Travels* – attractive but bogus – is omitted. With it disappears a more modern tall story, Ingram's account of his walk from Mexico to Nova Scotia. So the historian's judgement tempered the patriot's enthusiasm.

The *Principal navigations* has been called the prose epic of the modern English nation, and with reason; but it is an epic of struggle not only – not even primarily – against human enemies, but against the sea, against distance, against hunger and thirst and sickness. It is a source collection for maritime, not merely naval, history. This is the quality which gives special distinction to Hakluyt's patriotism. Foreigners, including hostile foreigners, who had made great voyages, are given their due. Hakluyt never belittles valiant achievement or depreciates distinguished skill. Even when writing of the arch-enemy, the Spaniard, he can be judicious, even appreciative. He admiringly describes Spanish institutions and customs which he wants his countrymen to imitate – the professional training of navigators, for instance. There are atrocity stories, derived chiefly from Las Casas, in the 'Discourse', but few in the *Principal navigations*. Hakluyt can exult over the Spanish squadron in the Narrow Seas, when Lord Charles Howard 'enforced them to stoope gallant and to vaile their bonets for the Queene'; but in recording the greatest English victory of his time, his mood is one of awed thankfulness, rather than boasting or vindictive pride: 'But why should I presume to call it our vanquishing when as the greatest part of them escaped us, and were onely by Gods outstretched arme overwhelmed in the Seas, dashed in pieces against the Rockes, and made fearfull spectacles and examples of his judgements unto all Christendome?' Hakluyt was not only a patriotic, conscientious and on the whole critical historian; he was a magnanimous one.

2

Richard Hakluyt, geographer

G. R. CRONE

Hakluyt's own account of his induction to geography by his cousin, Richard Hakluyt of the Middle Temple, some time before 1570, is justifiably famous and as often quoted.[1] The elder man let him see 'certeine bookes of Cosmographie' open on his table and 'a vniuersall Mappe' (a world map). When the young man displayed some curiosity about the latter, his cousin pointed out to him various physical features ('all the knowen Seas, Gulfs, Bayes, Straights, Capes, Riuers') and the political geography ('Empires, Kingdomes, Dukedoms, and Territories of ech part'), and the economic geography of the various regions ('with declaration also of their speciall commodities, & particular wants, which by the benefit of traffike, & entercourse of merchants, are plentifully supplied'). He reinforced his instruction from scripture, citing the Psalmist (Psalms cvii. 23, 24) 'that they which go downe to the sea in ships, and occupy by the great waters, they see the works of the Lord, and his woonders in the deepe'. Hakluyt says these words 'tooke in me so deepe an impression, that I constantly resolued, if euer I were preferred to the Vniuersity . . . I would by Gods assistance prosecute that knowledge and kinde of litera⁄ture'. The young Richard was certainly fortunate in having his interest aroused at such an impressionable age by an enthusiastic and instructed tutor, and one moreover versed in practical affairs.

When Hakluyt went to Oxford, he goes on to tell us that after he had furthered his routine studies he went on to study geography as he conceived it: 'I fell to my intended course, and by degrees read ouer whatsoeuer printed or written discoueries and voyages I found extant either in the Greeke, Latine, Italian, Spanish, Portugall, French, or English languages.' In this claim to linguistic breadth Hakluyt is undoubtedly accurate about his attainments

---

[1] *PN* (1589), sig. *2.

in 1589, but scarcely of when he graduated B.A. in 1574, but the range of his reading in geographical literature was certainly very wide, though we wonder how he found so many geographical books in the Oxford of his time: he may have done much of his reading on visits to his cousin in London.

He then claimed to have expounded his subject at Oxford: 'in my publike lectures [I] was the first, that produced and shewed both the olde imperfectly composed, and the new lately reformed Mappes, Globes, Spheares, and other instruments of this Art for demonstration in the common schooles, to the singular pleasure, and generall contentment of my auditory.' Mr J. N. L. Baker has shown he was not the first to engage in college teaching of geography, and that he had other contemporaries who taught undergraduates. He suggests that Hakluyt gave these discourses to a college audience, either when he was an undergraduate, or between taking his B.A. and his M.A.[1] Others have thought that he delivered them, after taking his M.A. in 1577, to a university audience. Perhaps they were an informal and personal venture, in an attempt to bring geographical teaching outside the walls of the colleges.

In the information he has given us he indicated the main types of sources available to contemporary geographers, but he does not specify particular works which he had in mind. The cosmographical treatises, compiled from classical authors, and illustrated by the old tripartite world diagram, had been displaced quite early in the sixteenth century by improved works such as Peter Apian's *Cosmographicus liber* (1524), the 1529 and subsequent editions being put out by Gemma Frisius.[2] Several editions of Ptolemy's *Geographia* containing modern maps were available also. Of these the most significant for the overseas discoveries were the Strasbourg edition of 1513, with modern maps attributed to Martin Waldseemüller, and the editions by Sebastian Münster at Basel in 1540 and later.[3] A large compilation by Sebastian

[1] J. N. L. Baker, *The history of geography* (1963), pp. 14–19, 89–90.
[2] For a brief note see L. Bagrow and R. A. Skelton, *History of cartography* (1964), pp. 130, 228–9.
[3] See G. R. Crone, *Maps and their makers* (4th ed., 1968), pp. 71–2; Bagrow and Skelton, *History of cartography* (1964), pp. 150–2; V. Hantzch, *Sebastian Münster* (Leipzig, 1898).

Münster, which was very popular, was his *Cosmographia* (Basel, 1544). This, containing the new maps from his edition of Ptolemy, was revised and enlarged by him in 1550.

To these should be added treatises on the use of the globes by Gemma Frisius, Mercator and others. As to the globes themselves, Gemma Frisius and Mercator had produced terrestrial and celestial pairs, respectively, in 1539 and 1541. The 'vniuersall Mappe' which he saw before 1570 might have been Sebastian Cabot's large world map of 1544, of which a second edition was published in England in 1548 or 1549: if the occasion was as late as 1569 it could have been the celebrated Mercator world map of that year. The 'new lately reformed Mappes' which he used at Oxford were probably those included in Ortelius' still fairly recent *Theatrum orbis terrarum* (Antwerp, 1570), though there were a number of important Mercator maps, not yet bound into atlas form, already in circulation which he may have seen. One thing is certain: among his general cosmographies, atlases and maps none of any significance was the work of an Englishman. Hakluyt, in fact, began his work at the moment when continental geographers and cartographers were far ahead of Englishmen, and it was Hakluyt who by his constant endeavour to keep in touch with the best work being done abroad, brought the new geography fully to the attention of his contemporaries. The position had changed considerably by the end of the century: with men like Robert Hues writing on the use of globes, Edward Wright on mathematical geography, Thomas Hood on instrument design, George Best and Giles Fletcher on the foreign scene, a strong English school of men who might well be called geographers was flourishing.

What statesmen and men of affairs required were reliable facts about the new discoveries and these Hakluyt set himself to supply in the interests both of policy and action. His approach to geography is therefore an empirical one. He was no theorist and he renounced all desire to state his geographical notions explicitly and to add to 'those wearie volumes bearing the titles of vniuersall Cosmographie . . . most vntruly and vnprofitablie ramassed and hurled together'.[1] This attitude is reflected in George Best's

---

[1] *PN* (1589), sig. *3v.

reference to the English voyagers in his dissertation on the habit⸗
able globe: 'I mention these voyages of our Englishemenne, not
so muche to proue that Torrida Zona may be, and is inhabited,
as to shew their readynesse in attempting long and dangerous
Nauigations.'[1]

There is little doubt that Hakluyt agreed with Richard Willes
in his assertion that 'the fyrste principle and chiefe grounde in all
Geographie, as great Ptolome sayth, is the historie of trauel, that
is, reportes made by trauaylers skylfull in Geometrie & Astro⸗
nomie, of al suche thinges in their iourney as to Geographie do
belong'.[2] This passage occurs in Willes' treatise on the North⸗
west Passage and is reprinted in *Principal navigations*.[3]

The sources from which Hakluyt obtained 'the chiefe grounde
in all Geographie' are analysed in other sections: his *Principall
navigations* and the enlarged edition which followed were produced,
as he claimed, with the help of 'Geographie and Chronology
(which I may call the Sunne and the Moone, the right eye and
the left of all history)', that is to say that Hakluyt's interests were
concentrated in time and place. He was thus one of the great
collectors of raw material from which modern geography was
later to develop, rather than an exponent of geographical method.
There are, indeed, few formal geographical statements in *Principal
navigations* outside the personal narrative already cited. Professor
E. G. R. Taylor has written that in his time 'the unity of nature
had yet to be recognized, and the collection of scientific material
for its own sake, or for the elucidation of some principle of
causation, had not yet begun'.[4]

If we take one short section, entitled 'A briefe description of
Affrike',[5] we find that it simply locates the kingdoms, their sub⸗
divisions and the chief cities, and comments briefly on the
peoples and their characteristics and the kind of trade offered

[1] G. Best, *A true discourse of the late voyages of discouerie; for finding a passage to Cathaya* (1578), sig. e ii r–v.
[2] R. Willes, *The historie of trauell* (1577), sig. Hh i.
[3] *PN* (1589), pp. 612–13; III (1600), 26.
[4] E. G. R. Taylor, *Later Tudor and early Stuart geography, 1583–1650* (1934), p. 21.
[5] *PN* (1589), pp. 84–5; II (1599), ii, 10–11.

by them. The main emphasis on physical features is on deserts and mountains, and only two rivers, the Nile and the Niger, are mentioned. Most of the colour is provided by the human geography; for example, 'In the said regions [of Guinea] are no cities, but onely certaine lowe cottages made of boughes of trees, plastered with chauke, and couered with strawe. In these regions are also very great deserts.' The description concludes with a piece of medieval legend on the Earthly Paradise: 'And some say that there are the trees of the Sunne and Moone, whereof the antiquitie maketh mention: yet that none can passe thither, by reason of great desarts of a hundred dayes iourney.' There is, indeed, little in the description which could not be shown better on a map, and it may perhaps have been inserted as a substitute for one. Hakluyt had earlier admitted that 'it would bee expected as necessarie, that the descriptions of so many parts of the world would farre more easily be conceiued of the Readers, by adding Geographicall, and Hydrographicall tables thereunto',[1] but his single general map in 1589 was not a satisfactory one, and if he did better in the second edition he still failed to give the regional maps which Purchas was later to supply in his *Pilgrimes*.[2]

Another small piece of a geographical character is that concerning monsoons, headed 'The times or seasonable windes called monsons, wherein the ships depart from place to place in the East Indies'.[3] Of Goa it is related that:

> the winter there beginneth the 15. of May with very great raine, & so continueth till the 1. of August, so that during that space, no ship can passe ouer ye bar of Goa, because through the continual shoures of raine all the sands ioyne together neere vnto a mountaine called Oghane, & all these sands being ioyned together, runne into the shoales of the barre and port of Goa, and can haue no other issue . . . but at the 10. of August it openeth by reason of the raine which ceaseth, and the sea doeth then scoure the sands away againe.

On such grounds it can be said that Hakluyt was at least an exponent of applied geography, and this attitude can be traced also in the various discussions of the northeastern trade route

[1] *Idem*, sig. *4v.   [2] See pp. 66–7.   [3] *PN* (1589), p. 219.

which it was hoped to establish. In the instructions to the expeditions, the advantages of islands as bases are stressed; Arthur Pet
and Charles Jackman, for example, are bidden to note:

> the Islands, whether they be hie land or low land, mountaine, or flat,
> grauelly, clay, chalkie, or of what soile, woody or not woody, with springs
> and riuers or not, and what wilde beasts they haue in the same. And
> whether there seeme to be in the same apt matter to build withall, as stone
> free or rough, and stone to make lime withall, and wood or coale to burne
> the same withall. To note the goodnesse or the badnesse of the hauens and
> harborowes in the Islands...

a statement of the necessities required for the building of a trading
post – not, perhaps, very profound but to the point.[1]

There are of course many passages in the narratives of greater
profundity geographically, a case in point being Giles Fletcher's
description of Russia.[2] He writes vividly of the benefit of the heavy
snow cover; how it protects the vegetation from the severe cold in
the early months of the year, and the early and lush growth
which follows the thaw, and linking this to the annual migration
of the Tatars who followed the retreating winter northwards with
their flocks enjoying the first growth and then swung south again
to benefit from the second growth. Though there is no direct
evidence, it is probable that Hakluyt appreciated the significance
of this phenomenon, for as can be seen in the sections on his
favourite North American themes which follow, he was interested in the classical association of climate with latitude, and the
evidence which the pioneers were gathering to show that the
correlation was not so close as antiquity had maintained. From
Anthony Parkhurst on the apparent anomaly of the Labrador
climate, the Hakluyts learnt that 'this colde commeth by an
accidentall meanes, as by the Ice that commeth fleeting from the
North partes of the worlde, and not by the situation of the
countrey, or nature of the Climate'.[3] It is then fair to say that,
within the limits of the subject as understood by his contem-

---

[1] *PN* (1589), p. 461; these instructions were by the elder Hakluyt.
[2] G. Fletcher, *Of the Russe common wealth* (1590); brief summary in *PN* (1589),
pp. 502–3; I (1598), 474.
[3] *PN* (1589), p. 675.

poraries, Richard Hakluyt was a geographer. His interest was primarily in people and their actions, in the geographical environment as the setting in which they voyaged, explored, and developed the resources bestowed upon man by his Creator. Those best qualified to assist his country's statesmen in establishing new trades and colonies abroad were not the classical cosmographers but those who had adventured there in the past and those presently engaged in blazing new trails across the world. What inspires the pages of *The principal navigations* is the exhilaration of newlyrevealed space. We can feel this when he says that he believes no seas are now unnavigable or land uninhabitable, so that this leaves the earth's surface open wide to Englishmen.

3
Hakluyt and the economic thought of his time

G. V. SCAMMELL

For those who had eyes to see – and there were many perversely blinded by 'opinion of their owne' – it was clear, argued Hakluyt in 1584, that England and her economy were in a desperate plight. The message has a familiar ring. Hard times had produced, for the first time in European history, acute and original discussion of economic phenomena. The middle decades of the century saw analyses of inflation from Azpilcueta in Spain and Bodin in France, and an admirable explanation of the many and varied merits of treasure from the author of the *Discourse of the common weal of this realm of England*. Hakluyt never aspired to such heights. By temperament and training he was a man of practical ability and industry rather than one drawn to what Dr Johnson described in a famous sally as the 'exercise of invention'. Economic assumptions are fundamental to his colonial theories, but they are simply the assumptions of current orthodoxy.

The crux of the matter, as he saw it, was that there was no outlet for the woollen cloth that was England's major product.[1] Wherever we might expect to trade there were difficulties. French taxation, for instance, was high, and in any case that ungrateful nation complained of the quality of English goods and was fostering a native industry. Worst of all we had fallen into an unwholesome dependence on Spain, a country whose religion and politics were of the most undesirable order, for the oils and dyes used in cloth-making. And if this were not in itself bad enough, Spain and her empire were increasing their own wool production. It

[1] The following summary of Hakluyt's views is from the 'Discourse of Western Planting', edited by Professor E. G. R. Taylor in her *Original writings and correspondence of the two Richard Hakluyts*, II (1935), 213–326.

was her deliberate intention to ruin England, and nothing could have been easier since she controlled access to many of our markets actual and potential, was the prime producer of vital raw materials, and had a constant hostage in English shipping – 'halfe of our nauye' – loading in Spanish ports.

The fundamental problem therefore was how to give England the strength to break Spain. Our basic weakness was that we had too many people doing too little. It was not that the country was over-populated, but that its population was ill-deployed: 'lustie youthes . . . be turned to no profitable vse'; and where there was unemployment there was disorder and rebellion. What was needed was some way of providing work; some outlet for all this talent and energy. The answer, as Iberian experience so clearly showed, was colonization. For here were two impoverished countries which in founding empires had 'sett (all) on worke'.

A colony in North America would bring employment 'for all sortes and states', from the halt and the lame to cosmographers, hydrographers, astronomers, historiographers and men of parts overthrown by youthful and other indiscretions. Above all it would solve the crisis in textiles by opening up a market of limitless opportunities, free from all the snares and delusions of the European trades. Instead of our cloth being 'finished' abroad that for the New World would of necessity be entirely home pro-duced. Moreover, with any luck, the colony would supply what we were now getting from Spain, together with other raw materials which, having been 'wroughte by a wonderfull multi-tude of poor subiectes', could then be re-exported. And so perhaps as many as 100,000 – 'beside sailers and suche as shalbe seated in those westerne discouered contries' – would find work.

Nor, since miracles never come singly, would this be all. Colonial produce, acquired from the innocent natives at the cost of a few trinkets, would be cheap, and certainly cheaper than what was to be had in Europe, where taxation and other hazards forced up prices. The enervating drain abroad of bullion in 'the pur-chasinge of forreine commodities in so great a masse at so excessiue prices' would thus end. The capital required in trade would fall; merchants need no longer borrow; prices would drop.

Indeed the prospects were boundless. As the colony grew there would be a steady demand for shipping, and so English maritime strength would increase – more ships, bigger ships, better seamen.

Thus regenerated England could destroy all competition. With full employment population would rise 'For when people knowe howe to lyue, and howe to maynetayne and feede their wyues and children they will not abstaine from mariage as nowe they do'.[1] We should become stronger whilst foreigners would be reduced to penury. And so it would be, and this is the heart of his argument, that we could break Spain. It was the treasure of the Americas that had converted her – poor, barren, 'hardly able to susteine [her] inhabitaunts' – to such a formidable power; which underlay all Europe's troubles; and which could well mean the end, 'the unreuocable annoy', of England. But stop this flow of bullion and Spain was ruined.

There was little in all this that was new. Well before Spain replaced France in popular estimation as England's main enemy there were many who had seen that the nature and basis of her power – a long sea route down Channel to the wealth of the Habsburg patrimony in the Low Countries, a longer one across the Atlantic to the gold and silver of the Americas – and her inadequacies at sea made her a particularly attractive prey. AngloSpanish trade was in difficulties from the 1530s. Catholic Spain, embattled with heretics and infidels, increasingly intolerant, looked with growing suspicion on merchants and seamen from Protestant England. There were recriminations and reprisals, and by the 1540s Spanish merchants were vainly urging that something be done about the privateers who blocked the Channel. Not that there was at this date an irreconcilable antagonism between England and Spain. Far from it. Nevertheless from the 1540s onwards there was a powerful, and with the passage of time increasingly influential body of opinion, to whom Spain was the enemy and Spanish wealth the prize. It was in these years that

---

[1] This is not a general theory of marriage and fertility, and is not developed. But it is an observation of the greatest interest, and certainly plausible, even if difficult to reconcile with what is at present known of population growth in the late sixteenth century. But the whole problem of the relationship between populations and their livelihood is only now being investigated.

there first appear schemes, sanguine enough it is true, to seize Spanish treasure at sea or even to control its sources. A large-scale attack on the bullion ships was planned in 1533.[1] The radical and ambitious Northumberland was involved in a project of sorts to occupy Peru in 1553. Some years later Mildmay was blatantly in-quiring about the wealth and defences of the Americas, and by 1570 there were plans for a settlement in the 'Kingdom of Magellanes' as a base against Peru and John Hawkins was arguing that Spain could be crippled by the disruption of the treasure shipments.[2]

The rest of Hakluyt's views had even lengthier pedigrees. No other English product had such demand abroad as woollen cloth, and a concern for the well-being of textiles was almost as old as the industry itself. It was particularly lively in the sixteenth century, the first half of which saw a rapid expansion in exports and the second half a series of crises. By modern standards the labour force in textiles was minute – and it certainly did not, as Spes confidently informed Philip II, comprise the 'greater number of the people'.[3] But it was, in part at least, a true proletariate, having, as was said in 1565, 'no other living but by spinning, weaving and making of cloths'.[4] If the industry ran into trouble it starved, and as the history of medieval Europe showed, none could fight more bitterly for the right to live than textile workers. Industrial depression was therefore equated with disorders or worse, as for instance by the author of the *Discourse of the common weal . . . of England* in 1549.[5] His reasoning is echoed by publicists and statesmen: laconically by Burghley, who in 1579 wrote 'by lack of vent tumults will follow in clothyng countreys'; epigram-matically by the elder Hakluyt who condemned (1582) 'idlenesse the mother of most mischiefs'.[6]

Thus to maintain order peasant discontents had to be allayed,

---

[1] See J. Gibbs, 'Richard Cooper and the Spanish plate fleet of 1533', *University of Birmingham Historical Journal*, VII (1959–60), 101–3.

[2] *Cal. S.P. Spanish, 1553*, pp. 361–2; *Cal. S.P. Spanish, 1568–79*, p. 137; J. A. Williamson, *The age of Drake*, pp. 114, 150; R. B. Wernham, *Before the Armada*, pp. 343–4.

[3] *Cal. S.P. Spanish, 1568–79*, p. 113.   [4] *Cal. S.P. Foreign, 1564–5*, p. 528.

[5] P. 88 in the edition of Elizabeth Lamond (1929).

[6] H.M.C., *Cecil*, II, 251; Taylor, *Hakluyts*, I, 195.

and in the language of the time men had to be set on work. There were powerful instances to illustrate the dangers of failure. Riots under Wolsey, when, as Shakespeare has it, improving a good tale in the telling, 'the clothiers . . . put off the spinsters, carders, fullers, weavers, who. . . in desperate manner daring the event to the teeth, are all in uproar'.[1] Worse was to come. In 1549 there was a rising of the 'poor commons' on a scale unknown since the revolt of 1381. Government disintegrated in those very south-eastern counties where the dynasty was fondly imagined to have its main support; communist schemes were aired. These experiences reinforced the ruling class' well-found dread of 'the fury of the inferior multitude', and imprinted indelibly in the minds of statesmen the hazards of disorder.[2] Their problems were formidable enough: rising food prices; low wages; growing pauperism; dislocation of traditional markets; changes in the organization of rural life. England was seemingly feeble – no army to speak of, inadequate revenues – her enemies and neighbours apparently populous and wealthy. Elizabeth's native conservatism was allied to that of a ruling caste educated in Renaissance ideals of obedience to 'governours', equating change with decay and obsessed with the preservation of the social order. To the natural concern of a capable ruler for the economic well-being of the country there was added – not always with the happiest results – the less disinterested influence the merchant community was able to exercise. Hence the constant endeavour to find new markets. Hence too the mass of legislation to regulate wages, to preserve the existing pattern of society, to provide for the destitute, to set men on work: to do in fact all those very things which figure so largely in Hakluyt's writings.

A popular nostrum, which both he and his cousin reiterate, was that native products should be worked up at home and exported as manufactures whilst manufactured imports, especially luxuries, should be rigorously controlled. By this simple stratagem we would enjoy full employment and our rivals be overthrown.

---

[1] *King Henry VIII*, I. ii.
[2] Earl of Bath to the Privy Council, 1596. H.M.C., *15th report*, appendix, part VII (Somerset county), p. 20.

The point is made by the omniscient Doctor in the *Discourse of the common weal . . . of England*, and the elder Hakluyt, having demonstrated (1582) the superiority of English wool from the moth-resistant longevity of 'old parliament robes', urged that textiles be exported only after 'as much labour of our people as may be'.[1] The creed was a venerable one. The expensive import of useless 'nifles and trifles' had been condemned in the early 1400s in the doggerel of the *Libelle of Englyshe polycye*, which Hakluyt knew and published. Such doctrines were not peculiarly English and were equally prominent in France and Spain. They reflect the impasse, familiar enough in the modern world, of basically agrarian societies where lack of skill and technique depressed agricultural productivity and profits and forced up food prices. Industrial workers, ill-paid farm labourers, and the majority of small farmers had therefore no surplus to spend on manufactures. With no demand from the bulk of the population ingenious minds saw the salvation of industry in the manipulation of foreign trade. Native production could be stimulated if imports of foreign manufactures were controlled; new overseas markets could absorb those things for which there was no domestic demand.

Moreover a properly organized commerce – one, that is, in which exports were the product of native industry, and as far as nature permitted, of native materials – had the infinite blessing that it attracted what was variously described as treasure, coin or money. And as the Estates of France were graphically told in 1484 'money is to the body politic what blood is to the human body'. This was no false doctrine of wealth. Men were exercised by 'treasure' since there was a constant need for abundant, accessible and sound money which neither the economy nor rudimentary and antiquated revenue systems could meet. Money enabled states to prosper: it was the principal means of exchange; it stimulated production. More than this it enabled them to survive. Without money they could neither pay an ever-growing body of officials nor those increasingly expensive mercenary troops whose martial zeal was notoriously dependent on the sight of their wages. It was a truism going back to Antiquity that money,

[1] *Discourse*, ed. Lamond, p. 126; Taylor, *Hakluyts*, I, 191.

as the *Discourse of the common weal* puts it, 'be not with out cause called ... the senowes of war'.[1] Recent experience reinforced ancient wisdom. There were plentiful instances of ambitious monarchs cut short in grandiose strategies by untimely failures of the funds. And there was the awesome spectacle of Spain, with apparently limitless treasure to command, with not only Europe but virtually the whole world in her grasp by the 1580s.

Such lessons had not gone unheeded. 'For the occupation of clothmakers' medieval English governments had periodically prohibited or restricted the export of wool and unfinished cloth. There was legislation to control the outflow of coin and bullion; to restrict alien merchants; to foster English shipping. As elsewhere such policies were intensified in the sixteenth century. The early years of Elizabeth's reign saw strenuous efforts to stimulate domestic production of things as various as gunpowder, alum and salt. There was even an attempt, by the desperate expedient of boiling sheep's feet, to find a substitute for the Spanish oils used in the preparation of wool.[2] 'The increase and maintenance of the navy' were a constant concern and every colonial project, like Gilbert's in 1566 or Grenville's in 1574, was confidently recommended by its author as a sure tonic for a languishing merchant marine.

It is not, however, merely in his basic assumptions, but also in their application to colonization that Hakluyt reflects current opinion and practice. There were many who felt that Europe was unequal to the task of supporting the population with which it had been burdened. In mid-sixteenth century the imperial ambassador to Constantinople remarking, as was the fashion, the degeneracy of the times compared with the great days of Antiquity, regretted the passing of slavery, and in language to become familiar in Elizabethan England, spoke of those who 'having nothing but life and liberty are driven by want into every conceivable crime'.[3] Already a hundred years earlier a Czech observer had noted, as both the Hakluyts were later to notice, the admirable and beneficial Portuguese practice of depositing delinquents and undesirables in 'the land of the heathen'. And in

[1] *Discourse*, pp. 86–7.   [2] *Cal. S.P. Spanish, 1568–79*, p. 186.
[3] R. B. Merriman, *Suleiman the magnificent* (Cambridge, Mass., 1944), pp. 152–3.

1566 Humphrey Gilbert was urging, as Hakluyt was subsequently to urge, that a colony would take those who 'through want at home are inforced to commit outragious offences, whereby they are dayly consumed with the Gallowes'.[1]

Nor is it simply on points of detail that Hakluyt is anticipated. His cousin, for instance, discusses how overseas expansion would break dependence on Spain, absorb what he describes with candid vigour as 'the offals of our people', and give access to raw materials. And with raw materials cheaper, as he remarks in another context, merchants could work with less capital, prices would come down and the whole economy be re-invigorated.[2] This common stock in trade was doubtless the outcome of much family discussion. But it was not the monopoly of a circle of initiates. Gilbert had argued in 1566 that there was a potential market for cloth in India and elsewhere, and indeed the possibilities of colonial markets had been discussed, as Hakluyt knew, under Henry VIII, and as early as 1541 the Privy Council had debated the chances of a new outlet for textiles in 'the northern regions' to be reached via Iceland and Greenland.[3] In 1574 Grenville, whose rival colonial schemes Hakluyt conveniently ignores, had urged among the many merits of his South Seas project that it would set men on work, provide new markets for manufactures and stimulate shipping. So too Christopher Carleill had warned (1583) against the dangers of economic dependence on Spain, the parlous nature of England's foreign trade, and the perils of 'oure poore sort of people which are very many amongst vs liuing altogether vnprofitable and often times to the great disquiet of the better sort'.[4] But to demonstrate that Hakluyt's economics were merely current orthodoxies is only to say that he was human. There are limits to what any man, polymath though he may be, can encompass. And after all it is a wise man who argues a new cause in terms of the preconceptions, even the clichés, of his time.

[1] *The travels of Leo of Rozmital*, ed. M. Letts (1957), p. 112; Taylor, *Hakluyts*, I, 20, 175–6; Quinn, *Gilbert* (1940), I, 160–1.
[2] Taylor, *Hakluyts*, I, 119 ff., 149, 188; II, 339 ff.
[3] *Cal. S.P. Spanish, 1538–42*, pp. 326–7.
[4] A. L. Rowse, *Sir Richard Grenville* (1937), pp. 91–2; Quinn, *Gilbert*, II, 351 ff.

4
Hakluyt's language

N. E. OSSELTON

'I thought the Captaines letter well worth the remembring, not for the circumstance of curious enditing, but for the substance and good meaning therein contained.' George Best's comment[1] on the hopeful but abortive letter Frobisher wrote in 1577 to the five English captives in Baffin Island might stand also for all the Hakluyt narratives: they were preserved for their matter rather than their manner, and it is not for any elaboration of style, any 'curious enditing', that we remember them today. Yet it could well have been otherwise, for the man who set himself the task of recording fact and event in English in the sixteenth century faced difficulties unknown both to the medieval and to the modern prose-writer.

Caxton was the first to formulate the linguistic problem of Renaissance writers who found themselves constrained to use the English vernacular, and in so doing he picked on the same word, *curious*, that George Best was to use later: 'som honest and grete clerkes haue ben with me, and desired me to wryte the moste curyous termes that I coude fynde. And thus bytwene playn, rude, and curyous, I stande abasshed.'[2] The English language had emerged from the Middle Ages finally stamped as hybrid in character, readily receiving foreign words, but still retaining a native capacity for forming its own, and this actual and potential richness of vocabulary was a chief source of embarrassment to writers of English prose during the hundred years that separate Caxton and Hakluyt. You might rely on the native resources of the language, compounding words as you needed them, such as

---

[1] *PN*, III (1600), 70.

[2] Prologue to *Eneydos* (1490). *The prologues and epilogues of William Caxton*, ed. W. J. B. Crotch (Early English Text Society, Original Series, vol. 176, 1928), p. 109.

threlike, for *triangle*, *fleshstrings* for *muscles* or *witcraft* for *logic*; you could borrow learned words, though always at the risk of obscu‐ rity and the cry of pedantry; you might define your new words as you went along – a cumbersome method adopted by Sir Thomas Elyot in *The boke of the governour*; or, more elegantly, you might pair off the native and the foreign in one rhythmical and self‐ explanatory phrase, such as those familiar to us from Cranmer's Book of Common Prayer – 'acknowledge and confess', 'dis‐ semble nor cloke', 'prevent and go before'. The copiousness ('copie') of the language is generally extolled at this time; in the very year of Frobisher's note we find Holinshed writing of the English language that 'There is no one speache vnder the sonne spoken in our time, that hath or can haue more varietie of words and copie of phrases'.[1] Paradoxically, others seem to have despaired of finding appropriate words at all; the logician Ralph Lever complains that there are 'moe things, then there are words to expresse things by'.[2] Yet all are conscious of the need to use new words, and to use words in new ways. The adequacy of the language for its new purposes was probably never seriously in doubt, though it was loudly proclaimed to be ineloquent by those who wished to justify their own embellishments of it.

The reader of narrative and descriptive passages in Hakluyt must be struck by an absence of contrived lexical effects which is very remarkable for an age of such acute linguistic self‐conscious‐ ness. Here, for example, is part of Hakluyt's account of the islands of St Vincent and St George:

> The Iland of St. Vincent is easely to be wonne with — men, by meane it is nether manned nor fortified, and being wonne it is to be kept with —.
>
> This Iland and the mayne adjoyning doth so abound with victual that it is able to victual infinite multitudes of people, as our people report that were there with Drake, who had oxen, hogges, hennes, citrones, lymons, oranges etc.
>
> Distant from the mouth of the strait is the Iland of St. Georges, which yeldeth fowle infinite, able to victuall armies. These flie not, and may esely be taken and eaten freshe or kept salte.

---

[1] *The firste volume of the chronicles* (1577), f. 5r. This quotation and the next are taken from R. F. Jones, *The triumph of the English language* (1953), pp. 197 and 69.
[2] *The arte of reason* (1573), 'The Forespeache'.

These ilands will yelde plentie of grayne if they be sowed.

There yeldeth plentie of good fish within the straights as it is con‑iectured.[1]

How little there is of Renaissance lexical ornament in this may be illustrated by setting alongside it the description of Java in the fourteenth‑century English version of Sir John Mandeville's travels:

> This yle is full wel enhabyted & full wel manned, there growen all maner of spicerie more plentyfouslich than in ony other contree, As of gyngeuere, clowegylofres, canell, . . . Manye other spices & many other godes growen in that yle, For of all thing is there plentee saf only of wyn. But there is gold & siluer gret plentee. And the kyng of that contre hath a paleys full noble & full merueyllous & more riche than ony in the world . . . And witeth wel that the kyng of that yle is so myghty that he hath many tymes ouer‑comen the grete Cane of Cathay in bataylle.[2]

There is an exactly similar proportion of foreign words in these two passages, and they are put to similar use: compare Hakluyt's 'nether manned nor fortified' with 'full wel enhabyted & full wel manned', 'plentie of good fish' with 'of all thing is there plentee saf only of wyn', and the lists of native products. Every French and Latin word in this passage from Hakluyt was already in use in the fourteenth or early fifteenth century, and the language of it would, one suspects, scarcely have seemed strange even to the contemporaries of Chaucer.

The language of such accounts may be derivative, but a study of the original writings from the hand of Hakluyt[3] shows clearly enough that he does not succumb to the delights of exotic vocabulary where the starkly simple will suffice. Yet he was 'well‑languaged' – awake to the possibilities for renewal and extension of the vocabulary of his time. We find passages where Hakluyt's use of learned words antedates the first recorded instance in the

[1] 'A Discourse of the Commodity of the Taking of the Straight of Magellanus', printed in Taylor, *Hakluyts*, 1, 141.

[2] *Mandeville's travels*, edited, from B.M., MS Cotton Titus C. xvi, by P. Hamelius (Early English Text Society, Original Series, vol. 153, 1919), p. 125.

[3] As collected in the two volumes of Taylor, *Hakluyts*. Page references for indi‑vidual words and phrases are to these volumes.

O.E.D.; such are 'this *cursorie* pamphlet' (p. 181), 'upon paine of *discommunicacion*' (p. 221), 'yf wee doe *procrastinate* the plant￢ inge' (p. 279), 'the first *excription* of a book' (p. 346), and '3. partes, or as it were *Classes*' (p. 403). But most of these and of the other fashionable sixteenth￢century Latinate words which he uses, such as *alacritie, civilitie, extant, facilitie, occurrent, prognosticated, resolucion* and *ruinated* are to be found in the dedications, prefaces, and the 'Discourse of Western Planting', where the rhetorical intention is clear.

He also at times shows a liking for French idiom and vocabul￢ ary, again antedating the record of *O.E.D* in 'the ardent love of my countrey devoured all difficulties' (p. 426) (cf. *dévorer les difficultés*; *O.E.D.* records instances in English only in 1642 and 1648), in referring to 'the base Contries' (p. 238) ('Lowe Countreys' occurs, but less often) and in using *my Lords* as a class￢noun ('divers my Lords in England were up in armes', p. 345). Other new Gallicisms are *firme* ('all the coste and tract of that firme of America ... the hither side of that Firme', p. 142; cf. L. *terra firma*, F. *terre ferme*), *Renegadoes* (p. 218), *portable* (in postposition, 'some grete ryver portable', p. 144) and *ramassed* in his memorable dismissal of rival cosmographies as being 'vntruly and vnprofitablie ramassed and hurled together' (p. 402).

In his use of the native resources of the language Hakluyt likewise shows a discriminating inventiveness. *Bymedlers* (p. 280), for 'participants', is a compound word apparently of his own creation, in the best tradition of the sixteenth￢century Saxonists, but in quaintness it stands quite alone. *Sea￢knowledge* is another original compound, coined to describe the purpose of the pro￢ posed lectures in navigation 'for the increase and generall multi￢ plying of the sea￢knowledge in this age' (p. 429), a phrase which stands neatly in contrast to 'our former grosse ignorance in Marine causes'. His use of the adjective *fame￢thirsty* in referring to the Spaniards' 'fame￢thirsty and gold￢thirsty mindes' (pp. 436–7), also antedates the first instance in *O.E.D.* Could it be that he here recalls the use of *gold￢thirsty* to describe the Babylonians (Isaiah xiv. 4) in the Bishops' Bible of 1568? It seems not unlikely, for Hakluyt only rarely resorts to this type of compound adjective, though it is rather common in Renaissance prose, and very common in poetry.

We notice very often in Hakluyt's own writings a preference for 'Saxon' words and derivatives, some of them obsolescent in his time, where more learned terms were to hand; he refers to 'muskels of mervelous *bignesse*' (p. 145), 'the *backe side* of America' (p. 177), the small *manred* of Spaine' (p. 247), the 'high spirit, and wonderful *towardlinesse*' of Lord William Howard (p. 427), 'the *rawnesse* of his Seamen' (p. 429), 'the *trending* of the land' (p. 469), the *populousnesse* of Mexico (p. 471), and expresses his regret that we have *foreslown* (that is, 'put off', 'been dilatory about') the possessing of lands (p. 175). All these and many other details suggest that Hakluyt's language must have appeared conservative, if not old-fashioned, to the readers of his time, and the general effect of native plainness which his vocabulary gives is enhanced by the absence of classical allusion: one non-nautical reference to Scylla and Charybdis (p. 217), a mention of Pan's oaten pipe (p. 443), but little else. Far more characteristic is his use of traditional homely proverbial idioms such as 'to cutt large thonges . . . of other mens hides' (p. 301), 'To harpe no longer upon this string' (p. 398), 'so wee shoulde beate the bushe and other men take the birdes' (p. 275), and 'they will come to late and a day after the faire' (p. 278).

In sentence structure as in vocabulary the prose-writer of Hakluyt's day had a wide range of choices to make. There was, it is true, an unbroken native tradition of narrative prose-writing going back to the age of King Alfred, a tradition unparalleled in any other European language; this had survived with its sentence patterns little changed, even through the Norman Conquest, doubtless because it had drawn always on the rhythms of oral narrative. But writers in the fifteenth and sixteenth centuries had been given to experiments with longer and more complex sentences than had been customary before then. There was as yet no settled way of managing such sentences in the vernacular, and sheer vigour of experiment often resulted in awkwardness, especially in an excessive piling up of parallel phrases and a failure to relate the parts of the sentence to each other. Add to this the conscious imitation of rhythmical periodic Latin sentence structure practised by many sixteenth-century writers, and the varieties of syntax at the time may be seen to range from the artlessly simple to the artificially complex. Nor was there agree-ment about what syntax suited which occasion.

When we reflect that oral narrative and description are never very far behind the native English accounts given in Hakluyt's *Principal navigations* it is not hard to see why so much of the writing in them is unobscure and readily readable today. The description of St Vincent and St George already quoted is an example. Here is a narrative passage from John White's account of the 1590 voyage to Virginia:

> When we had seene in this place so much as we could, we returned to our Boates, and departed from the shoare towards our Shippes, with as much speede as wee could: For the weather beganne to ouercast, and very likely that a foule and stormie night would ensue. Therefore the same Euening with much danger and labour, we got our selues aboard, by which time the winde and seas were so greatly risen, that wee doubted our Cables and Anchors would scarcely holde vntill Morning.[1]

Nothing is forced here, and though the language is different from modern English in some details of phrasing, the passage presents no difficulties to us; the relationship of each part to the whole is always clear. This is Hakluyt narrative at its best. For contrast we may quote a passage telling of events in Virginia in 1585-6; it is rather similar in content to the last one, but this time the badly-sagging would-be eloquent sentence illustrates some of the worst features of one kind of sixteenth-century prose:

> While these things were in hand, the prouision aforesayd being brought, and in bringing aboord, my sayd Masters being also gone aboord, my sayd barks hauing accepted of their charge, and mine owne officers, with others in like sort of my company with them (all which was dispatched by the sayd Generall the 12 of the sayde moneth) the 13 of the same there arose such an vnwoonted storme, and continued foure dayes, that had like to haue driuen all on shore, if the Lord had not held his holy hand ouer them, and the Generall very prouidently foreseene the woorst him-selfe, then about my dispatch putting himselfe aboord.[2]

[1] *PN* (1600), III, 293.   [2] *PN* (1600), III, 264.

On such occasions we could wish that Hakluyt had been more rigorous in editing the language of his narrators for, from his own original writings, we can see that where he does venture on more complex sentences he can manage them with considerably more skill than this. Indeed, in places he shows himself to be the master also of the elaborate Latinate period:

> But calling to minde that you had spent more yeares in France then I, and vnderstande the french better then my selfe, I foorthwith perceiued that you approued mine endeuour, not for any priuate ease or commoditie that thereby might redounde vnto you, but that it argued a singuler and especiall care you had of those, which are to be employed in your owne like enterprise...[1]

This is only one third of a sentence from the opening passage of a dedicatory epistle addressed in 1587 to Sir Walter Ralegh; it is well-controlled, rather a fine specimen of the kind of language then expected in a dedication.

Hakluyt's occasional taste for such mannered writing has in the past been put down to 'a mild attack of euphuism' to which he succumbed in later life.[2] This may, it is suggested, have something to do with the passing from the prime of manhood to middle age,[3] and it has been held to account for a change of style in the 1598–1600 edition of the *Principal navigations*. The explanation seems questionable. Euphuism was in any case hardly an affliction specially associated with middle age: Shakespeare's *Love's Labour's Lost* may stand as evidence for that. It is of course hard to determine what Hakluyt's real share was in shaping the text of the *Principal navigations*, and whether he indulged in a process of embellishing the second edition. But in his personal writings and correspondence at least we can see that such rhetorical flourishes occur only in the formal set pieces – the prefaces and dedications – and that they are not a mark only of his later style. The sentence quoted above was written even before the first edition of the *Principall navigations*, in the preface to which we may

---

[1] *A notable historie containing foure voyages ... vnto Florida* (1587), the Epistle Dedicatory. See Taylor, *Hakluyts*, II, 372.

[2] J. A. Williamson, *The ocean in English history* (1941), p. 78.

[3] Taylor, *Hakluyts*, I, 55.

also find plenty of well-turned, rhythmical and alliterative sentences, such as 'I accompt him vnworthy of future favours, that
is not thankefull for former benefites';[1] the man who can write
this has little to learn of euphuism.

Nor, we may add, is he likely to be either blind or indifferent
to broken-backed syntax elsewhere. Pope was to write in a more
authoritarian age

> True Ease in Writing comes from Art, not Chance,
> As those move easiest who have learn'd to dance.[2]

and it seems likely that Hakluyt's expertise in the antithetical
language of studied compliment has provided him with a
syntactical discipline so sadly lacking in much of the practical
prose of the time. His language exemplifies the process by which
imitation of classical models helped the vernacular in the sixteenth
and seventeenth centuries; his own peculiar strength lies in avoid-
ing the current excesses of embellishment both in the choice of
words and in the shaping of sentences.

---

[1] *Ibid.* II, 407.   [2] *Essay on criticism*, lines 362-3.

5
Hakluyt's nautical terms

G. P. B. NAISH

In the confined days of Queen Elizabeth I, when only a very few were able to visit foreign countries, the Englishman, and in particular the Londoner, knew and understood ships much better than he does today. Ships were of course smaller and simpler, and altogether easier to comprehend, and the seamen and merchants, who almost alone amongst Englishmen travelled about the world without hindrance except from pirates and the Queen's enemies, were regarded with awe and interest. Above all the Thames was a common highway. Wherries and tilt boats threaded their way through the crowded shipping, proof of London being the most important port in the kingdom. There were hazards too. Passing under London Bridge at half tide was so dangerous, for a combination of mill race and waterfall built up between the piers, that even a sailor so bold as Sir Walter Ralegh chose to land and rejoin his boat dryshod the other side of the bridge. Ships beckoned the adventurous to seek their fortunes beyond the seas.

Hakluyt was a man of vision who saw his country's future prosperity in overseas trade and colonization. He realized the need for the improvement of the art of navigation to make direct voyages and to avoid shipwreck. He published in full the journals of seamen and merchants so that the fullest use could be made of the information these men had gained so hardly. It is possible therefore to make from the voyages a manual of Eliza⁄bethan seamanship.

Although he never went himself on a distant voyage, Hakluyt must have made a close study of sea terms when engaged on his translations from foreign tongues. Fuller says of him in his *Worthies*:[1] 'His genius inclined him to the study of history and

[1] Thomas Fuller, *Worthies of England*, ed. John Nichols (1811), p. 453.

31

especially the marine part thereof, which made him keep constant intelligence with the most noted seamen of Wapping until the day of his death.' Hakluyt remarks of himself:[1] 'I grew familiarly acquainted with the chiefest Captaines at sea, the greatest Merchants, and the best Mariners of our nation.' Not only have both editions of Hakluyt's principal work been searched by the editors of the *Oxford English dictionary*, but they were also consulted by Doctor Samuel Johnson. His copy of the *Principall navigations* of 1589 is in the former Admiralty Library with a note in his hand: 'Such is the expense of time and money for my dicty! After marking much of this vol. behold there is a later edn. of this (1598), with two more vols.'

Much depends on the style and wordiness of the writer, and whether he be predominantly seaman, merchant or adventurer, as to the extent nautical terms get used. Indeed, even when pro﹍ fessional seamen hold the pen, sea language only breaks in on the narrative occasionally when something unusual happens: a particularly violent gale or bloody sea fight or disastrous ship﹍ wreck. Then the reader pays an unexpected visit to an obscure corner of the ship or watches the carpenters and shipwrights repairing damages by using objects for purposes other than that for which they had been supplied to make good the damage. 'All this day wee made shyft, and made another spritsayle yarde of our Topgallant maste, our Myssen topmast, our mayne Flagstaffe, oars, etc.'[2] This comes from the lengthy journal of an intended voyage towards China commanded by Mr Edward Fenton, written by Luke Ward, vice﹍admiral of the expedition who, as a naval officer, commanded the *Tramontana* in 1588. His account is particularly interesting for his notes on the seamanship. Hakluyt curtailed it drastically for his second edition.[3]

Hakluyt's authors are very varied and as one would expect the most brilliant exploit is not always the one best recorded. Nor does everyone get his deserts. Sir Richard Grenville showed a

[1] *PN* (1589), *2.

[2] *PN* (1589), p. 671.

[3] In *The troublesome voyage of Captain Edward Fenton* (1957), Professor E. G. R. Taylor has edited all the narratives and documents she could discover.

stubborn and reckless disregard of orders not obvious to a reader of Ralegh's scintillating narrative on the *Revenge*. Sir Francis Drake seems to have been loath to let Hakluyt have adequate logbooks of his exploits. Perhaps he had good reasons for his secrecy. Mr Edward Hayes, gentleman, captain and owner of the *Golden Hind*, wrote the familiar and epic story of Sir Humphrey Gilbert's untimely and pathetic end when the little *Squirrel* was overwhelmed in mid-Atlantic. Few remember his record of the unruly and piratical conduct of the ships' companies nominally under Sir Humphrey's command.[1]

The *Principall navigations* of 1589 had its less important voyages curtailed in the second edition and much interesting routine nautical matter excised.[2] This is understandable. On the other hand several additional journals of voyages already described were added. For example, George Best, a gentleman in Hatton's service, provided an account of the voyages of Sir Martin Fro-bisher, a rough old sea-dog whom he had served as lieutenant and captain.[3] Best, so to speak, brings to life the little ships which Frobisher and his men ladened so heavily with what they thought was treasure.

Alison Quinn's superb index for the 1589 edition if it does nothing else shows up the need for a similar index to the three volumes of the second edition. In 1600 big ships carried spritsail topmasts at the bowsprit end as we learn from the first voyage of the East India Company. In 1588 they did not, according to the rigging warrants of the ships of the Royal Navy which fought the Armada. In 1609 we know from Purchas[4] the *Sea Adventure*, of 300 tons, was steered by means of a whipstaff. In a gale 'six and sometimes eight men were not inough to hold the whipstaffe in the steerage, and the tiller below in the Gunner roome, by which may be imagined the strength of the storme'. In 1592 the great carrack, the *Madre de Dios*, captured by Sir John Burrough (or

[1] *PN* (1589), p. 695; and for piratical conduct, p. 686.
[2] See the introduction by Quinn and Skelton to *PN* (*1589*), I (1965), l–lii.
[3] *PN* (1600), III, 57–93. His narrative had already been published separately as *A true discourse of the late voyages of discouerie* (1578).
[4] *Pilgrimes*, IV (1625), 1735.

Burgh), had been steered by a tiller (apparently no one had thought of tiller lines and tackles) 'for the greatnesse of the stirrage requiring the labour of twelve or fourteene men at once, and some of our shippes beating her in at the sterne with their ordinance often times with one shot slew foure or five labouring at either side of the helme'.[1] An index for the second edition as good as Mrs Quinn's has proved itself for the first edition would convince the writer that he has not failed to notice a mention of spritsail topmast or whipstaff.

Luke Ward,[2] mentioned above in connection with Fenton's voyage, gives us a most generous selection of common sea terms. Here are some typical examples, such as will be found used throughout the many narratives. We 'broughte our tacks aboord and stood along . . . larboord tacked'. 'Master Ralfe Crane . . . he should be put into the Bilbowes'. We 'romaged our ship all the forenoone'.[3] 'This day John Johnson wroughte of the settles in my cabbin': one of the few references to cabin comforts. Wind and weather have many happy descriptions. 'A stiffe gale at Northeast': 'we lay to and fro driving' (in a calm): a 'small gale': 'a pretie gale at Northeast': 'Ternado of wind': 'we went roome', that is put the helm up and bore away before the wind: 'the winde scanted', that is headed the ship off her course: 'a flawne sheete and a franke gale', that is, a flowing sheet, the ship was sailing free or large: 'we went our course southwest, except sometime we had a lache to the westwards, after the Admirall', where lache must be the same word as lask, to lask being to sail large as in lasking along: 'as we were catting our anker, the cattrope, stopper and all brake'; 'Master Walker dyed, who had bene weake and sicke of the bloody flix 6. dayes, wee tooke a

---

[1] *PN*, II. ii (1599), 197.

[2] *PN* (1589), pp. 647–72.

[3] 'To Rumidge, in Navigation is to remove goods or luggage out of a Ships Howld: Whence it is also used upon other occasions', Edward Phillips, *The new world of words* (4th ed., 1678), s.v. 'Rummidge, signifies to remove things from one Place to another. This is one of those sea Terms which are brought into common use:', *The gentleman's dictionary* (1705). 'Rummage. The search by custom-house officers for smuggled goods', Admiral W. H. Smyth, *The sailor's word-book* (1867), s.v. This last use it has today.

viewe of his things, and prised them, and heaued him ouer boord, and shot a piece for his knell', so dead sailors were treated for centuries: 'spring tydes . . . horsed vs a pace to leewardes';[1] this is a good phrase, very expressive and the writer intends bringing it into use again.

It is astonishing how typical Luke Ward's language is and how it accords with that of the other seamen. Picturesque phrases abound.[2] 'Heaue out the top-sailes': 'we spooned before the sea': 'you must be sure to borrow hard abord the maine', that is to keep over to the mainland side of the channel and borrow in this sense is still used in pilotage: 'thwart my haulse', athwart my hawse, still in use: 'waued us amaine with their swords'; according to a naval officer this phrase is not still in use. But all the same it is surprising how many of Hakluyt's nautical terms are still used at sea.

It is interesting to consider the nautical flavour that Sir Walter Ralegh gives so successfully to his expert journalistic handling of the last fight of the *Revenge*.[3] For example, the Spanish Armada, consisting, we are reminded, of the 'greatest Argosies, Portugal Carracks, Florentines, and huge hulks of other countries' did not 'so much as sinke or take one shippe, Barke, Pinnesse, or Cock-bote of ours'. Later at the Azores 'our ship being all pestered and romaging everything out of order': 'in the Bonaventure not so many men in health as would handle her maine saile': 'our ships had scarce time to way their anchors, but some of them were driuen to let slippe their cables and set saile': Sir Richard 'was persuaded by the master to cut his maine sayle and cast about': 'but Sir Richard vtterly refused . . . perswading his companie that hee would . . . enforce those of Siuil to giue him way. Which hee performed vpon diuers of the formost, who, as the Mariners terme it, sprang their luffe, and fell vnder the lee of the Reuenge'. Perhaps the parenthesis is the mark of the gentleman sailor. The

[1] These phrases may be found in PN (1589), pp. 648–50, 655–6, 658–9, 662, 668, 672.

[2] *Ibid.* pp. 655–72.

[3] PN, II. ii (1599), 169–75 (*A report of the truth of the fight about the iles of Açores . . . betwixt the Reuenge . . . and an armada of the king of Spaine* (1591)).

earl of Cumberland's 'discreet and valiant captaine M. Nicholas Downton' uses it,[1] but speaking as a sailor himself: 'I com/manded to give her the broad side, as we terme it.'

In fact, Nicholas Downton, who was captain of the *Sampson*, is as eloquent as Ralegh in describing an action he took part in, being severely wounded early on. He sailed from Plymouth in 1594 with two consorts, the *Royal Exchange* and the *Mayflower*. They met a mighty carrack from the East Indies, *Las Cinque Llagas* or *The Five Wounds*. The *Sampson* gave her a broadside, 'as we terme it'. 'The Admirall laid her a boord in the mid ship: the May/flower comming vp in the quarter, as it should seeme, to lie at the sterne of the Admirall on the larboord side. The captaine of the sayd May/flower was slaine at the first comming vp: whereby the ship fell to the sterne of the out/licar of the Carack, which (being a piece of timber) so wounded her fore/saile, that they sayd they could come no more to fight, I am sure they did not, but kept aloofe from vs.' Sir Walter was the better writer but Downton holds our attention.

There are a number of official documents, orders, sailing instruc/tions and indeed a great mass of material there is no room here to consider but perhaps enough has been said to show that a most instructive and indeed an entertaining nautical dictionary could be extracted from Hakluyt's volumes.[2]

[1] *PN*, II. ii (1599), 199–200.

[2] Certain other contemporary voyage narratives should also be plundered, in particular *The observations of Sir Richard Hawkins*, ed. J. A. Williamson (1933), and the 'Voyage of the *Barbara* to Brazil, anno 1540', ed. R. G. Marsden, Navy Records Society, *Miscellany*, II (1912). And of course very many of the volumes published by the Hakluyt Society. As has been noted, nautical terms get used in a far more interesting way by some authors than by others. Whoever under/takes the compilation of such a book will derive much assistance from the pages of *The Mariner's Mirror*, and particularly from some of the articles contributed by Sir Alan Moore, who understood the Elizabethan ship as well as anyone except perhaps his great friend, the *Mirror's* first editor, L. G. Carr Laughton.

6

Hakluyt as translator

F. M. ROGERS

Nam qui exterorum laudes proponit,
suos, si non sunt stipites, prouocat.
(Dedication of *De nouo orbe* (1587))

As geographical publicist Hakluyt played a dual role: he presented the English contribution of Renaissance travel and discovery
– chiefly in the two editions of the *Principall navigations* – and by
his involvement with many translations he also presented a portion
of the foreign contribution.[1] For the latter task he was superbly
equipped because of his ability to read both printed and manuscript works in Greek, Latin, Italian, Spanish, 'Portugall', and
French. His sojourn in Paris from 1583 to 1588 – with occasional
visits home – provided him with an appropriate foreign experience and perspective, and a wide network of contacts with
merchants and mariners furnished him with the necessary leads.
Among those with whom he talked, he tells Sir Francis Walsingham in a letter dated Paris, 7 January 1584, was Dom António
of Portugal, Prior of Crato and an unsuccessful pretender to the
Portuguese throne after the death of Cardinal-King Henrique in
1580. He also talked with five or six of António's best captains
and pilots, one of whom had been born in the East Indies.

Hakluyt personally translated two individually published
books, Laudonnière's and that by the Gentleman of Elvas – from
French and Portuguese respectively – and reworked the anonymous translation of Galvão's Portuguese volume. In fourteen
instances he served not as translator of separate volumes but as
stimulator and promoter of translators, of translators into English
and also other languages, on occasion even arranging for the

[1] Boies Penrose, *Travel and discovery in the Renaissance 1420–1620* (Cambridge,
Mass., 1952), p. 319.

publication in the original foreign language of books which he then translated or caused to be translated into English or another language.

As is to be expected, Hakluyt incorporated translations of his own into the *Principall navigations* and into its predecessor *Divers voyages*. An example in the latter, as we learn from its epistle dedicatory, is Verrazzano's voyage, which Hakluyt translated from Ramusio's Italian. An interesting example in the enlarged edition of the *Principal navigations* concerns what is said to be the second book printed by Europeans in China. By the Portuguese Jesuit Duarte de Sande and printed in Macao in 1590, it treats the Japanese embassy which was received in the Roman curia in March 1585. The only known exemplar in the United States, in the Oliveira Lima Library of the Catholic University of America in Washington, D.C., is Alessandro Valignani's presentation copy to Dom Teotónio de Bragança, Archbishop of Évora.[1] Another exemplar was aboard the Portuguese carrack *Madre de Deus* along with considerable additional documentation when captured by the English in 1592. Hakluyt had access to this one, 'inclosed in a case of sweete Cedar wood, and lapped vp almost an hundred fold in fine calicut-cloth, as though it had beene some incomparable iewell', to quote his dedication of the second volume. He translated it and included it in the collection without Sande's name.[2]

A final example of Hakluyt's activity as translator concerns Theodor de Bry, to whom Hakluyt suggested the idea of publishing the famous illustrated volume on the New World which appeared in Frankfurt am Main in 1590 in Latin, English, French, and German. It was Hakluyt who retranslated into

[1] F. M. Rogers, comp., *Europe informed: an exhibition of early books which acquainted Europe with the East* (Cambridge, Mass.: Sixth International Colloquium on Luso-Brazilian Studies, 1966), no. 92. For additional information concerning Sande's book, see Armando Cortesão, *Cartografia e cartógrafos portugueses dos séculos XV e XVI (Contribuïção para um estudo completo)* (2 vols., Lisbon, 1935), I, 162–3.

[2] In *PN*, II (1599), ii, 88–98. See also Taylor, *Hakluyts*, I, 59; II, 461, and Donald F. Lach, *Asia in the making of Europe. Volume I (The century of discovery)* (two parts, Chicago and London, 1965), i, 214–15; ii, 809.

English (in S.T.C. 12786) the Latin captions of the pictures which in turn had been rendered from an earlier English into Latin by the botanist Charles de l'Écluse.

Apart from De Bry, the individual volumes of translations with which Hakluyt's name is associated were:[1]

Cartier, Jacques, 1491–1557. *A shorte and briefe narration of the two navigations and discoveries to the northweast partes called Newe Fraunce*, tr. Iohn Florio.
London: Henry Bynneman, 1580.
S.T.C. 4699.
Translated from Ramusio's Italian. See pp. 528–9 below.

Espejo, Antonio de. *Histoire des terres nouuellement descouuertes, ausquelles a esté ja trouué quinze belles Prouinces remplies de villes & villages: ausquelles Prouinces il se trouue grandes commoditez, & abondance de diuerses especes metalliques: lesquelles terres ont esté descouuertes par Antonio de Espeio & nommees le nouueau Mexico . . .*, tr. Martin Basanier.
Paris: Widow of Nicolas Roffet, 1586. See pp. 534–5 below.
Translated from the Spanish edition published in Paris in the same year at Hakluyt's expense. This Spanish edition was in turn extracted from the first edition of the expanded text of González de Mendoza's *Historia*; see below.

Espejo, Antonio de. *New Mexico. Otherwise, The Voiage of Anthony of Espeio, who in the yeare 1583. with his company, discouered a Lande of 15. Prouinces, replenished with Townes and villages, with houses of 4. or 5. stories height, It lieth Northward, and some suppose that the same way men may by places inhabited go to the Lande tearmed De Labrador . . .*, tr. A.F.
London: [Thomas East ?] for Thomas Cadman, [1587].
S.T.C. 18487. See p. 572 below.
Translated from the Spanish edition published in Paris in 1586 at Hakluyt's expense. The extent of Hakluyt's connection with this English translation, if any, is not certain. The translation differs from Robert Parke's version of the corresponding chapters of González de Mendoza's complete work; see below.

Laudonnière, René Goulaine de. *A Notable Historie containing foure voyages made by certayne French Captaynes vnto Florida: Whereine the great riches and fruitefulnes of the countrey with the maners of the people*

[1] I should like to thank the Harvard College Library, and in particular Miss Katharine Pantzer, for the opportunity to consult the materials compiled by my late colleague William A. Jackson for the S.T.C. revision.

hitherto concealed are brought to light, written all sauing the last by Monsieur Laudonniere, who remained there himselfe as the French Kings Lieuetenant a yere and a quarter . . ., tr. Richard Hakluyt.

London: Thomas Dawson, 1587.

S.T.C. 15316. See pp. 470–1 below.

Translated from the French edition (*L'histoire notable de la Floride*, ed. Martin Basanier, Paris: Guillaume Auvray, 1586), whose publica⁄ tion Hakluyt himself had arranged.

González de Mendoza, Juan, bp., 1545–1618. *The Historie of the great and mightie kingdome of China, and the situation thereof: Togither with the great riches, huge Citties, politike gouernement, and rare inuentions in the same*, tr. Robert Parke.

London: Iohn Wolfe, for Edward White, 1588.

S.T.C. 12003. See pp. 536–7 below.

Translated from the Spanish printed in Madrid in 1586 by Querino Gerardo Flamenco for Blas de Robles, the first edition of the expanded text containing Antonio de Espejo's full account of his expedition to New Mexico in 1583.

Meierus, Albertus. *Certaine briefe, and speciall Instructions for Gentlemen, merchants, students, souldiers, marriners, &c. Employed in seruices abrode, or anie way occasioned to conuerse in the kingdomes, and gouernementes of forren Princes*, tr. Philip Iones.

London: Iohn Wolfe, 1589.

S.T.C. 17784. See pp. 538–9 below.

Translated from the Latin which was published in Helmstadt in 1587.

Pigafetta, Filippo, 1533–1604. *A Reporte of the Kingdome of Congo, a Region of Africa, And of the Countries that border rounde about the same . . . Drawen out of the writinges and discourses of Odoardo Lopes a Portingall, by Philippo Pigafetta*, tr. Abraham Hartwell.

London: [John Windet, for] Iohn Wolfe, 1597.

S.T.C. 16805. See pp. 544–5 below.

Translated from the Italian published in Rome in 1591, which was in turn based on Duarte Lopes' dictation to Pigafetta.

Houtman, Cornelis de, d. 1599. *The Description of a voyage made by certaine Ships of Holland into the East Indies. With their aduentures and successe: Together with the description of the Countries, Townes, and inhabitantes of the same: Who set forth on the second of Aprill 1595. and returned on the 14. of August. 1597*, tr. William Phillip.

London: [John Windet ? for] Iohn Wolfe, 1598.

S.T.C. 15193. See p. 573 below.

Translated from the Dutch. Occasionally catalogued (as in the British Museum) under the name of the Dutch publisher, Bernardt Langenes or Langhenes.

Linschoten, Jan Huygen van, 1563–1611. *Iohn Huighen van Linschoten. his Discours of Voyages into ye Easte & West Indies. Deuided into Foure Bookes*, tr. William Philip.
London: [Iohn Windet, for] Iohn Wolfe, 1598.
S.T.C. 15691. See p.p 546–7 below.
Translated from the original Dutch edition published in Amsterdam in 1595–6.

Leo Africanus, Joannes, 16th cent. *A Geographical Historie of Africa, Written in Arabicke and Italian by Iohn Leo a More, borne in Granada, and brought up in Barbarie . . .*, tr. Iohn Pory.
London: [Eliot's Court Press, for] George Bishop, 1600.
S.T.C. 15481. See pp. 548–9 below.
Translated from the Latin edition published in Antwerp in 1556, possibly with the aid of the French translation contained in the volume of translations from the first volume of Ramusio published in Lyons in 1556 with the general title *Historiale description de l'Afrique*. The original account was written in 1526.

Galvão, António, d. 1557. *The Discoveries of the World from their first originall vnto the yeere of our Lord 1555. Briefly written in the Portugall tongue by Antonie Galvano, Gouernour of Ternate, the chiefe Island of the Malucos: Corrected, quoted, and now published in English by Richard Hakluyt, sometimes student of Christ church in Oxford.*
London: [Eliot's Court Press, for] George Bishop, 1601.
S.T.C. 11543. See pp. 522–3 below.
Translated from the original Portuguese edition (*Tratado. Que compôs o nobre & notauel capitão Antonio Galuão . . .*, ed. Francisco de Sousa Tavares, [Lisbon:] João de Barreira, 15 December 1563).

Neck, Jacob van, 1564–1638. *The Iournall, or Dayly Register, Contayning a True manifestation, and Historicall declaration of the voyage, accomplished by eight shippes of Amsterdam, vnder the conduct of Iacob Corneliszen Neck Admirall, & Wybrandt van Warwick Vice-Admirall, which sayled from Amsterdam the first day of March, 1598. Shewing the course they kept, and what other notable matters happened vnto them in the sayd voyage*, tr. William Walker.
London: [Simon Stafford and Felix Kingston] for Cuthbert Burby and Iohn Flasket, 1601.
S.T.C. 18417. See pp. 550–1 below.

Translated from the Dutch account of Van Neck's voyage.

Veer, Gerrit de, fl. 1595–8. *The True and perfect Description of three Voyages, so strange and woonderfull, that the like hath neuer been heard of before: Done and performed three yeares, one after the other, by the Ships of Holland and Zeland, on the North sides of Norway, Muscouia, and Tartaria, towards the Kingdomes of Cathaia & China; shewing the discouerie of the Straights of Weigates, Noua Zembla, and the Countrie lying vnder 80. degrees; which is thought to be Greenland . . .,* tr. William Philip.

London: [William White for] Thomas Pavier, 1609.

S.T.C. 24628. See pp. 552–3 below.

Translated from the Dutch account of the Barents voyages.

Fidalgo, Um, d'Elvas, pseud. *Virginia richly valued, By the description of the maine land of Florida, her next neighbour: Out of the foure yeeres continuall trauell and discouerie, for aboue one thousand miles East and West, of Don Ferdinando de Soto, and sixe hundred able men in his companie. Wherin are truly obserued the riches and fertilitie of those parts, abounding with things necessarie, pleasant, and profitable for the life of man: with the natures and dispositions of the Inhabitants. Written by a Portugall gentleman of Eluas, emploied in all the action . . .,* tr. Richard Hakluyt.

London: Felix Kingston, for Matthew Lownes, 1609.

S.T.C. 22938. See pp. 524–5 below.

Translated from the original Portuguese edition (*Relaçam verdadeira dos trabalhos que ho gouernador dom Fernando de souto & certos fidalgos portugueses passarom no descobrimento da prouincia da Frolida. Agora nouamente feita per hum fidalgo Deluas,* Évora: André de Burgos, 10 February 1557), often catalogued under 'Relaçam verdadeira dos trabalhos . . .'

Another issue of Hakluyt's translation, with variant title page, appeared in 1611:

> *The Worthye and Famous History of the Trauailes, Discouery, & Conquest, of that great Continent of Terra Florida, being liuely Paraleld, with that of our now Inhabited Virginia. As also The Comodities of the said Country, With diuers excellent and rich Mynes, of Golde, Siluer, and other Mettals, &c. which cannot but giue vs a great and exceeding hope of our Virginia, being so neere of one Continent. Accomplished and effected, by that worthy Generall and Captaine, Don Ferdinando de Soto, and six hundreth Spaniards his followers.*

London: [Felix Kingston] for Matthew Lownes, 1611.

· S.T.C. 22939. See pp. 526–7 below.

Lescarbot, Marc, 1571 ?–c.1630. *Noua Francia: Or the Description of That Part of Nevv France, which is one continent with Virginia. Described*

in the three late Voyages and Plantation made by Monsieur de Monts,
Monsieur du Pont-Graué, and Monsieur de Poutrincourt, into the countries
called by the French men La Cadie, lying to the Southwest of Cape Breton.
Together with an excellent seuerall Treatie of all the commodities of the said
countries, and maners of the said countries, and maners of the naturall inhabit-
ants of the same, tr. Pierre Erondelle.
London: [Eliot's Court Press, for] George Bishop, 1609.
S.T.C. 15491. See pp. 554–5 below.
Translated from Books IV and VI of the original French edition
published in Paris in the same year.
Anghiera, Pietro Martire d', 1455–1526. *De Nouo Orbe, or The Historie*
of the west Indies, Contayning the actes and aduentures of the Spanyardes,
which haue conquered and peopled those Countries, inriched with varietie of
pleasant relation of the Manners, Ceremonies, Lawes, Gouernments, and
Warres of the Indians, Comprised in eight Decades . . ., tr. Richard Eden
(Decades 1–3) and Michael Lok (Decades 4–8).
London: [Thomas Dawson] for Thomas Adams, 1612.
S.T.C. 650. See pp. 558–9 below.
Lok translated from the Latin edition published in Paris in 1587
through Hakluyt's efforts and with a dedication written by Hakluyt.
Arthus, Gothard, 1570–1630? *Dialogues in the English and Malaiane*
Languages . . . first written in Latin, Malaian, and Madagascar tongues, by
the diligence . . . of . . . G. Arthusius . . ., tr. Augustine Spalding.
London: Felix Kingston for William Welby, 1614.
S.T.C. 810. See pp. 568–9 below.
Translated from the Latin edition published in Frankfurt in 1613.

The epistle dedicatory to Sir Robert Cecil in the English
translation of Galvão's treatise clarifies Hakluyt's role in the
preparation of that volume for the press, and it also provides
insight into his theory of translation:

Now touching the translation, it may please you, sir, to be aduertised that
it was first done into our language by some honest and well affected
marchant of our nation, whose name by no meanes I could attaine vnto,
and that as it seemeth many yeeres ago. For it hath lien by me aboue these
twelue yeeres. In all which space though I haue made much inquirie, and
sent to Lisbon, where it seemeth it was printed, yet to this day [29 October
1601] I could neuer obtaine the originall copie; whereby I might reforme
the manifold errours of the translator. For whereas a good translator
ought to be well acquainted with the proprietie of the tongue out of

which and of that into which he translateth, and thirdly with the subiect or matter it selfe: I found this translator very defectiue in all three; especially in the last. For the supplying of whose defects I had none other remedie, but to haue recourse vnto the originall histories, (which as it appeereth are very many, and many of them exceed⁄ ing rare and hard to come by) out of which the authour himselfe drew the greatest part of this discourse. And in very deede it cost me more trauaile to search out the grounds thereof, and to annexe the marginall quotations vnto the work, then the translation of many such bookes would haue put me vnto . . .

By his own criteria Hakluyt had the makings of a 'good' translator. He knew the languages from which he translated. He was splendidly acquainted with the niceties of his native English, to whose prose formation in that Elizabethan era he made such a notable contribution. As for subject⁄matter, Hakluyt did not himself travel to the four parts of the world, but he was thoroughly acquainted with the vocabulary of those who did. In effect he spent his life immersed in the jargon of overseas discovery, exploration, and colonization, for he was engaged in publicity for all these activities, in the West Indies (notably in Virginia and in the search for the North⁄west Passage) as well as the East Indies.

The third criterion confirms the hypothesis that modern linguistic theory, on which all sound translation including and especially biblical translation must be based in our own day,[1] evolved out of the contacts in the Age of Maritime Discovery of individual Europeans with each others' living idiom and with the strange contemporary tongues of the new⁄found continents. Hakluyt realized that a language expresses a cultural reality. Bougainville less than two centuries later was to remind Parisians and other Europeans that a Tahitian possessed a different 'struc⁄ ture of content' than they, that his 'structure of expression' was therefore very different from theirs, that accordingly Aotourou naturally found French more difficult to acquire than did the Italians, English, and Germans.[2]

[1] Reuben A. Brower, ed., *On translation* (Cambridge, Mass., 1959).
[2] Louis Antoine de Bougainville, *Voyage autour du monde par la frégate du roi La Boudeuse, et la flûte l'Etoile en 1766, 1767, 1768 & 1769* (Paris, 1771), pp. 224–5.

A sampling comparison of Hakluyt's English with Laudon-nière's French and the Gentleman of Elvas' Portuguese reveals that the clergyman-nationalist stood very high in the two aspects of translation concerning which modern readers are most demand-ing. The one is mastery of technical vocabulary: fauna, flora, navigation, types and parts of ships, arms, armour, and scores of other fields. Hakluyt's command of the relevant areas of know-ledge was complete. The other is the unravelling of complicated syntax, and here Hakluyt's thorough familiarity with the struc-tures of the foreign languages stood him in good stead. Thus, at the beginning of the *Relaçam verdadeira dos trabalhos* the Portuguese reads:

> foy com Fernando Piçarro a conquistar ho Peru, donde segundo muitas pessoas de credito que alli se acharom deziam, assi na prisam de Atabalipa señor do Peru, como na entrada da cidade do Cuzco & en todas as outras partes onde acharam resistencia & se elle achou, se estremou antre os outros capitães & pessoas principaes.

The English, incorporating a judicious use of parentheses, reads:

> hee went with Fernando Pizarro to the conquest of Peru; where (as many persons of credit reported, which were there present), as well at the taking of Atabalipa, Lord of Peru, as at the assault of the citie of Cusco, and in all other places where they found resistance, wheresoeuer hee was present, hee passed all other captaines and principall persons.

Hakluyt was amazingly modern in another translational sense: he recognized the dangers of Europocentrism. He counselled those who journeyed to the Orient not to have too much con-fidence in Portuguese as a lingua franca in the East Indies but rather to learn Arabic and Malay. Thus, in notes he drew up for the newly established East India Company, he advised 'aboue al others, a trustie interpretour in the Easterne Arabian tongue, for by vsing the Portugal tonge, you are in greate danger of being betrayed, as the Hollanders were 7 tymes in their first voyage'.[1] Little wonder that Hakluyt translated Gothard Arthus' Malayan dialogues into English.

[1] Taylor, *Hakluyts*, II, 482.

Of course Hakluyt took certain liberties which the twentieth-century translator of a sixteenth-century work would not take. On occasion he expanded the text where we would add a note, as when he gave the full name 'Pamphilo de Narvaez' for the simple 'Narvaez' of the first occurrence in the Elvas Portuguese, or explained Laudonnière's French ('elle fut descouverte le jour de Pasques Flories') by writing 'it was discouered on Palme-sunday, which the Spaniards call Pascha Florida'. He was particularly fond of retaining an original technical term and supplying a rough equivalent at first occurrence ('mays' – 'maiz, or corne', or again 'ho alcayde mor' – 'the chiefe alcalde or justice'). And, like all translators, he retained the original when he could think of no equivalent term: 'cacique'. It is just such a foreign word which the *O.E.D.*, with copious references, admits into the English language as English.

The modern translator would not correct an error in an ancient text, but he would be most likely to do so in a contemporary text. Hakluyt, who must have checked Laudonnière's geographical coordinates carefully, naturally treated his originals as contemporary, and he changed the Tropic of Cancer from $25°$ N to $23\frac{1}{2}°$ N and the Strait of Magellan from $55°$ S to $53°$ S.

E. G. R. Taylor has noted a marked contrast in English style between the first or 1589 edition of the *Principall navigations* and the second or 1598–1600 edition: 'Hakluyt's prose style had altered and become more mannered, more stilted and more ornate.'[1] She suggests that the change may be explained 'by his passage from the prime of manhood to middle age, but also by the changing fashions of the times'. Hakluyt's translation of Laudonnière's French was published in 1587 and his English version of the Gentleman of Elvas' Portuguese appeared in 1609. As the interval 1587–1609 is obviously greater than the time span noted by Professor Taylor, one might look for a stylistic difference in the two translations. But Hakluyt was too skilful a translator to betray the style of his originals. In both cases the narratives were straightforward, written on the whole in unadorned prose, and so were Hakluyt's renderings. And if the original author employed

[1] *Ibid.*, I, 55–6, cf. pp. 29–30 above.

46

a picturesque term ('Christophle Colon, premier de tous, surgit en ceste terre'), Hakluyt retained its flavour ('Christopher Colon did first light upon this land').[1]

[1] In writing this chapter, in addition to the works already cited, I have drawn heavily on John Winter Jones' introduction to the edition of the *Divers voyages* published by the Hakluyt Society in 1850; Henry Thomas, 'English translations of Portuguese books before 1640', *The Library*, 4th ser., VII (1926-7), 1-30, reprinted in *Revista da Universidade de Coimbra*, XI (1933 – *Miscelânea de Estudos em honra de D. Carolina Michaëlis de Vasconcellos*), 690-711; Parks, *Hakluyt* (2nd ed., New York, 1961); John Parker, *Books to build an empire* (Amsterdam, 1965); and the introduction by David Beers Quinn and Raleigh Ashlin Skelton to the facsimile edition of *Principall navigations* (1589) published by the Hakluyt Society in 1965.

7
Hakluyt's maps

R. A. SKELTON

Like other eminent Elizabethans, Hakluyt was alive to the useful'
ness of maps as sources of geographical and political intelligence.
He had access to recent cartographic documentation, impressive
both in quality and in quantity, which plainly contributed to the
formation of his judgement on the problems of world geography
and of overseas discovery and plantation. Yet, if we look more
closely at his study and application of maps as illustrated by
references in his own writings and in works edited or compiled
by him, we become aware of certain limitations in perception or
method. These references yield surprisingly few traces of the
intensive and critical collation of maps habitually undertaken by
some of Hakluyt's English contemporaries. It is conceivable that
Hakluyt preferred not to expose his 'workings' or the premises
by which he arrived at conclusions. It is at least equally possible
that, more at home with textual than with graphic data, he chose
to devote his time and energy to securing 'the best & most
perfect relations', paying lip'service to the need for non'literary
illustration of his themes and indirectly forwarding the efforts of
others to publish such documentation in pictorial or cartographic
form. It is the purpose of the present paper to test these explana'
tions in the light of the map'materials available to Hakluyt and
of the use which he made of them.

By Hakluyt's own account, it was his cousin's exposition of 'an
vniuersall Mappe' that fired the young Westminster scholar's
enthusiasm for cosmography.[1] This may have been Ortelius'
cordiform world map published in 1564;[2] many copies were
supplied by Plantin to London booksellers, it was frequently

[1] PN (1589), sig. *2r.
[2] As suggested by E. G. R. Taylor, *Hakluyts* (1935), I, 77–8, n. 2.

cited in English geographical writings, and about this time
(1567–9) Hakluyt's cousin, the lawyer, sent to Ortelius proposals
for a more convenient method of constructing a large world map.[1]
Some ten years later, after taking his master's degree at Oxford,
Hakluyt delivered public lectures in which he 'produced and
shewed both the olde imperfectly composed, and the new lately
reformed Mappes, Globes, Spheares, and other instruments of
this Art'.[2] Whether this refers to the form or to the content of
maps, it implies critical study of them in a comparative or
historical context, at about the time of his encounter with
Ortelius who visited England in 1577.

The career of Ortelius in map production practically spanned
the reign of Queen Elizabeth, and it was largely from Latin
editions of the *Theatrum* that Englishmen of this period learnt the
facts of world geography.[3] Hakluyt must have owned a copy of
the *Theatrum* and received, as they were engraved, the new maps
which Ortelius introduced in successive supplements and editions
of his atlas. Thus the maps of the Spanish territories in the New
World 'this present yere 1584 published by Ortelius', in his third
Additamentum, enabled Hakluyt, in the 'Discourse of western
planting', to analyse the density and distribution of their occupation, inferring that 'the lymites of the Kinge of Spaines dom-
ynions in the West Indies be nothinge so large as is generally
ymagined'.[4] This political argument was perhaps due to Ralegh,
who echoes it in the *Historie of the world*: 'in the West *Indies*, of
which the *Spaniards* have the experience, in those places where
they found neither path nor guide, they have not entred the
Countrie ten miles in ten yeares'.[5] Hakluyt's 'Discourse', written
'at the requeste and direction of... Mr Walter Raghly', reflects
Ralegh's geopolitical ideas and colonial strategy at this time. The

[1] Hessels, *Epistulae*, no. 172, pp. 415–18. This letter has generally been attributed
to the younger Hakluyt; but correctly to the lawyer by Taylor, *Hakluyts*, I, 77–83.
[2] *PN* (1589), sig. *2r.
[3] Cf. R. A. Skelton, introduction to facsimile edition (Amsterdam, 1968) of
Ortelius' *Theatre* of 1606.
[4] Taylor, *Hakluyts*, II, 250–1.
[5] *The history of the world* (1614), bk. I. viii. 3.

association doubtless gave Hakluyt access to a valuable stock of cartographic materials for study, mainly (it seems) from Spanish sources.[1] In 1582 he cites 'Alonso di Chavez & Hieronimus di Chauez, whose works . . . I haue seene'; whether collected by Hakluyt or (as seems more probable) by Ralegh, these would have been *derroteros* or charts of North America.[2] Hakluyt's reference to 'a secret mappe of those partes made in Mexico the yeere before [i.e. in 1585] for the King of Spaine (which originall with many others is in the custodie of . . . M. Thomas Hariot)'[3] points to systematic map collecting by Ralegh in the 1580s, mainly from Spanish sources, in preparation for his North American projects; and ten years later Harriot was assembling maps for the Guiana voyages and collating Spanish sailing directions which Hakluyt was to print in 1600. In 1596 (as will be seen) Hakluyt in turn had lent French maps of Canada to Harriot.

Hakluyt was also closely connected with Ralegh's employment of artists and map-makers, arising from his colonial projects, and with the publication of their work. Not only was Hakluyt the virtual editor of the first two parts of Theodor de Bry's *America*, which presented the drawings and maps of Virginia by John White (1590) and of Florida by Jacques Le Moyne (1591), in

[1] Cf. R. A. Skelton, 'Ralegh as a geographer', *Virginia Magazine of History and Biography*, LXXI (1963), 131–49.

[2] *DV*, Epistle dedicatorie. The *derrotero* of Alonso de Chaves was preserved by Oviedo, *Historia general*, lib. xxi; the North American nomenclature is transcribed by Harrisse, *The discovery of North America* (1892), pp. 633–5. A map of Florida by Gerónimo de Chaves was engraved for Ortelius in or before 1584. [The suggestion that Ralegh and Hakluyt were in close contact in 1581–2 may well be premature, as may be the suggestion that Ralegh was independently assembling maps at that time. The possibility that Hakluyt may have seen versions of their work in the possession of Antonío de Castillo, Portuguese ambassador in London, whom Hakluyt had recently consulted, is raised below, pp. 274–5. D.B.Q.]

[3] *PN*, II (1599), dedicatory epistle. This seems to be the map referred to in John Brereton, *A briefe relation . . . of Virginia* (1602), p. 47: 'The large description and chart of which voyage [Espejo's] . . . made in Mexico by Francisco Xamuscado 1585 being intercepted afterward by the English at sea, we haue in London to be shewed to such as shall haue occasion to make vse of the same.' I owe this reference to D. B. Quinn.

each case engraved from originals executed at Ralegh's expense
or in his employment. As G. B. Parks has suggested,[1] the great
series of folios on the western and eastern voyages published by
De Bry and his sons form a pictorial and cartographic counter‑
part to Hakluyt's unillustrated travel collections and narratives.
It was as Ralegh's agent also that, in Paris in 1586, Hakluyt
commissioned from the exiled Portuguese cartographer André
Homem, 'the prince of the cosmographers of this age', a map to
illustrate Espejo's 'Voyage to New Mexico';[2] but this came to
nothing. Another Portuguese hydrographic manuscript, with a
somewhat curious history, was D. João de Castro's illustrated
roteiro from Goa to Suez (1541), which Ralegh obtained some
time after 1603 and 'gave Mr. Richard Hacluit to publish'; it
was among the papers conveyed by Hakluyt to Purchas, who
printed extracts from it, and it subsequently passed into Sir Robert
Cotton's collection.[3]

Hakluyt then, from 1584 at latest, was well supplied with
cartographic information about Spanish America. For the geo‑
graphy of the Atlantic seaboard northward and of the St Law‑
rence basin, he depended largely on earlier sources. Those
specified by him[4] are 'a greate olde rounde carde' (i.e. on a polar
projection) shown to him in Paris by Dom António in 1584;
an 'olde excellent mappe' by Verrazzano in the possession of
Michael Lok, with its delineation of a 'little necke of lande' or
portage in 40° N; 'an olde excellent globe in the Queenes priuie
gallery at Westminster', which he ascribed also to Verrazzano;
'the mappe of Sebastian Cabot, cut by Clement Adams [in
1549] . . . which is to be seene in her Maiesties priuie gallerie at
Westminster, and in many other ancient merchants houses'. We
may perhaps add the so‑called 'Harleian' manuscript planisphere
of about 1544 (by Pierre Desceliers or John Rotz ?), the only

[1] Parks, *Hakluyt*, pp. 161–3.
[2] Hakluyt to Ralegh, 30 December 1586, Taylor, *Hakluyts*, II, 355.
[3] B.M., Cotton MS, Tiberius D. IX. References are cited by Skelton, 'Ralegh as a
   geographer', p. 143, n. 71.
[4] *DV* (1582), 'Epistle dedicatorie'; and in 'Discourse of western planting', cap.
   17, Taylor, *Hakluyts*, II, 287.

map of the Dieppe group to show the Verrazzanian isthmus and sea.[1]

While in Paris in 1583–4, Hakluyt applied himself to the collection of intelligence 'about North America and about French projects for voyages to America, in the interests of his master, Sir Francis Walsingham'.[2] The evidence that he brought back to London maps, or copies of maps, which he made available to his English associates is indirect but sufficient. First, there is a note by Thomas Harriot, written in 1596: 'Mr Hackluit / of Canada summe mappes of it' (B.M., Sloane MS 2292, f. 41). Second, the information which Hakluyt obtained in France, or subsequently, about French expeditions to Nova Scotia and Maine (Étienne Bellenger, 1583) and up the St Lawrence (Jacques Noël, before 1587; Stevan de Bocall, in the 1590s) was very probably cartographic, as well as textual or oral, in character. As D. B. Quinn has demonstrated, it provided place-names and delineations, doubtless supplied by Hakluyt or from his collections, to the compilers of the Molyneux globe of 1592 and of the 'Wright–Mercator' world map in the *Principal navigations* (1598–1600).[3] Some of this information was also made available to Edward Hayes, who used it in a treatise written *c.* 1593 and revised for publication in 1602. This is perhaps the only unambiguous illustration of the processes by which Hakluyt obtained possession of maps and placed them at the disposal of English projectors and cartographers.

For the North-west Passage, Hakluyt betrays no direct knowledge of the other maps and globes (including that of Gemma Frisius) cited by Willes and Gilbert; but he doubtless had access

[1] B.M., Additional MS 5413. Cf. references cited by Skelton 'Ralegh as a geographer', p. 135, n. 12.

[2] D. B. Quinn, 'The voyage of Étienne Bellenger to the Maritimes in 1583: a new document', *Canadian Historical Review*, XLIII (1962), 328–43; cf. also D. B. Quinn and J. Rousseau, 'Les toponymes amérindiens du Canada chez les anciens voyageurs anglais, 1591–1602', *Cahiers de géographie de Québec*, année 10 (1966), pp. 263–77. The paragraph which follows is based on these two papers.

[3] Quinn, 'The voyage of Étienne Bellenger' (1962), pp. 337–8; Quinn and Rousseau, 'Les toponymes amérindiens' (1966), pp. 264, 266–8. See below, pp. 281–3.

to the 'cardes and instruments' assembled by Michael Lok and shown to Dee in May 1576; to the charts supplied to and brought back by Frobisher, perhaps through Lok or Burghley; and to the charts of John Davis, either directly or through William Sanderson. Similarly, for the North-east Passage, the records of the Muscovy Company lent to Hakluyt for use in the *Principall navigations* must surely have included maps by Anthony Jenkinson, and John Dee, though they are nowhere mentioned textually except in the instructions to Pet and Jackman.[1] On the geography of the north, Hakluyt had studied Mercator's world map of 1569 and his map of Europe, in the second edition of 1572, from both of which he transcribed notes.[2]

There is no evidence that Hakluyt ever set eyes on maps directly derived from the two English circumnavigations, other than such compilation materials as were to be used in Molyneux's globe of 1592 and in Hondius' engraved hemispheric world map of *c.* 1593. Cavendish did however supply him with a large 'map of China, made in that land on paper made of bark,'[3] from which he printed in 1589 'certaine notes or references'.[4] In general, Hakluyt's geographical ideas on the southern sea routes and on the Indian and Pacific Oceans were based on Mercator's world map of 1569, supplemented and modified in succession by Ortelius' maps of 1587 and the reports of the English circumnavigations, by the maps of Portuguese origin published by Plancius and Linschoten (from 1592), by the records of the Dutch expeditions (from 1595–7), and by materials brought back from voyages of the English East India Company (from 1601–3). These materials, which were to be published by Purchas from 'Master Hakluyts many yeeres Collections', certainly included maps, very few of which got into print. An exception is the map of China which

---

[1] He did print in 1598 Borough's dedication to the Queen of 'his exact and notable mappe of Russia' (I, 417–18), now lost (we do not know when it was completed).

[2] *PN* (1589), pp. 248–9, 505. Cf. R. A. Skelton, 'Mercator and English geography in the 16th century', *Duisburger Forschungen*, VI (1962), 158–70.

[3] Emanuel van Meteren to the Treasurer of Zeeland, 18 January 1595, Parks, *Hakluyt*, p. 145.

[4] *PN* (1589), pp. 813–15.

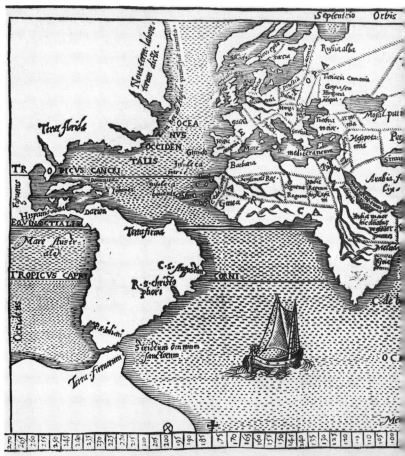

Septentrio Orbis

Rusia alba

OCEA
NVS
OCCIDEN
TALIS

TROPICVS CANCRI

Hispana zona
Eqvinoctialis

Mare Austr
ale

TROPICVS CAPR

Occidens

Terra firma

Terra firmorum

GRadus 180. demercationis Portugalensiū a terris isto ⊗ oppositis incipiunt, ac terminātur in gradus 16
huius cartæ versus orientem, secūdum computationem Hispanorum. Et sic insulæ Tharsis & Ophir dit,
mæ videntur extra illorum demercationem cadere, Portugalenses verò suam elevationem a terris isto signo
oppositis incipere aiunt, & terminare in gradus 180. huius carte, vt videantur prędictas insulas vtcūq; attingere, & gradus 180. demercationis Hispanorum a priore signo ⊗ secundum Hispanorum cōputationem. Vt
incipiunt a posteriore secundum Portugalenses versus occidentem, & terminantur in gradus 160. secundū
Hispanos, vel 180. secundum Portugalenses. Et sic, licet insulæ Tharsis & Ophir videntur attingere Portugale
ses, tamen insulæ Capo verde dictæ, quæ intra supradicta signa ⊗ ✠ cadunt, videtur omittere. Et sic dum
sulas Capoverde retinere volunt Portugalenses, illas Tharsis & Ophir non possunt attingere.

Fig. 1   Robert Thorne's world map of 1527. Reproduced

54

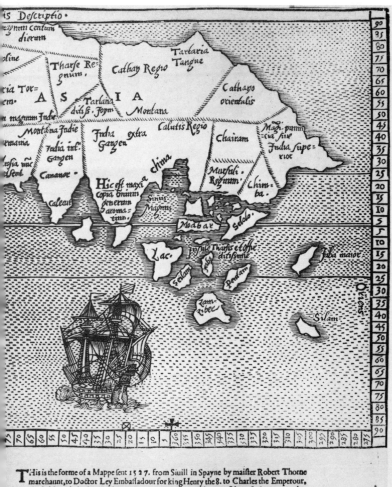

Tartaria
Tangue

Tharse Re-
gnum,

Cathay Regio

ria Tor-
em

A S I A

Tartaria
diuiss. Joph

Cathayo
orientalis

Montana

magnum Indie

Montana Indie

India extra
Gangen

Calutis Regio

Chairam

Magi. punu
cia siue
India supe-
rior

rmania

India inf.
gangen

Cananor

china

Hic est maxi
copia ბიიიი
generum
aromatum.

Mutfuli.
Regnum.

Chim-
ba.

caleat

Sinus
Magnus.

Moabar

Seba maior

Lac.

Selolo

Inste Tharfs etoffe
ditisfime

Selani

Pentam

Zam-
zibee

Silam

90
85
80
75
70
65
60
55
50
45
40
35
30
25
20
15
10
5
5
10
15
20
25
30
35
40
45
50
55
60
65
70
75
80
85
90

75 70 65 60 55 50 45 40 35 30 25 20 15 10 5 360 355 350 345 340 335 330 325 320 315 310 305 300 295 290 285 280 275

THis is the forme of a Mappe sent 1527. from Siuill in Spayne by maister Robert Thorne
marchaunt, to Doctor Ley Embassadour for king Henry the 8. to Charles the Emperour,
And although the same in this present time may seeme rude, yet I haue set it out, because his booke coulde not well be vnderstood without the same. The imperfection of
which Mappe may be excused by that tyme: the knowledge of Cosmographie not then be-
yng entred among our Marchauntes, as nowe it is.

for Richard Hakluyt (as a woodcut) in *Divers voyages* (1582).

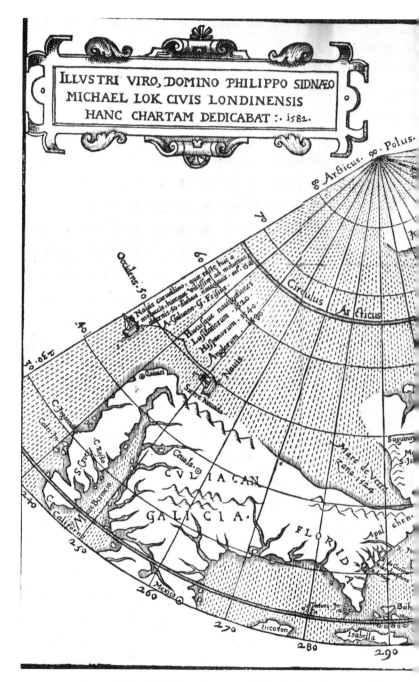

Fig. 2 Michael Lok's polar map of North America, 1582. Repr‹

56

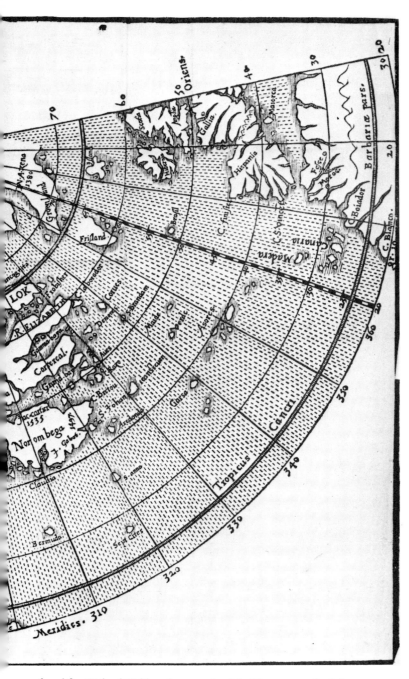

duced for Richard Hakluyt (as a woodcut) in *Divers voyages* (1582).

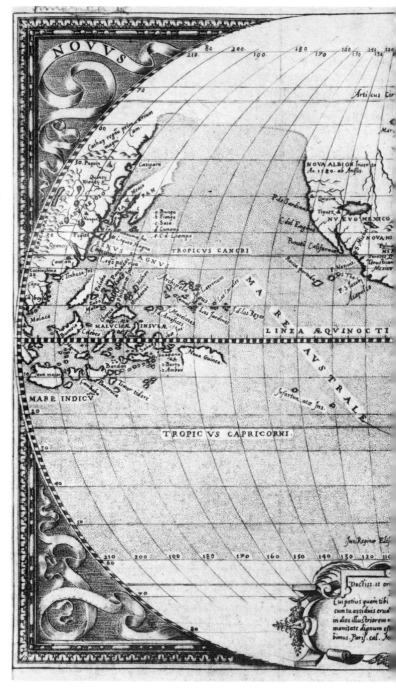

Fig. 3   The map of the Americas by F[ilips] G[alle]. Prefixed to

Hakluyt's translation of Pietro Martiro d'Anghiera, *Decades* (1587).

59

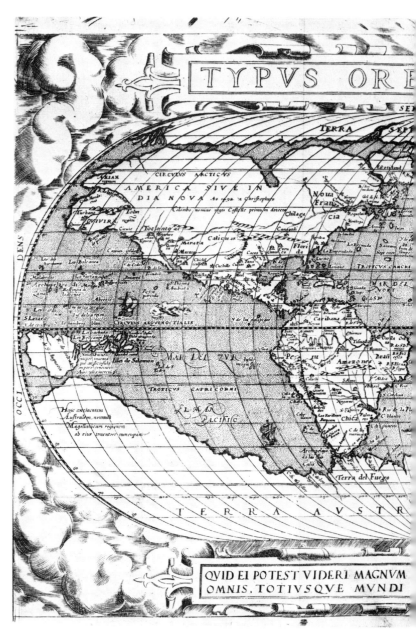

Fig. 4 World map (after Ortelius), 1589. Reproduced for Richard

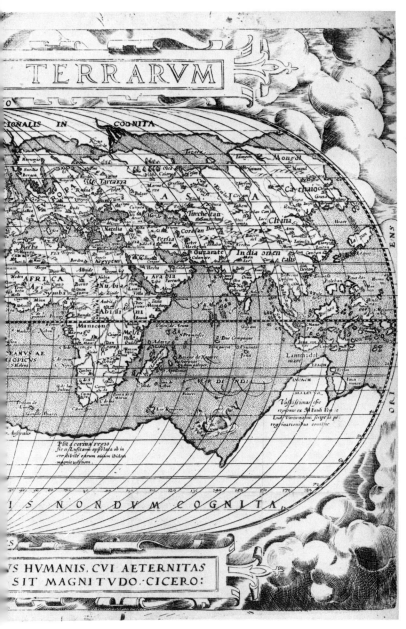

Hakluyt (as a copperplate), prefixed to *Principall navigations* (1589).

Fig. 5   The Edward Wright world map, 'a true hydrographical description of so
much of the world as hath beene hetherto discouered and is come to our

It appeareth by the discouerie of Francis Gaule
a Spaniard in the yeare 1584 that the sea betweene the west part of America and the most of Asia
which hath bene ordinarily set out as a straite
and named in most mapes the straight of Anian is
about 1200 leagues wide at the Latitude of 38 deg.
And that the distance betweene cape Mendozino and
cape California which most mapes and Cacharts
make to be 1300 or 1500 leagues is farre lesse then so

...en hath here reader a truely desographical description, so much of the world as hath
...owe helpe to discouered, and is easie to your knowl the Toledo, or Rieu in such, yet perform well, y...
...please begun set downe, have the same positions and distances that they haue in the olde, froma the
...skand in false longitudes and latitudes which they saue in this chart, which by the ordinarie sea-
...art can in use be performed. The way to finde the position or course from one place to
...her herein discribed. Assesseth notbing from this a middle, goe sell in the ordinarie sea chart.
...But to finde the distance, if both places haue the some latitude, see how many degrees of
...e meridian, taken til that latitude are contain betweene the two places, so so many, some...
...ques is the distance. If they differ in latitude, see how many degrees of the meridian...
...see about the middl of that difference are contained, betweene them and so many fore...
...begance is the distance.

knowledge'. State 1. Reproduced for Richard Hakluyt (as a copperplate),
prefixed to *Principal navigations*, II (1599).

'was by Captaine Saris . . . gotten at Bantam of a Chinese', given by him to Hakluyt in 1614, and engraved in the *Pilgrimes*.[1]

The reconstruction of the cartographic reference materials at Hakluyt's disposal must be made for the most part by inference only. Only once in his writings, in the 'Discourse of western planting', cap. 17, do we find him (like Willes) enumerating the maps he has consulted on a particular issue, and only in the 'Discourse' does he found a reasoned argument on maps rather than texts. Even if his geographical interests tended to lie at the periphery of knowledge, where cartographers had recourse to hypothesis and conjecture, this may suggest no very regular re/course to maps or lively confidence in their information. Indirectly, indeed, Hakluyt frequently writes as if a map or globe were on his table or in his mind's eye, stating with precision coordinates, bearings and distances. But we do not often have the impression, so forcibly conveyed in the writings of Dee or Ralegh and in the collections of Lord Burghley,[2] that he is positively thinking in a cartographic idiom, collating and annotating and even drawing maps to work out his argument. It is perhaps significant that in the *Principall navigations* only textual extracts are printed from the wall maps of Sebastian Cabot (in Clement Adams's version) and of Mercator.

This is the background against which we may consider Hakluyt's provision of printed maps in his publications. Those in *Divers voyages* (1582) have a certain air of extemporization.[3] The crudely engraved woodcut version of Robert Thorne's world map of 1527 is introduced by Hakluyt with the apology that 'his [Thorne's] booke coulde not well be vnderstood without the same', though he omitted it when reprinting Thorne's tract in the *Principall navigations*. An editorial failure is betrayed by the use of

[1] Purchas, *Pilgrimes*, III, 401.

[2] On Dee, cf. E. G. R. Taylor, *Tudor geography* (1930), chs. 5–7. On Ralegh: R. A. Skelton, 'Ralegh as a geographer', pp. 139–42. On Burghley: R. A. Skelton and Sir John Summerson, *A description of maps and architectural drawings in the collection made by William Cecil, first Baron Burghley, now at Hatfield House* (Rox/burghe Club, 1971).

[3] Cf. Quinn, *Richard Hakluyt, editor* (1967), pp. 17–26.

different prime meridians for the expression of longitude in the text and in the map respectively. The 'Lok map', a more accom⁄plished engraving, presumably prepared expressly for the *Divers voyages*, scarcely supports the principal thesis of the publication; it expresses Lok's geography of North America rather than Hakluyt's, the search for water routes into the Pacific in preference to territory for plantation.

With the finely constructed and executed map of America, signed 'F.G.S.' which accompanied his Latin edition of Peter Martyr's *Decades* (1587), Hakluyt plainly had more to do, as the dedication by the cartographer (Filips Galle ?) indicates.[1] Based on a Spanish original, and doubtless compiled and engraved in Antwerp, it includes data from Frobisher's north⁄western voyages, from Drake's circumnavigation and from Ralegh's colonial venture (the name Virginia here appearing for the first time in a printed map), which must have been supplied by Hakluyt. If hardly appropriate as an illustration of Peter Martyr, the map creditably reflects contemporary knowledge of the New World and the Pacific. The similarity of the map to the 'Silver map' of the world, the Drake medallion, has led some historians, notably Miller Christy, to suggest that the silver map was the source of the 1587 map, and, further, that the two works were executed by the same hand. The Drake medal is now known to have been made by Michael Mercator and put on sale by him in London in 1589.[2] Thus it would appear that the medal is partly derived from the 1587 map (or a common source), and not vice versa.

That the *Principall navigations*, like Ramusio's collection on which it was modelled, needed maps in illustration of its text, Hakluyt was evidently aware. For 'this singular and much to be lamented omission' (in J. G. Kohl's words[3]), he makes a lame

[1] On the sources and authorship of this map, cf. Quinn and Skelton, edd., *PN* (1589), I (1965), xlviii.

[2] R. M. Christy, *The silver map of the world . . .* (1900), pp. 41–4. A Drake medal bearing an inscription by Michael Mercator to this effect was sold at Christie's on 4 April 1967 (lot 138): and see H. P. Kraus, *Sir Francis Drake. A pictorial biography* (Amsterdam, 1970), pp. 104–5, 218–20.

[3] J. G. Kohl, *A descriptive catalogue of those maps . . . relating to America . . . mentioned in Vol. III of Hakluyt's great work* (1857), p. 5.

and disingenuous excuse: 'Nowe, because peraduenture it would bee expected as necessarie, that the descriptions of so many parts of the world would farre more easily be conceiued of the Readers, by adding Geographicall, and Hydrographicall tables thereunto ... I haue contented my selfe with inserting into the worke one of the best generall mappes of the world onely, vntill the comming out of a ... terrestriall Globe ... composed by M. Emmerie Mollineux ...' With some reason Kohl protested 'O good Hakluyt, how short, how unsatisfactory, how tyrannically spoken!' There were no regional maps; none of the numerous original maps mentioned in the printed documents was repro-duced; and the oval world map provided was a carelessly executed copy of the revised world map engraved for Ortelius in 1587. This failure is ascribed by D. B. Quinn, following Kohl, pri-marily to considerations of financial expense and to 'Hakluyt's determination to spare nothing to print every word he could afford'; and secondarily to the labour which would be involved in compilation of up-to-date maps.[1]

A travel collection on the scale of the *Navigationi et viaggi* or the *Principall navigations* could hardly be adequately illustrated except by a world atlas. The sheet-maps put out from Venetian shops in the middle decades of the century provided the cartographic counterpart of Ramusio's volumes. When Hakluyt was preparing his collections, competent map-engravers, Flemish or English, were available in London; but there was no native map-trade, and no entrepreneur or editor capable, like Ortelius, of the effort necessary to organize an atlas. Not until after 1600 was a world atlas to be published in England or with text in English.[2] Ortelius' *Theatrum*, which made an immeasurable contribution to geographical culture throughout Europe after 1570, did not contain the seeds of growth. The provision of new maps in its later editions tended to reflect Ortelius' historical interests rather than the increase of geographical knowledge; in his mapping of North America and the Pacific, for instance, he made no sub-

---

[1] Quinn and Skelton, edd., *PN* (*1589*), I (1965), xlviii–l.
[2] Cf. R. A. Skelton, 'The first English world atlases', in *Kartengeschichte und Kartenbearbeitung: Festschrift zum 80. Geburtstag von Wilhelm Bonacker* (1968).

stantial correction or revision after 1589. Thus, when Ortelius' nephew Jacob Cool transmitted in 1590 Hakluyt's request for a new map of 'that region which lies between the Mexican city and the Northern parts', Ortelius agreed to do so on the condition that Hakluyt supplied the materials.[1]

If the *Principall navigations* of 1589 (in D. B. Quinn's phrase) 'had to float on its sea of words alone', the globe of Emery Molyneux, compiled with Hakluyt's assistance and engraved by Hondius in 1592, was to contribute to the cartographic illustra-tion of the three-volume *Principal navigations* of 1598–1600. For the world map on Mercator's – or Wright's – projection included in the later collection was substantially a plane version of the globe, from which (as stated in the address to the reader on the map) the geographical data were transferred and replotted, per-haps by Edward Wright, with updating of detail from discoveries made since 1592.[2] This distinguished map, with 'its careful discrimination between actual discovery and conjectural geo-graphy',[3] is a reliable epitome of geographical knowledge at a turning-point in world history, and thus a worthy adjunct to Hakluyt's great compendium.

The compilation of the Molyneux terrestrial globe and of the 'Wright–Mercator' world map, with analysis of their sources and of their interrelationship, still awaits study in depth and detail, which cannot be attempted here.[4] That Hakluyt was in com-munication with Molyneux from 1589 or earlier is indicated by his reference to the globe in preparation, 'collected and reformed according to the newest, secretest, and latest discoueries, both Spanish, Portugall, and English', under the patronage of William Sanderson. Molyneux, in his address to the reader, cites as his

[1] Hessels, *Epistulae*, no. 184, p. 443.

[2] On this map see E. J. S. Parsons and W. F. Morris, 'Edward Wright and his work', *Imago Mundi*, III (1939), 68; A. M. Hind, *Engraving in England in the sixteenth and seventeenth centuries*, I (1952), 178–81.

[3] E. Heawood, *A history of geographical discovery in the seventeenth and eighteenth centuries* (1912), p. 13.

[4] Cf. H. M. Wallis, 'The first English globe: a recent discovery', *Geographical Journal*, CXVII (1951), 275–90; 'Further light on the Molyneux globes', *ibid.*, CXXI (1955), 304–11; and references on pp. 69–73 below.

sources in general 'castigatissimas chartas marinas quibus Hispani et Lusitani in suis Americis & Orientalibus Indicis nauigationib*us* vtuntur; Nec non et Anglicorum aliquot hominum excellentium probatissimas geographicas descriptiones in Septen-trionalibus . . . partibus'. Sanderson, to whom Molyneux was recommended by John Davis, could have given access to the geographical collections of his father-in-law Ralegh, which included 'chartas marinas'; and it is a reasonable (if as yet un-documented) inference that Molyneux also received compilation materials from Hakluyt, the most active contemporary collector of 'geographicas descriptiones', if not of maps.

In his studies of the St Lawrence region, D. B. Quinn has in fact identified certain features in the globe and in the world map which were, in all probability, supplied by Hakluyt. From 'a sketch of Étienne Bellenger's discoveries' may be derived the conspicuous delineation of the Island of St John ('I: S. Joan' in the globe; 'I: S. Iohn' in the map), off C. Breton Island, and the suggestion of the Bay of Fundy ('B. menin').[1] From a French source also, either Stevan de Bocall or Cartier's great-nephew Jacques Noël, Hakluyt must have obtained the name 'Tadouac' for the great lake, 'beyond the three Saults, where Jacques Cartier left to discover', as Hayes wrote.[2] This name occurs first in Hayes' treatise, and again in a marginal note by Hakluyt in the *Principal navigations*, III (1600), 378; and 'The Lake of Tadouac' appears in the world map, as the earliest representation of Lake Ontario in printed cartography. As early as June 1587, Noël, citing his own observations and Cartier's 'booke made in maner of a sea Chart', had criticized the world map of F.G., published in Hakluyt's edition of Peter Martyr (1586), which (as he noted) 'dothe not marke or set downe The great Lake, which is aboue the Saults'; but Noël's letter, as printed by Hakluyt in 1600, gives no name to the lake.[3]

[1] Quinn, 'The voyage of Étienne Bellenger', p. 338.
[2] Brereton, *A briefe relation* (1602), p. 21. Cf. Quinn and Rousseau, 'Les toponymes amérindiens' (1966), pp. 264, 266–8; and W. F. Ganong, *Crucial maps* (1964), pp. 456–61.
[3] *PN*, III (1600), 236.

From 1597 onward, various works whose translation or publication in English was promoted by Hakluyt included maps and
other illustrations, generally copied from those of the original
editions by London engravers, including (of those who signed
plates) William Rogers, Robert Beckit and Renold Elstrack. The
bookseller's imprint on the plates of the Linschoten (1598)
suggests that he paid the charges for engraving as part of the
publication costs of the book. To the development of cartography
in England they made no contribution.

Appendix
Edward Wright and the 1599 world map

HELEN WALLIS

The world chart added to *Principal navigations*, II (1599) was known for
many years as the Molyneux map or the Hakluyt–Molyneux map, on
account of its similarity to Molyneux's terrestrial globe, 1592, from which
much of its geographical information appears to have been derived. The
association of Edward Wright's name with the map has been suggested
mainly in the light of new evidence available over the last thirty years.
Edward Wright was famous in his lifetime and subsequently for his adaptation of Mercator's projection using mathematical formulae. In 1599 he
published his chart 'The voyage of the right Honorable the Earle of
Cumberland to the Islands Azores AD 1589' in *Certaine errors in nauigation*
(1599). A chart of the northeast Atlantic on Mercator's projection, which
appears to be a manuscript version (probably an earlier version) of the
printed map, is preserved at Hatfield House. For various reasons this is
believed to have been drawn *c.* 1595 and is attributed to Wright. If correctly
dated, it would be the earliest manuscript map on Mercator's projection
extant.[1] Wright lent his manuscript text on the projection to Jodocus
Hondius, who in 1596 anticipated him in publishing (without acknow

[1] R. A. Skelton and J. Summerson, *A description of maps and architectural drawings
in the collection made by William Cecil, first Baron Burghley, now at Hatfield House*
(1971), pp. 70–1, pl. 13.

ledgement to Wright) his so-called 'Christian Knight' map of the world, drawn on Mercator's projection as constructed by a graphical method. For this he incurred Wright's censure. In *Certaine errors* (1599) Wright published extracts from Jodocus Hondius' letters which expressed concern at his falling out with his one-time friend. The matter is also alluded to by Anthony Linton whose comments in *Newes of the complement of the art of nauigation* (1609) attest to Wright's reputation as the English authority on Mercator's projection: 'I answere & freely confesse, that the said M. Wright hath exceedingly wel-deserued of Nauigation, and specially in that proiection of the sea Mappe by him deuised, (according to which, the Mappe commonly annexed to the volumes of our English Discoueries, and the great quarter Maps published at Amsterdam by Iodocus Hondius, anno 1602, are framed).'[1] Thus it would appear that Wright, as the man publicly acknow-ledged to have introduced Mercator's projection to England, was responsible at least for the construction of the world map in *Principal navigations*. If anyone else had used the projection invented by him, Wright would pre-sumably have required an official acknowledgement.

Further evidence in support of Wright's authorship derives from the discovery of a world chart by Edward Wright, engraved by William Kip and published in the second edition of Wright's *Certaine errors* (1610), of which a unique example is preserved in the Bodleian Library, Oxford.[2] This chart is generally similar to that in *Principal navigations* but larger, and as well as being marked with observations of magnetic variation, has some major geographical revisions incorporated and explained in legends. For example, the west coast of South America is given an easterly trend, follow-ing Cavendish's discovery; the coast of Tartary is altered; and the Southern Continent is supplied from a large ancient sea chart. The discoveries of Quiros and Torres are also supplied, with an attached explanatory legend. In a further legend Wright states that he first published in his former edition of *Certaine errors* the method of applying Mercator's projection, and he goes on to say that Hondius had learnt of the technique from him, and used it for graduat-ing his map of the world and his maps of the four parts of the world. In 1657 Joseph Moxon, in his third edition of *Certaine errors* (pressmark B.M., C.31.e.25), includes a chart of the world which he describes as 'first set forth by Mr. Edw. Wright and now newly corrected . . . 1655'. This is a later edition of the Bodleian map of 1610. The plate has been altered to

---

[1] A. Linton, *Newes of the complement of the art of nauigation*, London (1609), p. 14; see also p. 41.

[2] E. J. S. Parsons and W. F. Morris, 'Edward Wright and his work', *Imago Mundi*, III (1939), 61–71.

incorporate further new discoveries. It is not clear whether Moxon is refer-ring to the map of 1610, or to the earlier one of 1599. Nevertheless, the similarities between the 1599 map and that of 1610, and Wright's statement about revisions, point to Wright as the author of the earlier map.

One other map which bears a family resemblance to the map in *Principal navigations* is a manuscript world map now in the duke of Northumberland's possession at Alnwick Castle. This has been known as the Leconfield world map, and is sometimes attributed to Edward Wright, presumably because it is similar in various ways to Wright's map of 1610, but the discoveries displayed show that the map was completed after 1616.

On the basis of this evidence it would appear that Edward Wright was mainly, or more probably wholly, responsible for the construction of the map. He had already collaborated in the making of Molyneux's globes. (The son of William Sanderson their financial sponsor wrote in 1656, 'When that excellent Mathematician Wright, and the rare Artisan Moli-neux, could not finde any other person, willing to disburse over 1000 l, to perfect them, my father did.'[1]) In 1599 commending to Lord Howard of Effingham the proposed 'Lecture in the Art of Nauigation', Wright was writing of Hakluyt as 'my learned friend', and referred to the first volume of Hakluyt's 'Discoueries' published a year previously.[2] The engraver of the map remains unknown. A. M. Hind suggested as one possibility, Jodocus Hondius (although by then he was settled in the Netherlands), because of the similarity of style to the Molyneux globes of which Hondius was the engraver, but this seems very improbable. Hind's other suggestion of Benjamin Wright as one whose style is similar is a more acceptable one.[3] It is perhaps significant that Benjamin Wright engraved the terrestrial and celestial charts for John Blagrave's *Astrolabium Vranicum generale* (1596), and that these maps are reductions from the Molyneux globes. Whoever was the engraver of the map in *Principal navigations*, the fact that Wright's map of 1610 was engraved from new plates by William Kip suggests that Wright did not secure possession of the plates. That he was not named on the map as the author, nor explicitly claimed it as his, may indicate that in the com-pilation of the map he was one of several collaborators.

Among other candidates for authorship Molyneux can probably be ruled out, although various historians made the natural assumption that he had

---

[1] Sir William Sanderson, *An answer to a scurrilous pamphlet* (1656), sig. A. 3v.
[2] E. Wright, Dedication to *The hauen-finding art* (1599), see below, p. 312.
[3] A. M. Hind, *Engraving in England in the sixteenth and seventeenth centuries*, I (1952), 181, 213.

had a hand in it,[1] and his terrestrial globe was a valuable source for material in the compilation. It is now known, however, that Molyneux had gone to the Netherlands in 1596 or 1597 and was settled there by January 1598 (and had died by 9 April 1599).[2] Thomas Harriot, on the other hand, had already in the 1580s worked on a mathematical solution to the construction of a map on this projection and had continued to do so in the 1590s, but his approach was more sophisticated than that of Wright and he was not satisfied with what he had done: it was not until 1613–14 that he eventually reached what was, for him, a satisfactory mathematical solution.[3] We have however no maps constructed on his tables, and the Wright map, constructed by his method set out in *Certaine errors* (1599) for the addition of secants, appears to contain no evidence of Harriot's influence so far as its construction was concerned. In 1595–6 Harriot was busy collecting and studying maps and sailing directions on a world-wide scale, and was closely associated with Richard Hakluyt in doing so.[4] The possibility that one or both of them contributed materials towards the compilation of the map remains open to further investigation. That Wright was responsible for its construction admits of little doubt.

The map was by far the most original of all Hakluyt's maps, and one of the most authoritative of its day. It was noteworthy in showing only discovered coasts, as the address to the reader indicated, for it described itself as 'a true hydrographical description of so much of the world as hath been hitherto discouered . . .' No southern continent was marked, in striking contrast both to Hondius' map of the circumnavigation of Drake and Cavendish, *c.* 1593, and to his 'Christian Knight map' (1596), in which the southern continent provided the stage for a major iconographic display. The *Principal navigations* map was altogether a very workmanlike production,

---

[1] For example, C. H. Coote in 'Shakespeare's New Map', *The New Shakespeare Society's Transactions* (1878), pp. 88–100; and 'Note on the New Map' in A. H. Markham (ed.), *The voyages and works of John Davis* (1880); also (amongst others) Henry R. Wagner, *Sir Francis Drake's voyage around the world* (1926), p. 422.

[2] Helen Wallis, 'Further light on the Molyneux globes', *Geographical Journal*, CXXI (1955), 307–8.

[3] See E. G. R. Taylor and D. H. Sadler, 'The doctrine of nauticall triangles compendious', *Journal of the Institute of Navigation*, VI (1953), 131–47; J. V. Pepper, 'Harriot's unpublished papers', *History of Science*, VI (1967), 17–39; *idem*, 'Harriot's calculation of the meridional parts as logarithmic tangents', *Archive for History of Exact Sciences*, IV (1968), 359–413.

[4] Most of the evidence is in B.M., Sloane MS 2292, and was discussed by D. B. Quinn in a so-far unpublished paper at the Thomas Harriot Seminar, Oxford, December 1971.

providing a faithful graphical depiction of discoveries printed in the text and especially those which Hakluyt himself highlighted. Thus the discoveries made by Drake and Cavendish on their circumnavigations are recorded (but their tracks omitted, in contrast to the Molyneux globe). Their achievement was acclaimed in a legend added to the plate in the second state,[1] which also referred to Pedro Sarmiento's discoveries. A separate legend noted the importance of Francisco de Gualle's voyage in revealing the width of the North Pacific, a discovery which Hakluyt had specially noted in his 'Epistle Dedicatorie'. The map's compiler thus gave foreign navigators their due, just as Hakluyt in his text indicated those achievements of foreign enterprise relevant to his theme. The map was a demonstration of the *known* distribution of land and sea, as revealed by actual voyages of discovery. It contained no armchair flights of fancy or theoretical conjectures about the unknown. Evidence of its immediate fame is provided by Shakespeare's allusion to it in *Twelfth Night* as 'the new map, with the augmentation of the Indies' (the somewhat cryptic phrase about the Indies was presumably a reference to the Solomon Islands, boldly depicted (but not named) to the east of New Guinea, and looking like an appendix to the East Indian archipelago). One other literary reference which probably alludes to the map is to be found in Thomas Dekker's *The guls hornbook* (1609) (ch. 1. 'The old world and the new waighed together'): 'What an excellent workeman therefore were he that could cast the Globe of it into a new mould: And not to make it looke like Mullineux his Globe with a rownd face sleekt and washt ouer with whites of egges; but to have it in *Plano*, as it was at first, with all the ancient circles, lines, paralels and figures.' Hind suggests that 'as it was at first' may refer to the world map copied from Ortelius in Hakluyt's first edition, for this was also a projection *in plano*, though in the form of a flattened globe.[2]

[1] Fig. 6, at the end of this volume.
[2] Hind, *Engraving in England*, I (1952), 180.

8

From Hakluyt to Purchas

C. R. STEELE

'My purpose is not to steale Master Hakluyt's labours out of the World . . . I had rather giue you new things.'[1]

Thus wrote the Reverend Samuel Purchas, the self-appointed successor to Richard Hakluyt, in his four-volume collection of travels *Purchas his pilgrimes* published in 1625. A study of the *Pilgrimes* and his earlier volume *Purchas his pilgrimage*, which appeared in 1613, 1614, 1617 and 1626, is essential in order to obtain a picture of Richard Hakluyt's collecting activity after 1600. The last volume of Hakluyt's *Principal navigations* appeared in 1600 but after this date Hakluyt continued collecting narratives of voyages and travels for a projected future edition. This edition had not appeared by the time of Hakluyt's death on 23 November 1616 and the material Hakluyt had collected was eventually obtained by Samuel Purchas. The result can be seen in the *Pilgrimes*, which contains one hundred and twenty-one items that are directly attributable to Hakluyt. The Hakluyt legacy was therefore no small one.

The historical reputation and image of Samuel Purchas, 1577–1626, has suffered from a constant comparison with Richard Hakluyt. Indeed G. B. Parks believed that 'to dwell on the contrast is to discover a growing dislike to Purchas, whose features gradually and irresistibly resolve into the features of Pecksniff'.[2] Other writers who have been equally critical of Purchas have been Sir John Knox Laughton, Sir William Foster and Richard S. Dunn.[3] More sympathetic writers, however, have emerged in

---

[1] Purchas, *Hakluytus posthumus or Purchas his pilgrimes* (1625), III, 808.

[2] Parks, *Hakluyt*, p. 224.

[3] *DNB*. W. Foster, 'Samuel Purchas' in *Richard Hakluyt and his successors*, ed. E. Lynam (1946), pp. 54–5; R. S. Dunn, 'Seventeenth-century English historians of America', in *Seventeenth-century America*, ed. J. M. Smith (Chapel Hill, 1959), pp. 206–7.

E. G. R. Taylor, Louis B. Wright and Loren E. Pennington, who have emphasized that Purchas must be viewed by the standards of his own time and not by those of the twentieth century.[1] As must, of course, Richard Hakluyt, but Hakluyt's vision and achievement manages to surmount the centuries. It is far more realistic, if comparisons have to be made, to compare Samuel Purchas with the editors who came after him, such as John Harris and John Stevens, rather than with Hakluyt. Purchas' editorial pruning and rigid organization of material can then be seen as a natural symptom of contemporary publishing and editing.

Samuel Purchas was very much a self-made man and praise is due to him for the enormous amount of work, in collecting, editing and proof-reading, that went into his large folio volumes. Purchas was born in Thaxted in Essex in 1577 and took his M.A. at St John's College, Cambridge, in 1600 before proceeding to a bachelor of divinity degree.[2] In 1601 he became curate of Purleigh and then in 1604 vicar of Eastwood in Essex. It was from Eastwood that Purchas brought to publication his first collection *Purchas his pilgrimage*, which appeared in 1613. This work was intended to 'bring Religion from Paradise to the Arke, and thence follow her round about the World, and (for her sake) obserue the World it selfe...'[3] It was therefore a sort of religious world gazetteer, covering Asia, Africa and America. Purchas acknowledged that 'this my first Voyage of Discouerie... hath made mee indebted to seuen hundred Authors, of one or other kind, in I know not how many hundreds of their Treatises, Epistles, Relations and Histories, of diuers subiects and Languages'.[4] Purchas places on record his debt to previous collections, in particular those of Ramusio and Hakluyt, although he did consult 'many Manuscripts, and many Relations from friends of mine yet liu-

E. G. R. Taylor, *Late Tudor and Early Stuart Geography 1583–1650* (1934), p. 62; L. B. Wright, *Religion and empire* (Chapel Hill, 1943), p. 116; L. E. Pennington, *Hakluytus posthumus: Samuel Purchas and the promotion of English overseas expansion* (Emporia, Emporia State Research Studies, 14, no. 3 (1966)), *passim*.
H. W. King, 'Ancient wills 7', *Transactions of the Essex Archaeological Society*, IV (1869), 166.
Purchas, *Purchas his pilgrimage* (1613), sig. ¶4r.
Ibid., sig. ¶2v.

ing',[1] Nevertheless, unlike Hakluyt, Purchas can be termed a static collector in his collecting of material from other countries. Indeed he admitted that he had never travelled more than two hundred miles from Thaxted in his whole life.[2]

Purchas' debt to Hakluyt at this stage was limited to what he could cull from Hakluyt's printed works, for the two men had not yet met. Purchas admitted the inspiration of Hakluyt who:

> of his Countri⁄men meriteth an euerlasting name, and to me (though knowne at this time, only by those portraitures of his industrious spirit) hath beene as Admirall, holding out the light vnto me in these seas, and as diligent a guide by land, (which I willingly, yea dutifully, acknowledge) in a great part of this my long and wearisome Pilgrimage.[3]

The publication of the *Pilgrimage* brought success and fame to Purchas, who saw himself 'leaping out of the Dungeon of obscuritie'.[4] The *Pilgrimage*, with its religious orientation, had considerable success in a book market dominated by theological works. Successive editions of the *Pilgrimage* appeared in 1614, 1617 and 1626 with King James I allegedly reading it seven times.[5] Small wonder therefore that ecclesiastical promotion soon followed for Purchas. In 1614 he became chaplain to his patron, George Abbot, archbishop of Canterbury, and in the same year was appointed rector of St Martins, Ludgate.

Samuel Purchas and Richard Hakluyt obviously met some⁄ time during 1613 for Purchas reveals in the second edition of the *Pilgrimage*, 'I haue beene much beholden to M. Hakluit for many written Treatises in this kinde'.[6] Hakluyt probably saw in Purchas the vigour and the energy which he could no longer bring to bear on the material he had collected. Purchas must have been over⁄ joyed at meeting Hakluyt and with gaining access to Hakluyt's vast store of manuscripts. The infusion of Hakluyt's material is the main reason for the increase in size of the second edition of the *Pilgrimage*. Purchas increased his stock of authors from over seven

[1] *Ibid.*, sig. A6r.   [2] Purchas, *Pilgrimes*, I, 74.
[3] Purchas, *Pilgrimage*, p. 653.
[4] Purchas, *Purchas his pilgrimage*, 2nd ed. (1614), sig. ¶2r.
[5] Purchas, *Purchas his pilgrimage*, 4th ed. (1626), sig. ¶4v.
[6] Purchas, *Pilgrimage* (1614), sig. A5r.

hundred in 1613 to just over one thousand in 1614, with a consequent increase in content from 752 to 918 pages. Purchas
dutifully acknowledged that much of this was done by 'the help
of my painful friend Mr. Hakluyt (to whose labours these of mine
are so much indetted)'.[1]

The *Pilgrimage* utilizes much of the material that appears in
enlarged form in the *Pilgrimes* and even a few items which do not.
An analysis of Hakluyt's collecting activity is, however, more
easily carried out from the *Pilgrimes*, for Purchas in the *Pilgrimage*
condenses and rewords Hakluyt's material to such an extent that
accurate analysis is not always possible. As Purchas himself
wrote, the *Pilgrimage* is 'mine own in matter (though borrowed)
and in forme of words and method: Whereas my Pilgrims are the
Authors themselues, acting their owne parts in their owne words'.[2]
Purchas' use of Hakluyt's manuscripts led to an increasing
emphasis in the *Pilgrimage* of its geographical and descriptive
elements. Purchas dutifully acknowledged that Hakluyt's 'helpes
in this second Edition, haue much more obliged me (that I say
not thee) vnto his laborious Collections; . . . and your poore
Pilgrime, with praiers for him, and praises of his paines in
getting and bountie in communicating, doth according to his
wit, without hacking, professe Hakluit (in this kinde) his greatest
Benefactor'.[3]

This amicable relationship was not to last and a disagreement
took place between the two men before Hakluyt's death in 1616.
Purchas notes that during his preparation for the third edition of
the *Pilgrimage*, published in 1617, 'I could not obtaine like kindnes
from him, I know not how affected or infected with emulation
or iealousie, yet shall his name liue whiles my writings endure, as
without whose helpes and industrious Collecions, perhaps I had
neuer troubled the worlde in this kinde'.[4] It is not clear when or
exactly why this quarrel took place but it is conceivable that
Hakluyt, aged and perhaps ill, resented either the success of
Purchas' *Pilgrimage* or Purchas' use of his material. Unfortu-

---

[1] *Ibid.*, p. 743.   [2] Purchas, *Pilgrimage* (1626), sig. ¶5r.
[3] Purchas, *Pilgrimage* (1614), pp. 782–3.
[4] Purchas, *Purchas his pilgrimage*, 3rd ed. (1617), p. 972.

nately the only remaining evidence is Purchas' cryptic account of the misunderstanding. Purchas certainly wanted to be Hakluyt's official successor although Hakluyt's will made in 1612 makes no reference to Purchas at all.[1] This is not too surprising when it is recalled that Purchas and Hakluyt did not meet until some-time in 1613. It is however puzzling to read that when talking about the Mexican Codex Mendoza Purchas states 'it remained amongst his papers [i.e. Hakluyt's] till his death, whereby (according to his last will in that kinde) I became possessour thereof'.[2] Purchas must surely only be referring to a verbal promise he had received from Hakluyt during their period of co-operation.

Nevertheless Purchas did manage to acquire Hakluyt's papers. He wrote in the *Pilgrimes*:

> As for Master Hakluyts many yeeres Collections, and what stocke I receiued from him in written Papers, in the Table of Authours you shall find: whom I will thus farre honour, that though it be but Materials, and that many Bookes haue not one Chapter in that kind, yet that stocke encouraged me to vse my endeuours in and for the rest. I was therein a Labourer also, both to get them (not without hard conditions) and to forme and frame those Materials to their due place and order in this Ædifice, the whole Artifice (such as it is) being mine owne.[3]

The phrase 'not without hard conditions' is significant, for it probably means that Purchas had to buy the documents from the executors of Hakluyt's will. Edmond Hakluyt was only twenty-three when his father died and probably needed the money derived from the sale of his father's papers. Purchas himself was certainly not rich at the time of Hakluyt's death nor for several years after. Indeed in his religious work *Purchas his pilgrim*, pub-lished in 1619, he talked of the deaths in his family in 1618 and 1619 and 'Myselfe almost executed by Executorship'.[4] In the

---

[1] Hakluyt's will is printed in Taylor, *Hakluyts*, II, 506–9; see pp. 326–7, below.
[2] Purchas, *Pilgrimes*. III, 1066.
[3] *Ibid.*, I, sig. ¶4v.
[4] S. Purchas, *Purchas his pilgrim. Microcosmus or the historie of man* (1619), sig. ¶4r.

Pilgrimes he indicated that 'If I had not liued in great part vpon Exhibition of charitable friends, and on extraordinary labours of Lecturing (as the terme is) the Pilgrime had beene a more agreeing name to me, then Purchas'.[1]

Purchas to his credit always remained faithful to the memory of Hakluyt as the full title of the *Pilgrimes* reveals. Purchas was often lavish in his praise of Hakluyt and never resorted to over-critical or underhand references to Hakluyt at a time when Purchas was better known to the reading public than Hakluyt. By 1700 the bookseller Thomas Bennet could price the five volumes of Purchas at 50*s* (i.e. the *Pilgrimes* plus the 1626 *Pilgrim-age*) and the three volumes in two of Hakluyt at 15*s*.[2] The main type of critical remark that Purchas makes in the *Pilgrimes* about Hakluyt is, for example, when he writes in volume three that 'I found this Worke translated in M. Hakluyts Papers; but I can scarsly call it English, it had so much of the Spanish garbe'.[3] This comment was made in reference to a translation Purchas published from the *Historia general de los hechos de los Castellanos* of Antonio Herrera y Tordesillas. Purchas indicates authors like Herrera that he obtained from Hakluyt in the contents list of the *Pilgrimes*. Thus items 'such as haue H. added, I borrowed from Master Hakluyts papers and such as haue H. and P. pertaine to both, beeing otherwise printed or in my possession written, wherein yet I made vse of some labour of his'.[4] There are, how-ever, twenty-three items which Purchas obtained from Hakluyt and which are not acknowledged in the contents list. Some of these Purchas acknowledges within the text or in the margins, but others are not mentioned, probably through hasty printing and proof-reading. Purchas did have an immense editorial task and his four huge volumes, with over four thousand pages, com-prised one of the largest publications in the English language at that time.

---

[1] Purchas, *Pilgrimes*, I, sig. ¶4v.

[2] N. Hodgson and C. Blagdon, *The notebook of Thomas Bennet and Henry Clements*, Oxford Bibliographical Society, n.s., VI (1956), 53.

[3] Purchas, *Pilgrimes*, III, 855.

[4] *Ibid.*, I, sig. ¶6r.

In the *Pilgrimes* Purchas derived the following items from Hakluyt:

	H	HP	(H)[1]		
Volume I	18	2	2 ⎫	29 ⎫	
Volume II	4	1	2 ⎭		121
Volume III	24	16	9 ⎫	92 ⎭	
Volume IV	27	6	10 ⎭		
	—	—	—		
	73	25	23		
	—	—	—		

The first two volumes of Purchas relate to those areas of the world known to the ancient world, whilst the last two cover all the world 'which the Ancients knew not'.[2] The figures 29: 92 therefore fully reflect Hakluyt's overall interest in the New World and English discoveries. Only fourteen items are reprinted from the *Principal navigations*, so that Purchas does adhere to his aim of not merely reproducing Hakluyt. The items printed in the *Pilgrimes* do not quite cover all the manuscripts Purchas obtained from Hakluyt's executors, for Purchas omits some accounts on Virginia and Newfoundland.

Volume one of the *Pilgrimes* reveals the increased collecting activity of Hakluyt after 1600 with regard to voyages and travels to the East, in particular of those voyages sent out by the East India Company. These accounts are concentrated in Books 3 and 4, and Purchas acknowledges his debt to Hakluyt with respect to voyages one to six, eleven and twelve. Walter Payton, who wrote an account of the twelfth voyage, arrived back in England in July 1614 so that the last date Purchas provides for Hakluyt's collecting activities on the East Indies is towards the end of 1614. Purchas maintained Hakluyt's tradition of collecting the accounts of these voyages although he notes:

> After this twelfth Voyage, the order of that reckoning is altered, because the Voyages ensuing were set forth by a ioynt stocke, and not by particular

[1] (H) being those items for which Purchas gives no symbol but which he derived from Hakluyt.

[2] Purchas, *Pilgrimes*, I, sig. ¶5v.

and proper ships, stockes, Factories, (as before) but promiscuous and generally accountable to the whole societie. Of which, all are not come to our hands: such as I haue (that which thence is meete for the publike view) giue I thee.[1]

The rest of Hakluyt's material on the East ranges widely both geographically and chronologically, from the medieval chronicle of William de Rubriquis to Diego de Pantoja's letter written in China in 1602.

The fact that Purchas prints only three items from Hakluyt on Africa is perhaps explained by the lack of activity by the English in this area and also by the fact that much material on Africa had already appeared. Apart from the appropriate sections in the *Principal navigations* Hakluyt had encouraged the English transla-tion of Duarte Lopes' *A report of the kingdome of Congo* in 1597 and then in 1600 of *A geographical historie of Africa* by Johannes Leo Africanus.

Hakluyt's collecting of narratives of voyages to the north was much more extensive. The encouragement and advice that he gave to the actual explorers is reflected by William Gordon writing of the voyage to Pechora in 1611, 'And in the after-noone, wee went on shoare with our shallop, and came to a Riuer, which wee called Hakluyts Riuer.'[2] Similarly in the voyages in search of the North-west Passage Robert Fotherby writes of 'Hakluyts Head-land' and 'Mount Hackluyt', while William Baffin refers to 'Hakluits Ile'.[3] These references indicate the esteem in which Hakluyt was held by those who carried out exploration. Hakluyt was similarly involved with those who sent out the expeditions like Sir Thomas Smith. Sir Thomas Smith, a key figure in English discovery, was, as a memorial to him indicates, 'late Gouernour of ye East-Indian Muscouia French and Sommer-Island Companies: Treasurer for the Virginian Plantations: Prime Vndertaker in the year 1612 for that noble Designe the Discouerie of the North-West Passage'.[4] Smith's

---

[1] Purchas, *Pilgrimes*, I, 500. [2] Purchas, *Pilgrimes*, III, 531.

[3] *Ibid.*, III, 721, 730, 847.

[4] Quoted in *The voyages of William Baffin 1612–1622*, ed. C. R. Markham (1881), p. vii.

contacts with first Hakluyt and then Purchas ensured the pre-servation and publication of much valuable source material that might otherwise have been lost. One explorer in touch with Hakluyt was Josias Logan, who wrote two letters in July and August 1611 from Russia. In his letter of 16 August Logan reported that the Samoyeds had met people that 'are not farre from Cataia and China. Thus haue I shewed vnto you the greatest secret, and the neerest to the truth that I know. Requesting you, if you thinke it meet, that the Right Honourable the Earle of Salisburie might haue a Copie there-of.'[1] The last date for Hakluyt collecting material on Russia is late in 1615, as William Gordon, whose account Purchas cites as the last derived from Hakluyt, did not reach Holland till September 1615. The pub-lication by Purchas of Hakluyt's material on the Russian voyages is especially valuable since the early records of the Russia Company were destroyed in the Great Fire of 1666.[2]

A similar vigour and enthusiasm is shown by Hakluyt in collecting material on the voyages to Greenland and Canada, particularly those in search of a North-west Passage. Hakluyt was, of course, one of the patentees of the North-west Passage Com-pany and was able to collect the accounts of the major explorations such as those written by Hudson, Fotherby and Baffin.[3] The dates of the Fotherby and Baffin narratives reveal that Hakluyt was collecting material as late as the beginning of 1616. Hakluyt does not seem, however, to have been so involved in collecting material on the French in Canada, for Purchas only records the 1603 voyage of Champlain. Hakluyt's collecting on Spanish and Portuguese America was more extensive with Purchas printing translations, for instance, of Léry, Cardim and Herrera y Torde-sillas. Most of Hakluyt's collecting on this area seems to have been carried out quite soon after 1600. The treatise of Cardim, for example, 'was taken by one Frances Cooke of Dartmouth in a

---

[1] Purchas, *Pilgrimes*, III, 546–7.
[2] T. S. Willan, *The early history of the Russia Company, 1553–1603* (Manchester, 1956), p. v. I am indebted to Mr J. S. G. Simmons, All Souls College, Oxford, for the information that Russian writings relating to these voyages are based on Purchas.
[3] Parks, *Hakluyt*, p. 208.

Voyage outward bound for Brasil, An. 1601. who sold the same
to Master Hacket for twenty shillings; by whose procurement it
was translated out of Portugall into English'.[1] Hakluyt seems to
have acquired or translated relatively little in his later years,
although several likely narratives of interest to him were published,
such as the first part of the *Commentarios reales* of Garcilaso de la
Vega in 1609. It was left to Purchas to publish a translation of
Garcilaso. It must be remembered, however, that the acquisition
and translation of a Spanish or Portuguese text was often time
consuming.

Hakluyt was deeply involved in the English colonizing
attempts after 1600 in the Americas and Purchas prints, albeit
sometimes in abbreviated form, Hakluyt's material covering the
abortive Guiana colony up to 1606. Hakluyt was personally more
involved in the fate of the Virginia colony and Purchas reflects
this interest although he admits to omitting some of Hakluyt's
material 'euen after I had with great labour fitted them to the
Presse'.[2] Again, as in the case of the northern voyages, a good
deal of material is unique to Purchas. The last date for Hakluyt
collecting on Virginia is the middle of 1613, but Purchas may
well have ignored later Hakluyt items because they duplicated
material already in his possession. By this time Purchas had his
own contacts within the Virginia Company, the most prominent
of these being Captain John Smith.[3]

Hakluyt and Purchas must therefore be considered together in
order to establish the true nature and genius of Hakluyt's collecting
activity after 1600. Certainly a study of the *Pilgrimage* and the
Pilgrimes reveals that J. A. Williamson was wrong when he
wrote of Richard Hakluyt that after 1612 'there is little record of
his customary activity'.[4] Hakluyt was in fact collecting as late
as the beginning of 1616, although this need not have been a
particularly arduous physical task. The works of Hakluyt and

[1] Purchas, *Pilgrimes*, IV, 1289.   [2] Purchas, *Pilgrimes*, IV, 1837.
[3] For the relationship of Purchas and Smith see P. L. Barbour, *The three worlds of
Captain John Smith* (1964), *passim*.
[4] J. A. Williamson, 'Richard Hakluyt' in *Richard Hakluyt and his successors*, ed.
E. Lynam (1946), p. 43.

Purchas together set a standard of achievement and enterprise which was not to be surpassed until modern times. They revealed the true nature of the overseas world to the English reader for the first time and ensured that the literature of travel and exploration became established in England free from the myths of the past and the simplicity of the compendiums.

Purchas/Hakluyt bibliography

The following is a list, arranged geographically, of the items which Purchas derived from Hakluyt, as printed in the *Pilgrimes*. An indication is provided after each item as to Purchas' use of his material, that is, whether it is printed in complete or abbreviated form. The letters H, HP and (H) have already been explained in the text (pp. 79–80 above).

General

(H) Drake, Sir Francis. The second Circum-Nauigation of the Earth: Or the renowmed voyage of Sir Francis Drake.
Volume I, book 2, pp. 46–57. (Only very minor changes from *PN*.)

(H) Pretty, Francis. The third Circum-Nauigation of the Globe: Or the admirable and prosperous voyage of Master Thomas Candish of Trimley in the Countie of Suffolke Esquire, into the South Sea.
Volume I, book 2, pp. 57–70. (Abbreviated from *PN*.)

(H) Galvão, Antonio. Briefe Collections of Voyages, chiefly of Spaniards and Portugals.
Volume II, book 10, pp. 1671–93. (Abbreviated.)

The East

H Wood, Benjamin. The Voyage of Master Beniamin Wood into the East Indies, and the miserable disastrous successe thereof.
Volume I, book 3, pp. 110–13. (Abbreviated.)

H Mildenhall, John. The trauailes of Iohn Mildenhall into the Indies, and in the Countries of Persia . . . written by himselfe in two Letters following.
Volume I, book 3, p. 114. (Complete.)

H The second Letter of Iohn Mildenhall to Master Richard Staper, written from Casbin in Persia, the third day of October 1606.
Volume I, book 3, pp. 114–16. (Complete.)

H   Davis, John. The Voyage of Captaine Iohn Dauis, to the Easterne India, Pilot in a Dutch ship; written by himselfe.
Volume 1, book, 3, pp. 116–24. (Complete, in that the only surviving record is in Purchas.)

H   Adams, William. William Adams his Voyage by the Magellan Streights to Iapon, written in two Letters by himselfe, as followeth.
Volume 1, book 3, pp. 125–9. (Complete.)
A Letter of William Adams to his wife from Iapan.
Volume 1, book 3, pp. 129–32. (Complete.)

H   [Davis, John.] The third Voyage of Iohn Dauis with Sir Edward Michelborne Knight, into the East Indies, in the Tigre.
Volume 1, book 3, pp. 132–9. (Complete, in that it is the only surviving record.)

H   A priuiledge for fifteene yeeres granted by her Maiestie to certaine Aduenturers, for the discouerie of the Trade for the East Indies, the one and thirtieth of December, 1600.
Volume 1, book 3, pp. 139–47. (Complete.)

H   [Lancaster, James]. The first voyage made to East India by Master Iames Lancaster, now Knight, for the Merchants of London, Anno 1600.
Volume 1, book 3, pp. 147–64. (Abbreviated, but the only surviving record.)

HP   Scot, Edmund. A Discourse of Iaua, and of the first English Factorie there.
Volume 1, book 3, pp. 164–85. (Abbreviated.)

H   Clayborne, Thomas. The second Voyage set forth by the Companie into the East Indies, Sir Henrie Middleton being Generall.
Volume 1, book 3, pp. 185–7. (Abbreviated, but the only surviving record.)

H   Keeling, William. A Iournall of the third Voyage to the East India.
Volume 1, book 3, pp. 188–205. (Abbreviated.)

HP   Hawkins, William. Captaine William Hawkins his Relations, of the occurrents which happened in the time of his residence in India.
Volume 1, book 3, pp. 206–26. (Abbreviated, but the only surviving record.)

H   [Middleton, David]. The Voyage of Master Dauid Middleton in the Consent, a ship of a hundred and fifteene tunnes, which set forth from Tilburie Hope, on the twelfth of March, 1606.
Volume 1, book 3, pp. 226–7 (correctly 229, but Purchas misnumbers). (Abbreviated.)

H   A briefe Narration of the fourth Voyage to the East Indies.

      1. Relations of the said Voyage, written by Thomas Iones.

Volume 1, book 3, pp. 228–32. (Abbreviated.)

      2. The report of William Nicols a Mariner . . . written from his mouth at Bantam by Henry Moris, the twelfth of September, 1612.

Volume 1, book 3, p. 232. (Abbreviated.)

      3. The vnhappie Voyage of the Vice-admirall . . . reported by a Letter which Master Samuel Bradshaw sent from Priaman, by Humphrey Bidulphe, the eleuenth day of March, 1609. written by the said Henrie Moris at Bantam, the fourteenth of September, 1610.

Volume 1, book 3, pp. 232–4. (Complete.)

      4. The Voyage of Master Ioseph Salbanke through India, Persia, part of Turkie, the Persian Gulfe, and Arabia, 1609. Written vnto Sir Thomas Smith.

Volume 1, book 3, pp. 235–8. (Abbreviated.)

H   Middleton, David. The Voyage of Master Dauid Midleton to Iaua and Banda, extracted out of a Letter written by himselfe to the Companie, this being the fifth Voyage set forth by them.

Volume 1, book 3, pp. 238–47. (Abbreviated.)

H   Middleton, Sir Henry. The sixth Voyage, set forth by the East Indian Companie in three ships.

Volume 1, book 3, pp. 247–74. (Abbreviated, but the only surviving record.)

H   Downton, Nicholas. Nicholas Dounton Captaine of the Pepper-corne, a ship of two hundred and fifty tunnes, and Lieutenant in the sixth Voyage to the East Indies, set forth by the said Companie, his Iournall, or certaine Extracts thereof.

Volume 1, book 3, pp. 274–314. (Abbreviated.)

H   Bonner, Robert. Notes taken out of Master Robert Boners Iournall, who was then Master in the Dragon.

Volume 1, book 4, pp. 479–81. (Abbreviated.)

H   Wilson, Ralph. The Eleuenth Voyage to the East India in the Salomon, begun in the yeere of our Lord 1611.

Volume 1, book 4, pp. 486–8. (Abbreviated.)

H   Payton, Walter. A Iournall of all principall matters passed in the twelfth Voyage to the East India.

Volume 1, book 4, pp. 488–500. (Abbreviated, but the only surviving record.)

H   Chan, Achmet. Sultan Achmet Chan, Sonne vnto the Sultan Mehemet Chan most inuincible, his Letter to King Iames.
Volume II, book 9, p. 1482. (Complete.)

H   [Meneses, Duarte de]. Don Duart de Meneses the Vice⁄roy, his tractate of the Portugall Indies.
Volume II, book 9, pp. 1506–33. (Abbreviated: it is possible that Hakluyt made the translation, see p. 295, below.)

(H)   Fitch, Ralph. The Voyage of Master Ralph Fitch Merchant of London to Ormus, and so to Goa in the East India.
Volume II, book 10, pp. 1730–44. (Reprinted from *PN*.)

H   Rubruquis, William de. The Iournall of Friar William de Rubri⁄ quis, a French⁄man, of the Order of the Minorite Friars, vnto the East parts of the World. Anno Dom. 1253.
Volume III, book 1, pp. 1–52. (Complete.) (Abbreviated Latin– English version in *PN*.)

H   Bacon, Roger. Tartarian and Northerne Relations written in Latin by the famous Friar Roger Bacon.
Volume III, book 1, pp. 52–8. (Abbreviated.)

HP   Hetoum, Prince of Korghos. The Historie of Ayton, or Anthonie the Armenian, of Asia and specially touching the Tartars.
Volume III, book 1, pp. 108–27. (Abbreviated.)

(H)   Mandeville, Sir John. Trauels and Memorials of Sir Iohn Mandeuile.
Volume III, book 1, pp. 128–58. (Abbreviated and translated from *PN* (1589).)

HP   Cruz, Gaspar da. A Treatise of China, and the adioyning Regions, written by Gaspar da Cruz a Dominican Friar.
Volume III, book 1, pp. 166–98. (Abbreviated.)

HP   Argensola, Bartolomé Leonardo de. Two Letters taken out of Bartolome Leonardo de Argensola his Treatise, called Conquista de las Islas Malucas, printed at Madrid 1609.
Volume III, book 2, pp. 309–10. (Abbreviated.)

HP   Pantoja, Diego de. A Letter of Father Diego de Pantoia . . . written in Paquin, which is the Court of the King of China, the ninth of March, the yeere 1602.
Volume III, book 2, pp. 350–79. (Abbreviated.)

Africa

HP   [Guinea]. A description and historicall declaration of the golden Kingdome of Guinea, otherwise called the golden Coast of Myna.
Volume II, book 7, pp. 926–70. (Abbreviated.)

H   A briefe Relation of the Embassage which the Patriarch Don Iohn Bermudez brought from the Emperour of Ethiopia, vulgarly called Presbyter Iohn, to the most Christian and zealous of the Faith of Christ, Don Iohn, the third of this Name, King of Portugall. Volume II, book 7, pp. 1149–74. (Abbreviated.)

H   [Ethiopia]. Late changes of State and Religion in Ethiopia, with other remarkable Obseruations ... An Armenian his report of Sussinus, the Emperour of the Abaxins, by vs vulgarly called Prester John, who came from the said Emperours Court twelue daies since. Volume II, book 7, pp. 1187–8. (Abbreviated.)

Voyages to Russia and the north (including North-east Passage)

(H) Barentszoon, Willem. This was written by William Barentson in a loose Paper, which was lent mee [Henry Hudson] by the Reuerend Peter Plantius in Amsterdam, March the seuen and twentieth, 1609. Volume III, book 3, p. 518. (Complete.)

H   [Finch, Richard]. A Note of the trauels of the Russes ouer Land, and by water from Mezen, neere the Bay of Saint Nicholas to Pechora, to Obi, to Yenisse and to the Riuer Geta ... translated out of the Russe by Richard Finch.
     Volume III, book 3, p. 530. (Complete.)

H   Gordon, William. A voyage made to Pechora 1611.
     Volume III, book 3, p. 530–4. (Complete, but the only surviving record.)

H   Finch, Richard. A Letter of Richard Finch to the Right Worshipfull Sir Thomas Smith.
     Volume III, book 3, pp. 534–8. (Complete.)

H   Logan, Josias. The Voyage of Master Iosias Logan to Pechora.
     Volume III, book 3, pp. 541–6. (Abbreviated, but the only surviving record.)

(H) Logan, Josias. Extracts taken out of two Letters of Iosias Logan from Pechora, to Master Hakluyt Prebend of Westminster.
     Volume III, book 3, pp. 546–7. (Abbreviated, but the only surviving record.)

H   Pursglove, William. A briefe relation of a Voyage to Pechora.
     Volume III, book 3, pp. 547–52. (Abbreviated, but the only surviving record.)

H   Gordon, William. Later obseruations of William Gourdon, in his wintering at Pustozera, in the yeeres 1614. and 1615. with a description of the Samoyeds life.

88

Volume III, book 3, pp. 553–6. (Abbreviated, but the only surviving record.)

H   Poole, Jonas. Diuers Voyages to Cherie Iland, in the yeeres 1604, 1605, 1606, 1608, 1609.
Volume III, book 3, pp. 556–66. (Complete, but the only surviving record: see Purchas, *Pilgrimage* (1614), p. 743.)

(H)   Gordon, William. A Voyage performed to the Northwards, Anno 1603 ... Written by William Gorden; being the first Voyage to Cherie Iland; which came to my hands since the former (or rather later Voyages) were in the Presse.
Volume III, book 3, pp. 566–7. (Complete.)

HP   Fioravanti, Christoforo and Michiel, Nicolo di. The shipwracke of Master Piero Quirino, described by Christophoro Fiorauanti, and Nicolo Di Michiel, who were present there: here contracted.
Volume III, book 3, pp. 611–19. (Abbreviated.)

HP   Jónsson, Arngrímr. Extracts of Arngrim Ionas, an Islander, his Chrymogaea or History of Island: published, Anno Dom. 1609.
Volume III, book 3, pp. 654–68. (Abbreviated: an earlier version in *PN*.)

H   Poole, Jonas. A Voyage set forth by the Right Worshipfull Sir Thomas Smith, and the rest of the Muscouie Company, to Cherry Iland: and for a further Discouerie to be made towards the North⁄Pole ... AD 1610.
Volume III, book 4, pp. 699–707 (pages 669–98 unpaged by Purchas in error). (Complete, but the only surviving record.)

HP   [Poole, Jonas]. A Commission for Ionas Poole our Seruant, appointed Master of a small Barke called the Elizabeth, of fiftie tunnes burthen, for Discouery to the Northward of Greeneland, giuen the last day of March 1610 [*recte* March 1611].
Volume III, book 4, pp. 707–9. (Complete.) (Contents list has 'last day of May, 1610' in error.)

(HP)   [Edge, Thomas]. A Commission for Thomas Edge our servant ... Giuen the 31. of March, 1611.
Volume III, book 4, pp. 709–10. (Abbreviated.)

HP   [Russia]. Of the miserable estate of Russia after Swiskeys deportation, their election of the King of Polands Sonne, their Interregnum and popular estate, and choosing at last of the present Emperour, with some remarkeable accidents in his time.
Volume III, book 4, pp. 782–91. (Abbreviated.)

H   [Ob]. Notes concerning the discouery of the Riuer of Ob, taken out of a Roll, written in the Russian tongue, which was attempt-ed by the meanes of Antonie Marsh, a chiefe Factor for the Moscouie Company of England, 1584. with other notes of the North-east.

Volume III, book 4, pp. 804–6. (Abbreviated.)

HP   Cherry, Francis; Lyndes, Thomas; Gaulle, Francis. The report of Master Francis Cherry a Moscouie Merchant, and Master Thomas Lyndes touching a warme Sea to the South-east of the Riuer Ob, and a Note of Francis Gaulle.

Volume III, book 4, p. 806. (Abbreviated.)

Gualle, Francisco de. Volume III, book 4, p. 806. (Abbreviated from *PN*.)

Voyages to Greenland and Canada (including the North-west Passage)

H   Baardarson, Ivarr. A Treatise of Iuer Boty a Gronlander, translated out of the Norsh language into High Dutch.

Volume III, book 3, pp. 518–21. (Abbreviated.)

H   Playse, John, and Hudson, Henry. Diuers Voyages and Northerne discoueries of that worthy irrecouerable Discouerer Master Henrie Hudson.

Volume III, book 3, pp. 567–74. (Complete.)

H   Hudson, Henry. A second voyage or employment of Master Henrie Hudson for finding a passage to the East Indies by the North-east: written by himselfe.

Volume III, book 3, pp. 574–81. (Complete.)

H   Juet, Robert. The third voyage of Master Henrie Hudson toward Noua Zembla.

Volume III, book 3, pp. 581–95. (Complete, and the only surviving record.)

H   Hudson, Henry. An Abstract of the Iournall of Master Henrie Hudson, for the discouerie of the North-west passage, begun the 17. of Aprill, 1610. ended with his end, being treacherously ex-posed by some of the Companie.

Volume III, book 3, pp. 596–7. (Abbreviated, but the only surviving record.)

(H) Prickett, Abacuk. A larger discourse of the same voyage, and the successe thereof, written by Abacuk Pricket.

Volume II, book 3, pp. 597–608. (Complete.)

(H) Widhouse, Thomas [Letter to Samuel Macham, p. 609]. A Note

found in the Deske of Thomas Widhouse, Student in the Mathe⁄
matikes, hee being one of them who was put into the Shallop.
Volume III, book 3, pp. 609–10. (Complete.)

HP   Marcolini, Francisco. The discoueries of M. M. Nicolo, and Antonio
Zeni, gathered out of their Letters, by Francisco Marcolino.
Volume III, book 3, pp. 610–11. (Abbreviated from *PN*.)

H   Poole, Jonas. A briefe Declaration of this my Voyage of discouery to
Greeneland, and towards the West of it.
Volume III, book 4, pp. 711–12. (Abbreviated.)

(H)   Poole, Randolph. [Description of same voyage as above – not titled
by Purchas.]
Volume III, book 4, pp. 712–13. (Abbreviated.)

H   Poole, Jonas. A Relation written by Ionas Poole of a Voyage to
Greeneland, in the yeere 1612.
Volume III, book 4, pp. 713–15. (Abbreviated.)

HP   Baffin, William. A Iournall of the Voyage made to Greeneland with
sixe English ships and a Pinnasse, in the yeere 1613.
Volume III, book 4, pp. 716–20. (Complete.)

HP   Fotherby, Robert. A Voyage of Discouery to Greeneland, &c. An.1614.
Volume III, book 4, pp. 720–8. (Complete.)

HP   Fotherby, Robert. A true report of a Voyage, Anno 1615. for
Discouerie of Seas, Lands, and Ilands, to the Northwards.
Volume III, book 4, pp. 728–31. (Complete.)

HP   Discoueries made by English⁄men to the North⁄west: Voyages of Sir
Sebastian Cabot, Master Thorne, and other Ancients: and Master
Weymouth.
Volume III, book 4, pp. 806–9. (Partially abbreviated from *PN*.)

(HP)   The Voyage of Captaine George Weymouth, intended for the dis⁄
coueries of the North⁄west Passag toward China, with two flye Boates.
Volume III, book 4, pp. 809–14. (Abbreviated.)

H   Hall, James. Iames Hall his Voyage forth of Denmarke for the
discouery of Greenland, in the yeere 1605.
Volume III, book 4, pp. 814–21. (Abbreviated.)

H   Hall, James. The second Voyage of Master Iames Hall, forth of
Denmarke into Greeneland, in the yeere 1606.
Volume III, book 4, pp. 821–7. (Abbreviated.)

H   Knight, John, and Browne, Oliver. The Voyage of Master Iohn
Knight . . . for the Discouery of the North⁄west passage, begunne
the eighteenth of Aprill, 1606.
Volume III, book 4, pp. 827–31. (Abbreviated.)

H Baffin, William. The fourth Voyage of Iames Hall to Groaneland. Volume III, book 4, pp. 831–6. (Abbreviated.)

H Baffin, William. A true Relation of such things as happened in the fourth Voyage for the Discouerie of the North-west Passage, performed in the yeere 1615.
Volume III, book 4, pp. 836–42. (Abbreviated.)

HP [South Sea]. A brief Discourse of the probability of a passage to the Westerne or South Sea, illustrated with testimonies: and a briefe Treatise and Mappe by Master Brigges.
Volume III, book 4, pp. 848–53, includes:
  Cowles, Thomas: Note, p. 849. (Complete.)
  Lok, Michael: A Note made by me Michael Lok the elder touching the Strait of Sea, pp. 849–52. (Complete.)
  Briggs, Henry: A Treatise of the North-west passage to the South Sea through the Continent of Virginia, and by Fretum Hudson, pp. 852–3. (Complete.)

H Champlain, Samuel. The Voyage of Samuel Champlaine of Brouage, made vnto Canada, in the yeere 1603.
Volume IV, book 8, pp. 1605–19. (Complete.)

H [Newfoundland]. The beginning of the Patent for New-found-land.
Volume IV, book 10, pp. 1876–7. (Abbreviated.)

Spanish and Portuguese America

HP Herrera y Tordesillas, Antonio. A Description of the West Indies.
Volume III, book 5, pp. 855–917. (Abbreviated.)

H [Codex Mendoza]. The History of the Mexican Nation, described in pictures by the Mexican Author explained in the Mexican language; which exposition translated into Spanish, and thence into English, together with the said Picture-historie, are heere presented.
Volume III, book 5, pp. 1066–117. (Complete.)

(H) [Clifford, George, third earl of Cumberland]. A Briefe Relation of the seuerall Voyages, vndertaken and performed by the Right Honourable George, Earle of Cumberland.
Volume IV, book 6, pp. 1141–9. (Partially abbreviated from *PN*.)

H Clifford, George, third earl of Cumberland. The Voyage to Saint Iohn de Porto Rico.
Volume IV, book 6, pp. 1150–4. (Abbreviated.)

H Layfield, John. A large Relation of Port Ricco Voyage.
Volume IV, book 6, pp. 1155–76. (Abbreviated.) (Contents list

indicates this is by a Dr Eglambie but was in fact written by Lay-field.)

(H)   [America]. The first Voyages made to diuers parts of America by Englishmen ... collected briefly out of Master Camden, Master Hakluit, and other writers.
Volume IV, book 6, pp. 1177–87. (Partially abbreviated from *PN.*)

H   Carder Peter. The Relation of Peter Carder of Saint Verian in Cornwall, within seuen miles of Falmouth which went with Sir Francis in his Voyage about the World, begun 1577.
Volume IV, book 6, pp. 1187–90. (Complete.)

(H)   Jane, John. [Cap. Davis his voyage into the South Sea reported by M. Iane.]
Volume IV, book 6, p. 1191. (Abbreviated from *PN.*)

H   Cavendish, Thomas. Master Thomas Candish his Discourse of his fatall and disastrous Voyage towards the South Sea.
Volume IV, book 6, pp. 1192–201. (Abbreviated.)

HP   Knivet, Anthony. The admirable aduentures and strange fortunes of Master Anthonie Kniuet, which went with Master Thomas Candish in his second Voyage to the South Sea, 1591.
Volume IV, book 6, pp. 1201–42. (Complete.)

H   Middleton, David. Certayne Notes of a Voyage made by mee Dauid Middleton into the West Indies with Captaine Michael Geare, An. Dom. 1601.
Volume IV, book 6, pp. 1246–7 (Purchas prints 1242–7 in error). (Complete.)

H   Sparrey, Francis. The Description of the Ile of Trinidad, the rich Countrey of Guiana, and the mightie Riuer of Orenoco.
Volume IV, book 6, pp. 1247–50. (Complete.)

H   [Leigh, Charles]. Captaine Charles Leigh his Voyage to Guiana, and plantation there.
Volume IV, book 6, pp. 1250–2. (Abbreviated.)

(H)   Leigh, Charles. Captaine Charles Leighs Letter to Sir Olave Leigh his Brother.
Volume IV, book 6, pp. 1252–5. (Complete.)

HP   Nicholl, John. A true Relation of the traiterous Massacre of the most part of threescore and seuen English men, set on Land out of a Ship of Sir Oliph Leagh, bound for Guiana.
Volume IV, book 6, pp. 1255–60. (Abbreviated.)

H   Wilson, John. The Relation of Master Iohn Wilson of Wansteed in Essex, one of the last tenne that returned into England from Wiapoco in Guiana, 1606.

Volume IV, book 6, pp. 1260-5. (Complete.)

H   Turner, William. Part of a Treatise written by Master William Turner, Sonne to Doctor Turner of London a Physitian, touching the former Voyage.

Volume IV, book 6, pp. 1265-7. (Abbreviated but the only surviv-ing record.)

(H)   [Marwin]. A Relation of the habitations and other Obseruations of the River of Marwin, and the adioyning Regions.

Volume IV, book 6, pp. 1283-6. (Complete.)

H   Cardim, Fernão. A Treatise of Brasill written by a Portugall which had long liued there.

Volume IV, book 7, pp. 1289-320. (Complete: see Purchas *Pilgrimage* (1614), p. 842.)

H   Cardim, Fernão. Articles touching the dutie of the Kings Maiestie our Lord, and to the common good of all the estate of Brasill.

Volume IV, book 7, pp. 1320-5. (Complete.)

HP   Léry, Jean de. Extracts out of the Historie of Iohn Lerius a Frenchman, who liued in Brasil with Monsieur Villagagnon, Anno 1557. and 58.

Volume IV, book 7, pp. 1325-46. (Abbreviated.)

HP   Schmidel, Ulrich. The Trauels of Hulderike Schnirdel in twentie yeeres space, from 1534 to 1554.

Volume IV, book 7, pp. 1347-64. (Abbreviated.)

H   [Englishman]. A briefe Relation of an Englishman which had beene thirteene yeeres Captiue to the Spaniards in Peru.

Volume IV, book 7, p. 1418. (Complete.)

H   Orsino, Allessandro. The Relation of Alexandro Vrsino concerning the Coast of Terra Firma and the secrets of Peru, and Chili, where hee had liued foure and thirtie yeeres.

Volume IV, book 7, pp. 1418-20. (Complete.)

(H)   Hakluyt, Richard. A note of Australia del Espiritu Santo. Written by Master Hakluyt.

Volume IV, book 7, p. 1432. (Complete.)

(H)   Vas, Lopes. The Historie of Lopez Vaz a Portugall . . . touching American places, discoueries and occurrents.

Volume IV, book 7, pp. 1432-47. (Abbreviated from *PN.*)

HP   Núñez Cabeza de Vaca, Álvaro. A True Relation of Aluaro Nunez, called Capo di Vacca, concerning that which happened to the Fleet

in India, whereof Pamphilo Naruaez was Gouernour from the yeere 1527. vntil the yeere 1536.
Volume IV, book 8, pp. 1499–528. (Abbreviated.)

(H) Soto, Hernando de. Ferdinando de Soto his Voyage to Florida.
Volume IV, book 8, pp. 1528–56. (Abbreviated.)

H Pérez, Martín. Extracts out of certaine Letters of Father Martin Perez of the Societie of Iesus.
Volume IV, book 8, pp. 1562–5. (Abbreviated.)

H Tribaldo Toleto, Luis. A Letter from Valladolid . . . touching Iuan de Onate his Discoueries in New Mexico.
Volume IV, book 8, pp. 1565–7. (Complete.)

The English in North America

(H) Gosnold, Bartholomew. Master Bartholomew Gosnolds Letter to his Father, touching his first Voyage to Virginia, 1602.
Volume IV, book 8, p. 1646. (Complete.)

H Archer, Gabriel. The Relation of Captaine Gosnols Voyage to the North part of Virginia.
Volume IV, book 8, pp. 1647–51. (Complete.)

H Pring, Martin. A Voyage set out from the Citie of Bristoll . . . for the Discouery of the North part of Virginia, in the yeere 1603.
Volume IV, book 8, pp. 1654–6. (Complete.)

H Canner, Thomas [and unknown author on p. 1658]. A Relation of the voyage made to Virginia . . . in the yeere 1603.
Volume IV, book 8, pp. 1656–8. (Complete.)

HP Rosier, James. Extracts of a Virginian Voyage made An. 1604. by Captaine George Waymouth.
Volume IV, book 8, pp. 1659–67. (Abbreviated.)

H Percy, George. Obseruations gathered out of a Discourse of the Plantation of the Southerne Colonie in Virginia by the English, 1606.
Volume IV, book 9, pp. 1685–90. (Abbreviated, but the only surviving record, except for *Pilgrimage* (1614), p. 768.)

H Archer, Gabriel. A Letter of Master Gabriel Archer, touching the Voyage of the Fleet of Ships, which arriued at Virginia, without Sir Thomas Gates, and Sir George Summers, 1609.
Volume IV, book 9, pp. 1733–4. (Complete.)

H Strachey, William. A true reportorie of the wracke, and redemption of Sir Thomas Gates, Knight; vpon, and from the Ilands of the Bermudas.
Volume IV, book 9, pp. 1734–58. (Complete.)

H   Argall, Sir Samuel. The Voyage of Captaine Samuell Argal from
     Iames Towne in Virginia to seeke the Ile of Bermuda.
     Volume IV, book 9, pp. 1758–62. (Complete.)

H   Argall, Sir Samuel. A Letter of Sir Samuell Argoll, touching his
     Voyage to Virginia, and Actions there.
     Volume IV, book 9, pp. 1764–5. (Complete.)

H   Stoneman, John. The voyage of Master Henrie Challons, intended
     for the North plantation of Virginia, 1606.
     Volume IV, book 10, pp. 1832–7. (Complete.)

H   [Mawooshen]. The description of the Country of Mawooshen, dis-
     couered by the English in the yeere 1602, 3, 5, 6, 7, 8 and 9.
     Volume IV, book 10, pp. 1873–5. (Abbreviated but the only sur-
     viving record.)

                            Spain

(H) [Cadiz]. A briefe and true report of the Honourable voyage vnto
     Cadiz, 1596.
     Volume IV, book 10, pp. 1927–34. (Abbreviated from *PN*.)

9

Tudor travel literature: a brief history

GEORGE B. PARKS

A history must have a theme if it is to be more than a chronicle, and the theme of this history would be the sudden efflorescence and maturing of travel literature in England as a conscious literary genre within the short space of fifty years. Not only England but all the West had shared in the expansion of Europe which began with the Crusades, and many landmarks of travel literature had recorded some phases of the expansion. We count the notable Crusade histories, and also the individual travel records of the Polo family, of Friar William de Rubruquis, and of Friar Oderico da Pordenone to the Far East; and in England the 'Wales' and the 'Ireland' of Giraldus Cambrensis, the 'Itinerary of Richard I' on his Crusade, and the 'Travels' of Sir John Mandeville (in so far as they were authentic). Whether as narrative of travel or as geographical description giving the results of travel, the records of medieval discovery by Europeans were generally known in England.

With the accelerated pace of travel in the age of the later European discoveries of India and America, all voyages in the public interest came to require a formal record. The voyages of both Portuguese and Spanish discoverers were official, and ships' logs and itineraries were obligatory. Though they were not published at the time, they formed the basis of the official histories of Peter Martyr, Oviedo, Barros, and Herrera, and appeared in their own name at last in the nineteenth century. It was the distinction of the Venetian official Giovanni Battista Ramusio that he saw the need of collecting and publishing, in his *Navigationi et viaggi* (1550–9), the travel records of recent centuries. His purpose was at the same time to bring up to date the classical geography and also to pay tribute to the discoveries, which he called the greatest achievement of his time. It was the double distinction of his English disciple Richard Hakluyt that he not only collected and published the like reports of travel by his compatriots in his *Principall navigations* (1589) and *Principal Navigations* (1598–1600) in order to record 'the search and dis∕couery of the world', but also insisted on the value of the primary documents of travel, even the bare itineraries or ships' logs. Ramusio published reports of significant travel. Hakluyt aimed to publish all the reports of the new travel by his countrymen, in addition to many of the reports of current travel by foreigners which supplemented them.

These two epic collections of travel literature, as they are entitled to be called, gathered up many important works of past and present, but could not include all. In Tudor England many important classical works of travel and geography were separately published in translation: Caesar's account of Britain (1530), Polybius (1568, part), the poem *The surveye of the world* [*Periegesis*] (1572) of Dionysius Afer, Herodotus (1584, part), the brief compendia of Pomponius Mela (1585) and Solinus (1587), the *Germania* of Tacitus (1598), and the notable Pliny (1601). Xenophon does not appear here, nor Strabo, nor Ptolemy. Medieval authors were published in translations of Ranulf Hig∕den's description of Britain (1480 and later), Mandeville (1496 and later), Marco Polo (1579), and in the Latin of Giraldus Cambrensis (1585). Hakluyt was to round out the medieval list by adding all the records, usually brief, of British travellers which he could find in the chronicles, as well as some notable reports of foreign travellers to Asia before and after Polo.

This record is given to show that the earlier travel literature was well known in Tudor England, and must have served at least some writers as models. In their turn, contemporary foreign works of travel came thick and fast into English translation, though not until the second half of the century. No fewer than four books on the Turks, an ever∕present danger to the West, were translated between 1542 and 1570, with more later. The English record of travel to America began in 1555 with the translation of Peter Martyr's first history, *The decades of the newe worlde*, of Columbus and his successors, plus the account of Magellan's voyage. Thereafter the reports of individual foreign travellers to the 'distant quarters of the Earth' were published in England in the characteristic acceleration of the new era: Ribault (1563) to Florida (1562), Varthema to India (1577), Cortes to Mexico (1578), Cartier to Canada (1580), Pizarro to Peru (1581), Nicolay and Pigafetta to Constantinople (1585), Laudonnière to Florida (1587), Federici to India and Mendoza to China (1588), and others.[1] Many of these authors had had to wait for decades for their English appearance, but by the time of Hakluyt's first active decade, the 1580s, and often by his initiative, the translation was likely to be done immediately. In the 1590s we record Guicciardini's Low Countries (1593), Pigafetta's Congo (1597), Linschoten to the East Indies with the first Dutch voyages (1598), and the already classic works of Leo Africanus on North Africa (1600) and Gasparo Contarini on the government of Venice (1599). The mere listing shows the interest of an awakened England in the whole global range of the new travel.

With respect to form, these works new and old varied from the descriptive treatise of Tacitus or of Leo Africanus to the straight narrative of Xenophon (who was of course read, if not translated) or Varthema, with alternate mixtures of little narrative and much description (Polo, Cartier) or much narrative and little description ('Itinerary of Richard I', Magellan). Since most of the new travel was by sea, where more accurate records had come to be required than was usual by land, we may expect the English narratives to be well detailed. Since the aim of Hakluyt was to record the discovery of the world, we may also expect as detailed observation as possible. Greater fullness and perhaps variety might then be the logical new desideratum.

The flood of foreign literature which I have outlined might have drowned out the native product had it not been for one individual obstacle and one social obstacle. The individual obstacle was Hakluyt's patriotic resolution to collect the full English record.

[1] See my bibliography in *Cambridge bibliography of English literature*, I (1940), 763–98, and *Supplement*, V, 330–3.

The social obstacle was the fact of the new commercial expansion of England overseas, which we may date from 1553, an expansion which aroused the national interest and inspired Hakluyt. England's steady trade had previously taken English ships to the Low Countries, to Bordeaux, somewhat less to Hamburg and Emden, also to Seville and even to Pisa or the Aegean. In 1553 a trading syndicate with official sanction set out on a voyage to find the North-east Passage to China, discovering instead a regular trade route to Russia by way of Archangel. Though the voyage thither was not as long as the one to Italy via the 'Straits of Maroc' which was well known to the English, it began a new and pioneer trade, and it led to a series of trading journeys overland from Moscow to Persia. These new voyages to the north and north-east seemed to Hakluyt a signal achievement of his country and therefore deserved first place in his collection.

They were followed up from 1576 on in a series of voyages to discover the North-west Passage, led by Martin Frobisher and then by John Davis, who in 1587 reached 72° N latitude, halfway up the west coast of Greenland. When no passage was found, Gilbert and Ralegh in turn sent out from 1583 expeditions to colonize North America, and later in 1595 Ralegh himself explored Guiana to the same end.

A parallel endeavour took English ships southward to trade beyond Seville, where an English merchant colony had long been settled, to Barbary from 1551, to Guinea and Benin from 1553, and thence in widening circles to the West Indies from 1564 in the slave trade, to South America on both the Atlantic and Pacific coasts and thence around the world in 1577 and 1586, and finally to the East Indies from 1591 around the Cape of Good Hope. Most of these southward voyages forced their trade on the Portuguese possessions in Africa and Brazil and on the Spanish territories in America, which were closed to foreign ships; force led to reprisals, which were in turn met by what must seem outright piracy, and presently to a virtual state of war on all the high seas. Except for the voyages to Russia and to North America, most Elizabethan voyages were warlike, and we are shocked to read of the burning of Negro villages in Africa, of the capture from private ships of the supplies for the voyage, and of the capture as prize of private property generally.

This challenge to Spanish sea power was made good by the defeat of the Armada in 1588, and in the next year Hakluyt published the voyage narratives which he had been collecting to show the might of England. Known to both the merchant adventurers in the commercial voyages and to the officials con‑ cerned with incipient colonial or actual naval enterprise, he was able in a sense to commandeer the voyage reports, or many of them, obtaining sometimes an official account, sometimes a mere ship's log, hoping always as we infer for an exact daily record. Instead of an official account, he might recover the diary of an officer or a gentleman volunteer or a ship's merchant. Or he might collect the story from the notes of a participant, and we suspect that he induced more than one traveller to surrender or even to draw up a report, perhaps improved by Hakluyt in the editing, based on a diary or other notes or recollections. He was the mid‑ wife of the new literary genre, which was called into being by a new national élan.

So Hakluyt saved the records of whole series of voyages which might otherwise have been forgotten. Sixteen accounts of current English travel had been published before 1589. For the *Principall navigations* Hakluyt brought together sixty‑four of any size, only seven of them being reprints. The sixty‑four included the voyages to Russia and Persia, most of the voyages to Morocco and beyond, the Frobisher and Davis voyages to the north‑west, the voyages to Newfoundland and to Ralegh's Virginia, the voyages to Mexico, and the two circumnavigations. His *Principal naviga‑ tions* (1598–1600) counted in its three volumes some 110 English narratives, plus a number of foreign ones. It added for the English mainly the naval voyages of the war with Spain, and the quasi‑ naval voyages to America and beyond, the reprinted Ralegh discoveries in Guiana, and the first English voyages to the East Indies. We should add to his great collection some ninety further English narratives which Hakluyt assembled before his death in 1616 and which were conveyed to Samuel Purchas for ultimate publication in 1625 in *Hakluytus posthumus or Purchas his pilgrimes*.

Perhaps 40 per cent of this enormous body of travel of all times and places was supplied by Hakluyt's legacy. The English records here would consist largely of the record of the successive voyages of the East India Company, and of the exploring voyages to north-east and north-west, especially those of Hudson and Baffin.

Altogether Hakluyt collected some two hundred English travel narratives. Of these, some 115 run to a minimum of 3,000 words each; twenty-three of them run to a minimum of, say, 10,000 words. Half-a-dozen other longer voyage narratives published separately and not reprinted by Hakluyt or Purchas bring to thirty the number of narratives of length or substance. At least as many more left in manuscript were printed later, and more may still come to light.

What can be said of this numerous collection, suddenly appear-ing as it did as a great body of documents of historical and patriotic interest? It should not *prima facie* expect high literary praise, for the reason that it was written mostly for a utilitarian purpose, by non-professional writers of only accidental skill, by writers more-over who would have no chance to develop skill in practice since most of them would write only once. As it happens, these are the normal conditions under which travel literature is written, and while some of it has undoubtedly been best done by professional writers from Xenophon to T. E. Lawrence, it can still draw a large audience when written by a non-professional Mandeville or Sir Edmund Hillary. Among the Elizabethans, Ralegh was not the only distinguished writer and not the only appealing one.

A more serious difficulty of appraisal is created by the variety of documents which Hakluyt collected: company charters, instructions to agents, letters to foreign kings, enemy reports. In later centuries, we have added many more like documents for every voyage: account books, letters, records of lawsuits, customs records. All these are needed for the full understanding of the travel, and indeed the Hakluyt Society has for more than a century devoted itself to amplifying the records available to Hakluyt. We cannot call all the documentation literature, and must limit our consideration to the key relations. At the same time, we may not forget the large body of documents which buttresses them and which demonstrates a large social movement enveloping the individual or the group travel. Hakluyt's *Principal navigations* are historical materials first, but they add up to a national record, which has been called by Froude 'the prose epic of the modern English nation'.

We must admit that the two hundred narratives, or the one hundred and fifteen of any length, which compose it can seldom be called literature: that is, self-sufficient writings possessed of substance, of adequate form, and of personality. Actually the modern maritime historians, Froude and Seeley and Laughton and Corbett and Williamson and Quinn, have written far more informative accounts of the voyages than any participant, not excepting even Ralegh or Sir Richard Hawkins. It is the task of the present historian to study the original narratives for themselves, and to arrive at some conclusions about their individual literary values.

The first narrative published in this period is the account of a voyage to Guinea in 1553 which was included by Richard Eden with his translation of *The decades of the newe worlde* in 1555.[1] Written by an unnamed participant, it is a complaint rather than a straight narrative, indicting a tyrannical captain of oppression of a competent foreign (Portuguese) pilot to the detriment of the voyage. The account has a theme and some personality, but is inadequate, for lack of details, as a report. A narrative of the subsequent Guinea voyage of 1554[2] begins as a pilot's log alone, being supplemented by the editor Eden, who was not a participant, with comments on the country and its products, partly derived from books and partly from the voyagers. This hybrid method was fortunately to be avoided by most travel accounts; indeed this report says almost nothing of the nature or results of the voyage, and does not even name the participants.

We must then look for the avoidance of these extremes, the Scylla of mere argument and the Charybdis of bare document, and we may take more satisfaction in the next printed examples.

---

[1] Pp. 345–8, reprinted *PN*, II (1599), ii, 9–14.
[2] Pp. 349–60, reprinted *PN*, II (1599), ii, 14–23.

The first voyage narrative separately published was that of John Hawkins,[1] giving in 1569 an account of his third slave-trading voyage to Africa and the West Indies, which had ended in the destruction of most of his ships by a Spanish fleet on the Mexican coast. This is written as a carefully and soberly framed indictment of Spanish treachery, passing discreetly over much of the African story but giving a lively if restrained account of the battle and of the dismal return of one ship (of the two surviving) to England. The method is that of argument, but vivid detail develops the theme of the armed conflict. The final theme of hardship at sea is left undeveloped and merely inferred, but the report remains impressive.

More light is thrown on the slave-raiding and the challenge to Spanish power by a longer narrative of the preceding (and successful) Hawkins voyage, a narrative which was not published then but which may effectively be contrasted with the brief Hawkins report. Written by an officer, John Sparke,[2] the lengthy narrative is not so well put together, but the details are especially vivid of the conflicts with the natives in Africa and with the local Spanish authorities in the West Indies who were compelled to buy the contraband. In addition to describing the conflict, the narrative adds new observation of the islands and of the natives both in the West Indies and in French Florida, which Hawkins reconnoitred.

Altogether the short Hawkins narrative and the longer Sparke narrative set a worthy standard of quality. Each has planned division into parts, the Hawkins story passing somewhat lightly over the African episodes, the Sparke story giving full narrative and observation. The latter can tell of triumph, the former can rise at moments to greater emotional heights in a story of disaster.

If the Hawkins narratives involve armed conflict, the next published accounts concern discovery. The Frobisher voyages seeking a north-west passage in the years 1576 to 1578, reaching as they did beyond Labrador, gave English sailors further experience, if only in the brief summer, of northern latitudes. The first

[1] *A true declaration of the troublesome voyadge* (1569), reprinted *PN*, III (1600), 521–5.
[2] In *PN*, III (1600), 501–21.

published account was that of Dionyse Settle (1577),[1] describing
the second voyage, its interest being in the natives and their living.
We wonder why the interest was sufficient to warrant publication
abroad in French, Latin, and Italian, the first such record of new
English enterprise; perhaps the title of the Italian version, the
discovery of the Arctic strait, indicates the interest as geographical.
The narrative is not very clear, and the account of the Eskimos
is not too perceptive ('their colour is not much vnlike the Sunne
burnt Countrey man, who laboureth daily in the Sunne for his
liuing').

Settle was followed in the next year by Thomas Ellis with a
brief report[2] of the third voyage which shows a master hand in
describing the dangers of ice, 'of fogge and hidious mist', and of
'boystrous blasts'. Fortunately all the ships but one endured the
dangers, and the report maintains an unusually cheerful tone
throughout its story of a safe if not a successful voyage.

In the same year, 1578, George Best, captain of a vessel in two
of the north-west voyages, published *A true discourse of the late
voyages of discouerie for the finding of a passage to Cathaya.*[3] The book
is the first new travel narrative of any size, running to perhaps
40,000 words including geographical commentary. The narrative
proper is framed in a somewhat elaborate (Latinate) style. The
theme of each account of the three voyages is the struggle with
ice and storm in the Hudson Strait region and the consequent
successful and vigorous encounter with the dangers. The manner
is formally rhetorical, the tone epic, and the work is the first
substantial triumph of the new literature.

We may arrive at a tentative scale of values in viewing this
writing. The theme of the narrative will be one of the three
observed: conflict with man, or conflict with nature, or both,
together with a more or less vivid observation of man or of nature.
This observation will not yet, it must be said at once, be usually
of a romantic sort, since the romantic view of either nature or man
will not appear for two centuries. The Eskimo of Settle's narrative,

[1] *A true reporte of the last voyage* (1577), reprinted *PN*, III (1600), 32–9.
[2] *A true report of the third voyage* (1578), reprinted *PN*, III (1600), 39–44.
[3] Reprinted *PN*, III (1600), 47–96.

for example, are brutish people who live on raw fish or flesh or 'such grasse as the Countrey yeeldeth'. Nor will the observation be very penetrating at first because both the natives and the observers will be apprehensive and all too prone either to do battle or to take fright.

If these are the three themes, mixed in varying proportions, the form of the relation may vary from the bare diary or log to the planned but only potentially developed account of Sparke or to the planned apologia of Hawkins, and occasionally, as with Ellis and Best, achieve the finished narrative. Here are three levels of achievement, to which we shall need in special cases to add a fourth, that of the finished description.

However critical our view, it must still be noted that few of Hakluyt's narratives, undeveloped though they may be, fail to light up in an emotional moment or in a brief vividness of descrip-tion. The reader today cannot fail to respond to such moments, which begin for him with the simple words, 'wee departed from Plimmouth with three tall ships and two barkes', or 'the wind came faire and wee hoysed our Anchors, and departed out of Tor Bay, directing our course towards the Ilands of Canaria'.

If we now turn back to the chronological order of the writing, as distinct from the publishing, of the new travel literature, we begin with the Russia–Persia voyages. Twenty-two voyage reports are extant altogether, including some not printed by Hakluyt, most of them official. As a body, they are not impressive narrative, being chronological records which rise only here and there to significant expression. The fact that the voyages describe a steady trade with Russia, which became an annual routine, may have obviated a dramatic interest, and indeed induced Hakluyt to omit many of them. We can form from them an idea of the routine voyage and the routine journey overland to Moscow, but an adequate idea of this travel needs to be fitted together from many more documents than these narratives.[1] We might have expected a special effort to chronicle the voyages in the new north-

[1] T. S. Willan has drawn the most complete picture in *The early history of the Russia Company, 1553–1603* (Manchester, 1956).

east enterprise. Ironically enough, a report of the first one was prepared in Latin by a schoolmaster Clement Adams, who was presumably commissioned to write it.[1] The irony is that the result is highly unsatisfactory. The writer was not a participant, and he paid slight attention to whatever narrative was shown him, though he did report many observations, casual to be sure, of Russian society and manners. In fact he lost the actual narrative of the voyage in his rhetoric, which aimed at panegyric, not history, and we do not learn from him the basic facts of the voyage. On the other hand, the report of Richard Chancellor, whose ship alone reached Russia, remains a report on Russia, not on his voyage.[2] A third report,[3] found in the ship in which the commander and his crews were frozen to death unprepared for an Arctic winter, gives an adequate account of stormy weather, but no more.

The same regretful judgement of casualness must be made of the reports of later exploration beyond the White Sea;[4] they should be impressive, but they remain mere ships' logs. The annual trading voyages themselves ceased to be discoveries, and Hakluyt recorded instead either diplomatic missions, which were aimed to secure trading privileges, and the reports may deal, perhaps indignantly, with rude or restricted living in Russia generally but with lavish plenty at the hands of the Emperor. They are most likely to note diplomatic encounters with the monarch or his attendants, usually ending after outbursts in a moment of surly good nature when the Emperor granted the English demands. After Chancellor's first mission, which set the pattern of description of Russian protocol, the next robust account is that of Anthony Jenkinson in 1572, his last mission,[5] which began with the news that the Emperor was angry with him, but which ended with his being shipped off successful but without his needed documents. A more forthright and complacent envoy was Sir Jerome Bowes, sent in 1583, who reported his sturdy inde-

---

[1] Printed in Latin, with an English translation, *PN* (1589), 270–9; no copy of the Latin edition of 1554 survives.

[2] In *PN*, I (1598), 237–54.   [3] *PN*, I, 232–7.

[4] *PN*, I, 274–85, 445–53.   [5] *PN*, I, 402–11.

pendence of manner towards the Emperor. The latter was indignant:

> challenging me, as he had done ere then, for my too much stoutnesse, reckoning vp great numbers of ambassadours that had come to him from many great princes, but that not any that bare himselfe so stout as I did, or would challenge his place to be so great.
>
> I desired his Maiestie to haue patience (for he had then none within my seeing) and not to iudge of me in his choller, and then he would finde that I had not at any time done ought that became me not . . . After these extreme iarres (wherin I vsed more patience then I had) we grew calmer, and parted such friends (reconciled as it were). . . [1]

Presumably this impertinence was the cause of the withdrawal of this version and the substitution of another, which was reprinted by Hakluyt in his second edition,[2] and though this shorter account is more concerned with business, it is still replete with 'stoutness', and adds an inimical account of the Emperor's secretaries. The bravado adds interest of a sort to the story of dealings with one who was later to become known as Ivan the Terrible. Altogether we may add Bowes to our list of competent authors.

The same 'stoutness' is displayed in several narratives of another envoy who fancied himself, Sir Jerome Horsey. His stories of twenty years in Russia,[3] which should have been most revealing since he made himself quite at home there, are less interesting as a whole, rising at times to vigour of detail in court dealings, dropping at others to mere self-display in Russia and on the way home by land.

The six overland trading journeys beyond Moscow to Asia carry much more interest, as it happens, partly because of the greater variety of travel – down the Volga, for which the English

---

[1] *PN* (1589), p. 494.

[2] *PN*, pp. 491–500 (Bowes leaves I), 491–6 (Bowes leaves II); *PN*, I (1598), 458–63.

[3] Hakluyt printed Horsey's account of the coronation of Tsar Feodor in 1584 and of Horsey's mission back to England in the same year and return in 1586, *PN*, I (1598), 466–73. Horsey's MS accounts of missions of 1585 and 1589 were edited by E. A. Bond in *Early voyages to Russia and Persia*, II (1866), 288–311. Horsey's survey of his travels, of which Purchas printed only an abstract, was edited from MS by Bond, I, 155–266.

built a special ship, across the dangerous Caspian, and by camel caravan – and because of the dangers from Tartar tribes on the frontiers. Anthony Jenkinson's pioneer journey in 1558 to Bokhara was reported in a workmanlike account,[1] in which the doughty Englishman faced Tartar chieftains with the Tsar's letters, or joined the native travellers in the caravans to beat off marauders. In reading his report, we are constantly aware of the historical overtones. Jenkinson was following in the footsteps of the elder Polos in their pioneer European journey from the Volga to Bokhara. He is the first Englishman known to have reached the ancient Silk Route to China. Yet his interest is limited to the immediate Tartar scene, its nomads and their camels, and Samar-kand, then in ruins, interested him only as the capital of Tamer-lane. Central Asia had no such glamorous quality as it has, in literary imagination, for us, and Jenkinson does not even mention Cathay. The report should be supplemented by Jenkinson's map of Russia (1562), more than half of which is actually given to the Asia still far beyond Russia's frontiers, a region which he dotted plentifully with camels and Tartar tents.[2]

We may count the report of this journey to Bokhara as a robust travel narrative, and should count the map with it as also a picturesque report. Jenkinson's next journey, which took him to northern Persia (Kazvin), is reported in a workmanlike account[3] of successful diplomatic dealings in a setting of royal pageantry, with an alert eye to the people and the country. The journey was however almost too successful to yield much interest, and it is increasingly evident difficulties of the distant trade to Azerbaijan which make the later reports more interesting. Indeed the last one, of 1579, included two winters in Astrakhan, encounters with Tartar raiders on the Caspian, and the need to unload a ship frozen in for the winter. It also included many difficulties with

[1] *PN*, I (1598), 324–35.

[2] The map was published in 1562, and reprinted in 1570 in the authoritative world atlas of Ortelius, *Theatrum orbis terrarum*; it was rather fanciful, however, and was soon modified (see J. Keuning in *Imago Mundi*, XIII (1956), 172–5). We must regret the loss of the map of Russia done by William Borough, a professional navigator, of which the dedication was printed by Hakluyt.

[3] In *PN*, I (1598), 417.

payments and brigands and with Turkish competition. The report is, however, inadequate, a daily record of dates and events and distances without unity.

Altogether in the reports of the north-eastern voyages we may count as self-sufficient narrative probably only Jenkinson's accounts taken together, especially to Bokhara, with his map, and Sir Jerome Bowes' two complementary accounts of his negotiations. We add one more item. The most important literature to result from the Russia voyages was the striking and authoritative treatise by another envoy, Giles Fletcher, *Of the Russe common wealth, or maner of government by the Russe emperour* (1591).[1] This is a classic description of the despotism, its edge sharpened by the ambassador's own difficulties in dealing with the government. It is the first systematic account of the structure of Russian society and its political organization. The descriptive treatise giving the results of travel was here more valuable than the envoy's brief report on his mission, and marks the climax of the literary achievement of the Russia voyages.

These voyages did not therefore occasion much important writing. Yet the reports of Anthony Jenkinson reflect a competent adult style, and the treatise of Fletcher is incisively written, and the report by Bowes is vigorous. We must still feel some compunction in dismissing the body of this literature. For it is clear that many bright intervals shine in the matter-of-fact records. The sea voyages report 'flawes of wind and terrible whirlewind' or 'the great and terrible abundance of ice'.[2] On land, it was not only diplomats who noted anxious moments, since merchants had the onerous charge to obtain privileges, to sell and to buy, but most of all to collect their due payments. An English agent was killed in Persia by thieves on the road, and at once his companion hastened to convey all the purchases on shipboard lest the law of the land require sequestration.[3] Another agent, though he pro-

---

[1] Reprinted in part in *PN*, I (1598), 473–92, and more fully in Purchas, *Pilgrimes*, III (1625), iii, 403–60. See *The English works of Giles Fletcher the elder*, ed. Lloyd .E. Berry (Madison, 1964); Giles Fletcher, *Of the Russe common wealth*, a facsimile, ed. Richard Pipes (Cambridge, Mass., 1966); *Of the Rus commonwealth*, ed. A. J. Schmidt (Ithaca, N.Y., 1966).

[2] *PN*, I (1598), 282.   [3] *PN*, I, 353.

fessed eagerness to proceed from Azerbaijan both to Ormuz and to Aleppo on mercantile reconnaissance, was still weary of his effort. As he wrote home:

> God graunt me in health to see your worships, for I haue had a carefull trauell, with many a sorowfull day and vnquiet sleeps. Neither had I the company of one English person, to whom sometimes I might haue eased my pensiue heart, as God well knoweth, who hath deliuered me from mine enemies.[1]

Anxiety to get the job done might be made the main themes of the exploring and the trading and the diplomacy, with brief bursts of conflict and doubtless with much underlying fear of the unknown, and correspondingly little interest in the appeal of the exotic.

In the north-west voyages, of which there are twelve accounts, we have recorded the two excellent ones after the Settle narrative which was the first published: the brief Ellis work and the sus-tained account of the three Frobisher voyages by George Best. Their theme is now the discovery of and conflict with nature. The reports of the three subsequent Davis voyages to Greenland[2] can hardly be said to be more than routine, despite the greater achievement of the discovery.

The same theme animates the colonizing voyages to America in the 1580s. Eight reports describe the Gilbert approach to New-foundland and the Ralegh settlements in Virginia. The account by Captain Edward Hayes of the luckless Humphrey Gilbert voyage of 1583[3] gives a leisurely and intelligible recital of events, especially the unprofessional casting away of the major ship on the sands, and later of the gallant end of Gilbert, choosing to sail home in the pinnace because 'we are as near to heauen by sea as by land' and being lost at sea in it. The narrative rises to the occasion, and the very ordinariness of the great dangers from wind and weather draws a dark veil over the whole relationship of man to sea.

The same simplicity, but with an opposite idyllic effect, informs

[1] *PN* I, (1598), 361.   [2] *PN*, III (1600), 98–120.   [3] *PN*, III, 143–61.

the first report on Virginia[1] by Captain Arthur Barlowe of Ralegh's reconnaissance team, which observed at Roanoke 'the most plentifull, sweete, fruitfull and wholsome (soile) of all the worlde' and 'the people most gentle, louing, and faithfull, voide of all guile and treason, and such as liue after the maner of the golden age' – a rare, because favourable, judgement of the 'saluages'.

The other side of the story is given in a second report by the governor of the now settled first colony, Ralph Lane.[2] It describes the first high hopes of friendship with the natives, the discovery of rich metal, the upriver reconnaissance which revealed native enmity, and the eventual need to crush Indian plots; it relates finally the discouraged return with Drake's fleet before the relief ships arrived. This report also makes a dignified story, with a striking picture of the difficulty of dealing even with well-disposed natives.

The Virginia colony gave rise also to a description of the people and the products in two media, brush and pencil. For the colony included by design a painter, John White, and a 'chorographer', Thomas Harriot. The latter produced a book, *A briefe and true report* (1588), the former a set of descriptive water-colours. After the publication of the book, Hakluyt procured its publication in four languages at Frankfurt (1590), together with engravings of a number of pictures.[3] The engravings provide a somewhat Euro-peanized Indian, and while neither book nor pictures give a systematic idea of the life or scene of Virginia, both are fresh and interesting.

We should add here the Ralegh voyages to Guiana, aimed to discover El Dorado as the last remaining site of a colony. Ralegh's *Discouerie of the large, rich and bewtifull empyre of Guiana* (1596)[4] is a full and sophisticated narrative of some 35,000 words. It is meant as propaganda, and therefore makes out a laboured case for the golden wealth of Manoa which had supported the Inca empire. But it also gives a reasoned and lavish account of Ralegh's long

[1] *PN*, III (1600), 246–51.   [2] *PN*, III, 255–64.
[3] Theodor de Bry, *America*, pt. i (Frankfurt, 1590). See P. H. Hulton and D. B. Quinn, *The American drawings of John White*, 2 vols. (1964), where all the White material has been published in full.   [4] Reprinted *PN*, III (1600), 627–66.

reconnaissance of the Orinoco Valley and of his careful attempt to build up the trust of the natives. The principal effect given by the narrative, though certainly unintended, is one of frustration, the flooded rivers and impassable terrain forbidding all approach to the illusory goal. Yet the tone is spirited, and the theme is that of gallant contention with hardship and failure.

The further reconnaissance for Ralegh in 1596 by Lawrence Keymis was also written up in an accomplished report,[1] which may be taken as a postscript of some length since it has no separate interest. Both narratives together survey a country which seems to be composed mostly of rushing waters and of scattered natives who, though obliging, were of little help towards discovery or even towards access to the inner land. Read in the light of Ralegh's last desperate venture to the same end twenty years later, the story is one of anxious self-delusion and futility.

The theme then of the voyages to north-west and west and now to Guiana is one of stout endeavour, with some successes and satisfactions, and with much more hardship and distress and failure. The motive was of course profit, which was however nil, and the achievement was one of endurance on the one hand, and some knowledge of the world, which must have been too overwhelming to grasp, on the other. The best records – of Ellis and Best, of Hayes and Barlowe and Lane and Harriot, of Ralegh and Keymis – might have been written by the same persons, excepting always the sophisticated Ralegh, in gallant endurance of the unknown.

Hakluyt's second category included the voyages to the south and south-east. We can say very little in praise of the reports of the eighteen voyages to Morocco and Guinea – not counting the Hawkins voyages which went on to the Spanish Main – for the records seldom rise above the mere diary or perhaps diatribe. In fact, the Africa voyage relations in Hakluyt[2] are scanty in number as well as in content. The charters of the Barbary Company of 1585 and the Senegal Company of 1588 seem not to have led to voyages which Hakluyt attended to, for his few reports are perfunctory.

[1] Reprinted *PN*, III (1600), 666–92.   [2] *PN*, II (1599), ii.

If we were obliged to find a representative report of an African voyage to stand beside John Sparke's account of slave-hunting, we would take one of the William Towerson voyages to Guinea – probably the second one in 1556.[1] The brief report on it gives a vivid idea of French and English and Portuguese and African co-operation and in rivalry, and it is most valuable for the picture of day-to-day trading for gold in river after river along the coast. The report has some continuity, and more direction than most.

Of the Mediterranean voyages, fourteen are recorded in Hakluyt. Actually English ships had sailed to Italy and the Greek Islands since the fifteenth century, but only with the founding of the Levant Company in 1581 did Hakluyt obtain a regular series of reports, which have some historical but not great intrinsic interest, and of course no interest as discovery. Of the fourteen accounts, a number deal adequately with the diplomatic missions to Constantinople, and several deal with uneventful voyages to Alexandria or Constantinople. The most detailed is the diary of Thomas Dallam,[2] who took out and installed a complex organ for the Sultan (1600), but his jottings have rather quantity than quality. The same thing is true of the lavish documents[3] – reports, notes, letters – of the merchant John Sanderson, who spent eighteen years in the Levant. Hakluyt paid no heed to these travellers, and perhaps he did not think the region needed attention since it had been well written up since the Middle Ages. He had however urged the publication in London in 1585 of an Italian report[4] of an overland journey to Constantinople, which was never translated into English. It was left to George Sandys and Fynes Moryson to record notable voyages thither.[5]

Three remaining Mediterranean narratives initiate a new kind,

---

[1] In *PN*, ii (1599), ii, 36–41.
[2] Not in Hakluyt: from MS, edited by J. T. Bent, *Early voyages and travels in the Levant* (Hakluyt Society, 1893).
[3] Not in Hakluyt: from MS, edited by Sir William Foster, *Travels of John Sanderson in the Levant, 1584–1602* (Hakluyt Society, 1930).
[4] Marc'Antonio Pigafetta, *Itinerario* (1585).
[5] Fynes Moryson was in the Levant in 1596–7, though his *Itinerary* was not published until 1617. Sandys was there in 1610, and *A relation of a iourney begun An. Dom. 1610* appeared in 1615.

the pure adventure and escape story. The first (1579) concerns a galley-slave, John Fox,[1] captured by Turks in an English ship off Spain in 1563. At the end of 1576 he plotted a slave rebellion in the galley quarters in Alexandria, which captured and made off with a galley to safety in Italy after arduous navigation. The narrative was written, or over-written, by a professional author, probably Anthony Munday, after the hero's return to England. It relates mainly the struggle with the keepers in Alexandria, and says little of the voyages. It is none the less a cogent reminder of the ever-present danger of captivity.

A rather better story of 'moving accidents' is that of the ship *Jesus* of London, trading to Tripoli in Africa in 1584 after the formal treaty of trade with the Turkish empire.[2] When a European held there as pledge for a debt was found smuggled aboard ship, the crew was enslaved, and the master and mate hanged, while two men were forcibly converted. The slaves were given shore employment, and one of them managed to get a letter home to England: whereupon the English envoy in Constantinople dispatched an embassy official with an order of release from the Sultan to the Pasha of Tripoli. The ship was apparently not recovered, for the 11 survivors out of 26 made separate ways homeward by Greek, English, Turkish, and (after capture) Venetian ships. Highly circumstantial though hardly well-wrought, the narrative is enlightening on the conditions of trade in the Mediterranean, and perhaps marks the first appearance of the embassy to the rescue.

The most varied series of individual adventures is given in the pitiful report of Richard Hasleton (1595).[3] He was taken captive by Moors, escaped to Spain only to endure the terrors of the Inquisition which included the rack, followed by several further escapes and back into the hands of the Moors. He was eventually

---

[1] Reprinted *PN*, II (1599), i, 131–6.

[2] Thomas Saunders, *A true description of a voyage* (1587). Reprinted *PN*, II (1599), i, 184–91.

[3] *Strange and wonderful things happened to Richard Hasleton* (1595); not reprinted by Hakluyt, it may be found in C. R. Beazley, ed., *Voyages and travels* (An English Garner), II (1903), 151–80.

rescued, and lived to write his story. Like that of another traveller of many but suspect adventures reaching to the land of Prester John, one Edward Webbe (1590?), the narrative is bare, a mere scenario without imparted meaning.

The incidental martial theme of these voyages becomes the principal idea of a final Mediterranean narrative of the beating off of a Spanish fleet off Tunis in 1586 by a convoy of English merchant vessels.[1] Written by the Rev. Philip Jones, a friend of Hakluyt's, this is a competent account of battle. Naval warfare off the Atlantic coast of Europe in the 1580s and 1590s is the subject of some fifteen remaining narratives in the south and south-east volume. These reported the battles of the Spanish war, and we can count only three outstanding. Walter Ralegh's *A report of the truth of the fight . . . of . . . the Reuenge* (1591)[2] is a somewhat laboured apologia, but a notable account of bravery, the most famous in the English record. Edward Wright's account of the earl of Cumberland's raid on the Azores in 1589 is most notable for its dramatic account of a storm.[3] Colonel Wingfield's narrative of Drake's raid on Portugal (1589, published abroad also in Latin and German) is a vivid military record of some length, rather more apologia than narrative, and rather more an account of battle than one of travel.[4] All three are creditable works.

We should have as satisfactory accounts of other noteworthy naval events, but in fact we have no better report of the battle with the Armada than that compiled by a Dutch historian which Hakluyt printed.[5] Likewise the principal account of the Essex–Ralegh raid on Cadiz in 1596 is rhetorical, uncritical, and factually inadequate,[6] while Ralegh's own account of his winning of the naval battle is a transparent claim of sole credit for the success.[7]

---

[1] In *PN*, II (1599), i, 285–9.

[2] Reprinted *PN*, II (1599), ii, 169–75.

[3] Published 1599, reprinted *PN*, II (1599), ii, 156–66.

[4] Reprinted *PN*, II (1599), ii, 134–55.

[5] *PN*, I (1598), 591–606.   [6] *PN*, I (1598), 607–19.

[7] 'The relation of the voyage to Cadiz, 1596', first printed 1700; reprinted in Ralegh, *Works*, VIII (Oxford, 1829), 667–81.

The most revealing account by Sir William Slingsby has detail, but little organization,[1] and we must turn to the modern historian.

The voyages to south and south-east thus reveal less interest than either northern or western voyages, probably for two reasons. They were not voyages of discovery, except as all travel is discovery for the traveller himself, and they were not pioneer voyages of any kind, and therefore seemed to include no special observation. The naval voyages have their own appeal, but we can count only three of them as adequate. We must still regret that the Africa voyages give only casual impressions of country and people.

Virtually all the westward voyages to the Caribbean and the South Atlantic and the Pacific involved acts of war, and armed conflict is therefore the common theme of the narratives. Most of them record plentiful conflict with wind and sea as well, so that our typical idea of an Elizabethan voyage narrative combines the two themes of storm and battle. We must add, to complete the picture, that most voyages failed to pay for themselves, that more men and ships were lost than survived, and that the oppressive air of suffering and failure and death hangs over these enterprises.

Beginning with John Hawkins' attempt to force the slave trade on the Spanish colonies in 1565, I count twenty-four reports of voyages south-westward (excluding Ralegh's Guiana voyages). I have already noted the value of John Sparke's full account of the second Hawkins voyage, and of Hawkins' own competent statement of the Spanish treachery at San Juan de Ulua, treachery which was made to justify all the subsequent acts of war which English ships were to commit at sight against Spanish ships and possessions. This justification was thought to be increased by the trial and tortures of English seamen by the Inquisition both in Mexico and Spain. The narrative of Miles Philips, one of the few refugees from the last Hawkins voyage who survived all dangers and reached home via Spain after sixteen years, is a notable example of the story of personal adventure.[2] Written down, or at

[1] Edited by Sir Julian Corbett in *The naval miscellany*, I (Navy Records Society, 1902), 137–92.
[2] In *PN*, III (1600), 467–87.

least reshaped, by a competent writer, it does not, it is true, create an adequate psychological narrative, but it is often as striking as many a romance or picaresque tale. The same cannot be said for the like report of the like adventures of Job Hortop,[1] which are made barely factual. As for David Ingram, who was thought to have walked from Mexico to Cape Breton, the confusion of his observations of scene and of savages in the variety of wild country he passed through prevents his recollections also from being listed with those of Philips.[2]

For the exploits of Drake and others in their silver raids on Panama in the 1570s, we must regret that the only adequate report, while quite competent, of Drake's success was very much rewritten and expanded when it was first published in 1626, and is therefore doubtfully authentic.[3] We may note only two other narratives of Caribbean adventure. One is the account (1589) of Drake's raid on the West Indies in 1585 which brought into the open the war which he had already long waged overseas against Spain.[4] This account is a full narrative of the capture of Santiago in the Cape Verde Islands and of Santo Domingo and Cartagena in the Caribbean. Even though it does not admit the failure of the voyage to carry out Drake's grand design to sweep the Spaniard from the western sea, it needs little supplementing for the under-standing of the enterprise. It is a notable naval narrative.

As much cannot be said of the reports of most of the other Caribbean raids which followed, including the disastrous last voyage of Drake and Hawkins in 1595, in which both died of illness, and which found the Spanish defences now too strong to permit the capture of Spanish treasure. The narrative of this voyage is, like many others, a barely developed diary with little continuity or point.[5] One of the last of Hakluyt's records may possess greater significance, in that the 1596 voyage of Sir Anthony Sherley, a newcomer to the Caribbean, was not only a pathetic

[1] PN, III (1600), 487–95.
[2] Hakluyt printed Ingram's story in PN (1589), pp. 557–62.
[3] Reprinted in C. R. Beazley, ed., Voyages and travels, II, 221–94.
[4] Reprinted in PN, III (1600), 534–48.
[5] PN, III, 583–90.

failure in itself but also a testimonial to the new Spanish strength which had already foiled Drake.[1] The implication of the narrative is that the game has played out, and that both the veteran Drake and the novice Sherley could try only wild and unlikely enter/ prises, even though both Sherley and his companion raider William Parker at least reached home. In the same year, the earl of Cumberland's own voyage to seize and hold Puerto Rico, which is described in great detail by the earl himself for a time and then by his chaplain, was defeated only by the tropical disease which carried off 600 out of his 1,000 men. Though the narrative[2] carries a buoyant air, the failure is none the less evident. Actually it is more impressive because the narrative is not written in the more expansive manner of 1600 and later.

In sum, the theme of arduous failure emerges clearly in the few good narratives, beginning with the first success and the first savage defeat of Hawkins in 1565 and 1568, going on to the long endurance and return of Philips, and to the triumph of Drake in 1585. Thereafter the narratives record failure and, with Sherley and Cumberland in 1596, hopeless endeavour; and the Ralegh voyages to Guiana in 1595 and 1596 emphasize the hopelessness even of discovery in the one region left free by the Spaniards, the flooded Orinoco delta. Piracy will still be possible, as the raids of the buccaneers a century later will show, but the disruption of the Spanish empire has proved a futile dream.

The same theme of early triumph and mounting defeat may be read in the voyages to South America and beyond, most of which followed Drake's initiative in seeking plunder in the Pacific. Of some twelve narratives, seven are of some fullness: the two narratives of Drake's circumnavigation (1577–80), the reports of the Fenton and the Cumberland voyages to Brazil (1582, 1586), of the Cavendish circumnavigation (1586–8) and of his dis/ astrous last voyage (1591), and Richard Hawkins' voyage in 1593 which led to his capture in the Pacific. We can say but little in favour of the narratives of circumnavigation: either the compressed account of Drake which Hakluyt printed,[3] or the notes of Drake's

[1] *PN*, III (1600), 598–602.   [2] In Purchas, *Pilgrimes*, IV (1625), 1150–76.
[3] In *PN*, III (1600), 730–42.

chaplain which were the base of the later published accounts[1] –
or on the other hand the report of 'The admirable and prosperous
voyage' of Thomas Cavendish.[2] They are adequate records of
events, and rise to much appeal in the account of the savage
weather of the Straits of Magellan, and they become lively indeed
in reporting the piracies of the Pacific which at first brought such
lavish profits; but they are otherwise routine, as are perhaps the
records of many of the world's most important travels, including
Magellan's.

The report of Fenton's voyage, which was to follow Drake but
did not reach the Straits, is likewise routine,[3] though the private
diary of the chaplain Richard Madox contains as much sharp
personal observation of the conflicts on board as any novelist
would make.[4] Fragmentary though it is, the diary ranks at least
with the reports of diplomatic encounters in Russia and Persia for
its shrewd perceptions. I cite a sample passage:

> Capten Skevington was hear also with a great complaynt agaynst his
> Master, with gawdy words, for euery Iack sayth I am a gentilman & I can
> tel how to gouerne & I wil gouern, yt is scarse worthy to syt & keep flies
> from a gawled horse bak. God send me discreet and wyse gouernowrs as
> be gentilmen indeed and not such crycket-catchers as neuer cam wher
> yt grew. in fyne we made al frends, L. Ward axed my opinion of Master
> walker, I told he myght be trust with any thing but with a fayr lasse.[5]

This all too rare observation could not of course be published.
Some degree of frankness was, as it happens, achieved in the
report of the voyage which the earl of Cumberland hoped would
reach the Pacific (1586) but which turned back to raid Bahia
for prize and treasure.[6] This report has sharp perceptions of the
conflict of the leaders, and is vivid furthermore in describing what
seems to us mere brigandage. James Lancaster's raid on Brazil

---

[1] All are collected in *The world encompassed*, ed. Sir Richard Temple (1926).

[2] In *PN*, III (1600), 803–25.

[3] *PN*, III, 757–68.

[4] Partially printed in *The troublesome voyage of Captain Edward Fenton*, ed. E. G. R.
Taylor (1959). A full edition has been prepared by Professor E. S. Donno.

[5] *Ibid.*, p. 169.

[6] In *PN*, III (1600), 769–78.

in 1594 has much the same vividness of unpleasant detail,[1] and both reports should be given credit.

Three narratives remain of quality above the usual. One was *The obseruations of Sir Richard Hawkins knight, in his voyage into the South Sea*, an account of his voyage in 1593 through the Straits to Peru, which led to his capture after a three-days battle by Spanish authority now prepared to defend itself. On his being ransomed after ten years as a prisoner of war, Hawkins wrote a full account of his voyage and its lessons, which was published posthumously in 1622. The work is not merely a narrative. It is a reasoned account of every incident or observation, explaining errors and necessary precautions against errors in the management of ships, in discipline, in strategy and tactics, and also spelling out observa-tions of tropical medicine and peoples and commodities. Alto-gether the book 'gives a fuller picture of life at sea than is to be found in any other Elizabethan work'.[2]

The other narratives are the two accounts of the last and fatal attempt of Thomas Cavendish to reach Peru in 1591. Of five ships, but one returned, with only sixteen survivors, the ship in perilous state with no anchors and with rags for sails. The narrative by John Jane,[3] on the ship of the veteran John Davis, is a record of despair unmatched in the collection, in which the overpowering perils of the sea were increased by the uncertainties and suspicions of men, so that only the sterling competence of John Davis (in Jane's eyes) succeeded in bringing the one ship back through the storms of the Straits. The pathetic counterpart of this narrative is Cavendish's own despairing account[4] of his trials, violent storms and (as he thought) the treachery of Davis and mutiny on his own ship. The final pathos is in his writing of the report in complete wretchedness on the homeward voyage during which he died.

The desperate trials of the sea sound the final sombre theme of the last overseas movement of the century. They darken even the

[1] *PN*, III (1600), 708–15.
[2] Sir Richard Hawkins, *Observations*, ed. J. A. Williamson (1933), p. xc.
[3] In *PN*, III (1600), 842–52.
[4] In Purchas, *Pilgrimes*, IV (1625), 1192–201.

one enterprise which in the end was to live up to its promise, the trade with the East Indies via the Cape of Good Hope. The first voyages, of 1591 and 1596, failed completely, the four ships which passed the Cape in the two voyages being wrecked. Meantime the Dutch began their successful trade with the east in 1595, and James Lancaster, who had been shipwrecked in the 1591 voyage, led the first successful English expedition in 1600. Despite the lavish backing of the voyage by court and city in the new East India Company, only two ships returned, and Lancaster was almost shipwrecked again in the South Atlantic on the return. The letter which he wrote to his employers in anticipation of death at sea is distinguished.

> Right worshipfull, what hath passed in this Voyage, and what Trades I haue settled for this companie, and what other euents haue befallen vs, you shall vnderstand by the bearers hereof, to whom (as occasion hath fallen) I must referre you. I will striue with all diligence to saue my ship, and her goods, as you may perceiue, by the course I take in venturing mine owne life, and those that are with mee. I cannot tell where you should looke for mee, if you send out any Pinnace to seeke mee: because I liue at the deuotion of the winds and seas. And thus fare you well, desir-ing God, to send vs a merrie meeting in this world, if it be his good will and pleasure . . .
>
> Your very louing friend[1]

The danger which reaches its climax in the letter darkens the narrative of his otherwise highly successful trading for pepper in Java. Fortunately triumph carried by a narrow margin, and he came safely home. The narratives of his failure and shipwreck in 1591[2] and success and near-shipwreck in 1603[3] are both effective and affecting. Indeed it may be that narrative technique has improved, if only because the report of the first voyage was written by Hakluyt from the notes of a participant. As for description of scene, the account in the second voyage of Java has begun to take

---

[1] In Purchas, *Pilgrimes*, I (1625), iii, 163.

[2] In *PN*, II (1599), ii, 102–10.

[3] In Purchas, *Pilgrimes*, I (1625), iii, 148–64; both were reprinted in *The voyages of Sir James Lancaster*, ed. Sir William Foster (1940).

on the greater extent which will be characteristic of voyage reports of the successful East India Company voyages, and will give them greater interest.

Before concluding the southern voyages, we must again note, as in the Mediterranean section, two further individual travellers who suffered 'moving accidents' and yet came safely home. Fox, Saunders of the *Jesus*, Hasleton and Webbe were limited to the Mediterranean. Peter Carder was lost with a boat's crew from Drake's ship beyond the Straits of Magellan, and was cast ashore a sole survivor in Patagonia. For months he lived with a cannibal tribe, improving their fighting skill. Then he passed over what seem to be three thousand miles to reach Bahia, found a degree of protection in the Portuguese colony instead of automatic con-demnation to the galleys, and there spent several years as plantation foreman and as coastwise trader. Eventually he smuggled aboard a Portuguese vessel which was captured off the Azores by English privateers, and so reached home safely in 1586 after eight years. His story is, however, altogether matter-of-fact, perhaps taken down at an interview, and striking only in two respects: it avoids stress on sufferings and complaints, and it gives a first English account of cannibals.[1]

A much more grilling story, and one reporting more hardships than any other in the century, is that of Anthony Knivet. Even when cut short by Purchas, who had it from Hakluyt, the story runs to about 30,000 words,[2] and the sheer weight of endurance and escapes is alone impressive. Knivet gives still a third view of the last ill-fated voyage of Cavendish, beginning with the disorderly capture and plundering of the town of Santos in Brazil on the way south, continuing with the disasters of storms and dispersion in the voyage to the straits and in the vain attempt to pass through, and recording the final attrition of the returning men and ships by the aroused Portuguese. The effect is far from heroic, as the desperate and unruly crews struggled to survive. Knivet himself was the most persistent struggler of all. Caught in the straits with-

---

[1] The narrative was collected by Hakluyt, but published only by Purchas, *Pilgrimes*, IV (1625), 1187–90.

[2] *Ibid.*, IV, 1201–42.

out suitable clothing (which had been lost at sea), he lay as one dead for what seem to be weeks of sailing northward in search of food. Being laid ashore on an island with other sick men, when 'my toes were raw, my body was blacke, I could not speak nor stirre', he was revived by the tropical sun, and was the only one to escape death, by his wits, at the hands of the Portuguese. Many months of bondage followed, now given to ignoble labour, now escaping to life in the woods or deserts or among the cannibals, as he calls the natives indiscriminately; now assigned to suitable labour, now loaded with leg-irons after a desperate escape, now engaged in interminable military marches through mountains and jungles. He even escaped by ship to Angola in Africa, hoping to enlist there as a soldier and eventually escape to Abyssinia and Turkey; but he was caught and brought back to Brazil. Eventually he sailed with his captor, the governor of Rio de Janeiro, to Lisbon, fell ill, was looked after by stray Englishmen, but was back in prison in Lisbon as the story is abruptly ended.

This narrative of ten years of endurance without end records hardship beyond belief, dangers innumerable, bondage and despair. Yet the tone is brisk and not hopeless, many intervals suggest a satisfactory routine of work as plantation or factory foreman or even as guest of the savages, and the theme is certainly the undying courage and adaptability of man. We have had earlier grim stories of captivity, that for example of Miles Philips, but I think none yet which have reported greater varieties of fortune. It is true that the narrative as we have it shows little planning or organization beyond the chronological, but its amazing content makes it the captivity story *par excellence*, and it antedates by a century the adventure narratives which gave Defoe the models for his fiction. With it the glamour of the 'prose epic' completely disappears.

We should at this point consider a somewhat similar kind of traveller, the extravagant or eccentric. His truth, or at least the truth of his personality, is stranger than fiction, whether he is Margery Kempe the shouter (of the fifteenth century), or Ludovico Varthema of Bologna, whose travels to India about 1500 make a long picaresque tale, or Mendes Pinto, whose travels to China about 1550 and whose hairsbreadth escapes have made him un-justly the symbol of the lying traveller. Perhaps the most striking such English figure in our time was Sir Thomas Stukeley, who called himself 'Duke of Ireland' and who actually acquired a papal armada to conquer that island; he died instead in the Portuguese defeat in Morocco in 1578.[1] Though a play was written about this swashbuckler at the time, I know of no single contemporary account of his travels.

A figure of intellectual rather than military bravura was the Scot known as the Admirable Crichton. At 22, he dazzled Venetian scholars with his brilliant public disputations in 1581 and 1582; but his story has had to be pieced together from a variety of evidences.

We do have long accounts of another dashing figure, Sir Anthony Sherley, whose Caribbean voyages we have seen above. He had been a soldier in the Low Countries and in France, he was to be a naval commander again in the Azores voyage of 1597, and he was sent by Essex in 1597 to command a company of volunteers to help defend Ferrara against the Pope. Since the defence had crumbled before he arrived, he revived with Essex as sponsor the grandiose scheme of a western alliance with Persia against the Turk. Through many dangers he reached Persia with his attending gentlemen, and impressed the Shah sufficiently to be made Persian ambassador to the western powers. He returned in splendour by way of Moscow, Archangel, Emden by sea; barred from England as an Essex partisan and a Catholic, he continued via Prague to Rome, where his mission ended. His Persian co-envoy continued to Spain, and so home, but Sherley moved on to other ends. He served the Emperor as envoy to Naples, and Spain as High Admiral there; but after 1610, when he was 45, he remained in Spain as a mere royal pensioner, unemployed except in devising further grandiose international designs.

Accounts of some of Sir Anthony's travels are extant in five languages, in print and in manuscript, but the best selection from

[1] His story has been written by John Izon, *Sir Thomas Stucley* (1956).

them tells only part of the story.[1] If we put together the Hakluyt narrative of the Caribbean voyage with Persian narratives: William Parry's *New and large discourse* (1601) and George Man-waring's *True discourse* (written 1600?, published 1825), we assemble a record notable for dangers, for pageantry, and for dashing self-display. Include all the narratives and contemporary notices in one volume, and we have a lively work of travel, in tone not epic but at the best romantic.

We may add here a word about the travellers to near-by countries who did not interest Hakluyt because they did not undertake discovery. Medieval travellers noted their itineraries, probably as information for others, or wrote lively letters if they were John of Salisbury or Peter of Blois, or included reports of travel in their autobiographies if they were St Willibald or Giraldus Cambrensis or Margery Kempe. With the renaissance, two new interests appear in the travel record. The reports of diplomatic missions are likely to be more regularly made, and may deal more or less with travel. For only one example, the official letters of Sir Richard Moryson and the private letters of his secretary Roger Ascham on their mission to the Emperor in Germany and Austria in 1550-3 make lively reading; indeed, one letter was begun as a *Report . . . of the . . . state of Germany*, which Ascham never finished, though it was published after his death. In general, the state papers contain many reports which have travel interest, such as those which Hakluyt published by the envoys to Russia and to Turkey. Some interesting travel litera-ture could be culled from reports like those the Venetian envoys regularly made to describe as a whole the country they returned from.

The second interest arises from the new emphasis on travel as education, praising Ulysses as the model 'for that he knew many mens maners and cities'. A gentle youth studying to be a statesman would keep a diary like Thomas Hoby, or write observant letters like Philip Sidney or Henry Wotton, or more ambitiously prepare

[1] Sir E. Denison Ross has edited *Sir Anthony Sherley and his Persian adventure* (Broadway Travellers, 1933); see D. W. Davies, *Elizabethans errant: the strange fortunes of Sir Thomas Sherley and his three sons* (Ithaca, N.Y., 1967).

to publish either an account of their travels or a study of foreign lands, like Ascham's *Report*. The most ambitious of these youths was Fynes Moryson, whose travels in Europe and the Levant from 1591 to 1597 led to his enormous *Itinerary*, published in part only in 1617, and to a complementary study of the countries he had seen, of which a part still remains in manuscript. The writing of these books falls after our period, and in any case his quantity does not add up to quality.

Of those whose work was done in the Tudor period, I mention four of some importance. The first is William Thomas, traveller in Italy from 1545 to 1548. Author of the first Italian grammar in English (1550), he also published an elaborate *Historie of Italie* (1549),[1] comprising for the most part translations of current Italian histories of the individual states, but including also chapters of description of Italian life and manners, partly from his own observations. This is the first substantial English work on Italy, and though most of it is translation, the original observation is a product of travel.

The second work is Anthony Munday's story, *The English Romayne life* (1582), of his travel to Italy and his stay at the new English college for priests in Rome. This is a journalist's account by a renegade, giving the first idea in England of the trials and jealousies of the exiles; it is amusing, but hardly more. A much more important work is *Roma sancta* (1581),[2] a description in English of the religious and charitable institutions of Rome done by Gregory Martin, the later translator of the Reims Bible, who arrived at the English Hospice in 1576. This is a substantial survey of nearly four hundred pages, intended doubtless to edify and strengthen English Catholics by an account of the majesty and the religious and charitable activity of the mother city of their faith. Transcending by far the usual guidebook for the religious pilgrim, it should have been written in Latin and published for all the world. For it antedates by twenty years, I believe, the

[1] *The history of Italy*, ed. G. B. Parks (Ithaca, 1963), contains selections, including all of Thomas' own observations.

[2] Edited by G. B. Parks (Rome, 1969), from a MS formerly in the possession of Lord Clifford of Chudleigh.

earliest published work of its kind, and demonstrates unusual scope and value as a survey of the Rome of the church.

A more ambitious work than any was Henry Wotton's proof of his education by travel, his *State of Christendom*, written in Geneva in 1594 though not published until 1657. This is an ambitious survey of international relations, involving knowledge of and conjecture about the major nations of Europe, with a study of their respective strengths and political needs and policies: in sum, a statesman's handbook. As observation of the foreign scene, it is the result of travel, and may be counted with Thomas' *Italie* and Martin's *Roma sancta* in the category which also includes Fletcher's *Russe common wealth* and Harriot's *Briefe and true report*.

Even after we have singled out some thirty or more of the most effective travel narratives and descriptions, we may still have some qualms over our piecemeal judgements. Not that we doubt the dignity of narrative of Best or the two Hawkins or Wingfield, or the workmanlike quality of the reports of Jenkinson and Sparke and Lane and Keymis and Harriot, or the adventurous appeal of Philips and Knivet and Sherley, or the distinction of Thomas and Gregory Martin and the trenchancy of Fletcher, or the final pathos of the voyages of the 1590s, or the superior writing skill of Ralegh. If these 'best' works were however segregated in an anthology, they might prove by themselves to make up only a pale story, suggesting a drowned range of hills of which only the tops can be seen. We still need to realize the range in its full depth.

For it is clear that the body of literature of which Hakluyt was the main inspirer is unique in that it records all, or nearly all, the new voyages of a significant period in a nation's history, and its consequent massiveness gives it a power which single stories do not convey. We can still not improve on Froude's phrase, 'the prose epic', for it is precisely the epic theme of daring and endurance which informs the narratives. The story is that of the *enfances* of empire, of experiment and failure more often than success, and failure here means disaster and multiple death. If the motive of the voyages was usually profit, the result was usually loss, often complete loss. The indirect result was some discovery of the world, and somewhat less understanding discovery of man. At least those few who survived learned a hard discipline of travel and travail in the struggle with the sea, with the enemy, with the strange peoples who were *ipso facto* enemy. This was real epic, not merely literature, with many heroes sung and unsung, in the search to know as well as to acquire a larger world.

I do not believe that one can point to any conscious develop' ment of form in this literature. An occasional work took the form of argument – the Latin history of the first Russia voyage, Ralegh's account of the *Revenge*. An occasional rather formal writing in elaborate Latin style was produced like George Best's book on the Frobisher voyages, and Ralegh's *Discouerie of Guiana* was a more facile work in this style. Yet in the end the character' istic form remains a straight chronology more or less elaborated, plus a straight description of the scene if called for. Undoubtedly Hakluyt's first collection in 1589 had its influence in establishing the mode of the 'round unvarnished tale', just as his own skill in writing, when it was called upon, probably encouraged the adding of body to the mere skeleton. At any rate, the standard travel narrative was for two centuries to emphasize the chrono' logical record and the needed description as statement of fact, with the added implication of rising to the emotional moment. It was not indeed until the time of Humboldt that travel literature became consciously romantic in tone.

Examples of Hakluyt's own idea of simplicity of style may be seen first in a narrative which he compiled in an interview with a traveller, which began:

Our fleet of the three tall ships abouenamed [in the long title of the first Lancaster voyages] departed from Plimmouth the 10 of April 1591, and arriued at the Canarie'ilands the 25 of the same, from whence we departed the 29 of April. The second of May we were in the height of Cape Blanco. The fift we passed the tropique of Cancer. The eight we were in the height of Cape Verde. All this time we went with a faire winde at Northeast, alwayes before the winde vntill the 13 of the same moneth, when we came within 8 degrees of the Equinoctiall line.[1]

[1] In *PN*, ii (1599), ii, 102.

This conciseness in the account of the beginnings of a voyage was a late development. Actually it might well give a wrong impres-sion of the most usual characteristic of these voyages, the long delays of head winds, which usually held ships back for weeks and months in the English Channel.

Again in the matter of style, it seems likely that Hakluyt helped to diminish overwriting. Before his collection was thought of, George Best wrote of a Frobisher voyage north-west:

> And albeit, by reason of the fleeting yce, which were dispersed here almost the whole sea ouer, they were brought many times to the extreamest point of perill, mountaines of yce tenne thousand times scaping them scarce one ynch, which to haue striken had bene their present destruction, considering the swift course and way of the ships, and the vnwieldinesse of them to stay and turne as a man would wish: yet they esteemed it their better safetie, with such perill to seek Sea-roome, than without hope of euer getting libertie to lie striuing against the streame, and beating amongst the Isie mountaines, whose hugenes and monstrous greatnesse was such, that no man would credite, but such as to their paines sawe and felt it.[1]

Contrast this characteristic Elizabethan elaborateness with a passage written after 1589:

> In the which time wee indured extreeme stormes, with perpetual snow, where many of our men died with cursed famine, and miserable cold, not hauing wherewith to couer their bodies, nor to fill their bellies, but liuing by muskles, water, and weeds of the sea, with a small reliefe of the ships store in meale sometimes.[2]

This will be the simple style of the travel narrative after Hakluyt. Whether he was also responsible for a third development I do not know: this would be a more elaborate account of the observa-tions of travel. Many of the Hakluyt narratives left to Purchas have more detail; so also has the account written by Richard Hawkins in 1602 or 1603 of his voyage,[3] and even more the version of Francis Drake's Panama raid of 1572 which was enlarged by his

[1] In *PN*, III (1600), 79.

[2] *PN*, III, 843.

[3] Sir Richard Hawkins, *The observations* (1622); edited by J. A. Williamson, 1933.

nephew and published in 1626. A narrative intended for publication was already lavish enough when Best wrote it in 1578 or
Ralegh in 1591 or 1596, but the reduction of Best's wordiness
allowed for more matter with less art. Doubtless the mere intent
to publish inspired more ample writing.

So much for form. For value, we must admit the inadequacies
of the epic. Few narratives succeed in telling the full story of the
travel, and we must always turn, as has been said, to the later
historian for complete information. It is the ordinary fate of the
historical report to grow obsolete, and inadequacy of fact is to be
expected. It is more important that the travel literature is inadequate in its report of the psychological. It is rare for a narrative to
describe the personal complications of the travel – enmities, dis-
content, divided counsels – often because revelations might be
dangerous, especially in print. A manuscript Hawkins account
describes,[1] for example, a scene of mutiny, which was as it
happened handled very creditably by Hawkins, but which did
not reach print at the time. On the other hand, we still do not
know the full truth of the parallel event on Drake's voyage, in
which Drake felt obliged to execute his subordinate rather than
forgive. Even if prudence permitted publication, it is probable
that the art of travel narrative could not yet manage such com-
plexities, having enough to do to recount both deeds and scenes.
Emotional outbursts and reactions could be handled, but not
probably continued emotional tension and scenes.

Another serious related fault in the literature is the lack of any
but formal characterization. Beyond question, the captain or
'general', or sometimes the master, is given credit for the conduct
of the voyage, or discredit, and something of his character can be
inferred. Frequently a clue will be given to his personality as
headstrong or cautious or clever, but there will be in general little
borrowing from the art of the historian or the biographer. Character is not yet very much on the mind of the writer of travel
literature. It is not very much on the mind of the writer either of
epic or of prose fiction in this period, as reference to the *Faerie*

[1] Printed in J. A. Williamson, *Sir John Hawkins* (1927), pp. 498–500.

Queene and the *Arcadia* will testify. Character is proclaimed by deeds, not words: this might indeed be the final motto of the literature of travel. It will be so generally for travel literature there, after, except for the best: which will aim either at systematic observation or at organized narrative, and add to either or both the values of emotional vividness.

10

Hakluyt's reputation

D. B. QUINN

The story of Hakluyt's reputation is still incomplete,[1] but it is now possible to see some of the elements, at times rather puzzling ones, which accounted for its survival and growth. In his own lifetime Hakluyt's achievement won him no spectacular rewards or exceptional literary prominence. An Oxford college fellowship, two country livings, two cathedral prebends, a Savoy chaplaincy, a modest fortune were his rewards as a scholar, business consultant and clergyman as well as a compiler and editor. He owed much of his rise in the little circle of voyage-promoters and voyage-recorders to his elder cousin, and it was largely through him that, in the first place, he made the essential contacts with merchants, maritime speculators, sailors and ministers of state. His role as consultant on certain overseas matters, more particularly on American prospects, to Walsingham, Burghley and Robert Cecil, between 1578 and 1612, was far from being a continuous one. From 1581 to 1588 he had some appreciable influence on Walsingham: though his contacts with Burghley went back to 1578, his close association with the elderly statesman on the St Lawrence voyages covered only a few years in the 1590s: from 1596 to about 1609 he had a rather limited range of connections with Robert Cecil and perhaps some influence with him during the crucial years 1605-7 when the Virginia Company was being created. He had very close connections with most of the North American adventures and adventurers between 1580 and 1607: besides the Virginia Company he had some share in determining the form and objectives of the East India Company in 1600 and

---

[1] A particularly useful estimate of the limits of what has already been done is that by Federico Marenco in his introduction to *I viaggi inglesi . . . di Richard Hakluyt*, I (Milan, 1966), 27–33. (This is the initial volume of the first extensive Italian translation of Hakluyt materials, a very generous selection from *PN* (1598–1600).)

the North-west Passage Company in 1612. Yet it is difficult to trace a continuous association between Hakluyt and very many of the individuals whose careers overlapped, as did Hakluyt's, the Elizabethan and Jacobean periods. Michael Lok he knew from at least 1581 and was still in fairly close touch with him in 1612. Ralegh he was close to between 1583 and 1589 but he was only loosely in contact with him from 1590 to 1603, and only occasionally, it is thought, after his disgrace in 1603. It seems probable that one of his most stable contacts in London from 1582 until his death was Thomas Smith, though we have few indications of precisely how close or continuous their co-operation was over either the East India Company or the Virginia Company.

Hakluyt had, it is true, other circles of influence. The little band of senior members of Christ Church which William Gager celebrated in Latin verse in 1583 included Hakluyt.[1] And in 1598 or a little later Gabriel Harvey noted, 'I looke for much, as well in verse, as in prose, from my two Oxford frends, Doctor Gager, & Master Hackluit: both rarely furnished for the purpose.'[2] Gabriel Harvey (d. 1630) and his brother Richard (d. 1623) both outlived Hakluyt and appear to have retained an interest in him for the rest of his life. At the same time, there is no indication that Archbishop Toby Mathew (d. 1628), or the mathematician, Nathaniel Torporley (d. 1632), both of whom were also included in Gager's gallery, kept up any contact whatever with Hakluyt. Such men could provide, however, some extension of his reputa- tion into the decade or two after his death. He was active also in the intellectual circle which included William Camden (d. 1623) and Sir Henry Savile (d. 1622), but our evidence of close contact with them is largely from the 1580s, and evidence of developing links with younger scholars in the years before his death is slight. His links with geographers in the Low Countries are not known to have survived the deaths of Mercator (1594) and Ortelius (1598), with the exception of some contact with Emanuel van Meteren (d. 1612). He did not leave, therefore, so far as we know,

[1] B.M., Additional MS 22583, the Hakluyt verse being on f. 62.
[2] Gabriel Harvey, *Marginalia*, ed. G. C. Moore-Smith (1913), p. 233.

a continental reputation, based on correspondence in his late years, behind him. Of the long list of men whom he had aroused to help him or to translate texts which he considered worth English editions, beginning with John Florio and including Martin Basanier, Philip Jones, Robert Parke, Abraham Hart' well, William Phillip, William Walker, Pierre Erondelle, John Pory and Michael Lok, none became his disciple and continued his professional interests, though Pory (d. 1635) may at times have aspired to do so. Captain John Smith continued to exploit Hakluyt's works with an occasional acknowledgement between 1612 and 1624,[1] as did William Strachey in his then unpublished 'Historie of Travell into Virginia Britania' (1610–12).[2]

It was left largely to Samuel Purchas to carry on Hakluyt's work, and on the whole, to enhance his reputation. The details of the transition in materials from Hakluyt to Purchas are given above[3] and are very important in the record of the transmission of Hakluyt's collections. The sequence of tributes too, between 1613 and 1625, which Purchas paid to Hakluyt were important as placing on record his most significant follower's appreciation of Hakluyt's work and in helping to consolidate his fame. Whatever problems Purchas encountered in acquiring part of Hakluyt's collections – and they still remain somewhat obscure – he did not shirk paying a due tribute to his master, most forcefully con' veyed in the engraved title to his last major work, *Hakluytus posthumus or Purchas his pilgrimes*, 1 (1625), even though the printed title'pages stress rather his own contribution and read *Purchas his pilgrimes* alone. After his immense labours, Purchas both in his titling and in his grumbles about the difficulties of obtaining some of Hakluyt's papers, which he expressed in his preface, was in two minds about precisely what tributes should

---

[1] John Smith, *Works*, ed. Edward Arber (1884), pp. 148, 267, 305, 465, 772. How far Smith had personal contacts with Hakluyt is not clear, but he claimed some.

[2] William Strachey, *The historie of travell into Virginia Britania*, ed. L. B. Wright and V. Freund (1953), p. xxvii; S. G. Culliford, *William Strachey, 1572–1621* (1965), pp. 48–50. Strachey could have encountered Hakluyt but we have no definite record that he did so.

[3] See pp. 74–96, above.

be paid to Hakluyt's example and memory, but it is clear that by attempting to distinguish materials culled from Hakluyt and those collected by himself, he was honestly concerned to establish and enlarge the reputation of his master, while not forgetting to claim originality for his own methods, 'the whole Artifice (such as it is) being mine owne'.

It would seem that shortly after 1600, the word 'Hakluyt' became a portmanteau expression for the *Principal navigations* or *Voyages* (as they were more generally known). Soon after their publication, Purchas' *Hakluytus posthumus or Purchas his pilgrimes* joined the *Principal navigations* under the general bracket of 'Hakluyt', and both collections came to be treated as a general store which could be employed and pilfered with little or no acknowledgement by geographical writers and littérateurs. Robert Burton, for example, used materials from Hakluyt freely in *The anatomie of melancholy* (1621 and subsequently), but he made only one reference to his collections in a long list of geographical writers.[1] Nathanael Carpenter, *Geographie delineated* (1625 and subsequently),[2] used Hakluyt freely without any acknowledgement whatsoever. Though Hakluyt had long been known to the Harvey circle, his death in November 1616 passed Richard Harvey by without any precise impact, but when he heard of it he thought it worth writing 'R^d Hakluyt dead, 1616–17' in his copy of Hakluyt's edition of Peter Martyr's *Decades* (1587):[3] the circumstance was important even if the particulars were vague and imprecise. This may well indicate the reputation which remained to Hakluyt after his death, his name was well enough known but the particulars of his achievements soon became somewhat unclear in men's minds.

Perhaps, George Hakewill's reference, in his influential book, *An apologie of the power and providence of God in the government of the world* (1631 and subsequently), marked the beginning of something of a revival in his reputation. Hakewill wished,[4] that *The*

---

[1] *Anatomy of melancholy*, ed. A. R. Shilleto, II (1903), 103 (though he bequeathed his *Principall navigations* (1589) to Christ Church where it still is).

[2] *Geography delineated* (Oxford, 1625 and 1635).   [3] B.M., pressmark 45.b.10.

[4] *An apologie* (1631), p. 253 (3rd edn., 1635), pp. 310–11.

principal navigations in their original form (he almost certainly means that of 1598–1600) and as 'lately enlarged and perfected' (i.e. by Purchas in 1625) could be translated into Latin: 'it were to be wished as well for the honour of the English name, as the benefite that might thereby redound to other Nations, that his collections and relations had been written in Latin, or that some learned pen would be pleased to turn them into that Language.' What Hakewill is saying, it is clear, is that the collecting and editing work of Richard Hakluyt was of such high quality and intrinsic interest that it should be made fully available not merely to those who read English but to the learned world of continental scholarship. The texts with which Hakluyt had supplied De Bry in 1588 had been used and reused on the continent and other borrowings were made before and after his death for voyage collections published then, but the complete translation of *The principal navigations*, not to mention the *Pilgrimes*, was too much for even the most energetic Frankfurt or Amsterdam entrepreneur. The myth of a French translation of *The principal navigations* in 1629 is a hardy one,[1] but there is clearly nothing in it. It seems to have stemmed from careless references to the works of Pierre Bergeron. His *Traicté de la nauigation et des voyages de descouuerte et conqueste moderne* (Paris, 1629), and *Relation des voyages en Tartarie* (Paris, 1634), utilized extensively, and with due acknowledge ment, first Hakluyt's more modern contributions and then, in more depth, his medieval contributions. He referred to him in the first work as 'le docte et laborieux Richard Hakluit' and in the second as 'le docte Geographe', thus placing his name before a French readership not too long after his death.[2]

The publication in 1658 of Sir Ferdinando Gorges' tract on his New England enterprises and of a rewritten version of it by his grandson, another Ferdinando Gorges, in 1659,[3] provided an occasion both for acknowledging Hakluyt's work on providing materials on North America and reviving the link between his promotional activities and those of an entirely new generation.

[1] Reappearing, for example, in M. van Durme, ed., *Correspondance Mercatorienne* (Antwerp, 1959), p. 161.

[2] *Traicté*, pp. 51–2; *Relations*, sig. a3r.   [3] *America painted to the life* (1659).

Hakluyt had a certain following in Restoration England. Thomas Fuller's posthumous *Worthies of England* (1662)[1] had a useful and amusing though rather inaccurate notice of Hakluyt (though Aubrey wholly ignored him), which helped to revive his reputation, notably his reference to the 'useful Tracts of *Sea Adventures*, which before were scattered as several Ships, Mr. Hackluit hath embodied into a *Fleet*, divided into *three Squadron*, so many volumes, a work of great honour to England', which usefully characterized and commended *The principal navigations*. Thomas Dinely, noting in 1680 several Hakluyt tombs in Leominster Church,[2] remarked, 'of this family of Hacluit is Richard who wrote learnedly, as a traveller concerning Geography & History'. (It may be noted that Dinely seems to have thought that some of Hakluyt's 'Voyages' were his own.) Anthony à Wood in his *Athenae Oxonienses*,[3] again writing not wholly accurately on the man, speaks of *The principal navigations* as being 'performed with great care and industry' which 'cannot but be an honour to the Realm of England', in the last words echoing Fuller.

The French connection also continued into the later seventeenth century. Melchisedech Thévenot had used Hakluyt and Purchas when preparing his voyagecollection and included their names in his titlepage, *Relations de divers voyages curieux, que n'ont point esté publiés ou ont esté traduit d'Hacluyt, de Purchas et d'autres voyageurs*[4] but in fact he took only one Anthony Jenkinson narrative from Hakluyt and nine others (some of which had come from Hakluyt in the first place) from Purchas. Nonetheless, Thévenot remained genuinely interested in Hakluyt. He had picked up from Purchas the information that not all the voyagenarratives collected by Hakluyt had been included in his own collection. When a friend of his, one N. Toinard (or Thoynard), was writing to John Locke on 24 August 1680 (N.S.), Thévenot added a note of his own to inquire whether there was any hope of finding these

[1] Ed. John Nichols (1811), p. 453.
[2] *History from marble*, ed. J. G. Nichols (1867), p. clvii.
[3] *Athenae Oxonienses*, I (1691), 350; ed. P. Bliss, II (1815), cols. 186–8.
[4] Paris, 1663–72, 4 parts in 5 volumes.

unpublished pieces which he might possibly then translate and publish.[1]

Locke was himself a connoisseur of voyage literature and owned a copy of *The principal navigations*,[2] but he was unable to locate (as indeed his modern successors have been) the Hakluyt papers, used and unused, which Purchas had had.[3] Thévenot's attitude to sources would have pleased Hakluyt himself: his inquiry too may have been the first time a question on the fate of Hakluyt's papers was asked (we still do not know the answer).

There are some indications towards the end of the century that, however much his publications may have been cherished by their owners, and his memory kept alive by biographers, compilers and collectors, Hakluyt was thought to be fading out of the historian's ken as his works became less accessible through want of a new edition. Edmund Bohun, in his *Character of Queen Elizabeth* (1693),[4] was rather pessimistic in tone: 'Mr. *Richard Hacluit*, who

---

[1] 'Japris par la lecture de Purchas, que de son temps cest adire vers lannee 1625 il y avoit encores des ecris d'Hackluit qui n'avoient point este Imprimés, Purchas en parle commes de pieces qui meritent d'estre données au public, Il fauderoit s'informer en quelles mains peuvent estre tombes ces ecrits, et Sauver ces ouvrages en faveur du Public et dun homme dont on se souviendera tousjours pour lobligation que nous luy avons de nous avoir sauvé beaucoup de bonnes choses

il a sauvé des pieces et des ouvrages de quelques uns de nos conquerans Francois, Je vouderois bien estre assez heureux pour luy rendre la pareille et sauver de loubly par ce soin que J'en prens quelques uns de ses ouvrages

ce seront une diligence a faire encore pour les ouvrages de Purchas il est difficle quil ne soit reste quelques pieces quil avoit ammassées pour en enrichir son receuil.' Bodleian Library, MS Locke C. 21, ff. 55–6. I owe this reference to Dr Esmond de Beer.

[2] In the collection of Mr Paul Mellon, see Peter Laslett and John Harrison, *The library of John Locke* (Oxford Bibliographical Society, n.s., XII, 1965), p. 28.

[3] Locke to Toinard, 30 August [1680]: Et si quid post se reliquit Hacluit quod nondum editum est id totum interijsse credo.' B.M. Additional MS 28728, ff. 9–10. This reference also I owe to Dr de Beer. Locke transcribed a section on Russia from Hakluyt (headed 'excerpts from Principall Navigations') in Bodleian Library, MS Locke C. 30, ff. 56–7 (reference from Mr Colin Steele).

[4] P. 264. A selection of seventeenth and eighteenth century views of Hakluyt may be found in C. W. Moulton, ed., *Library of English and American literary criticism*, I (New York, 1910), 445–6. An unpublished sketch by William Fulman (1632–88) is in Corpus Christi College, Oxford MS 308, f. 43v.: the sketch by

lived in these times, took a particular care to collect and publish the journals of all these Voyages, by which he deserved very well of the Nation; and it is a great pity that his works are becoming so scarce and so little known, and that no man has since pursued the same method; these Discourses being of great use for all Mariners, and serving very much for the enlarging and clearing the Geography of the World.' Though there was still a long way to go before a new edition of Hakluyt was to be possible, 'the same method', or at least a comparable method, if not so scholarly or comprehensive as Hakluyt's, was to produce a long series of general voyage-collections, from the beginning of the eighteenth century onwards until the early nineteenth. These were frequently to invoke the name of Hakluyt on their title-pages, though some-times with less justification even than Thévenot, and were to be, in a sense, substitutes for the real thing, Hakluyt reissued and restored. G. R. Crone and R. A. Skelton point out[1] that most of these collections were not produced for purely geographical or scientific reasons, or even for political ones, but almost solely to provide desultory reading for educated country gentlemen, and were consequently distinguished rather by 'eclecticism and amateurism' than by scholarship or practical value. The effect was to keep the name of Hakluyt alive indeed, but also to annoy, even infuriate, the few who were devoted to his text. William Oldys may have been an unusually articulate representative of this view, but it is possible to sympathize with him when he complained in 1757 that 'Hakluyt went on, to be pillaged, abridged, and reduced, as he had been; to be transposed and transformed; so he has been published and republished, little or much of him, from one end to the other, in a confused, or indis-tinct conjunction with other collections; and no true genuine Hakluyt, or grateful acknowledgement to Hakluyt, after more than one hundred and fifty years, revived yet'.[2]

White Kennett (1660–1728) in B.M. Lansdowne MS 983, f. 273, also remains unpublished.

[1] 'English voyage collections, 1625–1846', in E. Lynam, ed., *Richard Hakluyt and his successors* (1946), pp. 66, 78–9.

[2] *Biographia Britannica*, IV (1757), 2472.

However, the first of the major eighteenth-century collections, *A collection of voyages and travels* (4 vols. 1704), best known as *Churchill* from its publishers, contained in its first volume a long discourse[1] entitled 'The catalogue and Character of most Books of Travels'. This was first advertised as being by Edmond Halley, though afterwards was 'supposed to be written by the celebrated Mr. Locke'. The attribution to Locke is false; that to Halley very doubtful, and the author was most probably some Churchil-lian hack. Not without interest as reflecting eighteenth-century taste and knowledge, the critical remarks on Hakluyt help to indicate why it was not in this period easy to contemplate a new edition of the original text. Hakluyt was starred as 'the first Englishman that compil'd any Collection of Travels now extant', but the *Principal navigations* was characterized as both too bulky and too uncritical. Hakluyt is said to have been responsible for 'stuffing his Work with too many Stories taken upon trust, so many trading Voyages that have nothing new in them, so many Warlike Exploits not all pertinent to his Undertaking, and such a multitude of Articles, Charters, Letters, Relations, and other things little to the purpose of Travels and Discoveries', and to have failed to concentrate on what 'was really authentick and useful'. Viewed as a historical source-book, this is a bad misjudgement of *Principal navigations*, but in the context of eighteenth-century taste and of the amateur readership of the time it was not unreasonable. Nor is it unfair to say that Hakluyt's reputation with the broader reading public in the later nineteenth and twentieth centuries has been based on rigorous selection in anthologies of his more dramatic and colourful pieces. Hakluyt was valuable to the Churchills, as was frankly admitted, 'for the good there is to be pick't out', though the selection made in 1704

---

[1] [Awnsham and John Churchill], *A collection of voyages and travels ... with a general preface giving an account of the progress of navigation from its original to this time*, I (1704), xcii–xciii. Curiously enough, the writer found Ramusio's *Navigationi et viaggi* 'judiciously compiled and free from the great mass of useless matter, which swells our English Hakluyt and Purchas'. John Harris, *Navigantium atque itine-rantium bibliotheca*, II (1705), i–ii, speaks well of Hakluyt. Other editors tend to ignore him, as did John Knox, *A new collection of voyages*, I (1767), iv, when he commended in turn Purchas, Churchill and Harris.

was not unconscientious. Purchas too was regarded very similarly, following Hakluyt, 'whom he has imitated too much'. How much and how little the travel collections in fact exploited Hakluyt can be gleaned from Crone and Skelton and need not be laboured in detail. When the Abbé Prévost began his extensive work, *Histoire générale des voyages*, he prefaced his first volume in 1746 with a tribute to Hakluyt.[1] He had used both the 1589 and the 1598–1600 editions and regarded them as sheet-anchors in a general collection such as he aimed at, remarking that with Hakluyt and Purchas the English had an advantage over any other country in putting the voyages of their countrymen on record. He paid a special tribute to the detail in which earlier English enterprises were known.

A collection of voyages and travels . . . Compiled from the . . . library of the late earl of Oxford published by Thomas Osborne,[2] had rather a different character from those which took items or snippets or abstracts from *Principal navigations*, as it consisted largely of reprints of earlier volumes of travels, including Hakluyt's trans-lation of Galvão and three other books translated at his prompting, all of which helped to increase the Hakluyt material in circulation and enable a more comprehensive view to be taken of his achieve-ment. William Oldys, however, proved that a new edition of *Principal navigations* was not yet a practical proposition. His 1736 prospectus was for a 300-sheet edition in weekly parts to be

---

[1] Antoine Francois Prévost, *Histoire générale des voyages* (20 vols. Paris, 1746–79), I, i–ii: 'Mais il n'y a point de plus de Nation qui en ait publie plus que les Anglois, de qui nous en avons déja trois générales, . . . ; celle de Hakluyt, en trois Tomes in folio celle de Purchass, en quatre Tomes, . . . & celle de Harris, en deux. He criticized Harris for leaving out many of the best narratives in Hakluyt, and said that while the intention of the collectors was to put together the best authors from the beginnings of commerce and discovery down to their own times, their fear of multiplying volumes (which was not to deter Prévost) led them to suppress many excellent pieces. 'C'est par cette raison que Hakluyt est borné aux Auteurs Anglois, & que n'écrivant pas plus de cinquante ans après les premieres naviga-tions de ses Compatriotes, il n'a pas laissé d'en omettre plusieurs, qui n'ont pas même trouvé place dans son Supplement.' (He had already noted that 'Hakluyt se crut obligé en 1599, c'est a-dire, dix ans après sa première Addition, d'en donner une Seconde avec un supplément considerable.')

[2] 2 vols., 1745.

assembled in a single folio volume. Not only was the whole of the 1598–1600 edition to appear, but also biographical material, some notes and corrections and an appendix of Hakluyt's 'remains' from Purchas were to be added.[1] This would surely have made up one of the bulkiest and most indigestible volumes it is possible to imagine, and it is perhaps, for all Oldys' enthusi-asm and scholarship, a good thing for Hakluyt's reputation that he did not reappear in this form. There was insufficient response, and Oldys had to content himself with a full analysis of the contents of *Principal navigations* and a further plea for its republica-tion in his *British Librarian*.[2] It is now clear that Oldys' bio-graphical knowledge of Hakluyt and his enthusiasm for his works made his contribution of his Hakluyt article to *Biographia Britannica* in 1757,[3] though unsigned, a real turning-point in the history of Hakluyt's reputation. Oldys understood, as earlier critics had not done, both the precise nature and extent of Hakluyt's labours in compiling and editing his collections, pay-ing tribute to 'his vigorous endeavours' and to 'this undiscour-ageable spirit' with which he went about his task. His assessment is entirely contrary to that in the Churchill collection: 'For this edition is built up on a very comprehensive plan, and may, at all times, be no less serviceable many ways, than reputable to the nation; as it is a magazine, so nobly stored with some of the most adventrous atchievements of our ancestors, that were of the most national concern, attested by eye-witnesses, as well as other most credible and authentic vouchers.' Oldys' biographical infor-mation cleared up many problems and was authoritative for another century, while his bibliographical data were comprehensive and accurate. If his eulogy sounds at times a little excessive, it should be remembered that the article was deliberately aimed to rescue a major historical authority, for so Oldys considered him, from undeserved misunderstanding and neglect. Subsequent bio-graphical studies in the eighteenth century, for example, that in Joseph Towers, *British biography*,[4] largely followed Oldys.

One factor in arousing and maintaining an interest in Hakluyt

[1] *Biographia Britannica*, IV, 2472. [2] No 3, March 1737, pp. 136–58.
[3] *Biographia Britannica*, IV, 2461–74. [4] III (1767), 299–302.

in the eighteenth century was the rise of naval history. But the earlier naval historians, as Oldys was to point out about Joseph Burchet's *Most remarkable transactions at sea* (1720), paid very little attention either to the Elizabethan period or to Hakluyt. Yet Hakluyt's significance as a source-book in this field had previously been pointed out, Fuller having remarked that 'his Genie urging him to the study of History, especially to the Marine part thereof'. Thomas Lediard in *The naval history of England*[1] both used and acknowledged Hakluyt, stating, 'I have given my Readers an Abridgement of the most curious Accounts contained in Hackluyt and Purchas.' To Oldys he was, as so much else, 'our most eminent and worthy Naval Historian in the reign of Queen Elizabeth'; but there was a chauvinistic purpose too to be served by reviving Hakluyt. The argument here was that Hakluyt had both recorded and stimulated overseas exploration and aggression: now in an era of world-wide war with France might he not be used again for a similar purpose? Oldys winds up with a rhetorical call to Englishmen to 'animate their posterity to dispise all hazard,...bloodshed and death itself, for a knowledge of the uncultivated world, and the honour that may be reaped in it, to their own advantage, and the aggrandizement of their country'. The revival of Hakluyt in a scholarly manner was thus to be involved once,[2] and, similarly, again, in the later nineteenth century, with the glorification of British imperialism.

The growth of bibliographical studies in the hands of men like Oldys, Joseph Ames and William Herbert, and the appearance of reasonably reliable catalogues of the major libraries, made it possible for interested students or scholars to find out what pub-lished works, besides *Principal navigations*, Hakluyt had been responsible for, so that both *Principall navigations* (1589) and *Divers voyages* (1582) came to light again in that way.[3] The eighteenth century too saw the first beginnings of an interest in the biblio-

---

[1] I (1735), sig. A2r.

[2] The eighteenth-century boast is echoed in his own manner by William Robert-son, *The history of America* (1777), bk. ix, on Hakluyt 'to whom England is more indebted for its American possessions than any man of that age'.

[3] See Quinn, *Richard Hakluyt, editor*, pp. 40-2.

graphy of the history of North America for its own sake. White Kennett's *Bibliothecae Americanae primordia* (1713) was the pioneer work in English in this field and it contained, some twenty-four years before *The British Librarian*, a full catalogue of the contents of *The principal navigations*. An occasional American colonist had already begun to collect books on the North American past in England:[1] and to add to the stocks brought over by earlier settlers. The *Bibliotheca Americana* (1789), apparently compiled by Leman Thomas Rede, continued to feature Hakluyt's writings. The way was thus opening for men like John Carter Brown, Obadiah Rich, and James Lenox, not to mention Henry Stevens, who put Hakluyt's publications into the front ranks of growingly expensive Americana.

Thomas Zouch in 1808 could write[2] that 'Every reader conversant in the annals of our Naval transactions will cheerfully acknowledge the merit of Richard Hakluyt'. They might indeed do so, but largely on the basis of second-hand recommendations, for copies of the original editions were by now genuinely scarce. However, buoyed up by the boom in publishing and bookselling of those years, Robert Harding Evans was well on the way to publishing the first edition of Hakluyt for over two hundred years. A successful bookseller and auctioneer, Evans was also an old boy of Hakluyt's school, Westminster, so that piety may have worked with him as well as profit. His introduction was a puff for his publication ('This elaborate and excellent collection') as well as a boost for Hakluyt. It was so useful to authors in cosmography, navigation and history, and 'a LEADING STAR TO THE NAVAL HISTORIES since compiled'.[3] However, the edition lived up to its advertisement. The text of *Principal navigations* was well produced in four stout volumes, as well as a few additional items from *Principall navigations* (1589), and volume five (1812) added *A selection of voyages . . . chiefly published by Hakluyt, or at his*

---

[1] Either William Byrd I or William Byrd II had acquired a copy of *The principal navigations* during a visit to England, which was in the family library when it was dispersed in 1777–8 (C. L. Cannon, *American book collectors* (1941), pp. 16–18).

[2] *Life of Sir Philip Sidney* (York, 1808), p. 317. John Stanier Clarke, *The progress of maritime discovery* (1803), pp. xii–xiii, has a favourable sketch of Hakluyt.

[3] I (1809), xxvi–xxvii.

suggestion, but not included in his celebrated compilations, comprising Hakluyt's own translations and most of those published under his inspiration. Therefore, although the Evans edition was a limited one of only 325 copies and was expensive, it made up at last a coherent body of Hakluyt material in an unabridged form, from which the greater part of his output could be read, studied and judged.

From 1812 onwards we are in rather a different world so far as Hakluyt scholarship is concerned. Study of the early expansion of Europe overseas, for which Hakluyt was essential, and the continued preoccupation of Englishmen and others with the exploration of the less accessible parts of the earth's surface, meant that Hakluyt formed part of the basic reading of geographers, explorers, and even civil servants engaged in some way with distant colonies. After 1815 curiosity tended to replace xeno⁄phobia for a time in the international sphere and in relation to the lesser⁄known regions: the atmosphere for this became more favourable as concepts of free trade and *laissez⁄faire* became more general. Sir William Foster has explained the circumstances under which the Hakluyt Society came into existence in 1846 as the result largely of the efforts of the geographer, William Desborough Colley.[1] It was a time when the names of eminent Elizabethans such as Matthew Parker and William Camden were being used to cover the activities of publishing societies. As the Camden Society published historical texts and the Parker Society ecclesi⁄astical texts, so the Hakluyt Society was 'formed for the purpose of printing, for distribution among the members, the most rare and valuable voyages, travels, and geographical records, from an early period of exploratory enterprise to the circumnavigation of Dampier'. Thus launched, the Society might have proceeded, as indeed the Camden Society proceeded, with little regard for its guiding light, but there were enthusiastic Hakluytians amongst its members from the first, and John Winter Jones' fine edition of

---

[1] 'The Hakluyt Society, a retrospect', in Lynam, ed., *Hakluyt* (1946), pp. 143–5. J. Payne Collier, 'On Richard Hakluyt and American discoveries', *Archaeologia*, XXXIII (1849), 282–92, however questionable some of its statements, also reflected the revival of interest in Hakluyt.

Divers voyages in 1850, with its copious additions to the Oldys biography of Hakluyt in its introduction, ensured that Hakluyt's reputation and its furtherance remained a primary purpose of the Society. This was reflected by the gradual appearance of editions of his and his pupils' translations and the slow sorting out and editing of sections of the voyage collections along with new and hitherto unpublished material. By 1898, the year following Queen Victoria's diamond jubilee, the Society had put out one hundred volumes and thought it time to begin a second series.

The Hakluyt Society had, however, missed an opportunity to publish the most important Hakluyt work which still remained in manuscript, 'A particuler discourse concerninge the greate necessitie and manifolde comodyties that are like to growe to this Realme of Englande by the Westerne discoueries lately attempted written in the yere 1584, by Richard Hakluyt of Oxforde.' Leonard Woods, searching for materials on the history of Maine, located the only surviving contemporary copy at Middle Hill (as Phillipps MS 14097) in 1868, and had it recopied for publication with the blessing of Sir Thomas Phillipps. Charles Deane com-pleted the editing of Wood's edition, to which was given the short title, *Discourse on western planting* (which has, with a few minor variations, held the field since 1877 when it appeared as *Documentary history of the state of Maine*, II (Cambridge, Mass., 1877), and also separately). Even though it was not sufficiently appreciated then, and has not always been since, that this was a confidential paper, prepared for the use of Queen Elizabeth and her advisers without any idea of publication, the contents of this work as the first major prospectus for the English occupation and exploitation of North America on a grand scale, won for its author an additional and significant place in the history of the beginnings of English enterprise in America as a major con-tributor to the foundation of the colonies from which the United States emerged.

I have written elsewhere[1] that 'the Hakluyt Society was a typical expression of Free Trade optimism, the English belief that

[1] Comité International des Sciences Historiques, XIIe Congrès International des Sciences Historiques, *Rapports*, 1 (Vienna, 1965), 54.

their right to penetrate the farthest corners of the earth to sell their goods had a strong historical foundation which would be strengthened by the publication of well-edited materials on how exploration and European expansion came about'. But this too was to alter rapidly; Hakluyt was to change in the period of the new imperialism of the late nineteenth century from the great Free Trader to the protagonist of nationalistic empire. It is not without significance that it was J. A. Froude, as the prophet of imperial revival, who should have characterized the Evans edition, as early as 1852,[1] as 'the Prose Epic of the modern English nation'. The Elizabethan period was to him an epoch of heroic endeavour, an inspiration for future generations: 'They [the Voyages] contain the heroic tales of the exploits of the great men in whom the new era was inaugurated; not mythic, like the Iliads and the Eddas, but plain broad narratives of substantial facts, which rival legend in interest and grandeur.' He pays a scholarly tribute too by saying that 'very little which was really noteworthy escapes the industry of Hakluyt himself', but he saw the voyages, in inflated rhetorical terms, 'which with their picturesqueness and moral beauty shone among the fairest jewels in the diamond mine of Hakluyt'. The Hakluyt Society was reproved for its scholarship: it should, instead, have been publishing Hakluyt in penny numbers, since 'What the old epics were to the royally or nobly born, this modern epic is to the common people'. Hakluyt's approach was, of course, that of a strongly biased English nationalist, and so statements from his writings could be used in support of the later British Empire and its makers. At the same time these fluctuations in the ideological context in which he was seen, with consequent changes in his reputation, did not affect the continuing study of his work and the growth in the appreciation of its historical value.

It will be evident that to a considerable degree Hakluyt's reputation with scholars has depended on knowledge of and accessibility of his works. Edmund Goldsmid's edition of the *Principal navigations*, published elaborately in sixteen volumes in Edinburgh

[1] 'England's forgotten worthies', *Westminster Review*, July 1852, reprinted in *Short studies in great subjects*, II (1867), 102–59.

between 1884 and 1890, added to the number of texts of the work available to students and collectors, but the editorial apparatus was, unfortunately, almost valueless. It was only in 1899 that the Hakluyt Society at last seriously considered publishing a critical edition.[1] By 1903, when one volume was nearly ready, it was found that the firm of James MacLehose of Glasgow were about to publish an edition of their own. A portion of this edition was eventually adopted by the Society for its extra series, and has remained a mainstay of all students of Hakluyt since its completion in 1905. It contained, in volume twelve, a vivid and penetrating study of the book and, incidentally, of its compiler by Professor Walter Raleigh which became and has remained a classic of its kind. There was a full index of names and places, many illustrations, and an almost entirely reliable text. There was loss, however, as well as gain in the abandonment by the Society of its own project. C. Raymond Beazley's version of *The texts and versions of John de Plano Carpini and William de Rubruquis*, added by the Society to the extra series in 1903, contains collations of Hakluyt's texts, notes and explanations, intended to appear in the first volume of the Society's projected edition, which, if maintained in quality, would have gone far beyond the handsome MacLehose edition in scholarly value. Indeed, the formidable task of producing a critical edition of Hakluyt still remains a challenge which the Hakluyt Society has never, so far, managed to meet. This does not mean that it has abandoned the attempt to build on what Hakluyt laid down. Many of its volumes have continued the earlier policy of the Society by incorporating sections from Hakluyt's texts in wider annotated collections of material, so that scattered throughout its publications critical annotation of much of what Hakluyt published is to be found. In 1928 the Society obtained a stimulus from an outside source. The American Geographical Society published *Richard Hakluyt and the English voyages* by a young professor of English literature, George Bruner Parks. This was the first full study of Hakluyt inside the context of his own time. It revealed also the significance of the profession (or occupation) of geographical consultant in Tudor England,

[1] Lynam, ed., *Hakluyt* (1946), p. 162.

and so made possible a much more accurate assessment of Hakluyt's role in Elizabethan overseas enterprise. Its scholarly appendices also contained comprehensive lists of the material on Hakluyt and his elder cousin which still survived. This stirred the Hakluyt Society to publish in 1935, under the devoted editorship of E. G. R. Taylor, two volumes of *The original writings and correspondence of the two Richard Hakluyts*, with a characteristic introduction placing the Hakluyts still more firmly in their geographical setting.[1] It now became possible for the first time, through George Parks' book and the Taylor texts, to estimate the respective contributions of the elder and younger Hakluyt in their roles as collectors and advisers (with some redress of the balance in favour of the older man). The younger Hakluyt's efforts to rake in material from every possible source and his own willingness to supplement those sources by his own writings if he was at the last resort unable to get a firsthand account of an enterprise which he felt should be recorded, stood out more clearly. Moreover, the weight and scholarship of 'A particuler discourse' ('Discourse of western planting', was the form chosen for a short title) became more evident in the edition of it contained in Professor Taylor's second volume: Hakluyt emerged as a peculiarly learned and formidable advocate of western expansion by the Elizabethan state.

In the 1950s the advance of photolithography enabled the Hakluyt Society to contemplate the republication of Hakluyt's *The principall navigations* (1589), still largely unknown in its original form to many scholars. Full annotation did not seem practicable, as the main objective was to make a usable text available fairly rapidly. Accordingly, the editors, D. B. Quinn and R. A. Skelton, and the indexer, Alison Quinn, concentrated on providing a mainly bibliographical introduction and a fully analytical index. Though a blackletter text offers some discouragement to casual readers, it has some corresponding advantages for scholars who can see from it precisely what the author and

---

[1] Her *Late Tudor and early Stuart geography* (1934), pp. 1–38, had already presented a succinct and searching review of Hakluyt's geographical achievement and reputation.

his printers put into their text, but it is a far from complete substitute for a fully annotated version. A similar technique was subsequently adopted for the publication by a private firm of *Divers voyages* (1582) and *A shorte and briefe narration of the two navigations to newe Fraunce* (1580).[1] It will be unfortunate if some further attempt is not made to grapple with the problems of a fully explanatory edition of the work by which Hakluyt is rightly and most universally known, *Principal navigations* (1598–1600).

We might even, with perhaps undue optimism, envisage a programme which began with a facsimile edition of the second edition on similar lines to those employed for the first edition. It might proceed with a facsimile edition of the manuscript of 'A particuler discourse' (1584) with a transcript and notes. It could then go to a multi-volume edition, with full elucidations, of all Hakluyt's works and those he influenced. Some of these suggestions may well be accomplished in due course if humane scholarship survives. But it would be a mistake to regard the publication and editing of Hakluyt's works as an end in itself: they are not, after all, the sacred texts of an inspired writer. Yet they are to an increasing degree basic sources for a widening range of inquiry. Hakluyt assembled invaluable materials on the reciprocal relations between the European and the non-European world at a formative stage in their many and varied aspects. They are not limited in interest to 'the English nation' but contain vital elements of the early history of many more recent nation states. The catholicity of Hakluyt's interests and the integrity of his documentation – however this was limited by the conventions and circumstances of his own time – ensure to his collections both an enduring and expanding place in the fields of historical, geographical and anthropological scholarship on a world scale.

Hakluyt's reputation is not something static, but one reflecting the scholarly values of each generation of students of his work and of the society in which he lived. Continued scholarly concern with his works is the means by which successive groups of scholars can review and revise Hakluyt's status and significance

---

[1] Edited by D. B. Quinn, under the general title, *Richard Hakluyt, editor*, 2 vols. (Amsterdam, Theatrum Orbis Terrarum, 1967).

within Elizabethan and Jacobean England, reconsider and refine opinions on his editorial capacities and limitations, and may, above all, exploit the materials he collected for new and varied ends. By these means Hakluyt's reputation can, continuously, be re-assessed, his changing relevance estimated. Hakluyt's reputation is not, however, only a matter for scholars. His popular reputation not only survives but grows through repeated selections and anthology pieces from his collections. These circulate more widely, it might seem, in each decade. For those who continue to read books, the narratives he collected, told, or got others to tell have a continuing and lively appeal. His name and something of his fame adheres.

Appendix
Prices

Some indications of the rises and falls in the reputation of *Principal navigations* (1598–1600) may be given by the prices it fetched. Mr Colin Steele has given me the following list taken from the unrivalled collection of early sale catalogues in the Bodleian Library. They have been grouped for purposes of emphasis.

1678 Worsley	£1	18s	0d
1678 Brooke, Lord Warwick		8s	2d (one volume)
1680 Digby	£1	4s	6d
1682 Smith	£1	7s	6d
1698 Bernard		19s	0d*
1700 Bennet		15s	0d
1713 Salmon		12s	0d
1725 Killigrew	£2	12s	6d†
1726 Bridges	£2	17s	0d
1756 Hyde	£2	2s	0d
1773 James West P.R.S.	£1	14s	0d
1800 George Stevens F.R.S.	£7	0s	0d†
1881–3 Sunderland	£18	10s	0d

* Significant fall † Significant rise

PART TWO

HAKLUYT'S USE OF THE MATERIALS AVAILABLE TO HIM

11

Northern Europe

G. D. RAMSAY

Portions of northern Europe, particularly the Netherlands and the Rhineland, were as well known to sixteenth-century Englishmen as anywhere else in the world, Italy not excepted. About the region there existed a profusion of information waiting to be gathered – from City merchants and their factors, from sailors, from the soldiers who since 1572 had been fighting in the Netherlands, from ecclesiastics, from former political and diplomatic agents of the queen who had completed missions on the continent, and even from a few play-actors and tourists. Much valuable material had been tucked away in state papers, Admiralty records and documents personal to the lord treasurer Burghley or other ministers of the queen, and was accordingly accessible only with difficulty or not at all. However, there was much to be learnt by tackling individuals directly, whether in writing or by word of mouth. Hakluyt was usually ready to do this. But for northern Europe he deliberately refrained from exploiting such sources of information. As he pointed out in the preface to the first edition of the *Principall navigations*, 'I stand not vpon any action per-fourmed neere home, nor in any part of Europe commonly frequented by our shipping.'[1]

Nevertheless, when the time came for him to prepare a second edition, his mind had changed. His purposes and methods had significantly deepened. He was now anxious to rectify any im-pression that he might have conveyed to the effect that 'our forren trades of merchandise haue bene comprised within some few yeeres, or at leastwise haue not bene of any long continuance'.[2] Therefore, while purging his collection of the narratives of Mandeville and other dubious writings, he decided to introduce extracts from a whole array of sources from Tacitus and Bede

[1] *PN* (1589), *3v.   [2] *PN* 1 (1598), *5v.

155

onwards, to illustrate the antiquity of English commerce. He was thereby turning himself in some measure into a historian of the overseas interests of Englishmen and the English interests of foreigners in the Middle Ages and – like all other historians worth their salt – venturing upon paths that might lead him through an unexpected countryside. Not surprisingly, he was ready to include accounts of such military forays as Edward III's invasions of France, and the expedition of Henry of Lancaster into Prussia. But the identification of the mainspring of English relations with the outer world as the need 'to find out ample vent of our wollen cloth, the naturall commoditie of this our Realme'[1] brought him into a different sort of field. He could not neglect, in the light of this, the origins of Hanse traffic in England, nor the development of the commercial policy of the Plantagenet kings. So in went, among many other things, the *Carta Mercatoria* of 1303 and the charters on which the privileges of the merchants of the Steelyard were grounded. For the fifteenth century, *The Libelle of Englyshe Polycye* lay conveniently to hand, with its accounts of the wool traffic to Calais and Flanders, the cloth trade to the fairs of Brabant, and the resources of the Baltic in timber products and other shipbuilding materials. With his usual sense of fitness, Hakluyt then capped his collection of medieval documents with the charter issued in 1461 by Edward IV to the Merchants Adventurers trading to the Netherlands.

At this point, he stopped. As soon as his collection began to move into the sixteenth century, he virtually ceased to interest himself in the doings of Englishmen in northern Europe west of Muscovy. This is surprising, if only because the most 'ample vent' of English woollen cloth was still restricted to this nearby quarter of the world. Indeed, it never acquired much of a market across the Atlantic until a couple of centuries later, or in the East at all. At the end of the sixteenth century, English foreign trade was still heavily concentrated upon north-western Europe, and still chiefly in the hands of the Merchants Adventurers.[2] If room

[1] *PN* II (1599), *4r.
[2] This point has been considered at length by L. Stone, 'Elizabethan Overseas Trade', *Economic History Review*, 2nd series, II (1949–50), 30–58.

could be found for their 1461 charter, it is difficult *prima facie* to see why their even fuller charter of 1564 could not be admitted.[1] It was not that the history of their Company lacked daring and colour in the reign of Elizabeth I. They were, perhaps, too generally prosperous and therefore unenterprising during the first half of the sixteenth century, shipping cloths in ever greater quantity to their established mart at Antwerp.[2] But the con-ditions of their traffic were transformed during Hakluyt's own lifetime. He was certainly not ignorant of the mercantile drama of 1564, when the cloth fleet of the Merchants Adventurers, shut out from its usual destination in the Netherlands, after some anxious weeks of negotiation and organization boldly sailed to the little-known port of Emden in East Friesland, guided by pilots specially recruited for the exploit.[3]

Nor was he unaware of the even more startling developments of December 1568 and the following months, when the export trade of England, violently barred from its usual outlets, was once again diverted to a German port, this time Hamburg. The enter-prise was an even more dangerous one. It involved the organiza-tion of a convoy of nearly thirty merchantmen carrying a cargo, mostly of cloths, believed to be worth not far short of a quarter of a million pounds sterling.[4] The ships were escorted by men-of-war from the Royal Navy; in addition, the merchantmen carried a number of well-armed gentlemen exultantly travelling in hopes of a scrap, boasting that they would pass the shores of the Nether-lands 'with the utmost bravado possible'.[5] The English govern-

---

[1] It has been printed more than once, e.g. by G. W. Prothero, *Select statutes and other documents illustrative of the reigns of Elizabeth and James I*, 3rd ed. (Cambridge, 1907), pp. 461–4. Summary in *Calendar of patent rolls 1563–6*, pp. 178–80.

[2] For the generally upward nature of the trend see the figures and graphs printed by E. M. Carus-Wilson and O. Coleman, *England's export trade 1275–1547* (Oxford, 1963), pp. 112–19 and 141.

[3] There is a reliable modern account by B. Hagedorn, *Ostfrieslands Handel und Schiffahrt im 16. Jahrhundert* (Berlin, 1910), pp. 170–86. See also the reference in Taylor, *Hakluyts*, I, 236.

[4] I.e. 700,000 écus. French ambassador to Charles IX, 30 April 1569, printed in *Correspondance diplomatique de B. de S. de la Mothe-Fénelon*, ed. A. Teulet, I (Paris, 1838), 355.

[5] 21 March 1569, *ibid.*, p. 272.

ment was well aware that the Spanish ambassador was urging Alva to intercept the convoy, and it was strongly rumoured at London that a fleet of warships was being got ready in the Netherlands for this purpose. Upon the success of the voyage hung the fate of the whole Elizabethan régime.[1] As it happened, the convoy reached its destination intact. But most of the informa- tion available to the historian about its organization and passage comes perforce from the dispatches of the French and Spanish ambassadors at London, for lack of any native chronicler.[2]

The establishment of a major cloth mart on the Elbe hence- forth brought English merchants into much more frequent and intimate contact with Germany. As a result of the Emden voyage and the Hamburg mart, Englishmen were much more often to be met at the fairs of Frankfurt-am-Main and Leipzig. They began to make regular visits to the little weaving towns at the foot of the Erzgebirge, to buy Saxon linens. A settlement of the interloping English merchants who flouted the regulations of the Merchants Adventurers' Company was established at Nuremberg, on the invitation of the government of the free city. After some years, the enmity of the Hanse Towns compelled the Merchants Adventurers to remove their mart from Hamburg back to Emden and then to Stade on the Elbe, while in the Baltic the English merchants organized themselves into the Eastland Company and moved their headquarters from Danzig to Elbing.[3]

[1] Even J. A. Froude, not given to overestimating the importance of mercantile activities, was of this opinion (*History of England*, IX (1870), 74).

[2] The fullest and best account of the Hamburg adventure is still that of R. Ehren- berg, *Hamburg und England im Zeitalter der Königin Elisabeth* (Jena, 1896), pp. 107–10.

[3] There is information about Elizabethan merchants and their agents in Germany in various secondary authorities, including: G. Aubin and A. Kunze, *Leinener- zeugung und Leinenabsatz im östlichen Mitteldeutschland zur Zeit der Zunftkäufe* (Stuttgart, 1940), pp. 216–18, 252–3 etc.; L. Beutin, *Hanse und Reich im handels- politischen Endkampf gegen England* (Berlin, 1929), *passim*; A. Dietz, *Frankfurter Handelsgeschichte*, II (Frankfurt, 1921), pp. 272–4; R. Ehrenberg, *Hamburg und England*, pp. 120–2 *et passim*; B. Hagedorn, *Ostfrieslands Handel und Schiffahrt, passim*; *ibid.*, *Ostfrieslands Handel und Schiffahrt vom Ausgang des 16. Jahrhunderts bis zum Westfälischen Frieden (1580–1648)* (Berlin, 1912), pp. 1–66 etc.; E. Kroker, *Handelsgeschichte der Stadt Leipzig* (Leipzig, 1925), pp. 80 ff.

For anyone concerning himself with the 'ample vent' of English cloth, these were stirring deeds, and there were plenty of men in the City who could have told Hakluyt all about them. For instance, Thomas Aldersey, who led the Emden voyage in 1564, was living in London as a merchant until his death in 1598.[1] But, to the loss of future generations, Hakluyt did not avail himself of their information. As far as northern Europe in the sixteenth century was concerned, the only addition to the second edition of *Principal navigations* was an account of the defeat of the Spanish Armada.

Since Hakluyt was too percipient a historian not to grasp that the quest for a market in which to sell English cloths had for long been the chief driving force behind the 'Navigations, Voyages, Traffiques and Discoveries', why did he apparently shrink from drawing the full consequences of this observation? It is impossible to dismiss him as merely a romantic collector of stories, whose imagination could be fired only by tales of far-away lands, or of memorable deeds in distant ages. The author of 'Discourse of Western Planting' was keenly interested in the fortunes of the City and was closely following the great controversy that for a number of years from 1564 onwards divided the protagonists and the enemies of the traditional mart at Antwerp. But he was not tethered to any counting-house, much less to a ledger-book of immediate profit and loss. He appreciated the arguments of those who feared the debilitating consequences of an almost total reliance upon the Netherlands market, political as well as economic. Indeed, he carried them a stage further than the City advocates of change thought of doing. They might urge Emden, Hamburg or some other German port as suitable replacements for Antwerp, but he was ready to appropriate their arguments and give them a novel twist by pointing to the temperate regions of America or eastern Asia as better still, offering illimitable markets for the woollen cloths that could not be absorbed in Europe.[2]

This was doubtless welcome to his influential friends, who belonged to the seafaring or exploring wing of the Elizabethan world of action – Hawkins, Ralegh and Jenkinson. The City

[1] His will is in P.R.O., Prob. 12, formerly P.C.C. 10 Kidd.
[2] Taylor, *Hakluyts*, I, 218–42 *passim*.

merchant singled out by Hakluyt as his patron was Richard Staper, whose venturesome career spanned the tense period in English foreign trade from the last undisturbed years of the Ant' werp mart in the 1560s to the first voyages of the East India Company in the early seventeenth century. Staper's factors were often to be met at the periphery of commercial penetration, while he himself was adept enough to avoid bankruptcy, the frequent fate of the over'bold trader.[1] But Staper was not at all repre' sentative of City merchants, most of whom had a different view of risky trades – indeed he was not even a Merchant Adventurer.[2] The sad truth is that Hakluyt's business contacts at London were meagre or unrepresentative. Yet he did not lack means of intro' duction to City men with ordinary trading interests, for instance through his lawyer cousin and namesake who sat with a number of them on the commission appointed in 1571 to investigate the levying of customs duties at London,[3] or through Hawkins; but he does not seem to have used such opportunities. Certainly, if Jenkinson ever introduced him to his hard'headed father'in'law John Marsh, for many years Governor of the Merchants Adven' turers, who survived until 1578, we must conclude that little passed between the two men.[4] Perhaps prudent City merchants were put off by the unrealistic zeal of the clergyman seeking information about out'of'the'way places. Whatever the reason, the resultant lop'sided nature of Hakluyt's City connections was not compatible with an attempt to chronicle the contemporary trade to the traditional markets in northern Europe – without the profits of which it would have been hard indeed to finance the far' flung expeditions that provided the stuff of *Principall navigations*.

[1] For information about the career of Richard Staper as a merchant, see T. S. Willan, *Studies in Elizabethan foreign trade* (Manchester, 1959), pp. 191–3.

[2] He was listed among exporters not belonging to the Company in 1577–8, B.M., Harleian MS 167/3, ff. 75–80.

[3] The report of the commission, bearing the elder Hakluyt's signature (with others), is in the P.R.O. at E 178/1358. See also the references in Taylor, *Hakluyts*, I, 7, 93.

[4] The will of John Marsh is in P.R.O. Prob. 12, formerly P.C.C. 2 Bakon; many of his letters are in the State Papers (S.P. 12 and S.P. 70). He is frequently mentioned by O. de Smedt, *De Engelse Natie te Antwerpen*, 2 vols. (Antwerp, 1950 and 1954).

12

Russia

J. S. G. SIMMONS

The materials in *Principall navigations* (1589) relating to Muscovy (and they amount to between a quarter and one-third of the total text of the first edition) have been characterized as the finest body of materials in the book.[1] The compliment is deserved and is a tribute both to the compiler and to his opportunities. London was the bridgehead of the Muscovy trade via the northern sea route, and Hakluyt – the son of a member of the Skinners' Company, the cousin of the Richard Hakluyt who was an early advisor to the Muscovy Company, and the friend of such Company stalwarts as William Borough and Anthony Jenkinson – was admirably placed to obtain information from Company sources, both official and unofficial. His connections with Burleigh and Walsingham facilitated his access to complementary sources of information such as the reports and conversation of returning diplomats – to say nothing of state papers. Hakluyt was energetic and enterprising and not slow to cultivate his opportunities – the materials that he obtained from Sir Jerome Bowes and his inclusion of extracts from Giles Fletcher's *Of the Russe common wealth* two years before it was published are but two examples of the harvest that such contacts could bring.

With such sources available to him Hakluyt would have had little need to turn to published accounts even if these had been numerous, reliable, and up to date. They were none of these things, and Hakluyt's sparing use of them is understandable.[2] He took Clement Adams' account of Chancellor's 1553 voyage

[1] Quinn and Skelton, edd., *PN* (1589), I (1965), xxxviii.
[2] See F. Adelung, *Kritisch-literärische Übersicht der Reisenden in Russland bis 1700*, 2 vols. (St Petersburg–Leipzig, 1846; repr. Amsterdam, 1960; Russian translation in *Chteniya v Imp. Obshchestve istorii i drevnostey rossiyskikh*, III (1847), no. 9; IV (1848), no. 1; 1863, bks. 1–4; 1864, bk. 1. See also V. I. Kordt, *Chuzhozemni podorozhni po Skidniy Yevropi do 1700 r.* (Kiev, 1926).

from a now no longer extant London pamphlet of 1554;[1] he drew on the then standard work, Sigismund von Herberstein's *Rerum Moscoviticarum commentarii* (visits in 1517 and 1526; seventeen editions, 1551–89) in *Principal navigations* (1598–1600) only for its accounts of the infrequently visited Pechora and Ob areas. The more recent *Moscovia* (visit in 1582; four editions, 1586–7) of Antonio Possevino he does not refer to, but the omission may be condoned since the account would have added little.

If Hakluyt's relative neglect of published materials is excusable on the grounds of their inferiority to his own sources, the accusa-tion of carelessness which some later scholars have advanced against him is not a venial one – where the fault can be proved. This it is not easy to do with confidence since we cannot certainly identify his originals and compare them with his printed versions. But some cases are clear and damaging. The Russian historian Hamel[2] pointed out that a change in the Tsar's titles gratuitously introduced in the second edition led Karamzin (author of the classic history of Russia) to state that Muscovy laid claim to sovereignty over Astrakhan and Lithuania several years earlier than the facts warrant.[3] And in this particular case, Hamel suggests that apart from this blunder there are variations between Hakluyt's printed text and the text of the actual document which he believed to have served as his original.[4] Other examples could

[1] The surviving source for the text is C. Marnius and J. Aubrius, *Rerum Mosco-viticarum auctores varii* (Francofurti, 1600), pp. 142–53.

[2] Joseph Hamel (Iosif Khristianovich Gamel', 1788–1861) was the pioneer investigator of English archives for the history of early Anglo-Russian relations. His book was published at St Petersburg and Leipzig in 1847 as *Tradescant der Ältere 1618 in Russland*. A two-volume Russian translation (*Anglichane v Rossii v XVI i XVII stoletiyakh*) was published as supplements to vols. VIII and XV of the *Zapiski* of the Imperial Russian Academy of Sciences in 1865–9. This edition includes a chronology and some corrections and additions but omits much of the documentation. The version by J. S. Leigh (*England and Russia*) published in London in 1854 is even less well documented.

[3] Hamel, *Anglichane*, VIII, 27.

[4] Hamel's second charge is not proven. None of the three manuscripts which he connects with Hakluyt's text (they must now be B.M. Additional MS 6113, Cotton MS Otho E III, and Lansdowne MS 141) can be shown with certainty to have served as Hakluyt's original.

be quoted:[1] it is clear that *caveat lector* applies – it is vain to expect diplomatic accuracy of the texts of documents which descend to us not only through an Elizabethan editor but through Elizabethan compositors.

By a curious chance an example of the excellence of technical representation to which Hakluyt could attain is offered by the very document which Hamel used to convict him of editorial care-lessness: he is punctilious in giving his readers information about its script and pendant seal – he leaves us in no doubt as to its genuineness and makes it clear that he saw it himself.[2] His presentation of other documents (especially in the more leisurely second edition) shows similar care: he indicates authorship when this is known to him, and he uses shoulder-notes to explain obscurities or emphasize points of interest in the text.

Principal navigations (1598–1600) also shows advances in quanti-tative terms in spite of the fact that Hakluyt made a few cuts, e.g. he prints the English text only of Clement Adams's account and only a single narrative (Hugh Smith's) of the Pet and Jackman navigation of 1580. A rationalization of another kind is the moving of Richard Johnson's account of Cathay from the 1567 area to its proper place with the other materials relating to 1558.

The actual additions of 1598–1600 amount to about a third as much again over the Muscovy material in 1589. They include material from literary sources, e.g. the 'Genealogy of the Emperor of Muscovy',[3] a large slice of Fletcher's *Russe commonwealth*, and

---

[1] Examples are: (1) 1588 for 1568 as the date of the instructions to Bassendine (*PN* (1589), p. 406; *PN* I (1598), 383); (2) in the 'corrected' Bowes leaves (*PN* (1589), sig. 2Y1r) the dates 1582 and 1581 appear in lines 2 and 13 re-spectively instead of the correct 1583 and 1582 which appear in the original version; (3) 1567 for 1568 at the foot of the letter from Queen Elizabeth I to Tsar Ivan IV (*PN* I (1598), 375). The meaningless 'Zenopskie' occurs for 'zempskie' (or the like) in both *PN* (1589), p. 404, and I (1598), 380; Hakluyt should have known better, as the concept of the *zemshchina* is ex-plained in Fletcher's *Of the Russe commonwealth*.

[2] *PN* (1589), p. 293; *PN* I (1598), 255. The original Russian text seems to have perished.

[3] The source of this first work on Russian history to appear in English has not previously been identified. It must have been translated directly or indirectly from the anonymous *Edictum serenissimi Poloniae regis ad milites* (Coloniae: M. Cholinus,

the extracts from Herberstein (with something from Ramusio sandwiched in), referred to above. The most valuable new matter, however, consists of state papers and letters and documents (many dating from before 1589) dealing mainly with Muscovy Com-pany affairs and supplied by persons connected with it, such as Henry Lane,[1] William Hawtrey, and the two Sir Jeromes – Bowes and Horsey.[2] Most of these were conveniently and appropriately added at the end of Part 3 of *Principal navigations* (1598–1600), since they relate mainly to the 1590s; the others find their proper places earlier in the work.

1580; Estreicher, XII (1891), 406–7), where it appears in Latin on sig. E4v *seq.* as *Magni Moscoviae ducis genealogiae brevis epitome.* Its last three paragraphs consist of the text (published anonymously) of the letter of 22 May 1576 of Gotthard Kettler, last Grandmaster of the Teutonic Knights and first Duke of Courland, addressed to Daniel Printz von Buchau, one of the Imperial ambassadors to Muscovy in 1575–6 (see E. Winkelmann, *Bibliotheca Livoniae historica* (Berlin, 1878), no. 5525, and Kordt, *Chuzhozemni podorozhni*, pp. 43–6). Printz von Buchau may well have been the compiler of the *Brevis epitome*: he was avowedly the author of its continuation (*Narratiuncula de successione Moscoviae principatus*) which accompanies it in the *Rerum Moscoviticarum auctores varii* (1600) at sig. 3*1. Hakluyt's translation preserves – among other errors – the blunder (572 for 862) in the traditional date for the 'calling of the Varangians', though the year is correctly given *stilo Moscovitico.*

[1] From their positioning at the end of Part 1 of *PN* (1589) it would appear that Lane had earlier supplied stop-press material for that edition. Among the fresh documents he contributed to *PN* (1598–1600) (cf. I, 375) is the text of a letter (otherwise unknown) from Sigismund Augustus of Poland to Queen Elizabeth I on the Narva problem (I, 337–8). Hakluyt incorrectly dated it and placed it under the year 1559. G. [Yuriy] Tolstoy prints the text in part (from Hakluyt) in his *First forty years of intercourse between England and Russia* (St Petersburg, 1875), pp. 30–1, dating it correctly 6 December [1569]. There is no reference to Sigis-mund Augustus in *PN* (1589) *pace* the index-entry in the 1965 reprint – the reference is not to the Polish king but to the Imperial diplomat, Sigismund von Herberstein.

[2] Horsey's account of the coronation of Tsar Fedor Ivanovich in 1584 and his text of the 1587 privileges were slipped in at the end of *PN* (1589), but neither edition includes his 'Relacion' of his adventures in Muscovy; this was published in epitome in Purchas and in full by E. A. Bond (*Hakluyt Society*, XX, 1856). A further important absentee from Hakluyt's panel of informants is Sir John Meyrick (d. 1638), but he was notoriously discreet and no substantial materials by him are known to survive.

The differences between the two editions are not, however, explicable in terms of availability alone. It is clear that both omissions and alterations in the second edition were in certain cases dictated by considerations of policy. Two striking examples are the treatment which Hakluyt extends to the account of the Bowes mission of 1583 and his handling of Fletcher's *Russe commonwealth*. Bowes provided Hakluyt with a long, circum‚ stantial, tactless, and lively account of his mission, written in the first person, and this text is found in slightly over one‚third of the surviving copies of *Principall navigations* (1589). In the other copies the leaves from the beginning of Bowes's narrative to the end of Part 2 (2X5, 6 and 2Y1–6) are cancelled and a reset gathering (2Y6) is substituted which contains a much watered‚down third‚ person account – a substitution which can only be explained in terms of second thoughts on Hakluyt's part, or of government or Muscovy Company pressure. Similar considerations applied to his handling of Fletcher's text.[1] Fletcher had returned from his mission in the autumn of 1589 in time for Hakluyt to be able to obtain stop‚press materials from him which occupy a couple of pages at the end of Part 2 of *Principall navigations* (1589).[2] Hakluyt added the circumspect comment that Fletcher was not proposing to publish his work immediately. By the time that Hakluyt was preparing materials for the second edition Fletcher's book had long since been both published (in 1591), and sup‚ pressed at the instigation of the Muscovy Company. However, Fletcher's text was evidently too attractive to be passed over: Hakluyt printed thirteen of its twenty‚eight chapters – five as they stood, and the other eight with excisions. The excisions and the omitted chapters consisted of the matter critical of Muscovite conditions that had disturbed the Company nine years earlier. In this case Hakluyt was giving his readers less than the full story

---

[1] This brief account is based on the detailed study of Hakluyt's procedure by R. O. Lindsay, 'Richard Hakluyt and *Of the Russe commonwealth*', *Papers of the Bibliographical Society of America*, LVII (1963), 312–27.

[2] For Hakluyt's 'scoop' and his treatment of Fletcher's book, see Professor Richard Pipes' introduction to the facsimile edition of *Of the Russe common wealth* (Cambridge, Mass., 1966), especially p. 18.

(in spite of the fact that much similar 'anti-Russian' matter occurs elsewhere in his book).[1]

Hakluyt's compromise over the potentially embarrassing Bowes and Fletcher texts cannot be said to detract from the general effectiveness of his coverage of *res Moscoviticae*. The emasculated versions may lack some picturesque details but the impression that remains is not thereby falsified; and there are in any case plenty of other texts in *Principal navigations* (1598–1600) which round out the picture. To say this is to draw attention to the outstanding feature of the materials relating to Muscovy that Hakluyt provides – their adequacy both in number, content, and genre. There are first-hand accounts of every early navigation, of the country and of its rulers, inhabitants, customs, laws, trade, and coinage; there are the texts of royal letters, of ambassadorial instructions and of diplomatic dispatches; there is even George Turbervile's verse. Moreover, for the vast bulk of this material Hakluyt remains the only source; little of it was taken from printed books and almost all his manuscript originals have perished – in particular the pre-1666 records of the Muscovy (later, Russia) Company and the private papers of individuals whom he tapped for his book. Evidence for the continuing importance of his Russian materials is provided by the footnotes in every modern work that deals with Anglo-Russian relations during the second half of the sixteenth century.[2] In spite of his inaccuracies, misprints, errors, and tactful omissions, Hakluyt's

---

[1] Hakluyt could also temper the wind to domestic lambs. A 26-line passage critical of Sir Jerome Horsey which appears in the contemporary English translation (B.M., Cotton MS Otho B VIII, f. 24v) of Tsar Fedor Ivanovich's letter to Queen Elizabeth I of January 1592/3 is absent from Hakluyt's printed text (*PN* I (1598), 503; after the opening paragraph).

Nearly half the references to contemporary sources in the first chapters of both T. S. Willan's *Early history of the Russia Company, 1553–1603* (Manchester, 1956) and K. H. Ruffmann, *Das Russlandbild im England Shakespeares* (Göttingen, 1952) are to *PN*. The text has also served philologists (see H. Leeming, 'Russian words in 16th-century English sources', *Slavonic and East European Review*, XLVI (1968), 1–30, and XLVII (1969), 11–36). A tribute of another kind is provided by the numerous partial Russian translations of which the earliest dates from 1826; the most recent (edited by Yu. V. Got'ye) was published in Leningrad in 1937 as *Angliyskiye puteshestvenniki v Moskovskom gosudarstve v XVI v.*

contribution to the sources relating to sixteenth-century Muscovy remains without rival both as regards its splendid literary form and its comprehensive factual content. Modern scholars, however, should not confuse comprehensiveness with exhaustiveness; they should, moreover, use *Principal navigations* with the caution reserved for sixteenth-century printed texts – until such time as they have produced the systematically annotated text which the work so clearly deserves.

13
The Caspian

W. E. D. ALLEN

Hakluyt's materials for the description of the Caspian and adjoining countries derive from the same sources which he used for Russia – notably his contemporaries Stephen and William Borough and Anthony Jenkinson.[1] While he was principally concerned with English contributions to the exploration of the northern and eastern regions of the Eurasian land mass, Hakluyt printed in full in the second edition of 1598 the classic accounts of the missions of John de Plano Carpini (1246) and William de Rubruquis (1253) to the Mongols in the middle of the thirteenth century. The only Englishman whom he could cite for the same period was Sir John de Mandeville, printed in the first edition, but omitted from the second.[2] Hakluyt made use of a Latin version of Mandeville where the account of the countries round the Caspian lacks many of the details given in the Egerton and Paris MSS of the late fourteenth century.[3] Whether or not he actually visited the countries described, the Egerton text establishes

[1] For detailed discussion of documentation of these sources see Quinn and Skelton, edd., *PN* (*1589*), I (1965), xxxvii–xli.

[2] For the omission of Mandeville's text from the second edition, see remarks of Quinn and Skelton, *op. cit.*, pp. xxvi–xxvii. It appears that Hakluyt used an abbreviated Latin text of Mandeville, printed *c.* 1485. The first Englishman recorded in the Caucasus was Petrus Geraldus, Roman Catholic bishop of Sukhum as early as 1330 – two years before Mandeville left England on his travels, cf. W. Heyd, *Histoire du commerce du Levant au Moyen Age* (re-impression, Leipzig, 1923), I, 192, citing Raynald, *Ann. eccl.*, ad an. 1330. But Bagrat IV of Georgia (1027–72) employed a Varangian Guard which was surely recruited through Byzantium. After the Battle of Hastings in 1066, a number of English *émigrés* joined the Varangian Guard and it is likely that some found their way into the service of the Georgian kings, cf. W. E. D. Allen, *A history of the Georgian people* (1932), pp. 90, 264.

[3] See Malcom Letts, *Mandeville's travels*, 2 vols., Hakluyt Society (1950–1), I, 176–83 (Mandeville's chapters XXVII–XXVIII).

Mandeville as the earliest English source for Caucasia and Turkestan. In the Egerton MS Mandeville distinguishes between the two Georgian Kingdoms of Abkhazia and Kartli and gives what may well be an account of the remote region of Svaneti; this seems to be derived from the Armenian King Haiton (who actually states that he had visited 'Hamson') and perhaps also from Masudi (with whose work Mandeville may have become familiar during his stay in Egypt).[1] In chapter 27 of the Egerton text, Mandeville gives quite a down-to-earth description of central Asia where he mentions the towns of Eccozar (Oçerra in Haiton – identified by Malcolm Letts as Farab, south-east of the Sea of Aral) and Corasme (Khorezm). Again following Haiton, Mandeville gives the Tartar name of the Volga (Etill = Itil). He records that 'in that land men lie in tents and lodges and dry beasts' dung and burn it for default of fuel'. The pest of flies which he remarks was suffered by Jenkinson in Astrakhan. It derived from the custom of hanging sturgeon out to dry.[2]

Hakluyt was familiar with the work of Ramusio, but he does not incorporate in his materials the important information which had been provided by Genoese and Venetian merchants and diplomatic agents at intervals over the period between the thir-teenth and fifteenth centuries.[3] The accounts of Christopher

[1] *Swan-eti* in Georgian signifies 'land of the *Swan-ni*'; cf. Strabo's *Soani*, medieval Russian *Sonskaya zemliya*, *Soni*. Douglas Freshfield, *The exploration of the Caucasus* (1896), I, 203, prefers to *Hamson* the MS variant *Hanyson* and suggests that it is an anagram of *Soany*.

[2] *PN* (1589), p. 349.

[3] For the thirteenth century, Polo states that 'of late the merchants of Genoa have begun to navigate this sea, carrying ships across and navigating them thereon', cf. Sir Henry Yule, *The book of Ser Marco Polo*, 3rd ed. (1929), p. 52 (*bis*). Further, Polo goes near to giving the correct length of the Caspian from north to south – 700 miles. For the fifteenth century, Ramusio, *Navigationi et viaggi*, printed the travels of Josafa Barbaro (1436); and of Ambrogio Contarini, Caterino Zeno and Giovan Maria Angiolello in the 1470s. For Englished versions, see *Travels of the Venetians in Persia* (Hakluyt Society, 1873). For modern studies in detail: Heyd, *Histoire du commerce*, II; G. I. Bratianu, *Recherches sur le commerce Génois dans la Mer Noire au xiiie siècle* (Paris, 1929), chapters V–VI; F. S. Zevakin & N. A. Panchko, 'Ocherki po istorii Genuezskikh koloniy na zapadnom Kavkaze v xiii i xv vv.', in *Istoricheskiye Zapiski*, III (1939). It is

Borough and other agents of the Muscovy Company are revealing on economic and social conditions in Shirvan, Azerbaijan and Georgia, but naive on politics and personalities when compared with more worldly Italian and Spanish contributions.[1] It should be remembered, however, that Hakluyt's theme was English

> becoming clear that apart from the Tana–Don–Volga route the Genoese had established a line of access to the Caspian from Sukhum via the Klukhor pass into Kabarda and along the river Terek to a port and factory at Tyumen on the coast of the Caspian. Place names on early Italian maps (e.g. *Tusci, Cobi*) suggest also a fork from Kabarda through the Daryal gorge to Tbilisi.

[1] For the Spanish contribution see: *Historia del Gran Tamorlan...y enarracion del viage y relacion de la embaxado que Ruy Gonçalez de Clavijo le hizo, por mandado del muy poderoso Señor Rey Don Henrique Tercero de Castilla. Y vn breue discurso fecho por Gonçalo Argote de Molina, para mayor inteligencia deste libro* (Seville, 1582), second ed., 4to, Madrid, 1782. (The Hakluyt Society brought out a translation by Sir Clements Markham in 1859; the Spanish text was edited with a Russian translation by I. Sreznevskiy and published by the Academy of Sciences in St Petersburg in 1881; Guy Le Strange made an English translation for the Broadway Travellers Series in 1928.) Clavijo's travels covered the years 1403–6. See also *Andanças é viages de Pero Tafur por diversas partes del mundo avidos.* The only known manuscript, which appears to have been an eighteenth-century copy of an earlier MS, was first printed in Madrid in 1874 as *Colección de Libros Españoles raros ó curiosos*, vol. VIII. An English translation, *Pero Tafur, travels and adventures, 1435–1439* was edited by Malcolm Letts (Broadway Travellers, 1926). Chapters XV and XVI cover the empire of Trebizond, Caffa and the Don region.

A third work in Spanish which was printed six years after the appearance of *Principal navigations* (1598–1600), but which comes within the range of sources available to contemporaries of Hakluyt is *Relaciones de Don Juan de Persia, dirigidas a la Magestad Catholica de Don Philippe III. Rey de las Españas...donde se tratan las cosas notables de Persia* (Valladolid, 1604). Of this work there are said to be only four known copies. There is an English rendering by Guy Le Strange, *Don Juan of Persia: a Shi'ah Catholic, 1560–1607* (Broadway Travellers, 1929). Starting in July 1599, as a member of a diplomatic mission from Shah Abbas to Tsar Boris Godunov and other European potentates, Don Juan (or Ulugh Beg as he then was) took two months crossing the Caspian from Gilan to the mouth of the Volga. The Englishman, Sir Anthony Shirley, was in the same party. They touched at Mangyshlak on the eastern shore forty years after Jenkinson had been there. Don Juan gives the length of the sea as 800 miles – as against Polo's 700 miles – and exaggerates the breadth to 600. From Moscow Don Juan came out of Russia by Kholmogory and Archangel and, after two months at sea, reached the mouth of the Elbe.

voyages and English contributions to exploration rather than a detached and objective description of countries such as is to be found in Herberstein's *Rerum Moscouiticarum commentarii* (1549) and Olaus Magnus's *Historia de gentibus septentrionalibus* (1555). Thus there is in Hakluyt's work an undertone of propaganda – justified indeed by his intention to inspire Englishmen to take a strenuous part in the contemporary expansionist drive of the western European maritime nations.

As Quinn and Skelton have observed: 'the finest body of material in the book is that relating to the Muscovy Company.'[1] The principal contribution to this material for the period 1557 to 1572 – the formative years of a special relation between England and Russia which was to endure until the execution of King Charles I in 1649 – was the truly heroic figure of Anthony Jenkinson. Within days of his arrival in Moscow in late December 1557 he attracted the interest of Tsar Ivan IV, and soon enjoyed a confidence and prestige which no foreigner had attained since Baron Sigismund von Herberstein at the court of Tsar Ivan III, nearly half a century earlier. In the spring of 1558 Jenkinson started on his celebrated journey down the Volga to Astrakhan which at that time had only been in Russian hands for four years. From there by boat he made a perilous circuit of the northern and eastern shores of the Caspian as far as Mangyshlak where he joined a caravan of a thousand camels and proceeded by way of Khiva to Bukhara. On 26 December 1558, a year and a day after his first audience of Ivan IV, Jenkinson was received by the Amir Abdulla-bin-Iskender Khan – the greatest, perhaps, of the Usbek rulers of Transoxania. He was the first Englishman – and the first diplomatic representative of the Russian Tsar – to be received in this most conservative of the cities of Islam.[2] Jenkinson reached

---

[1] See Quinn and Skelton, edd., *PN* (1589), 1 (1965), xxxviii.

[2] In another age, the Volga route and the shores of the Caspian had been familiar ground to the Norsemen if not to Englishmen. See B. Dorn, *Kaspii: o pokhodakh drevnikh Russkikh v Tabaristan s dopolnitel'nymi svedeniyami o drugikh nabegyakh ikh na priberezhya Kaspiyskago Morya*, published as *Prilozheniye k xxvi'mu tomu Zapisok Imp. Akademii Nauk*, no. 1 (St Petersburg, 1875). Sailing down the Volga the Norsemen raided the coasts of Shirvan, Gilan and Tabaristan. For the tenth century Togan cites Arab sources for the penetration of Norse merchants as far

Moscow again in September 1558. After an interval in England and his return to Moscow, Jenkinson was again in Astrakhan on his way with letters from Queen Elizabeth and from Tsar Ivan to the Persian Shah Tahmasp. He passed through Derbent and was received by the Shirvanshah Abdulla in Shemakha – then the centre of the industry in rugs and fabrics. The prosperity of Shemakha was at its zenith before the outbreak, in 1576, of the long wars between the Ottomans and the Persians which were to continue into the first decade of the seventeenth century. From Shemakha Jenkinson proceeded to Kazvin but his negotiations with the crabbed and suspicious Shah were unsuccessful and in May 1563 he was back in Moscow.

Jenkinson was clearly familiar with Herberstein's *Rerum Moscouiticarum commentarii*. His own map, edited in London in 1562, follows in many details the Herberstein map of 1549 – with the improvement that Herberstein's Latin names are given by Jenkinson in Russian (e.g. *Lacus Albus = Biala ozera*).[1] East of the line of the rivers Ob–Yaik is Jenkinson's original composition. In delineating *Kitaia Lacus* (the Aral Sea) Jenkinson follows Herberstein's error in showing it as the source of the Ob. The *Sur* (Syr Darya = Jaxartes) is correctly shown as flowing north into the Aral while the *Amow* (Amu Darya = Oxus) is drawn as an affluent of the Syr Darya. The *Ougus* (Amu Darya = Oxus) is depicted as another river flowing westward to the Caspian. Here, in Jenkinson's mind, would seem to be reflected the old

east as Khorezm, see his *Documents on the Khorezmian Culture*, part 1, p. 35, Introduction in Turkish and English to the *Khorezmian Glossary of the Muqaddimat al-Adab* (Istanbul, 1951).

[1] No example of Jenkinson's original print of 1562 is known to survive, but it was reproduced in Ortelius' *Theatrum orbis terrarum*, first published 20 May 1570 (no. 46). For a detailed discussion of Jenkinson's map, see E. Delmar Morgan and C. H. Coote, *Early voyages and travels to Russia and Persia by Anthony Jenkinson and other Englishmen*, Hakluyt Society (1886), I, cxix–cxlviii. For the composition of Herberstein's map and the role of Anton Wied and the contributions of the Russians Gerasimov and Latskiy to the cartography of Russia in mid-sixteenth century: see the important article by Leo Bagrow, 'At the sources of the cartography of Russia' in *Imago Mundi*, XVI (Amsterdam, 1962), 33–48; for a review of different reprints of the map, Joh. Keuning, 'Jenkinson's Map of Russia', *ibid.*, XIII (1956), 172–5.

controversy about the date of the change in the course of the Oxus (Amu Darya). He has in effect tried to give both versions. It is interesting to note that despite the clear indication on his map, Jenkinson does not include the name *Ougus* among the rivers which he names in a subsequent report as falling into the Caspian. The confusion in Jenkinson's mind doubtless reflects conversa/ tions, perhaps rather muddled and incorrectly interpreted, which he held with merchants in Bukhara.[1] As a useful appendix Jenkinson adds to his reports the notes of his companion Richard Johnson on itineraries between Astrakhan and Bukhara, and from Bukhara through Tashkent to Kashgar (*Cascar*) and to Cathay.

Jenkinson gives a fair approximation of the lie of the principal cities of Turkestan: *Urgeme* (Urgenc), *Boghar urbs* (Bukhara), *Shamarcandia* (Samarkand), Tashkent and *Balgh* (Balkh). But although he was the first English navigator of the northern and north/eastern shores of the Caspian, he follows the traditional error of giving the sea a circular bag/like shape.[2] He places Mangusha (Mangyshlak) due east of Astrakhan, and the Cau/ casian towns *Durben* (Derbent), *Backow* (Baku), and *Shamagi* (Shemakha) to the south instead of to the east of the great sea. Thus no space is left for the location of Kazvin – which he visited when his map had already been published, on his second journey in 1562–3, after passing through Derbent, Shirvan and Azerbaijan. Jenkinson's map of the Caspian certainly compares un/ favourably with the Italian maps prepared a hundred years earlier.[3]

[1] For the continuing controversy on the changes in the course of the Oxus, see arts. 'Amu Derya', in *Islam Ansiklopedisi* by A. Zeki Velidi Togan, and 'Amu Darya', in *The Encyclopaedia of Islam* (2nd edition) by B. Spuler. Both Bartold and Togan have adduced evidence for the shifting back of the Amu Darya to the Aral Sea in the years between 1573 and 1578 – that is within twenty years of Jenkinson's visit to Bukhara.

[2] Following, of course, the Ptolemaic delineation. Here the conservatism of cartographers is amazing; as early as 1485 a surprisingly accurate representation of the Caspian coasts had been in circulation. It is believed to have been of Venetian origin, see art. by Erich Woldan, 'A circular copper/engraved mediaeval world map', in *Imago Mundi*, XI (1954), 13–16.

[3] For early Italian cartography of the Caspian, see art. by G. Caraci, 'The Italian cartographers of the Benincasa and Freducci families and the so/called Borgiana Map of the Vatican Library', in *Imago Mundi*, X (1953), 23–50, particularly

An intrepid traveller and an acute man of affairs, Jenkinson was the first Englishman to sail the Caspian and to penetrate to Bukhara. As an explorer of his contemporary world, he ranks with – but certainly not above – Ruy Gonçales de Clavijo, the Castilian ambassador to Tamerlane, who travelled to Samarkand more than a century and a half before Jenkinson was in Bukhara. The account of Gonçales de Clavijo, first published by Gonçalo Argote de Molina in Seville in 1582, seems to have been over-looked by Hakluyt. This is perhaps indicative of the limited resources which Hakluyt and Walsingham's office had at their disposal for checking on recent foreign publications.

Hakluyt was primarily the editor of materials on the English contribution to the expansion of knowledge of the world beyond Europe during the sixteenth century. As such he worked with a thorough and conscientious enthusiasm and he has produced a superb documentation on the English epic of those days. Hakluyt was familiar with a certain range of foreign travels in central Asia and, somewhat illogically in the second edition of his *Principal navigations*, includes the missions of Plano Carpini and Rubruquis. He knew his Polo and could draw on Ramusio and on the published *Commentarii* of Herberstein. But beyond some inquiries about Abul Fidā (first printed in Europe in 1650) he had no

pp. 40–2 and pl. 6; also art. by L. Bagrow, 'Italians on the Caspian', *ibid.*, XIII, 3–10. The map found in the Dalmatian monastery of Lesina and dated to the last quarter of the fifteenth century, gives 130 place-names round a surprisingly accurate delineation of the Caspian coasts. Incidentally, it shows the infall of the Oxus into the Caspian. Bagrow concludes: 'I should like to draw attention to the mistrust with which Venetian and other 16th century cartographers regarded this (to them) new representation of the Caspian. When Jacopo Gastaldi, the famous Venetian cartographer, who certainly had access to all available materials provided by contemporary explorers, was in 1553 entrusted with the compilation of a map of Asia . . . he chose for the Caspian the typical representation after Ptolemy . . . The Netherlands cartographer Christian Sgrooten, on his map of 1572 in 10 sheets, also gives the Caspian a Ptolemaic shape. It is thus not surpris-ing that in 17th century maps the Caspian still takes different shapes according to its representation in the maps of Anthony Jenkinson (1562), Adam Olearius (1647) and Nicolas Witsen (1687). Only Waldseemüller, who had followed Portuguese maps of the Caspian, gave in his world map of 1516 a similar outline to Fra Mauro's though rather crudely executed.'

access to the lore surviving in Arabic and Hebrew and Persian
and Turkish sources.[1] A thirteenth-century Armenian source like
Haiton came to him only in distorted form through Mandeville.[2]
But it would be otiose to expect Hakluyt to have edited the
English 'Navigations' by embodying them in a general evaluation
of the state of contemporary knowledge on each country. His
object was to publicize – and perhaps a little to exaggerate in
terms of priority – the substantial English contribution to the
knowledge of the age. His achievement was to publish the documentation of the English voyages and in doing so he rendered a
signal service to geographers and historians. In the expansion of
the knowledge of the countries bordering the Caspian Jenkinson's
first voyage was a great feat and in sixteenth-century Russia it was
recognized as such.

[1] For instance, the masterpieces, widely known in the Islamic world, of Rashid-
al-Din (1247–1318); of Ulugh Beg (1393–1449), known to John Graves in
Oxford only in the 1640s; and of the Emperor Babur (1482–1530), translated
from Turki into Persian in 1590 and into English in 1826.

[2] He makes no reference to, and perhaps did not know, the English version,
Hetoum, Prince of Gorigos, *Here begynneth a lytell cronycle*, R. Pynson [1520 ?],
S.T.C. 13256 (for which see pp. 187–8 below).

14
The Near East:
North and North-east Africa

C. F. BECKINGHAM

The area with which this chapter is concerned extends from the Atlantic to the Persian Gulf and from the Mediterranean to the Sahara and the Arabian Sea. It comprises North Africa within the Straits of Gibraltar, Egypt and the valley of the Nile, Ethiopia, the Horn of Africa, the Arabian peninsula, the Fertile Crescent and Asia Minor. When Hakluyt lived most of these countries were included in the Ottoman Empire, though Morocco, Ethiopia, the Fung Kingdom of Sennar and some principalities in Arabia maintained an independence that was sometimes precarious. Many of them had belonged to the Roman Empire and had therefore been familiar to the geographers of classical antiquity, and they were now under the government of one of the most powerful states in the world. They were not unexplored and there was no need for Hakluyt to collect topographical descriptions. There were, of course, some parts, such as the interior of Arabia and Ethiopia, of which the ancient writers had known very little. For these, however, with a few notable exceptions, such as the works of Varthema and Alvares, the sources he could have consulted were not much better than theirs had been. Insofar as he had a consistent purpose in this section it must be assumed that it was to publicize the English connection, to show what opportunities there were for English merchants, and to record information that might be useful to them.

The earliest British travellers to the East whom he mentions are soldiers of the Roman army. In his preface he writes: 'I read in Ioseph Bengorion a very authenticall Hebrew author, a testimonie of the passing of 20000 Britains valiant souldiours, to the siege and fearefull sacking of Ierusalem under the conduct of Vespasian and Titus the Romane Emperour, a thing in deed of all the rest most ancient.' The reference is to the so-called *Sepher Yosippon*, which was attributed to Joseph ben Gorion, usually identified with the historian Josephus. In fact, Josephus (Joseph ben Mattathiah) was not Ben Gorion, who did not write the book, which is by no means 'authenticall'. It was probably written in southern Italy in the tenth century.[1] Sebastian Münster, who pub-lished a Latin translation of part of the work in 1541, and who believed it to be by Josephus, recognized that it contained allu-sions that an author of the first century could not have made; he concluded that there had been interpolations.[2] Hakluyt doubtless had a smattering of Hebrew but he probably consulted the English translation by Peter Morwyng (1558, S.T.C. 14795).[3] The phraseology of the relevant passage is curious: 'So the Lordes of the straunge nacions chose out of their armies . . . xx thousand english Britons.' In the Hebrew text there is no word cognate with 'English'; it says merely 'twenty thousand of the men of Britain'. The same sentence does, however, include an anomalous refer-ence to the 'men of Burgundy' and Hakluyt should have been suspicious.[4]

[1] See S. W. Baron, *A social and religious history of the Jews*, 2nd edn., VI (1958), 195, 419, 420; M. Waxman, *A history of Jewish literature*, I (1960), 419–21.

[2] 'citantur quaedam gentes quae longe post Iosephi tempora in mundo surrexerunt, ut sunt Franci, Gothi, Lombardi, Bulgari, &c. haec plane arguunt Iosepho quaedam accessisse per posteros Iudaeos.'

[3] *A compendious and moste marveylous history of the latter times of the Jewes commune weale.* There is no copy of the first edition in the British Museum. S.T.C. records only a copy in the Huntington Library. There is, however, a copy, with the title-page missing, in the Lucien Wolf collection in the Mocatta Library at University College, London. The passage is on fol. ccxii verso. The second edition, dated 1561, is in the British Museum; the passage is on f. clxxxxvii verso. Neither edition is divided into chapters.

[4] There are several versions and arrangements of the text which has a complicated history. The *editio princeps* was printed at Mantua about 1480 by Abraham Conath; it does not contain the final, which is the relevant portion of the work. This was first included in an edition printed at Constantinople in 1510; the passage with which we are concerned occurs in chapter 88. The same arrange-ment is followed in the modern edition by H. Hominer (Jerusalem, 1956). In the well-known edition by J. F. Breithaupt (Gotha, 1707), which is accom-

Principall navigations (1589) begins with short accounts of medieval English visitors to the East. They are given in Latin, followed
by English translations, and are arranged more or less chronologically. It has been shown that most of them were taken from
John Bale's *Scriptorum illustrium maioris Brytanniae . . . catalogus*,
and that Hakluyt used the edition published at Basle in two
volumes in 1557 and 1559. Bale gave a short biography of each
writer, followed by a list of his writings whether these had survived or not. He was a learned, industrious, atrabilious and
uncritical compiler; Hakluyt is misled by him into confusing
Ranulf de Glanville and Ranulf de Blundeville.[1] He usually
omits all or nearly all of Bale's lists of books. In the notice of
Robertus Ketenensis he even deletes his translation of the Koran,
which had been printed in 1543, and a work *Super doctrina
Mahumeti*, which one might have expected him to record as
evidence of English study of the dominant religion of the region.
Otherwise he abridges little, when at all, occasionally condensing
a phrase or excising an item of theological interest, as he does in
the life of Pelagius. It cannot be said that his editing of Bale is
systematic, and he was not thorough in his examination of his
source. He ignores Daniel Morleye (Bale, pp. 229–30), who
went to Toledo to study mathematics and 'Arabum scrinia
excussit'; Petrus Canonicus (pp. 276–7), who translated a book
De terra Palaestinae from French; Ranulf Fresburne (pp. 284–5),
who went to Carmel some years after the return of Richard I and
brought back a companion with whom to establish the Car-
melites in England; John Tiptoft, the famous earl of Worcester
(pp. 620–1), a fifteenth-century pilgrim to Jerusalem, whom
Bale states to have lived there for some time and to have travelled
in the neighbouring countries; and William Lily (pp. 649–50),
the grammarian, who had visited Jerusalem. These omissions
were not repaired in *Principal navigations* (1598–1600).

Most medieval English travellers to the East of whom we have

panied by a parallel Latin translation, it is in lib. vi, cap. xli (p. 772). A Hebrew
word cognate with 'Angli' does occur in the text, though not in the passage to
which Hakluyt refers. See, e.g., Breithaupt, p. 4; Hominer, p. 45.

[1] See Quinn and Skelton, edd. *PN* (*1589*), 1 (1965), xxv.

any knowledge were either crusaders or pilgrims. Hakluyt evidently made no attempt to compile anything like a comprehensive
list of either. For Richard I he used the fourth edition of Foxe's
Actes and monuments (1583, S.T.C. 11225), by no means the best
source available to him. He adapts the text slightly, omits passages
about events in England, the death of Barbarossa, and the King's
conversations with Abbot Joachim, but his editing is perfunctory.
The name of Richard's father-in-law, Sancho VI of Navarre,
appears both as Zanctius (p. 8) and as Rancon (p. 10); he
copied this obvious error from Foxe. For William Longsword
he relied on Matthew Paris, omitting everything about the earl's
stay in Cyprus. In his second edition Hakluyt includes brief
accounts of a few more English crusaders. One might reckon
among them Sir Thomas Chaloner, counsellor to the English
ambassador in Madrid, whom he and two other Englishmen
accompanied on Charles V's expedition against Algiers in 1541.
The note about Chaloner's exploits is described as 'drawen out
of his booke De Republica Anglorum instauranda'. In fact it is
translated from the dedication, written by William Malim, High
Master of St Paul's School. Hakluyt does not mention something
stated in the same dedication, that Malim had been in Antioch,
Constantinople, Jerusalem and 'several other famous cities and
provinces of Asia and Europe'. Malim had published an English
translation of Nestor Martinengo's *Relatione di tutto il successo di
Famagosta* (Venice, 1572), entitled *A true report of all the successe
of Famagosta* (1572, S.T.C. 17520). In the dedication of this work[1]
he refers to 'these barbarous Mahometistes: whose crueltie and
beastly behauour I partly know, and am able to iudge of, hauing
bene in Turkye, amongest them more than 8. monethes together'.
He had also visited Chios and Cyprus before the Ottoman
conquest of these islands and included with his translation
'A breefe description of the Iland of Cyprus'. It occupies
little more than three pages, the content is principally historical,
and when it is descriptive it is concerned with classical times.
This is typical of the writings of many scholarly travellers of

---

[1] The article on Malim in the *DNB* refers to this dedication but does not exploit
it fully.

the next two and a half centuries, and it is of no relevance to Hakluyt.[1]

There were many pilgrims to Jerusalem who described their own travels or who compiled manuals of useful information for others. These writings vary considerably in length, interest and accuracy. *Principall navigations* (1589) includes only one, the best known but among the least typical and least authentic, the narrative that purports to be by Sir John Mandeville. The text is a widely known Latin version commonly called 'the vulgate', first printed at Strasbourg about 1484. Hakluyt's decision to incorporate it has caused surprise and it may be significant that he did not provide an English translation, as he did for every other text that he published in a foreign language.[2] In *Principal navigations* (1598–1600) it is omitted and it has been suggested that this is because he had doubts about its reliability. It is unthink-able that Hakluyt should not have been sceptical about some of Mandeville's statements, but he also used a description of the Guinea voyage in which there are some comparable items cited, not always with complete accuracy, on the respectable authority of Gemma Frisius. Bale's biography of Mandeville is also included, for he was supposedly English, and if so, was certainly the most famous of English travellers. There had been six printed English editions of his book, and when Martin Frobisher's first voyage was organized, it was thought worth while to spend a shilling on a copy of one of them.[3] Moreover, Mandeville's modern reputation is not wholly justified. Some of his strangest stories give superb opportunities to the illustrator. The delightful woodcuts of the Augsburg and Basle editions of 1481 have often been reproduced and are perhaps more familiar than the text. They are apt to give the impression that more of the book is about such creatures as sciapods than is really so. Many of these cele-brated monsters are mentioned only briefly. The greater part of

---

[1] 'It is perhaps important that his interests remained modern, that in his publica-tions there is no trace of the humanist impulse.' (Parks, *Hakluyt*, p. 214.)

[2] See Quinn and Skelton, pp. xxvi, xxvii, for a discussion of this.

[3] *The three voyages of Martin Frobisher*, ed. R. Collinson (Hakluyt Society, 1867), p. x.

the work is a description of Egypt, the Holy Land, Cathay and India. India is the fabulous India of Prester John's letter, but the others are real countries, and Mandeville's information, confused, exaggerated and distorted though it is, often has some basis in fact.

The narratives of English pilgrims which Hakluyt ignored were nearly all in manuscript in his time. The earliest of these travellers was St Willibald, the eighth-century English Bishop of Eichstätt. Bale has a brief notice of him but says nothing of his having travelled in the East. Our knowledge of this journey, in the course of which he and, for at least part of the time, seven compatriots, visited Cyprus, many of the cities of Lebanon and Syria, Constantinople and Nicaea, as well as the Holy Land, derives from the *Hodoeporicon* and the *Itinerarium*. Both were published for the first time by Canisius in 1603 from manuscripts in Germany.[1] Another pilgrim was Saewulf, a part of whose Latin narrative was among the manuscripts given by Archbishop Parker to Corpus Christi College, Cambridge.[2] Saewulf's route included Paphos and a voyage along the Syrian and Anatolian coasts. Henry, earl of Derby, the future Henry IV, was a notable pilgrim, whose itinerary is recorded in his treasurer's accounts. His journeys had been described, not always accurately, by the chroniclers, but were ignored by Hakluyt in 1589. In *Principal navigations* (1598–1600) there is an account of his first expedition to Prussia, but not of the second, nor of the short visit to Jerusalem which he then made before coming home. Hakluyt also quotes a passage from Polydore Vergil in which Henry is said to have joined a Franco-Genoese expedition to Barbary, from which he had in fact withdrawn at the last moment, and another relating to the preparations to go on a Crusade that he was making when

---

[1] *Antiquae lectionis tomus IV* (Ingolstadt, 1603), pt. II, pp. 475–513, and 705–18 respectively. English translations of both by W. R. Brownlow were published in *The Library of the Palestine Pilgrims' Text Society*, III (1897).

[2] First published by d'Avezac in *Recueil de voyages et de mémoires publié par la Société de Géographie*, IV (1839). *The Library of the Palestine Pilgrims' Text Society*, IV (1897), includes the Latin original and an English translation by W. R. Brownlow.

he died.[1] In 1392 Sir Thomas de Swynburne, castellan of Guines and later Mayor of Bordeaux, went to Jerusalem by way of Alexandria, Sinai, Gaza, and Hebron, and returned by Damas‚ cus and Beirut; his companion Thomas Brygg left a brief account of their journey.[2] William Wey, a Fellow of Eton, visited Jeru‚ salem in 1458 and again in 1462. The manuscript, probably a holograph, is now in the Bodleian, but was privately owned in Hakluyt's time.[3] The *Pylgrymage of Sir Richard Guylforde* had been printed.[4] It is a short narrative, written by his chaplain, of a journey that he made in 1506 to Palestine where he and his companion John Whitby spent twenty‚three days. The diary of Sir Richard Torkington, Rector of Mulberton in Norfolk, who was a pilgrim in 1517, is preserved in the British Museum.[5] There were a number of other itineraries or guides to the Holy Land which Hakluyt might have found in libraries and which are still unpublished, sometimes deservedly. It is sufficient to cite as examples Queen's College, Oxford, MS 357, ff. 9–41v, which is illustrated;[6] University College, Oxford, MS 99, pp. 274–97, by M. T. de Ashburne;[7] *Loca peregrinationis terre sancte*, a MS of 15 folios in Bodley Rawlinson C 958 (Röhricht 260); and

[1] L. Toulmin Smith, *Expeditions to Prussia and the Holy Land made by Henry earl of Derby* (Camden Society, New Series, no. 52, 1894). See also T. F. Tout's article on Henry IV in *DNB*.

[2] The MS is in the library of Gonville and Caius College, Cambridge, no. 449. It was published by Riant in *Archives de l'Orient latin*, II (1964), 378–88.

[3] *The itineraries of William Wey* (Roxburghe Club, 1857).

[4] *This is the begynnynge and contynuance of the pylgrymage of Sir Richarde Guylforde*, 1511 (S.T.C. 12549). It was edited for the Camden Society by Sir Henry Ellis in 1851.

[5] B.M., Additional MSS 28561 and 28562. It was printed in the *Vellum‚Parchment Shilling Series of Miscellaneous Literature*, VI (1884), under the title *Y*e *Oldest Diarie of Englysshe Travell*, edited by W. J. Loftie.

[6] This is a guide‚book, not a 'narrative' as it is described in Coxe's catalogue of MSS in Oxford colleges. By mistake it is entered twice in Röhricht's *Bibliotheca Geographica Palaestinae* (1890), as no. 268 (p. 101) and as no. 531 (p. 155). Both entries are inaccurate. In the first the number is given as 375 (for 357); in the second the location is stated to be 'Oxford, Bodlej. Colleg. Regin.'

[7] Now kept in the Bodleian Library. Röhricht, no. 253 (p. 98), gives the author's first name as Johannes, though his initials are given correctly by Coxe.

Itinerarium cujusdam Anglici, in Corpus Christi College, Cam-bridge, MS 370, ff. 85b–95b (Röhricht 202), an account of the pilgrimage of three Englishmen who set out from Avignon in October 1344, including a description of Cyprus. All these narratives and descriptions, however, of which Hakluyt was not aware, or which he decided to omit, are not only much less amusing than Mandeville; they are also much less informa-tive, even though such information as they do contain is more reliable.

The contemporary travellers whose writings are included in *Principall navigations* (1589) were mostly seamen, merchants or their agents. We cannot often be sure of the nature or extent of Hakluyt's editorial work on their narratives. However, the rather sensational account by Thomas Sanders of the voyage of the *Jesus* to Tripoli (pp. 192–9) had already been published as a pamphlet with the title *A true discription and breefe discourse, of a most lamentable voiage, made latelie to Tripoli in Barbarie in a ship named the Iesus* (1587, S.T.C. 21778). Hakluyt changed the spelling of the author's name from Saunders to Sanders,[1] omitted the brief preface, the dedication to Julius Caesar, most of which is merely the story of Androcles and the lion as recounted by Guevara, and some of the marginal headings, and made some slight changes. A few place names become more recognizable: Oezãt is amended to Zante, Saffalonea to Cephalonia and Ierbby to Gerbi. In Laurence Aldersey's second voyage, known only from Hakluyt (pp. 224–7), such editorial help would have been welcome. Some of the spellings are bizarre, e.g. Bickbert for Abu Qir, Caramasate for *karamürsel,*[2] and Singonina, which seems to be Nisyros. The 'second voyage to Guinea' (pp. 89–98) includes descriptive matter about Africa translated from Gemma Frisius. The originals of these passages are to be found in chapters XV and (mostly) XVI of the *De orbis diuisione et insulis, rebusque nuper inuentis.* It is not an exact version. Some sentences have been

---

[1] This has caused him to be bisected in the B.M. catalogue into Saunders (Thomas) *Captive at Tripoli* and Sanders (Thomas) *Captain.*

[2] In *PN* (1598–1600) these appear in the slightly preferable forms Bichieri and Caramusalin.

added and there are omissions that make it more dogmatic and more sensational than Gemma's text. Thus, in translating with reference to Meroe, 'ei foeminas praefuisse ferunt', and of the Blemmyes, 'capite carentes oculos et os in pectore habere creduntur', the last word of each phrase is ignored; 'in qua solitudines montesque plures occurrunt, vario genere animantium impleta' becomes 'in the which are many horrible wildernesses & mountaines, replenished with diuers kindes of wilde and monstrous beasts and serpents'. The sentence 'A great part of the other regions of Afrike that are beyond the Equinoctiall line, are now ascribed to the kingdome of Melinde' misrepresents the Latin which refers to Azania, not to Africa.

Hakluyt's book is incomparably the most important source of our knowledge of English activity in these countries in his own times, though his account is by no means exhaustive, any more than it is for the Middle Ages. His 'Epistle Dedicatorie' enumerates some of the achievements of which his contemporaries were entitled to be proud: 'Who euer saw before this regiment, an English Ligier in the stately porch of the Grand Signor at Constantinople? who euer found English Consuls & Agents at Tripolis in Syria, at Aleppo, at Babylon, at Balsara . . . ?' The establishment of commercial and diplomatic relations with the Ottoman Empire was, for his purpose, the most important event in the recent history of the Near East and much of his material is relevant to it. The first English envoy to the Porte, William Harborne, who left London in July 1578, had been sent to obtain a trading licence; it was only later that he came to be concerned with political objectives, such as inducing the Ottomans to attack the Spaniards. The two aspects of AngloTurkish relations were inseparable throughout Elizabeth's reign. In his preface Hakluyt mentions that 'more specially in my first part, Master Richard Staper Marchant of London, hath furnished me with diuers thinges touching the trade of Turkie, and other places in the East'. Staper and Sir Edward Osborne were the principal organizers of the undertaking, and it is no doubt because of the compliance of the former that Hakluyt was able to procure so many of the relevant documents. These have been the subject of two important studies.[1] There are six Turkish documents in *Principall navigations* (1589) and another eleven were added in *Principal navigations* (1598–1600). Professor Paul Wittek estab-lished that they conform to Ottoman diplomatic practice and that there is no reason whatever to question their authenticity.[2] When he wrote, the Turkish original of the charter of privileges granted to the English in June 1580 ((1589), pp. 166–70) had already been identified in the Bodleian Library. Dr Susan Skilliter, who has published the Turkish text of the letter of Ṣāfiye Sulṭān to Queen Elizabeth (*Principal navigations*, II, i (1599), 311) has since discovered in the Mühimme Defteri (the register of important affairs) at Istanbul the originals of the letter of 15 March 1579 ((1589), p. 163) and of several of the documents in the second edition. It is obvious that there must have been many more documents which Hakluyt did not publish. Professor G. B. Parks remarks that the records of the Levant trade 'were not so complete and were not made so complete in the final edition' as those relating to other parts of the world. He suggests that it 'may have been that a certain censorship hedged about the new trade, which had to consider the strong and jealous foreign competition' and that this might explain why the elder Hakluyt's notes on the Turkish trade were not published in *Principall navigations* (1589). He also suggests that 'the Turkish trade was a settled one, having been in the hands of the Italians since the Crusades and recently of the French, and therefore needed small illumination. Hakluyt may therefore have felt justified in making no note of the annual voyages except for noteworthy reasons.'[3] Professor Wittek com-ments on the fact that only one of the documents printed in

---

[1] P. Wittek, 'The Turkish Documents in Hakluyt's "Voyages"', *Bulletin of the Institute of Historical Research*, XIX (no. 57, for November 1942), 121–39, and S. A. Skilliter, 'Three Letters from the Ottoman "Sultana" Ṣāfiye to Queen Elizabeth I' in S. M. Stern, ed., *Documents from Islamic chanceries*, 1st series (1965).

[2] Professor Wittek's article was written and published in wartime when it was not possible to verify some of his suggestions. B.M., Cotton MS, Nero B XI, 377, is not the 'full Latin version of the sultan's letter', but another copy of Sinan Pasha's letter (*PN*, II, i (1599), 294); the *Casul-bas* (i.e. Qizilbash) of the printed text is an improvement on the MS reading *Rasul bas*.

[3] Parks, *Hakluyt*, pp. 127–8.

Principal navigations (1598–1600), Sinan Pasha's letter to Queen Elizabeth of June 1590, is political in content. By quoting from the Queen's correspondence with the Emperor he illustrates its value as propaganda for the English government. He concludes that it was specially released for publication by the authorities.

As we have seen Hakluyt did not need to describe the topography of the area with which this chapter is concerned and his work is not in the tradition of the classical or medieval Arabic geographers. Even to the former he makes few references; Parks could find no evidence 'that he had anything to do with the appearance of various geographical classics during his lifetime'.[1] Among the latter he knew of Abul Fidā's treatise; Newbery tried to obtain a copy for him at Tripoli ((1589), p. 208) and he mentions it in a letter to Van Meteren of 4 December 1594;[2] he does not refer to Idrīsī, part of whose work was available in Latin. Nevertheless the merit of *Principall navigations* (1589) as a source of geographical information about the region must be evident to anyone who considers what had been published about it in English by 1589, for Hakluyt's work is comparatively free from three conspicuous defects of much of this writing, credulity about marvels, topographical confusion, and gross errors of translation.

In the 1589 edition the marvellous is still represented by parts of Mandeville and a few passages from Gemma Frisius, but there were many works in circulation in the sixteenth century which made much greater demands on credence. In Caxton's *Mirrour of the world*, a translation of a thirteenthcentury French poem which was very popular in the later Middle Ages, the Earthly Paradise is in Asia, protected by fire and by giants; in Cappadocia there is 'a manner of Mares that conceyve of the wynde' and in Ethiopia is a river that is frozen by day but so hot at night that animals cannot drink from it. The inaccessible paradise recurs in a booklet printed about 1535 called *Mappa mundi. Otherwyse called the compasse, and cyrcuet of the worlde* (S.T.C. 17297). This provides precise, if not always accurate, information about distances between places and also the location of hell, under the earth 'in the myddes of Affryke; also a man may se in Affryke

<hr />

[1] *Ibid.*, p. 214.   [2] *Ibid.*, p. 144.

openlye two hylles that be soupitall of hell, and they cease not neyther daye nor nyght & be ever brenyng with fiers fyre'. Some curious nonsense occurs in a very popular compendium by a great scholar, Sebastian Münster's *Cosmographia uniuersalis*. An anonymous English translation of selections from this was pub-lished in 1572 with the title *A briefe collection and compendious extract of straunge and memorable thinges, gathered out of the cosmographye of Sebastian Munster* (S.T.C. 18242), of which there was another edition in 1574 (S.T.C. 18243). This includes the statement that in Carmania no man marries until he has decapitated an enemy; he takes the head to the king who cuts the tongue into small pieces, mixes it with bread and gives it to the man and his 'familiers' to eat. As one would expect, the chapter 'Of Prester Iohannes Lande' contains some startling matter. In Ethiopia are found animals with seven horns, white bears, two-horned horses, birds that carry off oxen and horses to feed their nestlings, horned men, men with one eye in front and two behind, men who eat their parents, men with horses' feet, and Amazons.

The topographical confusion is sometimes inextricable in these works. In the *Mirrour of the world* Persia is part of India, Sheba is in Chaldaea, 'thereby' is Tarsus, and Assyria is in Egypt. The confusing use of India to mean Ethiopia persists even in the famous book of Damião de Góis, *Legatio magni Indorum imperatoris Pres-byteri Ioannis* (1532), translated by Sir Thomas More's son John as *The legacye or embassate of the great emperour of Inde prester John* (1533, S.T.C. 11966),[1] although Góis must have known as well as we do the difference between the two.

A few examples of disastrous mistranslations will suffice. In the *Mirrour of the world* we read that in Persia grows 'a pese which is so hoot that it skaldeth the handes of them that holde it'. The word translated *pese* is *poiz*, 'pitch'. Haiton's *La flor des estoires de la terre d'Orient* was translated by order of the duke of Bucking-

---

[1] S.T.C. mentions only the copy in the library of Emmanuel College, Cam-bridge. There is another at Lambeth Palace, which was described by S. R. Maitland, *A list of some of the early printed books in the Archiepiscopal Library at Lambeth* (1843). No other copy is recorded. There is a description of the book in F. M. Rogers, *The quest for eastern Christians* (1962), pp. 145–54.

ham. The translation has no title-page and begins: *Here begynneth a lytell cronycle translated and imprinted at the cost of Rycharde Pynson* (S.T.C. 13256); there is no date; the B.M. catalogue assigns it tentatively to 1515 and S.T.C. to 1520. Here we read the extraordinary statement that Mesopotamia 'is called Grioise'. The French text is different but not less surprising: 'La langue du pais est appellee grioise'. The true reading appears in a MS in the Escorial: 'Aquesta tierra es clamada Mesopotamia en lengo gergesco'.[1] The first English version of Marco Polo, *The most noble and famous travels of Marcus Paulus* (1579, S.T.C. 20092), was made by John Frampton from the Spanish of Rodrigo Fernández de Santaella.[2] N. M. Penzer, who published an edition of this text in 1929, claims that Frampton's knowledge of Spanish was 'very considerable'. He nevertheless made some bad mistakes. Santaella included with Polo a *Cosmographia breve*, which Frampton also translated. In this it is stated that a city called Africa gave its name to the continent. *Africa cibdad que dio nombre a su todo.* This becomes 'the name so given by Asu'. Cyrene becomes Syria and the word *sertano*, 'hinterland', is twice treated as a place-name.

Nevertheless, for all his superiority in these respects, it cannot be claimed that Hakluyt made available, even to those who could read no language but English, much new information of geo-graphical importance about this area. The parts of it about which the classical writers had known least were inland Arabia, and Ethiopia. During the sixteenth century two books had been published which made substantial additions to European know-ledge of these countries, the *Itinerario* of Varthema (1510), which included a description of his travels in the Hijaz and the Yemen, and *Ho Preste Joam das Indias* (1540) of Francisco Alvares, which described his journey from Arkiko to Shoa. The former had been translated into English by Eden (1577, S.T.C. 649); the latter was accessible only in Portuguese and Italian. Neither western

[1] *La Flor de las ystorias de Orient*, ed. W. R. Long (1934).
[2] The founder of Seville University. See Joaquín Hazañas y La Rua, *Maese Rodrigo, 1444-1509* (Sevilla, 1909). Santaella used an Italian MS which is pre-served in the Biblioteca del Seminario at Seville.

Arabia nor Ethiopia was of any political interest to the English government and neither was at all easy of access to European traders; no Englishman is known to have visited either until long after this date. It is significant of his purpose that Hakluyt should make no reference to either author.

15

Morocco, the Saharan coast, and the neighbouring Atlantic islands

P. E. H. HAIR

The chronological sequence of English commercial expansion into the south-west Atlantic was from trade with Portugal and Spain, to trade with the nearer Atlantic islands, particularly the Canaries;[1] to trade with Atlantic Barbary, that is, modern Morocco;[2] and, finally, to trade with Guinea. The organizational interconnections of the sequence have not yet been fully examined: one scholar argues that the Guinea voyage was 'naturally and historically a development of the Barbary voyage', another scholar comments that the connection has been exaggerated, that the two trades were separate ventures, and that ships almost never sailed to both coasts in a single voyage.[3] Again, the role of Spanish traders in the Canaries in encouraging and assisting

[1] See G. Connell-Smith, *Forerunners of Drake: a study of Elizabethan trade with Spain in the early Tudor period* (1954); T. S. Willan, *The Muscovy merchants of 1555* (Manchester, 1953), pp. 25–6, 85.

[2] English material on Morocco has been fully reprinted and excellently edited in H. de Castries, *Les sources inédites de l'histoire du Maroc, Archives et bibliothèques d'Angleterre*, I and II (Paris, 1918–25). See also J. Caillé, 'Le commerce anglais avec le Maroc pendant la seconde moitié du XVIe siècle', *Revue Africaine*, LXXXIV (1940), pp. 186–219; T. S. Willan, *Studies in Elizabethan foreign trade* (Manchester, 1959), 'Elizabethan trade with Morocco', pp. 92–312. In Elizabethan usage, 'Barbary' included a large part, if not all, of the Saharan coast, south of modern Morocco. While English seamen seldom landed on the Saharan coast, they regularly raided the Portuguese and Spanish fishing fleets which operated off-shore, particularly off Cap Blanc: Hakluyt records several such raids, which provided fish for expeditions going to Guinea or America (Towerson, 1556–7; Hawkins, 1564–5; Winter, 1577–9; Cavendish, 1586–8; Lancaster, 1594–5; Dudley, 1594–5; Ralegh, 1596–7).

[3] J. W. Blake, *Europeans in West Africa, 1450–1560* (1942), II, 250; Willan, *Elizabethan foreign trade*, p. 100.

English voyages to Guinea (and to America) has not to date been adequately investigated:[1] contemporary documentation, both Spanish and English, of course tended to conceal rather than to record such activities. Hakluyt undoubtedly provides material for the study of these and related problems, though it is not easy to assess the overall value of his material.

A notable and curious feature of Hakluyt's material is that the greater part of it was added in the second edition, and that the additional material includes most of the items earliest in time. In the first edition there were few items specifically on this region: on Morocco, only papers relating to the English embassies of 1577 and 1585, and the patent of the Barbary Company granted in 1585,[2] on the Atlantic islands, only an extract from a Portuguese chronicle concerning the alleged discovery of Madeira by Macham the Englishman in 1344. Hakluyt even failed to include Nichols' printed account of the Canaries, published anonymously in 1583.[3] Yet, in the accounts of Tomson's voyage to New Spain in 1555, of Towerson's voyage to Guinea in 1557–8, and of Hawkins' voyage to Guinea and America in 1562, there are references to English merchants living in the Canaries and to English trade with the islands. The account of Hawkins' first voyage is introduced with a pregnant statement: 'Master John Haukins having made diuers voyages to the yles of the Canaries, and there by his good and vpright dealing being growne in loue and fauour with the people, informed himselfe amongst them by diligent inquisi

---

[1] For some discussion, see A. Rumeu de Armas, *Los viajes de John Hawkins a America* (Seville, 1947); and for discussion of the conflict of economic interests between the Canaries and the Spanish crown, see F. Morales Padron, *El comercio CanarioAmericano* (Seville, 1955), and P. Chaunu, *Séville et l'Atlantique (1504–1650)*, VIII (i) (Paris, 1959). It is conceivable that local interests in the Portuguese possessions, Madeira and the Cape Verde islands, similarly encouraged English activities, but there is no evidence of this in Hakluyt.

[2] This material is reprinted and annotated in De Castries, *Sources inédites*, I, 239–49, 468–75, 510–12, and discussed in Willan, *Elizabethan foreign trade*, pp. 148–52, 225–9.

[3] *A pleasant description of the fortunate Ilandes called the lands of Canaria . . . Composed by the poore Pilgrime* (London, T. East, 1583). [B.M., G. 7074], reprinted and annotated in A. Cioranescu, *Thomas Nichols, Mercader de azúcar, Hispanista y Hereje* (Tenerife, 1963).

tion, of the state of the West India, whereof he had receiued some knowledge by the instructions of his father, but increased the same by the aduertisements and reports of that people.' The account of Hawkins' second voyage not only includes a brief description of the Canaries but refers openly to the assistance Hawkins received from the Canarian merchant, Pedro de Ponte. Similarly, there are passing references to earlier English trade with Morocco. Bodenham's account of a voyage to New Spain mentions an attempt by this Englishman, then living and working in Spain, to trade with Fez in Barbary at an unspecified date before 1564. The account of Fenner's voyage to Guinea of 1566 mentions an English ship visiting Agadir in south Morocco, presumably to collect sugar, and there attacked by Portuguese vessels. We now know that Englishmen were reconnoitring the south Moroccan sugar trade as early as the 1530s.[1] But the earliest specific item on Morocco in Hakluyt's first edition is of date 1577. It is tempt-ing to link this editorial lack of interest in English ventures to Morocco with the disparaging remarks about the early Barbary trade, made in Hakluyt's 1584 discourse recommending English expansion westwards across the Atlantic.[2]

Whether it was partisan lack of interest, or simply a failure to locate documentation, which brought about the sparsity of material on the Atlantic islands and Morocco in the first edition, in the second the picture changed. In the 1590s, Hakluyt, perhaps having come to realize the importance of the early stages of English expansion in the south-west Atlantic, sought – or sought more successfully – documentation, particularly from his merchant acquaintances. In his 1599 'Epistle Dedicatorie' he proudly announced: 'I haue here set downe the very originals and infancie of our trades to the Canarian Ilands, [and] to the kingdomes of Barbarie', as well as to Guinea. In the second edition, he re-printed Nichols' account of the Canaries in the 1560s, supplying the author's name, and prefaced it with a note on English trade

---

[1] Roger Barlow, *A brief summe of geographie*, edited by E. G. R. Taylor (1932), pp. xxiii, 100.

[2] Taylor, *Hakluyts*, II, 218; cf. similar disparaging remarks in Carleill's discourse in Hakluyt, 1589, on p. 719.

to the islands in the 1520s. He further added two documents relating to what were probably the earliest regular English voyages to Barbary, in 1551 and 1552,[1] and a description of Arguin on the Saharan coast written by a Portuguese in 1591. Only on the Cape Verde islands could he still print nothing specific. How-ever, a series of visits there by English voyagers, at first merely to water and take provisions from the uninhabited islands but of later date directed against the Portuguese settlements, led to descriptions being incorporated in accounts of several voyages, the descriptions being fullest in texts new to the second edition.[2]

Apart from Nichols' account, none of the material specifically relating to Morocco, the Saharan coast, or the Atlantic islands, had been printed before; and none of the manuscripts used by Hakluyt appears to be extant. As in the case of the Guinea voyages, it looks as if there was only one manuscript copy of each item and this was destroyed during printing. The material on Morocco in the first edition was official in character and most likely formed part of a large collection of Barbary and Levant papers which came to Hakluyt, more or less direct from the companies.[3] But the material on the Barbary voyages of the 1550s in the second edition was of a different character: it had been written long after the events described, the account of the second voyage possibly at Hakluyt's request, and if so, in the 1590s. Both documents probably reached Hakluyt through his merchant friend, Michael Lok. The account of Arguin in 1591, apparently an intercepted Portuguese letter, possibly came from the same source as the papers which precede and follow it, papers relating

[1] Reprinted and annotated in De Castries, *Sources inédites*, I, 14–20; reprinted in Blake, *Europeans in West Africa*, II, 304–7 (the 1552 voyage erroneously attributed to Hakluyt's first edition, on p. 251), and discussed in the same, pp. 271–2, and in Willan, *Elizabethan foreign trade*, pp. 96–100. Hakluyt also added a brief extract from a Portuguese source referring to the death of Thomas Stukeley at the battle of Ksar el Kebir in 1578.

[2] Substantial material on these islands can be found in the accounts of the following voyages: 1558 (Towerson, to Guinea), 1566–7 (Fenner, to Guinea), 1576–7 (Barker, to America), 1577–80 (Drake), 1583 (the *Edward Cotton*, to Guinea), 1585–6 (Drake), 1596–7 (Sherley).

[3] Quinn and Skelton, edd., *PN (1589)*, I (1965), xli–xlii.

to the trade of the Dassel family in Morocco and Guinea in the early 1590s and presumably handed over to Hakluyt by the Dassels. The note on trade to the Canaries in the 1520s was 'gathered out of an olde ligier booke', very possibly by the hand of the prebendary of Bristol himself.

Hakluyt published material on the earliest regular voyages to Morocco, but not on those that followed. It is unlikely that there were no accounts of the many voyages in the three preceding decades extant in the 1590s, or available to Hakluyt, and it is almost certain that he was here select in his documentation. Unlike the Guinea trade, the trade to Morocco was soon operated on a permanent basis, that is, 'it ceased to be organised in those separate, self-contained annual voyages which Hakluyt clearly preferred to recount'.[1] Unfortunately what Hakluyt did not choose to use has now been lost: 'none of the business records of the merchants seem to have survived'.[2] But a great deal of material has in recent years been found in the records of the High Court of Admiralty[3] (which were probably not available to Hakluyt), and it is probable that the same collection contains important material on the trade to the Atlantic islands. There is much further material among the general state papers – references to Morocco in diplomatic reports from the 1540s, petitions from English merchants of 1567 and 1572 (which if published by Hakluyt would have made it clear that English trade to Morocco was continuous between the voyages of the 1550s and the establishment of the Barbary Company), an important paper of 1577 by the ambassador, Edmund Hogan, on the saltpetre trade, an extraordinary proposal of 1579 from the merchant Roger Bodenham for an Anglo-Moroccan alliance and an English naval base at Mogador to threaten the Canaries and the Indies.[4] Hakluyt may well have seen some of these, since copies were probably held by the London merchants. While certain of the

[1] Willan, *Elizabethan foreign trade*, p. 101.

[2] *Ibid.*, p. 121.

[3] Material up to 1560 is printed and discussed in Blake, *Europeans in West Africa*, II, 273–82, 347–54, 433–40; this and later material is discussed in Willan, *Elizabethan foreign trade*, *passim*.

[4] All these papers are printed in De Castries, *Sources inédites*.

papers related to secrets of state, the publication of most of them would surely have been impolitic only in the mildest degree by 1598–1600: Spanish and Portuguese opinion no longer mattered; Moroccan opinion was not formed by reading English publica-tions. Presumably, therefore, Hakluyt deemed these records to be outside his strict terms of reference, though some of them were no more so than several of the documents published in his sections on 'Ambassages, Treatises, Privileges, Letters and other observa-tions'. Most probably Hakluyt failed to see Roger Barlow's manuscript translation of Enciso's geography, which contained interpolated material on the translator's contacts with the Canaries (and Azores) and with south Morocco in the late 1520s and early 1530s: the translation was among the royal papers.[1] Our present knowledge of sixteenth-century trade between England and Morocco is therefore drawn only to a limited extent from Hakluyt's documentation, though there are details about the earliest voyages which appear only in documents Hakluyt pub-lished, including some which he rescued or even had written. Our knowledge of English trade with the Canaries is similarly based largely on sources other than Hakluyt, principally official Spanish records – not least those of the Inquisition.[2]

The internal history of Morocco is of course extensively docu-mented from sources in other European languages and in Arabic, and the material in Hakluyt is of slight value. Interest in Morocco, and in the many dramatic events there, was keen in late Eliza-bethan England and was catered for by a series of books and pamphlets. However Hakluyt published information on one event – and that an event of some moment in the history of Africa – which may well have not been known about previously in England. His information came from a reliable source, and his documents are valued by the African historian. This event was the successful Moroccan invasion of the western Sudan in the early 1590s, which was reported in two letters of 1594 from an agent of the Dassels in Morocco. Comment in these letters on the

[1] Barlow, *A brief summe of geographie*, pp. 100–3.
[2] L. de Alberti and A. B. Wallis Chapman, *English merchants and the Spanish Inquisition in the Canaries*, Camden 3rd series, 23 (1912).

gold obtained by the conquest helped to stimulate English interest in both Morocco and west Africa.[1] Lastly, as regards the internal history of the Atlantic islands, though Nichols' account has been reprinted and edited by modern historians of the Canaries,[2] we must expect that the progressive exploitation of Portuguese and Spanish archives will render Hakluyt's documentation of slight importance.

[1] E. W. Bovill, *Caravans of the old Sahara* (1931), ch. 6.

[2] H. Bonnet Reverón, 'Descripción de las Canarias en el año 1526 [sic], hecha por T. Nicols, factor inglés', *Revista de Historia* (Tenerife), v (1933), 206–16; Cioranescu, *Thomas Nichols*, pp. 83–4 (describes Nichols' account as 'un papel importante en el desarrollo de la historiografía canaria').

16

Guinea

P. E. H. HAIR

In his 1598 Preface, Hakluyt distinguished between the voyages in the northern seas, where the English were explorers and innovators, and the voyages in the more southern seas, where they were only following up the Portuguese and the Spaniards. Africa, being wholly to the south, therefore received less attention than did, say, Muscovy or North America. In terms of full continents, the material on Africa comes a poor third to the material on America and Asia – the proportion of pages devoted to Africa being only about one-tenth, compared to about one-third and one-quarter devoted to the other continents. Moreover, the printed voyages concentrated on a small part of Africa. Apart from accounts of North and North-east Africa, and apart from two accounts of Lancaster's voyage of 1591 to the East, which briefly visited the Cape of Good Hope and the east African coast, Hakluyt's material on Africa was limited in geographical cover-age to the first fifteen hundred miles of the four thousand miles of coastline of middle Africa, that is, to the Guinea coast up to the Benin river. Before Lancaster's voyage, the coasts of southern and eastern Africa were virtually unknown to English seamen: in his first edition, Hakluyt's only references to these coasts were to ships passing, and sometimes sighting, the Cape of Good Hope. How-ever, if *Principal navigations* thus fairly reflected the severe limitations of contemporary English activity in Africa, it has to be recollected that Hakluyt sponsored the translation of two works by foreign writers whose publication revealed to English readers great tracts of the continent as yet closed to English influence, Leo Africanus' account of North Africa, the Sahara, and the west and central Sudan (originally published 1550, translated by Pory and published in 1600), and Pigafetta's account of the Congo (originally published 1591, translated by Hartwell and published in 1597).[1]

About a score of the voyages narrated in any detail in *Principal navigations* were to Guinea and contain material on the region.[2] But nearly half of these were voyages to America as well as to Guinea, and often the material on Guinea is briefer and less detailed than the material on America. It is clear that sometimes the Guinea narrative was abbreviated, before or after reaching Hakluyt's hands, in order to increase the dramatic impact of the episodes in America: the various accounts of the Hawkins voyage of 1567–8 are typical in this.[3]

A small part of the Guinea material had already appeared in

[1] Furthermore, English activity in southern Africa increased greatly between 1600 and 1616, the year of Hakluyt's death. The papers which Hakluyt collected during this period, and which were subsequently published by Purchas, include much material on southern Africa in the following accounts of voyages to the East Indies: on the Cape of Good Hope, in accounts of the first and sixth voyages (Lancaster, Middleton, Downton); on Madagascar, in accounts of the third and twelfth voyages (Middleton, Payton); on east Africa, in the account of the fourth voyage (Jones). There is also material on Angola in Anthony Knivet's account of his experiences as a prisoner of the Portuguese. Thus, had Hakluyt published a third edition in 1615, the concentration on Guinea would have been much less evident.

[2] Accounts of the following voyages contain material on Guinea (an asterisk indicates supplementary material added in the second edition; a dagger indicates material only in the second edition): *c.* 1530 (William Hawkins), 1553–4 (Wyndham), 1554–5 (Lok/Gaynsh), 1555–6 (Towerson), 1556–7 (Towerson), 1558 (Towerson), 1562–3 (Baker/Rutter),* 1562–3 (Hawkins), 1563–4 (Baker), 1564–5 (Carlet), 1564–5 (Hawkins), 1566–7 (Fenner), 1567–9 (Hawkins),* 1577–80 (Drake),* 1582–3 (Fenton), 1583 (Cotton), 1585–6 (Drake),† 1586–7 (Cumberland), 1586–8 (Cavendish),* 1588–9 (Newton/Walsh),* 1590 (Newton),† 1591 (Rainolds/Dassel),† 1596 (Shirley).† In addition, there is material on the organization of the following voyages, proposed or undertaken, and of trade in general: 1482 (Tintam/Fabian), 1561–2 (Lok),† 1588 (patent to Exeter merchants), 1592 (patent to Taunton merchants).† Finally, Keeling's account of the third voyage to the East Indies, which includes material on Sierra Leone, was among the papers collected by Hakluyt and eventually published by Purchas.

[3] Whereas the account of the voyage in the Cotton MS, Otho E. VIII, ff. 17–41v (printed in J. A. Williamson, *Sir John Hawkins* (1927), pp. 491–534) considered the Guinea episodes sufficiently important to devote over 5,000 words to them.

print – two out of the three accounts of the 1567–8 voyage (published 1569 and 1591),[1] two poems by Robert Baker concerning
voyages begun in 1562 and 1563 (published probably in 1568),[2]
and the accounts of the first two voyages of the 1550s. The latter
were first published by Richard Eden in 1555, and reprinted by
Richard Willes in 1577. (It is of some interest, and does not
appear to have been noted before, that Hakluyt copied the texts
from Willes, not from Eden: he follows Willes in a cut reducing
Eden's animadversions on Captain Thomas Wyndham.)[3] Eden's
Guinea accounts have of course a wider significance than their
African content, since they represent the earliest attempt by an
Englishman to collect and print narratives of contemporary
English voyages to any part of the new-found world. Even the
style of their presentation by Eden – an introduction and commentary in the first person (describing, for instance, a visit to a
dockyard to inspect one of the ships, and a call at a merchant's

[1] *A true declaration of the troublesome voyadge of M. Iohn Haukins . . . in . . . 1567. and
1568.* (1569) (S.T.C. 12961); *The rare trauailes of Iob Hortop* (1591) (there is a
facsimile reprint, with notes by G. R. G. Conway, Mexico, 1928), which was
revised and re-issued as *The trauailes of an Englishman . . . By I. H.* (1591) (S.T.C.
13828). Hakluyt used the revised version, which was perhaps made in order to
bring Hortop's first recollections into line with the accounts of the same voyage
published by Hakluyt in 1589.

[2] Perhaps from *The brefe dyscource of Roberte Baker in Gynney India Portyngyule and
Fraunce . . .*, a work licensed by the Stationers' Company to Frances Coldoke
in 1568 (Arber, *Transcript*, I, 363), but of which no copies are extant. Should
it be subsequently discovered that this work was not the source of Baker's poems,
we would have to revise our judgement that Hakluyt borrowed all available
printed sources on Guinea voyages.

[3] Twelve lines on Wyndham's character in Richard Eden, *The decades . . .* (1555),
p. 345v, were cut in Richard Willes, *The history of trauayle . . .* (1577), p. 338v,
as they are in Hakluyt, 1589, p. 85. A textual error in Hakluyt also shows that
he was following Willes. The error involves the omission of eight words in the
very first (and very long) sentence of Eden's first narrative (p. 343): '. . . fortresses,
or rather [blockhouses amonge naked people, thinke them selues woorthy] to bee
lordes of halfe the worlde'. The omission of the words in brackets by Hakluyt
makes the sentence grammatically and semantically incomplete, therefore the
omission was not deliberate. The omitted words do not form a line in Eden,
but they do in Willes (p. 336v, line 12), therefore Hakluyt was copying
Willes.

house to study the skull of an elephant), and an original feature, the inclusion of a faithfully copied sea log[1] – must have influenced Hakluyt a generation later.

Hakluyt appears to have borrowed all the available printed accounts of Guinea voyages; but how successful was he in obtaining manuscript and oral narratives? He was in a strong position to obtain such as were available. He seems to have obtained the manuscript account of the voyage of 1564–5 from John Hawkins himself; and to have persuaded Hawkins to supply information about the 1562–3 voyage, and about his father's pioneering voyages to Guinea and Brazil *c.* 1530. Since the chief adventurers of almost all the other Guinea voyages of the 1550s and 1560s were a group of London merchants involved in other ventures overseas, particularly in Muscovy, and since Hak-luyt obtained from this circle a notable series of records relating to the Muscovy trade, it is almost certain that he tapped the same source for many of his Guinea accounts.[2] He was persistent in his search for information. When he dropped Baker's rather uninformative poems in 1598, he replaced them with an unpub-lished account of the 1562 voyage;[3] and he added to the later

---

[1] Or, at least, a lightly edited sea log; in the printed text, there are no entries for some days at sea, which presumably indicates editing. It has been pointed out that this log constitutes the earliest known English 'rutter' for Atlantic (though not, of course, for trans-Atlantic) voyaging: D. W. Waters, *The art of navigation in England in Elizabethan and early Stuart times* (1958), p. 91.

[2] On Hakluyt's connections with the London merchants, see Quinn and Skelton, edd., *PN (1589)*, I (1965), xxxviii–xlii. The Guinea adventurers have not been systematically studied as a business group (though there are useful notes in an unpublished thesis, K. M. Eliot, 'The beginnings of English trade with Guinea and the East Indies 1550–1599', University of London, 1915), but almost all the leading individuals are to be found in a list of Muscovy adventurers, with biographical details, in T. S. Willan, *The Muscovy merchants of 1555* (Manchester, 1953), pp. 75–135.

[3] Hakluyt states that Baker's first poem and Rutter's account relate to the same voyage, although the title of the poem gives October as the date of departure while Rutter describes a voyage which began in the February following. (It is wrongly stated in Quinn and Skelton, edd., *PN (1589)*, I (1965), l, n. 3, that it was Baker's second poem which Hakluyt claimed to replace.) The details by which Baker's voyages can be identified and dated appear solely in their titles,

edition documents about the organization of voyages in 1561 and 1564, and an additional account of the 1588 Benin voyage, as well as accounts of voyages since the first edition appeared, to Benin in 1590 and to the Gambia in 1591. Possibly Hakluyt only came on the additional material relating to the voyages of the 1560s after 1589, since he noted in the second edition that he had searched in vain for an account of the 1564 voyage: 'I could not by any meanes come by [one], although I have vsed all possible indeuour for the obtaining of the same'. On the other hand, the possibility cannot be ruled out that in 1589 he kept some accounts up his sleeve, perhaps those which he considered less significant or less interesting. Conceivably, he preferred the literary flavour of Baker's poem to the prose account in 1589, but changed his mind in 1598. While it can be said that today we know of very little additional material on many of Hakluyt's Guinea voyages – and this additional material is mainly in archives which were not open to Hakluyt (e.g. the records of the High Court of Admir-alty)[1] – it would be rash to assume that what is available today represents all that was available either in 1589 or in 1598.

The English-backed voyage of Bartolomeu Bayão to the Cape Verde islands and perhaps to Sierra Leone in 1564, an unsuccessful English voyage to Mina in 1565, Lovell's voyage to Guinea in 1566–7, a Hawkins-backed voyage in 1571, William Hawkins' voyage to the Cape Verde islands and perhaps to the Guinea mainland in 1582–3 – these voyages out of England are briefly reported in archives but are not documented by Hakluyt.[2]

the texts being vague in the extreme about time and place; the titles may very well have been supplied by Hakluyt, and there are other grounds for supposing that some of the details in the titles are inaccurate.

[1] Quinn and Skelton, edd., *PN* (*1589*), I (1965), xlv. However, it should be noted that at one point in his second edition Hakluyt speaks of employing 'proofes of record in the Admiralty' (in Barker's voyage 1576, *PN*, III (1600), 83.

[2] On these voyages, see Williamson, *Hawkins* (1927), pp. 99 (Bayão), 114 (1565), 122–6 (1566–7), 231 (1571), 403–5 (1582–3); A. Álvares d'Almada, *Tratado breve dos rios de Guiné* (*1594*) (Lisbon, 1946), p. 86 (Bayão). Hakluyt also failed to publish (in this case, presumably, to find) any English material on the Tintam/Fabian proposed voyage of 1482, probably the earliest English display

There is no reason to assume that Hakluyt intended to provide an account of every English voyage, but on the other hand it also cannot be assumed that the reason why he omitted mention of these particular voyages was that no accounts were extant when he began collecting. Since the last three of the named voyages were carried out by agents or relatives of John Hawkins, it is difficult to believe that it was impossible for Hakluyt to obtain at least oral narratives. It is perhaps significant that one voyage recorded in the first edition was not recorded in the second: when Baker's poem relating to the 1563 voyage was dropped, no substitute account was provided. Of course Hakluyt was not intending a work of strict historical inquiry and documentation. If he was prepared to leave out one voyage in his second edition, apparently in order to economize in space, it is reasonable to suspect that he was also selective, for the same reason – and possibly for other reasons – in his choice of voyages in the first edition; and therefore that some manuscript accounts available to him may have been set aside.

In the case of two voyages to Guinea and then to America, we know that substantial documentation was not employed by Hakluyt. Journals now in the Pepysian Library (Magdalene College, Cambridge) and the British Museum were not used for Fenton's voyage of 1582, and a very full account (unusually full on the Guinea episodes) also in the British Museum was not used for Hawkins' 1567-8 voyage.[1] Though it is unfortunately not known where these manuscripts were in Hakluyt's day, it is likely that they were within easy reach of, if not directly with, either Hawkins or the London merchants. We can only speculate why these manuscripts did not reach print. But it may be relevant, and might indicate that Hakluyt deliberately disregarded them, that in each case other material on the voyage was printed.

of interest in Guinea: see D. B. Quinn, 'Edward IV and exploration', *Mariner's Mirror*, XXI (1935), 275–84, on pp. 279–80.

[1] See E. G. R. Taylor, *The troublesome voyage of Captain Edward Fenton* (1957), and Williamson, *Hawkins*, pp. 143, 491–534. The extracts from Madox's diary printed by Professor Taylor give an inadequate impression of the richness of material on Guinea in this source; a complete edition is being prepared by Professor Elizabeth Storey Donno of Columbia University.

Moreover, as far as the Guinea section of each voyage is concerned, there were delicate matters involved (quarrels among the
leaders and nautical incompetence in 1582, secret trading relations
with the Portuguese in 1567–8) which may have made the
owners of the papers, or Hakluyt, consider it inadvisable that
fuller details should appear in print. Whatever the reason for the
failure to print these sources, no adequate account of the Guinea
section of the voyages could be written today without recourse to
them; and we should have to add for the 1567–8 voyage, not
only the Spanish manuscript sources (in Seville and Mexico)
which were of course inaccessible to Hakluyt, but also some
documentation which was among the English state papers in
Hakluyt's day but which was not suitable for his design, the book
of Portuguese complaints of 1568.

Hakluyt's editorial treatment of the manuscripts he printed
cannot now be exactly assessed, since none of the originals appears
to be extant. But he copied faithfully and fully the printed sources
(though we might fault him for copying Willes rather than Eden),
apart from numerous verbal and other minor emendations (most
obvious in the spelling of names, e.g. Senegal, Jalofo and Antony
Anus Pinteado instead of Eden/Willes' Senega, Jaiofo and
Antonides Pinteado). However, he was less faithful to his own
text of 1589 in his second edition: he abbreviated five of the
Guinea accounts, three only slightly but two severely.[1] For this

---

[1] Cuts were made in the accounts of the following voyages: 1554–5, 1555–6,
1556–7, 1564–5 (Sparke), 1582–3, the cuts becoming more severe, curiously,
in this chronological order. But it must also be noted that Hakluyt occasionally
added small details in his second edition. For instance, whereas the account of
the 1554–5 voyage, in Eden and in Hakluyt's first edition, named only one
officer in the expedition, Gaynsh, the master of one ship and probably the author
of the account, in 1599 Hakluyt added a note, 'The captaine whereof was M.
John Lok' – information he presumably received after 1589 from some person
who had been involved in this voyage forty years earlier. Another useful addition
and correction in the second edition concerned an even earlier voyage, or rather set
of voyages, those of William Hawkins to Guinea and Brazil. In 1589 the brief
account was entitled 'a voyage . . . in the yeere 1530', but in 1600 this was changed
to 'A brief relation of two sundry voyages . . . in the yeere 1530 and 1532'. Possibly the additional date had been supplied by John Hawkins. Yet, very strangely,
even the corrected title is inadequate, for the text clearly describes three voyages.

cutting – as for the failure to mention certain voyages – political reasons have been suggested, principally changes in English official attitudes to Portugal and to France.[1] In detail, this theory is difficult to maintain. Examination of the cut passages shows that the vast majority were omitted merely for reasons of economy in space and drama in narration: thus, as a general rule, entries in sea journals for days when only routine navigational details were noted were cut in the second edition. Possibly a few cuts were made in the interests of English prestige: entries relating to errors in seamanship were suppressed, and in Ward's journal of the 1582 voyage some of the cuts removed evidence of quarrels between the leaders. On the other hand, a good deal of evidence on both points was allowed to remain. Two cuts in the accounts of the 1556 and 1558 voyages related to French defeats, yet it really must be doubted whether the cuts were made to spare French feelings since substantial evidence relating to the defeats was retained.[2] Finally, since the cut material was already in print in the first edition, alterations in the second edition do not necessarily tell us much about Hakluyt's approach to the editing of unpublished manuscripts, when the cutting of material could produce total suppression.

We must therefore reserve judgement on many points relating to Hakluyt's editing of his Guinea material. We can be more certain about the value of the published material. The English were late arrivals in Guinea, and their activities between 1550 and 1600 were limited, in frequency and geographical range, com‑ pared with those of the Portuguese, who had established intimate trading and social relations with the African peoples of the coast a century earlier; or even compared with those of the French, who began visiting the coast in strength in the 1530s. On the face of it, English accounts might be expected to have contributed little to contemporary knowledge of Guinea. But, as it happened, the

[1] Quinn and Skelton, edd., *PN* (*1589*), 1 (1965), lii, n. 1; cf. Williamson, *Hawkins*, p. 404, and Parks, *Hakluyt*, p. 128.

[2] In the 1558 account, the entry for 5 April describing the English seizure of French ships was retained, while the entry for 22 June listing the Frenchmen captured and the victuals they were given was cut.

Portuguese had not published their fullest accounts, apparently for reasons of policy, and French accounts were surprisingly few and thin. The English therefore went to Guinea knowing little about the region, and this no doubt encouraged them to describe their experiences, on their return, at some length. Sheer ignorance gave the English accounts freshness and informality: they displayed a curiosity about the detail of the African background which must have seemed to the better-informed Portuguese mere naivety. These qualities made the English accounts thoroughly readable: they appealed to the English reader of the time as they still do to the English reader of today. They helped to inspire later Guinea voyages and ventures; and we are told of one voyage of 1607 during which a copy of the *Principal navigations* was produced and consulted, to enable the navigators to decide on a suitable watering-place in Guinea. Purchas, who published the anecdote, noted: 'M. Hackluits books of Voyages are of great profit. This saued the Company, as Sir Th. Smith affirmed to me, 20000. pounds, which they had bin endamaged if they had returned home, which necessitie had constrayned, if that Booke had not giuen light.'[1] No doubt the accounts also influenced English attitudes to the peoples of Africa (envisaged as 'Othello's countrymen' by a modern African scholar):[2] in general, the English found the Africans curious, barbarous and untrustworthy (and they reserved their strongest contempt for the superstitious and malevolent Portuguese).

Nevertheless, however influential for a time, Hakluyt's material on Guinea was fairly soon superseded, for the English reader, by accounts of later English voyages in Purchas (1625), by the Jesuit letters from Upper Guinea (in Portuguese 1603–11, in French 1614, summarized in Purchas), by Jobson's detailed account of the Gambia (1623, also in Purchas), and above all by Dutch sources, beginning with De Marees on the Gold Coast

---

[1] Purchas, *Pilgrimes*, 1 (1625), 188.

[2] Eldred Jones, *Othello's countrymen* (1965), ch. 1. Hakluyt's Guinea voyages are also scrutinized in Winthrop P. Jordan, *White over Black* (Williamsburg, 1968), to provide evidence of racial intolerance on the part of the Elizabethan English towards black Africans.

(in Dutch 1602, summarized in Purchas), continuing through Dutch maps and translations of Dutch coastal guides, and reach' ing full flood in Dapper's account of all Africa (in Dutch 1668, English translation 1670) and Bosman's account of Gold Coast and Benin (in Dutch 1704, English translation 1705). Barbot's lengthy compilation on Guinea, written in French but partly prepared in England and finally published only in English (1732), borrowed heavily from seventeenth-century writers but made no use of Hakluyt.[1]

In the twentieth century, systematic study of the internal history of Guinea has begun, and *Principal navigations* is being em' ployed as historical documentation, not only of European trade and influence on the coast, but also of the local ethnohistory. At the moment of writing, they provide a fairly substantial part of the available documentation for the period 1550–1600: thus, a recent article on tribal wars in Sierra Leone in the 1550s leans heavily on evidence drawn from the accounts of the Hawkins' voyages in the following decade.[2] In general, *Principal navigations* has not yet been thoroughly investigated by historians of Africa, and evidence from it is likely to prove even more useful during the next few years of research. However, the evidence from English sources will eventually be outweighed, quantitatively and prob' ably qualitatively, by evidence from the vast but as yet unorganized Portuguese archives (enough has already been revealed to make this clear), and much also remains to be discovered in Dutch archives (though this generally relates to a slightly later period). What this amounts to is that Hakluyt published the greater part of the relatively slim English documentation contemporaneously. Had there been a scholarly interest in Guinea history during the next three centuries, Hakluyt's published evidence on the later sixteenth century would have been of major importance. But in

---

[1] Though Barbot named the early English voyagers: J. Barbot, *A description of the coasts of North and South Guinea* (1732), p. 146.

[2] W. Rodney, 'A reconsideration of the Mane invasions of Sierra Leone', *Journal of African History*, VII (1967), 219–46. The lists of words in African languages in Hakluyt's account of the 1555–6 voyage have been examined in D. Dalby and P. E. H. Hair, '"Le langaige de Guynee": a sixteenth century vocabulary from the Pepper Coast', *African Language Studies*, V (1964), 174–91, on p. 188.

the later twentieth century, we must expect Hakluyt's evidence, though indispensable at certain points – and in particular for the study of English influence on the coast – to be only of increasingly minor importance for the general history of Guinea.

The history of English mercantile venture in Guinea, as part of the history of English overseas enterprise, is of course an older study, and for a century Hakluyt has provided a basis and frame work for research in this field. However, during this period, scholars have also ransacked libraries and archives for manuscript sources, with considerable success, and it may be fairly said that the printed *Principal navigations* continue to be used, apart from the reason of convenience of consultation, only because the manu scripts on which the text was based are no longer extant. Non survival is so regularly the case that it would seem that Hakluyt collected the only manuscript copy of any account, and that this copy was destroyed in the printing process. It follows that we must ask an ungracious question: would we now be better off for sources if Hakluyt had not made his collection? On the one hand, manuscripts collected by Hakluyt are not now extant (and whatever we think of Hakluyt's editing, we know that the texts he passed on to Purchas were mangled in printing), while manu scripts he did not collect are extant. Yet, on the other hand, Hakluyt has preserved for us Baker's poems, whose original print has not survived. Surely some of the manuscripts would have been similarly lost in the course of centuries; and may it not have been the good influence of the *Principal navigations* which enabled some of the accounts which were not included to survive?

17
India

M. F. STRACHAN

There is no record of an Englishman setting foot in India between the Bishop of Sherborne's visit in 883 and the arrival at Goa of the Jesuit Father, Thomas Stevens, in 1579. Hakluyt therefore had a relatively easy task in presenting a picture of purely English achievement which was his aim in the first edition of the *Principall navigations*. At the time of its publication the first English trading reconnaissance to India led by John Newbery and Ralph Fitch was still uncompleted. Hakluyt knew both leaders personally and supplied them with such information as he possessed before they left. This included Thomas Stevens' letter to his father written within a few days of his arrival at Goa, which probably reached Hakluyt through his cousin, who knew the Stevens family. Stevens was no doubt surprised, when he befriended Newbery and his party in Goa, to discover that they knew so much about his adventures; but these cannot have been of much practical use to Newbery and Fitch who travelled overland from Aleppo, as the whole letter, save a few lines at the end, concerns his voyage round the Cape of Good Hope.

Apart from Stevens' letter and some letters from Newbery and Fitch, of which all but two were written before they reached India, the only up-to-date information in the first part (voyages to the south and south-east) of the first edition are some notes made by William Barrett the consul at Aleppo. Barrett's contribution includes a freight tariff from Ormuz to Chaul, Goa, and Cochin, notes on Indian customs charges, the weights, measures and money of Goa and Cochin, a table of monsoon winds and a list of commodities and their places of origin which is by no means confined to Indian produce. This information is derived primarily from sources which are neither English nor Indian and its incompleteness is a measure of English ignorance about India at that time.

Queen Elizabeth's letter[1] to Akbar which Newbery carried to India is another example of this ignorance. The letter was addressed to 'Yeladin el Kubar', a rough phonetic rendering which is improved upon in the second edition, and Akbar is described as King of Cambay. At this time the Great Mogul had reigned for over a quarter of a century, and Cambay was a mere province in the vast territories of northern India over which he ruled.

If the first edition of the *Principall navigations* is inevitably short of hard facts, it is rich in propaganda and hopeful speculation. Hakluyt was interested quite as much in how to get to India as he was in what India was like when one arrived there. He collected material about all the routes, both known and supposed; not only the route of the Portuguese via the Cape of Good Hope, the established overland route via Aleppo and Baghdad and the route via Russia into northern India, but also the supposed North-east and North-west Passages. Robert Thorne's 'A declaration of the Indies', written as early as 1527, Sir George Peckham's *A true reporte of the late discoueries* (1583) and Sir Humfrey Gilbert's *A discourse of a discouerie for a new passage to Cataia* (1576) all pointed to the Portuguese achievements and urged that England should not be left behind. One may smile at Gilbert's suggestion that the description in the Book of Esther of the pomp of King Ahasuerus 'who reigned from India euen vnto Ethiopia' is evidence that English cloth would be popular in India, but he is on surer ground when he asserts that one of the advantages of opening up a commercially competitive route to India would be to rid the country of 'loiterers, vagabonds and such like idle persons' because there would be 'occasion to set poore mens children to learne handie crafts, and thereby to make trifles and such like, which the Indians . . . doe much esteeme'.[2]

In the second edition of *Principal navigations* all the material about India in the first edition is retained except that Sir John Mandeville's travels are replaced by the account of Friar Odoric of Friuli (Odoric da Pordenone), who was the original source of Mandeville's information. The date of the first English traveller to reach India is, in the second edition, pushed back to 883 when,

[1] *PN* (1589), p. 207.   [2] *PN* (1589), p. 609.

according to William of Malmesbury, Bishop Sighelm of Sherborne took alms to the Christians of Saint Thomas on behalf of King Alfred and returned home safely bringing many precious stones and costly spices.

The pattern of the second edition allowed for the inclusion of foreign authors. It can be stated with certainty that no Indian sources were available to Hakluyt. There was no Indian navigational literature and the manuscript chronicles would have been of little interest to prospective merchant adventurers even if they had been procurable. Arab manuscripts were similarly inaccessible, and Hakluyt failed to acquire the works of an Arab cosmographer[1] which he asked Newbery to obtain for him. The obvious and potentially most fruitful foreign sources of information about India were the Portuguese. They had been in India longer than the Moguls; their main base at Goa had been established for nearly a century and from it a chain of fortress trading posts extended along the west coast and up the east coast of India. Their navigators, merchants and administrators were observant and literate, yet Portuguese contributions to the *Principal navigations* are virtually nonexistent. This was not accidental. Hakluyt knew the Portuguese language and was well aware of their navigational and trading achievements. In Paris he had talked with several of Dom António's best captains and pilots. He had translated and published the Portuguese António Galvão's *The discoveries of the world* (1601) and his annotations to that work show that he was conversant with the writings of Barros, the historian who was Galvão's original source for the section on India. Admittedly there is nothing much in either Barros or Galvão to help English navigators or merchants. The Portuguese took care not to broadcast information which could be useful to their competitors, but we know that Hakluyt also obtained much Portuguese intelligence which was never published. Among the documents which Hakluyt gave Newbery before his departure for India were notes by a Portuguese, Francisco Fernandes. Hakluyt never made these notes public, possibly because they contained too much useful commercial information. When Sir John

---

[1] Ismael Abulfeda, *PN* (1589), p. 208.

Borough took the *Madre de Deus* in the Azores in 1592 the geographical materials, including maps and the Portuguese 'Register of the East Indies', were handed over to Hakluyt. According to the unknown writer of the account of the action, the English gained by the capture 'the broad light of full and perfect knowledge' of 'those secret trades & Indian riches, which hitherto lay strangely hidden and cunningly concealed from vs'.[1] This may be true; neither Hakluyt nor the official censor saw fit to exclude or qualify the statement.

Yet there is some evidence that Hakluyt did not realize the full importance of the Portuguese in India. He made a curious marginal comment on Fitch's letter from Goa which he did not amend in the second edition: 'The Italians our great enemies for the trade in the East.'[2] The immediate cause of this comment was that an Italian had contrived the imprisonment by the Portuguese of Fitch and his companions. Though in this instance Hakluyt's observation was strikingly wide of the mark, it is a fact that a Venetian merchant, Cesare Federici, provided the most valuable addition, English or foreign, to the second edition. The translation of Federici's *Viaggio* by Thomas Hickocke, which Hakluyt used, had already appeared in London in 1588, the year after its publication in Venice. This account, based on eighteen years travelling and trading, mainly in India, vividly records the author's adventures, local customs and trading conditions together with much sound practical advice, even down to details of the effects and furniture with which a visiting merchant should equip himself.

As regards English activities since the publication of the first edition, Newbery had perished, either in India or on the way home. Fitch had returned home safely, but his published account is a great disappointment. He was the first Englishman to travel through central India, present himself at the Great Mogul's Court, sail down the Ganges to Bengal, visit Ceylon and Cochin, and come home to tell his story. Yet that story is an almost slavish copy of Federici whenever their routes coincide, and when he is covering new ground the narrative is extraordinarily meagre. Hakluyt says that on Fitch's return home in 1591 he presented 'an

[1] *PN* (1598–1600), II, ii, 198; see pp. 296–7, 305–6, below. [2] *PN* (1589), p. 212.

ample relation of his wonderfull trauailes' to Lord Burghley,[1] which this certainly is not. Here may well be another case of the censorship which presumably prevented Hakluyt from printing information from Portuguese sources, and almost certainly accounts for the fact that he makes no mention of Newbery's first journey to Syria and Palestine, or his second to Ormuz during which he had learnt much about the routes between India and Persia and had come to the conclusion that commerce with India overland was perfectly feasible.

The historian, and indeed the general reader, will always be grateful that Hakluyt presented the material of the *Principal naviga-tions* whole and, so far as one can judge, uncut. How often does one wish that his successor, Purchas, had done the same. Hakluyt's method of arranging his material and the fact that his own index is rudimentary do, however, mean that important information about India lies hidden in sections of the *Principal navigations* other than that devoted to voyages to the south and south-east. For example Anthony Jenkinson produced useful intelligence about commerce with India on his journey from Moscow to Bukhara in 1558. Securing privileges of trade with India was one of Jenkinson's aims on the Muscovy Company's eighth journey three years later, and in 1568 Arthur Edwards, another servant of the Muscovy Company, urged the opening of a trade route to India via Russia and Persia, based on his own observations and experience.[2] Alison Quinn's splendid index to the 1965 reprint of the first edition of the *Principall navigations* has helped to bring this scattered information to light.

The appearance of the second edition of the *Principal navigations* coincided with the birth of the East India Company and the real start of English enterprise in India. Hakluyt played an important role as advisor to the new Company.[3] The memoranda which he drew up for the East India Company have survived[4] and are

[1] *PN* (1598–1600), II, dedication to Sir Robert Cecil.
[2] *PN* (1589), pp. 356, 363, 414.
[3] For fuller details, see Parks, *Hakluyt*, pp. 153–8.
[4] Bodleian, MS Arch. Selden B 8, printed in *Divers voyages*, ed. J. Winter Jones (Hakluyt Society, 1850), pp. 151–71 and Taylor, *Hakluyts*, II, 476–82.

remarkable for the incomplete and fragmentary nature of the information which they contain. While the sources upon which he drew include some captured manuscript material, most are from printed works and the two most important authorities are Cesare Federici, and Linschoten whose *Itinerario* had been trans'lated and published in 1598 at Hakluyt's instigation.

Hakluyt continued to collect accounts of voyages to India cer'tainly until 1615, the year before his death, and now in the last decade of his life there was plenty of English achievement to record and preserve. Purchas, who published what escaped his own and the cen'sor's editing, is scrupulous in acknowledging what he received from Hakluyt, and so we know that virtually the whole of Purchas, *Pilgrimes*, part 1, book 3, was inherited from him. This contains the travels of John Mildenhall, Captain William Hawkins' account of his experiences at the Court of the Great Mogul, Sir Henry Middleton's account of the East India Company's sixth voyage and extracts from the journal of his lieutenant Nicholas Downton.

If attention has been drawn to the sketchy knowledge of India which can be gained from Hakluyt's work, nevertheless the *Principal navigations* gives a full account of English achievement down to the publication of each edition. From an early date the book was carried on board East India Company vessels and there is at least one recorded instance in which the practical navigational information it contained saved the Company a great deal of money.[1] That was in 1607 and no doubt caused Hakluyt satis'faction. He must have been pleased also when, in 1611, the Company sent out a consignment of literature to its factory at Surat including 'Master Hackluites Voyadges, to recreate their spirittes with varietie of historie'.[2] But the most important aspect of Hakluyt's work is his activity as a successful propagandist and persistent advocate of trade with India. No doubt the East India Company would have come into existence in any case, but its early history might have been different and we should certainly know less about the forerunners and early pioneers if Hakluyt had never lived.

[1] Purchas, *Pilgrimes*, I (1625), iii, 188.
[2] G. Birdwood and W. Foster, edd., *The first letter book of the East India Company* (1893), p. 419. See pp. 324, 326, below.

18

The Far East

D. F. LACH

Examination of Hakluyt's materials on the Far East reveals that he published *only* those accounts written by observers who had actually travelled in Asia (including therein Russia and the Levant). He reproduces no writings from antiquity or the early Middle Ages. Substantial texts on the Far East begin with the thirteenth-century accounts of John of Plano Carpini and William of Rubruquis, and conclude with the latest (*c.* 1590–6) Jesuit reports on Korea and 'Zuegara' (northern Japan).

In both editions Hakluyt used the best English sources available. But, as he clearly realized, the direct contacts before 1600 of the English with the Asian countries were few, sporadic, and superficial. Consequently, in his second edition he sought to supplement the English writings with a few selections from the earlier travel collections of Ramusio, Eden and Willes and from the separately published continental writings on Asia.

In his first edition the Asian materials were limited to a few Newbery letters on India, the report of Cavendish on maritime south-east Asia and China, and incidental references to eastern Asia in the narratives of the north-eastern and Levantine travellers. These materials were reprinted in the second edition and were given background by the addition of scattered medieval references to early English contacts with India, of the narratives of the overland missions of John of Plano Carpini, William of Rubruquis, and Odoric of Pordenone, of the letters from Mercator and Ortelius commenting on the geographical implications of the medieval explorations, and of a brief passage translated from Ramusio on the Arab voyages.

Hakluyt also added new materials on the Far East to the modern sections of the second edition which were derived from both foreign and domestic sources. The most important of these were the translation of the voyage of Cesare Federici (Anglicized as Caesar Frederick), the 'excellent treatise' on China by Duarte Sande, the account of China by Galeote Pereira, the Jesuit letters on Japan and Korea, and the description by Francisco Gali (de Gualle) of the round-trip voyage across the Pacific between Acapulco and China. These foreign authorities were supple-mented by the addition of Ralph Fitch's account of India and south-east Asia, the narratives relating to the circumnavigation of Drake, and the accounts by three participants in James Lancaster's voyage to the East Indies. Hakluyt also included in his second edition a substantial amount of supporting material: the letters of Queen Elizabeth to China and Cambay, the brief report by Linschoten on the imprisonment in Goa of Newbery and Fitch, the letters from the field of Thomas Stevens and Frey Peter of Lisbon, the notes and instructions prepared for some of the expeditions, and William Barret's tables on moneys, weights, and measures used in the Eastern trade.

Hakluyt evidently tried, though not always successfully, to avoid reprinting accounts that had already appeared in earlier travel collections or in works previously published separately such as those prepared by John Frampton, Thomas Nichols, and Robert Parke. For example, he does not republish Ludovico Varthema's *Viaggio* (first published at Rome in 1510) as trans-lated by Eden and published in English by Willes in 1577, or the *Marco Polo* translated by Frampton from Spanish and pub-lished separately in 1579, or Mendoza's *China* translated from Spanish by Parke and published separately in 1588. On the other hand, he republished Pereira's account of China (1565) issued in English by Willes in 1577, as well as the extracts from the Jesuit letters on Japan which Willes first brought over into English. Evidently the guiding principle, here as elsewhere, was to include only the most recent first-hand accounts available.

While undoubtedly aware of the high quality and comprehen-sive character of the Portuguese sources, Hakluyt selected for publication only Pereira's account of China from among the relatively large number of first-hand Portuguese materials that were available in his day. The invaluable accounts of maritime

Asia (the epitome of Duarte Barbosa and the extracts from Tomé Pires) that were published in Ramusio he does not include among his selections from the great Italian collection. Though Nichols' translation of the first book of Castanheda's *História* was published in 1582, Hakluyt makes no attempt to bring into his collection any part of Castanheda's large work (eight books of which were published at Coimbra between 1551 and 1561 and seven books of which were translated into Italian and published at Venice in 1577-8) even though it was based in substantial part on the author's lengthy experience in India. Likewise, he makes no effort to include anything from the *Tractado* (Evora, 1569) of Gaspar da Cruz, the first post-discovery book on China written on the basis of the author's experiences there. Hakluyt seems to have been totally unaware of or completely disinterested in Garcia da Orta's *Coloquios* (Goa, 1563) and the Latin versions of it first published at Antwerp in 1567 by Charles de L'Écluse (Clusius) and reissued by the Plantin press in revised editions four times before the end of the sixteenth century. The *Commentarios* of Albuquerque (Lisbon, 1557; rev. ed., 1576) compiled by the great Captain's son seem likewise to have escaped Hakluyt's attention. Nor did it seem to occur to him that the *Lusiads* of Camões, first published in 1572, could be used as a primary source for Eastern names, places, and practices; but Jan van Linschoten, Hakluyt's Dutch contemporary, freely borrowed from the *Lusiads* in the preparation of his monumental *Itinerario* (Amsterdam, 1595-6).

Of the writings of non-Iberian continental voyagers, Hakluyt included in his collection only the accounts by John of Plano Carpini, William of Rubruquis, Odoric of Pordenone, and Cesare Federici. He ignores the letters of the early Florentine factors published in Ramusio, the separately issued *Meerfahrt* (Augsburg, 1509) of Balthasar Springer, and the series of Indian travelogues by Venetian emissaries and merchants included in the *Viaggi fatti alla Tana* (Venice, 1543). While these travel accounts may have been disregarded because they were not of recent enough date, this same basis for omission could not have applied to the *Viaggio* of Gasparo Balbi published at Venice in 1590. Essentially a commercial handbook, Balbi's work would have provided data on trade in India that was more recent and more reliable than that given in Federici's account. The neglect of Balbi can probably be best accounted for by the fact that Ralph Fitch's account was presumably even more recent and certainly better on the interior regions of India.

Hakluyt's strict adherence to the rule of publishing only the writings of observers and participants was probably responsible for his failure to include relevant materials from the available histories, cosmographies,[1] scientific books, maps, and engravings, many of which were based on primary sources not generally available. Most notable is his omission of all reference to João de Barros' *Décadas da Ásia*, the first three Decades of which were published at Lisbon between 1552 and 1563 and the first two Decades of which were issued in Italian versions at Venice in 1562. Hakluyt's neglect of so vital a source may possibly be ascribed to the fact that the Decades actually in print in the sixteenth century only carried the story of the Portuguese enterprise in the East down to the year 1525. It is far more difficult, however, to account for his omission of relevant excerpts from the monumental history of the Jesuit mission to the East by Father G. P. Maffei entitled *Historiarum Indicarum libri XVI* (Florence, 1588). This elegant Latin history based on the latest Jesuit letters was repeatedly reissued on the continent before the end of the sixteenth century for general distribution, and it was also translated into Italian. While religious bias might have made an official Jesuit history suspect in Elizabethan England, it should be recalled that Hakluyt did publish excerpts from Jesuit letters.

On the basis of these omissions, as well as from his failure to include materials on Asia which could have been extracted from the wonderful books of Clusius on flora and fauna and from the remarkable engraved books on peoples and costumes that were published in the last generation of the sixteenth century at Antwerp and Venice, one is led to conclude that Hakluyt intentionally avoided bringing materials from the European scholarly tradition into his collection of primary materials on overseas

[1] According to Hakluyt, 'wearie volumes', *PN*, I (1598), preface to the reader.

navigation. The absence of all illustrative material and special maps[1] likewise supports the conclusion that he was determined to limit his collection to first-hand literary accounts of the sort that he conceived of as being most directly beneficial to English navigation and trade.

As a rule, Hakluyt gives the source for his document in the caption which prefaces each. The Latin texts of the overland travellers, John of Plano Carpini and William of Rubruquis, were copied from the manuscripts in the library of Lord Lumley. The original versions are followed by verbatim and accurate English translations; the same procedure is followed in presenting the text of Odoric of Pordenone. In his extracts from Ramusio he gives the original Italian text followed by a translation. He does not, however, give the texts in the original language of any of the other continental accounts of travels to Asia,[2] not even the Jesuit letters. He has excerpted materials from certain of the more important Jesuit letters on Japan and Korea without indicating anything more about his method than to say that these are items 'collected' from certain letterbooks about which he gives only the dates and places of publication.

The editorial device regularly employed is the marginal note. It is used as a quick reference guide for citation of authorities (usually classical authors), for explanation of unclear passages, for cross-references, and for his own remarks and observations on the text. He also makes occasional cross-references in the marginal notes to similar or contrasting passages in the other documents included in his collection. But such marginal captions are tantalizingly brief and too infrequent. They provide only minimal explanations of obscure passages and almost never explain terms,

---

[1] Instead of providing his readers with engraved illustrations, he suggests that they should view the overseas curiosities in the collections of Richard Garth and Walter Cope; see Quinn and Skelton, *PN* (*1589*), I (1965), xlvii–l.

[2] Thomas Hickock's translation of Federici, for example, is not preceded by the original Italian text. It was nonetheless a faithful rendition, even though it contains a number of omissions and mistranslations. For a thorough comparison of Hickock's with the original see E. Teza, 'Il viaggio di Cesare dei Fedrici e la versione inglese dell' "Hickocke"', *Atti del reale istituto veneto di scienze, lettere, ed arti*, LXVIII (ser. 8, vol. XI, 1908–9), 327–37.

names, or practices which must have been completely unknown to his contemporaries. While he must have been uncertain what to say editorially about the strange flora and fauna, customs, and institutions of the Far East, Hakluyt could have readily thrown more light on these matters by making reference to the natural scientific works and cosmographies that were then available.

The most important lapse in his editorial work comes in his presentation of the travels of Cesare Federici and Ralph Fitch. These are presented almost side by side (II, i, 216–44, 250–65), but he does not indicate that Fitch borrowed heavily from Federici's narrative for accounts of the places in India and Pegu where both travellers had visited. Perhaps it was because Fitch wrote his account from memory, under pressure from Hakluyt, that Fitch's mild plagiarizing was left unnoticed. Fitch evidently did not utilize Balbi's book, for he seems not to have extracted anything from it. Still Fitch is independently valuable as a source because he comments on interior places not visited by either Federici or Balbi.[1] On the whole Hakluyt may be judged an earnest and reliable but unimaginative editor – one who is content to let the documents speak for themselves while providing only the barest minimum of editorial amplification.

As Hakluyt makes abundantly clear in his prefaces, he was interested in collecting material on those parts of the Far East (Tartary, northern China, Korea, Japan and Yezo) which could be most easily reached by the northern routes, where English woollens could be sold most readily and advantageously, and where English explorers and merchants would not be forced to compete directly with the entrenched Portuguese and Spanish interests. But, unfortunately for his purposes, the authoritative materials available in his day were not as full on north-eastern Asia as were the accounts of the overland travellers of the late Middle Ages. His preoccupation with this northern region did have the effect, however, of bringing rapidly to England the Jesuit and Portuguese accounts of the wars of Hideyoshi in Korea and of the revelation of northern Japan and Yezo. On

[1] For further discussion and more detail on these matters see D. F. Lach, *Asia in the making of Europe*, I (Chicago, 1965), 215, 479, 499.

Japan proper he presents information from a few Jesuit letters, but his selection from the numerous printed letters available was far from comprehensive.

On China his documentation is better than on any other Asian nation. It is derived mainly from the accounts of the medieval travellers, Pereira, Cavendish, and Duarte Sande. Galeote Pereira, a Portuguese merchant, was imprisoned in southern China from 1549 to 1553. While languishing in prison, he evidently wrote up his observations of Fukien and Kwangsi provinces. These were first published in abridged form in 1565 as an appendix to a Venetian compendium of Jesuit letters. This shortened version was translated into English and published in 1577 in Willes' collection. Pereira's account is particularly valuable for its observations on Chinese justice, punishments, and prison life. Cavendish's notes on China are obviously based on data extracted from a Chinese gazetteer and they include valuable information on population, military forces, and political organization. The treatise in dialogue form of Duarte Sande, a Jesuit, is particularly useful for its survey of Chinese religion and culture, probably the best available in sixteenthcentury Europe. Taken together, these three accounts are not as comprehensive as Mendoza's synthesis of the materials on China. But since Mendoza was already published in English, Hakluyt supplied important supplementary information by firsthand observers.

The routes to the Spiceries come in for considerable attention, especially in the circumnavigations and in the descriptions of the Acapulco–Manila–China run by Francisco de Gualle and Henry Hawks. The description of Drake's reception at Ternate provides the occasion for a brief but informative discussion of the political conditions prevailing in the Moluccas in 1578–9. The effort to break the Portuguese monopoly of the route around Africa to the East Indies is related in the Lancaster narratives describing the reconnoitring of the route and the pillaging of the Portuguese fleets in the East. While the narratives contain only brief glimpses of the East Indies themselves, they are nonetheless valuable because of the paucity of contemporary materials on the eastern archipelago. On continental southeast Asia, the accounts in

Hakluyt are limited entirely to the materials on Burma and Malacca in the writings of Federici, Fitch, and Frey Peter of Lisbon. Nothing of moment is to be found here on Siam or Indo-China, two regions about which the Portuguese and Spaniards were relatively well informed at the end of the sixteenth century.

In summary, Hakluyt gives a balanced, adequate picture of China, very sketchy and inadequate representations of Japan and India, and an uneven portrayal of south-east Asia. His documentation is especially good on the routes to the East Indies and is up-to-date on the latest discoveries of the Portuguese and Jesuits in north-eastern Asia. Were we to judge about England's subsequent Asian interests on the basis of Hakluyt alone, we should conclude that England would by-pass India and concentrate its efforts upon the Moluccas, north-eastern Asia, and China.

Hakluyt's materials relating to trade are still useful, but are by no means unique. Most of his other documents have appeared in later and fuller versions in Purchas, other travel collections, and in separate books. For the modern student a few of his documents, such as the 'Excellent treatise . . . on China' by Duarte Sande are still of importance, usually because they have received no more recent translation or editing. On the whole, however, Hakluyt's collection is today of only marginal importance for the study of the Far East in the sixteenth century.

List of relevant materials
in 'Principal navigations' (1598-1600)

John of Plano Carpini A.D. 1246. I, 21–53 (Latin), 53–71 (English).
William de Rubruquis A.D. 1253–78. I, 71–92 (Latin), 93–117 (English).
Russia Company Articles, 1555, land route to Cathay. I, 261.
Letter of Anthony Jenkinson, 1559, Tartar girl. I, 305.
Anthony Jenkinson, 1558, merchandise of Asia. I, 332–3.
Anthony Jenkinson, 1559, Cathay. I, 336.
Anthony Jenkinson, 1562, Indian merchants. I, 350.
'Certaine directions giuen . . . to Hubblethorne, Dier, sent into Persia, 1579' – to learn about Chinese dyes. I, 432.

Commission to Pet and Jackman, 1580, Cathay. I, 433.

John Dee to Pet and Jackman, 1580, geography. I, 437.

Hakluyt's Notes for Pet and Jackman, 1580, China. I, 439.

Mercator's letter, 1580, Cathay. I, 443–4 (Latin), 444 (English).

Herberstein's description of North and East, 1588. I, 494.

Notes from Ramusio out of Abilfada Ismael (Ismael Abulfeda), 1588. I, 495.

John Balak, 'A learned Epistle written 1581' – North'east Passage to Cathay, China, and the Malucaes. I, 509–10 (Latin), 511–12 (English).

Note from Ramusio, 1557. I, 512–13 (Italian and English).

Odoric of Pordenone, 1330–1. II, i, 39–52 (Latin), 53–67 (English).

Caesar Frederick, 1563–81, part on Asia. II, i, 216–44.

Queen Elizabeth to King of Cambay, 1583. II, i, 245.

Queen Elizabeth to King of China, 1583. II, i, 245–6.

Ralph Fitch, 1583–91. II, i, 250–65.

Linschoten on Newbery and Fitch, 1583. II, i, 265–8.

William Barret's moneys, weights, etc., 1584. II, i, 273–7.

The second Levant Charter privilege for East Indies, 1592. II, i, 297.

Pereira's account of China, translated by Willes, 1565. II, ii, 68–80.

'Of the Island Iapan' by R. Willes, 1565. II, ii, 80–8.

'An excellent treatise . . . of China', 1590. II, ii, 88–98.

Thomas Stevens' letter from Goa, 1579. II, ii, 99–101.

Frey Peter of Lisbon on Pegu, 1589. II, ii, 102.

James Lancaster to East Indies, 1591–2. II, ii, 102–7.

Capture and cargo of the *Madre de Deus*, 1592. II, ii, 198.

Extract on New Mexico, 1583, taken from Mendoza. III, 389–96.

Voyage to China from Acapulco of Francisco Gali (de Gualle), 1584 (gives route both ways; first time known in England). III, 442–7.

Henry Hawks on China–Manila–Acapulco, 1572. III, 467–8.

Henry May voyage to East Indies, 1591–3. III, 571–2.

Drake's circumnavigation, 1579–80. III, 736–42.

Instruction to Edward Fenton, 1582. III, 754–7.

Discourse of Lopes Vas, 1586. III, 801–2.

Cavendish's circumnavigation, 1587. III, 817–22.

Thomas Fuller's Notes, 1588. III, 832–4, 835–6.

Cavendish's Notes of China, 1588. III, 857–9.

Queen Elizabeth's letter to Chinese emperor, 1596. III, 852–3 (Latin), 853–4 (English).

'Three Seuerall Testimonies. . . of Coray', 1590–4. III, 854–61.

A Brief Note on 'Zuegara', 1599. III, 861–2.

19
The Pacific

HELEN WALLIS

In North America, his 'Westerne Atlantis', Hakluyt centred his immediate hopes for the expansion of the English enterprise overseas. Yet beyond America the South Sea held compelling if more distant objectives which were never far from Hakluyt's thoughts in his vision of empire. For centuries the quest for Cathay had symbolized and given direction to Europe's yearning for the wealth of the Orient. Hakluyt himself (as G. B. Parks has noted)[1] made the study of Cathay and the way thither one of the guiding motives of his career. His proposed colonies in North America, in addition to their intrinsic advantages, fitted into his wider scheme; for a North American base would provide a halfway house to Asia and would aid the search for the North-west Passage to Cathay.[2] This route seemed the most suitable for England's exploitation, in view of her situation in north-west Europe and the fact that the other practicable routes were already discovered and appropriated by Spain and Portugal. Neverthe-less, the route which engaged Hakluyt's attention in his earliest pamphlet (1579–80)[3] was that through the Strait of Magellan, the only western passage to Asia so far discovered.

England had played no part in South Sea discovery hitherto. At Darien in 1573 Drake had been the first Englishman to cast eyes on the waters of the Pacific (a sight, as Camden recalled, which fired his ambition to sail those seas). John Oxenham, sailing a pinnace off the coast of Darien in 1575, is recorded by Hakluyt in 1589[4] as the first Englishman to sail a ship in the Pacific. Englishmen were also ill-informed about the activities

[1] Parks, *Hakluyt*, p. 188.
[2] Hakluyt, 'Particuler discourse' ('Discourse of western planting'), cap. 17, in Taylor, *Hakluyts*, II, 283–9.
[3] *Ibid.*, I, 139–46.   [4] *PN* (1589), sig. *4r, 595–6.

of other nations in this sphere, as Hakluyt's *Principall navigations* (1589) reveals. It is significant too that Hakluyt's information about the early ventures of Drake and Cavendish on the coast of Darien came from 'one Lopez a Spaniard', corrected in *Principal navigations* (1600) to 'one Lopez Vaz a Portugall borne in the citie of Eluas'.[1] Lopes Vas was a Portuguese, captured by the earl of Cumberland's fleet in the River Plate in 1587, whose depositions included valuable information on Drake's voyage, which Hakluyt did not use in 1589, but added as supplementary material in 1600. For the series of Spanish voyages across the Pacific to establish a trade route to the East, following Magellan's voyage, and for Mendaña's voyage, 1567–9, to find lands in the south Pacific, Hakluyt had no direct access to Spanish sources, for as chaplain to the English ambassador in Paris his personal contacts with the Hispano-Portuguese world (united in 1580 under the joint crowns of Spain and Portugal) were mainly through the Portuguese pretender Dom António. He depended primarily on the Anglo-Spanish merchant group, among whom Roger Bodenham and Henry Hawks were the most notable. Hawks provided the elder Richard Hakluyt – whom his cousin names with Sir John Hawkins and Sir Walter Ralegh as his 'cheefest light' on the western discoveries – with the important memorandum on New Spain and the Pacific printed in 1589.[2] This contained the first English report on Mendaña's discovery of the Solomon Islands in 1568, news of which had spread through Mexico while Hawks was there on business. Hawks also gives information on the Spanish trade route to the Philippines. All this was authoritative material, for its chief source was Diego Gutierrez, the Spanish pilot and cartographer and former royal cosmographer to the emperor Charles V, with whom Hawks had become well acquainted while in Mexico.[3] Hakluyt's other sources were secondary. Sir Humphrey Gilbert's 'Discourse'

[1] *PN*, III (1600), 525, 726.

[2] *PN* (1589), sig. *4v, pp. 545–53.

[3] *PN* (1589), p. 551. Hawks describes him as 'the first Pilot that euer went to that Countrey of the Phillipinaes'. His map of America, 1562, is one of the most important maps of the sixteenth century.

on the North-west Passage, reprinted by him in 1589,[1] although mainly an academic exercise derived from learned authorities, contained two interesting pieces of information. One was a report on Friar Andrés Urdaneta obtained by Gilbert from a Spanish nobleman Salvatierra in 1568, stating that Urdaneta had found the North-west Passage. This somewhat garbled report appears to have confused Urdaneta's discovery of the return route from the Philippines to Mexico in the north Pacific with a rumour of a supposed voyage round North America. The other intelligence concerned the voyage of Bernardo de la Torre who had sailed from New Spain to the Moluccas on Villalobos' expedition in 1542, and had twice attempted to discover the return route to America, making valuable observations on ocean currents which Gilbert used as evidence for his theory of a North-west Passage to Asia.[2]

The history of Pacific discovery prior to Drake and Cavendish thus received from Hakluyt, of necessity, a treatment less systematic and more restricted than its importance justified. Hakluyt was well read in Spanish literature and paid tribute to Spanish seamanship, but Spain's secretiveness over her activities was a serious obstacle in the search for information, and means of access to confidential sources were not open to him in the 1580s. Nor were such data strictly within his terms of reference, in that his main concern was English voyages. The balance should therefore have been redressed by the voyages of circumnavigation by Drake (1577–80) and Cavendish (1586–8), which the title-page of *Principall navigations* offered as the triumphant conclusion to the whole work. A symbol of England's independence and thrusting enterprise, these voyages inspired the poetic rhetoric of Hakluyt's dedicatory epistle:

> what English shippes did heeretofore . . . passe and repasse the vnpass-able (in former opinion) straight of Magellan, range along the coast of Chili, Peru, and all the backside of Noua Hispania, further then any

[1] *PN* (1589), pp. 547–610.
[2] *PN* (1589), p. 601. Both Ramusio (1550) and Galvão (1563) give reports of De la Torre's voyage and could have been Gilbert's source.

Christian euer passed, trauers the mighty bredth of the South sea, land vpon the Luzones . . . traffike with the princes of the Moluccaes, . . . & last of al returne home most richly lade*n* with the co*m*modities of China, as the subiects of this now florishing monarchy haue done ?[1]

Drake's voyage had been the talk of the man in the street and the sailor on the quayside. That Drake had 'shot the gulf' remained a popular saying among sailors for more than a hundred years. In official circles, however, a curtain of silence was imposed through the queen's prohibition on publication, and this re-mained in force for nearly ten years after Drake's return. Only when Spain had been vanquished through the defeat of the Armada in 1588 was the prohibition removed. Hakluyt then received permission to publish. By this time he had another major enterprise to record, the second English circumnavigation from which Cavendish had returned on 10 September 1588. Hakluyt here had no problem of secrecy to contend with, and, being related to Cavendish by marriage (his wife Douglas was Caven-dish's cousin), he had ready access to available sources. Hakluyt's difficulty in handling both these voyages was pressure of time, for the first section of *Principall navigations* was ready for printing early in 1589.

In his preface Hakluyt records that for Drake's circumnavigation he had taken 'more then ordinarie paines, meaning to haue inserted it in this worke: but being of late (contrary to my expecta-tion) seriously delt withall, not to anticipate or preuent another mans paines and charge in drawing all the seruices of that worthie Knight into one volume, I haue yeelded vnto those my freindes which pressed me in the matter, referring the further knowledge of his proceedinges, to those intended discourses'.[2] It is surmised that Drake may have been intending to publish, or to sponsor the publication of an account of his voyage, and then cancelled or postponed his plans.[3] As *Principall navigations* had now been run

[1] *PN* (1589), sig. *2v–3r.   [2] *PN* (1589), sig. *4v.

[3] E. M. Tenison, *Elizabethan England*, IX (1950), 555, challenges the assertion that Drake was out of favour in 1589 after his Portugal voyage, a reason suggested to explain the alleged change of plan. Cf. Quinn and Skelton, edd., *PN (1589)*, I (1965), xxii.

off Hakluyt had to cut his account to about 10,000 words, and print it on paper of the right format. Comprising six extra un-numbered leaves, it was inserted between pp. 643 and 644 in nearly all the copies ready for sale.[1]

Hakluyt's compilation entitled 'The famous voyage of Sir Francis Drake into the South Seas and there hence about the whole Globe of the Earth', was derived from two main sources. John Cooke's narrative (B.M., Harleian MS 540, ff. 93r–110v), which ends with Drake's entry into the South Sea, was the basis for the first part of the voyage, and was later used by John Stow for his account published in 1592. The manuscript is in John Stow's hand, and bears the heading 'Ser Francis Drake. Anno dñi 1577 (not 'For Francis Drake', a misreading by W. S. W. Vaux[2] which is also repeated in his reading of the final note, and which in turn misled Wagner).[3] Cooke was critical of Drake's behaviour to Thomas Doughty, but Hakluyt omits the sections which refer to the quarrel between the two men. The second source is the anonymous narrative 'A discourse of Sir Francis Drakes iourney & exploytes after hee had past ye Straytes of Megellan into Mare de Sur, & throughe the rest of his voyadge afterward till hee arived in England. 1580 anno' (Harleian MS 280, ff. 83–90).[4] This is preceded in the same volume by a memorandum in the same hand (ff. 81–2) on various incidents of the voyage. As the main 'discourse' begins at the point where Cooke's account leaves off, it is possible that Hakluyt himself obtained this account to complete the record of the voyage. As Wagner points out,[5] the fact that Hakluyt misplaced a note about the island of Caño and the capture of the Spaniard Sanchez Colchero which was also out of place in the manuscript suggests that he only had this manuscript as his source for these events.

---

[1] Quinn and Skelton, edd., PN (1589), I (1965), xxii–xxiii. W. H. Ker, 'The treatment of Drake's Circumnavigation in Hakluyt's Voyages', Bibliographical Society of America, Papers (1940), 281–302.

[2] W. S. W. Vaux, ed., The world encompassed (Hakluyt Society, 1855), appendix IV, pp. 187, 218.

[3] H. R. Wagner, Sir Francis Drake's voyage around the world (1926), p. 241.

[4] Misprinted f. 23 by Wagner, p. 243.

[5] Wagner, Drake's voyage, pp. 240, 267 n.

In reprinting 'The famous voyage' in 1600 he attempted to correct the error. As suggested by Corbett, the author of the anonymous discourse could have been William Legg, listed (on f. 89) in 'Partyes that were priuey to this voyadge', presumably the 'gentlemen'. The fact that Legg was one of those who did not sign his own name to the deposition concerning Doughty does not necessarily mean, as Wagner infers, that he was an uneducated seaman.[1] Hakluyt also seems to have had access to Fletcher's manuscript account,[2] using it for sections where his other sources were inadequate (or alternatively, he was using a common source). This would explain the similarities of Hakluyt's wording with that in *The world encompassed* (1628), and the marked differences between Hakluyt and the anonymous narrative for the later sections of the voyage. The exact relationship between Hakluyt's 'Famous Voyage' and Fletcher's account cannot be established, as the second part of Fletcher's manuscript is missing.

In Professor Walter Raleigh's view Hakluyt 'speaks somewhat slightingly of Drake's great voyage', showing 'a certain tenderness of conscience with regard to sheer piracy'.[3] This interpretation is not borne out by Hakluyt's references to Drake. In *Divers voyages* (1582) he writes in flattering terms: 'seeing God hath blessed him so wonderfully . . . the worthie and good Knight',[4] carefully worded phrases intended as commendation of the voyage while publications about it were forbidden. Michael Lok's map printed in *Divers voyages* was the first to record Drake's discoveries, marking the visit of English ships on the northwest coast of America. Clearly Hakluyt knew something of Drake's activities in Nova Albion, although nothing was in print. That he was on familiar terms with Drake in the period immediately following Drake's return is revealed by his account of his dealings with him on the proposed lecture on navigation, 1581–2.[5] Hakluyt's writings show plainly his resentment at the arrogant division of the world by Spain and Portugal, and their monopoly

---

[1] Wagner, *Drake's voyage*, p. 244. [2] B.M., Sloane MS 61.
[3] Walter Raleigh, 'The English voyages of the sixteenth century', *Principal navigations*, XII (1905), 53–4.
[4] *DV*, sig. ¶3. [5] *DV*, sig. ¶3–3v.

of the practicable routes to the Orient. He must have rejoiced as much as any one in Drake's successful challenge to Spain. He would see Drake's voyage not as an act of piracy but as a major step forward in England's policy of expansion overseas.

When Hakluyt thought himself debarred from including Drake's voyage in the main body of his work, he contented himself instead with that of Cavendish. For the account of the circumnavigation Hakluyt had to obtain his material from Cavendish in some haste. His main source was the narrative by 'N.H.', which gives a straightforward account of the voyage but lacks colour or detail. The identity of N.H. is not known. It has been suggested that Robert Hues the mathematician who accompanied Cavendish may have helped Hakluyt to collect and edit the Cavendish material.[1] The globemaker Emery Molyneux, who was of course well-known to Hakluyt, used N.H.'s account for plotting the track of the voyage on his terrestrial globe which was in preparation between 1589 and 1592, as Hakluyt records. It is interesting to note that Molyneux took Cavendish's track to the west instead of the east of Celebes, misled by an ambiguous passage in N.H.'s account. The fact that the globe gives three eye-witness legends does however suggest that Molyneux had access to one of the participants, such as Robert Hues. Hakluyt added to N.H.'s account a letter from Cavendish to the lord chamberlain, Henry Carey, Lord Hunsdon, giving a concise summary account of the voyage. A third document comprised notes on China translated from the legends on the large map of China which Cavendish brought home and evidently passed to Hakluyt. Hakluyt also interrogated two intelligent men from Japan and the Philippines whom Cavendish had brought home, but he did not make any notes for publication.[2]

For his new edition of *The principal navigations* Hakluyt had the opportunity of much enlarging his material on the Pacific. Many

---

[1] Quinn and Skelton, edd., *PN* (1589), I (1965), xliv; but the suggestion that Hues might be the author of the narrative if N.H. is a misprint for M.H. (Master Hues) seems rather unlikely, especially in view of certain ambiguous geographical statements in the account.

[2] Taylor, *Hakluyts*, I, 48.

restraints were now removed, and new sources were accessible. Improved relations with Spain meant that he could extend his circle of international contacts. The free exchange of information among those interested in cosmography and maritime affairs of the 1590s was much more congenial to him than the atmosphere of secrecy and suspicion prevailing in the previous decade. Further, Hakluyt now released himself from his rule that in general he would include only English enterprise, stating that 'where our owne mens experience is defectiue, there I haue bene careful to supply the same with the best and chiefest relations of strangers'.[1] In the Pacific sphere, as elsewhere, this policy enabled him to fill some serious gaps. As well as adding to his material, Hakluyt substituted one account for another where he considered the alternative superior in detail.

By 1598 the voyages of Drake and Cavendish were still the only major English enterprises in the Pacific. Although Hakluyt had had nine years to add to his sources, he failed to improve his coverage of Drake's circumnavigation from sources controlled by Drake himself. Drake had dedicated a narrative to the Queen in 1592, which must have been a version in some form of that eventually published in 1628 as *The world encompassed*, but he did not proceed to publication, and he did not make it available to Hakluyt before he sailed on his last voyage in 1595. Hakluyt reprinted 'The Famous Voyage'[2] and added John Winter's voyage,[3] covering only the Atlantic phase (as Winter's ship had separated shortly after entering the South Sea and returned home in 1579). This was written by Edward Cliffe, one of the sailors. Hakluyt added intelligence from two foreign sources, Nuño da Silva[4] and Lopes Vas. Nuño da Silva, Portuguese pilot for the viceroy of New Spain, had been carried by Drake from the Cape Verde Islands to Guatulco. The accounts given by da Silva at different times are regarded as one of the most reliable for this phase of the voyage, partly because they are among the earliest written, and also because they have suffered less editing.[5] Lopes

[1] *PN*, III (1600), sig. A2v. [2] *PN*, III (1600), 730–42.
[3] *Ibid.*, pp. 748–53. [4] *Ibid.*, pp. 742–8.
[5] Wagner, *Drake's voyage*, p. 335.

Vas included his account of Drake's voyage in 'A discourse of the West Indies and South Sea',[1] comprising a miscellany of information on Spanish America and the South Sea. His material for Drake's voyage he had obtained in writing from Nuño da Silva, as he himself states.[2] Wagner suggests that he obtained the information from Da Silva in Spain,[3] and that his account includes some details which Lopes Vas himself obtained at Lima shortly after Drake had been on the west coast of South America. Numerous discrepancies with official Spanish reports suggest that Lopes Vas' evidence for Drake's voyage is not very reliable in detail.[4]

For Cavendish's navigation Hakluyt had the advantage of closer personal contacts, and he was able to obtain, probably from Cavendish just before he set sail on his last voyage in 1591, the fuller and more graphic account of Francis Pretty, 'lately of Eye in Suffolk', a gentleman who had sailed with Cavendish.[5] This he substituted for N.H.'s useful but dry narrative of *Principall navigations* (1589). He added notes by Thomas Fuller of Ipswich, master in the *Desire* of Cavendish's fleet.[6] This document includes useful geographical tables of places on the coast of Chile and Peru and among the islands of the Philippines and East Indies, of islands in the South Sea, and of distances in the Pacific, as well as navigational records of the voyage, with depths and winds. Cavendish's letter to Lord Hunsdon and the notes from the map of China were retained. Finally, a major addition to the record of the two voyages was also included in the form of Edward Wright's map, which recorded the discoveries made by Drake and Cavendish. Although it did not display the tracks of the circumnavigations, the second state of the map highlighted their achievements through the addition of a legend.

Among the additions of foreign intelligence in 1600 one of the most important was Lopes Vas' Discourse, containing 'diuers rare things not hitherto deliuered by any other writer'.[7] Besides

[1] *PN*, III (1600), 778–802.
[2] *Ibid.*, p. 791.
[3] Wagner, *Drake's voyage*, p. 396.
[4] *Idem.*
[5] *PN*, III (1600), 803–25.
[6] *Ibid.*, pp. 825–37.
[7] *Ibid.*, p. 778.

the report on English voyages, these included much valuable data on the Pacific, including detailed information on the activities of the navigator Pedro Sarmiento de Gamboa. Vas records the colonization of the Philippines and the discovery of the Solomon Islands by Mendaña with Sarmiento as lieutenant.[1] Hakluyt himself probably knew Sarmiento, who had been in London in 1586 as an honoured prisoner enjoying the hospitality of Sir Walter Ralegh. Sarmiento's discoveries also gain special mention on Wright's map, and so does Francisco Gualle's revelation of the great width of the ocean (running to more than 1,200 leagues) between Cape Mendoçino and Cape California (Cape San Luas). Gualle's narrative had appeared in *Reysgheschrift* (1595), the second part of Linschoten's *Itinerario*, of which an English edition was published in 1598 at Hakluyt's suggestion. Hakluyt printed a version of the voyage in 1600.[2] This was one of the references to foreign enterprise which Hakluyt expressly mentioned and justified in his 'Epistle Dedicatorie', pointing to the geo⁄graphical importance of Gualle's discovery that a wide ocean lay where many maps showed the narrow Strait of Anian. It was vital information for Hakluyt because of his special interest in the North⁄west Passage as England's most suitable trade route to Asia.

In its underlying theme the later edition of *Principal navigations* confirms and develops the lines of thought in the earlier. Hakluyt was primarily interested in the Pacific as an oceanic highway, with the Orient as its focal point. He was not greatly concerned with geographical speculations about the Southern Continent or rich Pacific archipelagoes, although attentive to any reports of Pacific discoveries, hence his record of the discovery of the Solomon Islands. In an interview with Simão Fernandes, a pilot of Lisbon, in March 1604, he learnt of Quiros' voyage from Peru (evidently that of 1595), and his note on this, written after 1607, reports a captain of quality (i.e. Quiros) at Madrid solicit⁄ing support for a further expedition.[3] The shores of the Pacific

[1] *Ibid.*, pp. 801–2.
[2] *PN*, III (1600), sig. A2v–3r, 411, 442–7. See H. R. Wagner, *Spanish voyages to the north⁄west coast of America in the sixteenth century* (1929), p. 356.
[3] Taylor, *Hakluyts*, II, 489. Purchas, *Pilgrimes*, IV (1625), 1432.

littoral nevertheless offered the more tangible rewards. As a high-way the Pacific must have seemed even more formidable a route in 1600 than in 1589, for all the additional Spanish records used by Hakluyt tended to emphasize the great size of the ocean. All this would recommend the advantages of the known route round the Cape of Good Hope. Further, Grotius' *Mare liberum* (1608) which Hakluyt translated under the title 'The Free Sea' in 1609, strengthened his conviction that England, like the Netherlands, had a right to freedom of action on the seas, and could challenge the claims of Spain and Portugal to a monopoly in the use of certain sea routes.[1]

For the materials which Hakluyt acquired after 1600, *Purchas his pilgrimes* provides the main evidence. In his Spanish collections on the Orient a major addition was an account of Miguel López de Legaspi's voyage to the Philippines, 1565, and of the establish-ment there of the first Spanish colony.[2] These later collections must have reinforced the impression that the Orient was England's legitimate and most promising objective and that the route to it lay not westward but eastward. When Hakluyt died in 1616 England had her foothold in the Orient, but there had been no successful English voyage into and across the South Sea since Drake and Cavendish. These two voyages thus might seem in retrospect a flash in the pan, bold acts of piracy rather than well-conceived projects in the movement of English imperial expan-sion, and some historians have represented them as such. Hakluyt had a truer sense of history in hailing them as 'the two renowmed and prosperous voyages ... round about the circumference of the whole earth'.[3] By first carrying the English flag across the seas they were a practical demonstration of Hakluyt's dictum derived from Robert Thorne: 'there is no sea innauigable, no land vnhabit-able'.[4] The high seas were all legitimately open to English ships venturing their way to the remotest shores of Asia and America, and seeking out the 'secret trades and Indian riches' of the Orient.

---

[1] See below, pp. 324–5.   [2] Purchas, *Pilgrimes*, III (1625), 284.
[3] Title-page, *PN*, III (1600); see below, p. 000.
[4] Parks, *Hakluyt*, p. 73.

20

Latin America

K. R. ANDREWS

The contents of the two editions of *Principal navigations* reflect changes during Hakluyt's lifetime in the character of English activity in the Spanish-dominated region of the West Indies, South and Central America. In 1589 intelligence supplied by New Spain traders and those who had attempted trade in the Caribbean and Brazil occupied an important place alongside the records of enterprise inspired by growing hostility towards Spain. Though much of the interesting information in the English reports was in fact picked up from Spaniards and Portuguese, Hakluyt made little direct use of Iberian sources. In 1600 he trebled the space devoted to Latin America, reporting many more voyages, but the war which occasioned most of these also stopped the flow of English reportage on the Iberian-occupied areas. The privateering narratives did not fill this gap, but the raiders made up for this by capturing first-class Iberian documents in the shape of letters, reports and rutters, to which Hakluyt now added the whole of the 'discourse of the West Indies and South sea' by Lopes Vas, from which he had printed only short extracts in 1589. His avowed purpose now was 'to publish such secrets of theirs, as may any way auaile vs or annoy them'. On the English side he included new and better material on the two circumnavigations and a substantial new section on Guiana.

Both editions supplemented contemporary public knowledge of Latin America with lively and often up-to-date, if not comprehensive, observation, though not all the contributors saw the point. Bodenham, who must have known a great deal about New Spain trade, ended his meagre story by referring the reader to the Spanish histories. Of course Spanish literature did give the Elizabethans their groundwork of information and Hakluyt acknowledged its importance, not only by his 'owne extreeme trauaile in the histories of the Spanyards', but by republishing the whole of Peter Martyr's *Decades* in Latin[1] and by inspiring its translation into English.[2] He passed on to Purchas a translation of Herrera,[3] and it may have been partly out of interest in the Spanish record that he encouraged the translator of González de Mendoza.[4] In *Principal navigations*, however, he made little use of Spanish publications relating to this area. Most of the few refer/ ences to Peter Martyr and Oviedo,[5] for example, concern North America. The one excerpt from Oviedo referring to Spanish America, cited from Ramusio, was a misquotation which merely caused confusion.[6] Gómara, whom he cited more often, but usually with reference to North America, was an inferior source, and Hakluyt used him uncritically.[7] By 1598 Acosta was avail/ able, but apart from short extracts concerning Guiana, which Hakluyt had translated for Cecil, the 1600 volume made no use of the book, though it contained, for example, a discussion of the Strait of Magellan based on Sarmiento de Gamboa's recent experience.[8] Cieza de León's work,[9] remarkable not only for social description but also for a detailed survey of the west coast of South America, is mentioned only once in 1600 (by Ralegh), though Hakluyt knew it, for he referred to it in his edition of

[1] *De orbe nouo Petri Martyris Mediolanensis . . . decades octo* (Paris, 1587).

[2] *De nouo orbe, or the historie of the west Indies* (1612), translated by Michael Lok.

[3] Antonio de Herrera, *Historia general de los hechos de los castellanos*, 8 vols. (Madrid, 1601–15). Purchas, who found the translation among Hakluyt's papers, con/ demned it, but does not state that it was Hakluyt's own work: Purchas, *Pilgrimes*, III (1625), 855.

[4] Juan González de Mendoza, *The historie of the great and mightie kingdome of China . . . Translated out of Spanish by R. Parke* (1588).

[5] Gonzalo Fernández de Oviedo y Valdés, *Historia general y natural de las Indias* (Seville, 1535, 1557).

[6] J. A. Williamson, *The voyages of the Cabots and the discovery of North America* (1929), pp. 255–62.

[7] Francisco López de Gómara, *La historia de las Indias y conquista de Mexico* (Zara/ goza, 1552). The second part was translated by Thomas Nichols as *The pleasant historie of the conquest of Weast India, now called New Spayne* (1578).

[8] José de Acosta, *Historia natural y moral de las Indias* (Seville, 1590), translated by Edward Grimston as *The naturall and morall historie of the East and West Indies* (1604).

[9] Pedro Cieza de León, *La crónica del Perú* (Seville, 1553).

Galvão.[1] English interest in the sensitive southern outposts of Iberian America perhaps warranted some mention of Ercilla's epic,[2] Schmidel's work on La Plata[3] and Léry's on Brazil,[4] but Hakluyt gave no hint of their relevance, though he had copies of the last two when he died. It is arguable, therefore, that he might here and there have made more effective use of Spanish published work, but in general his restraint was justified. What was already in print had less claim on his space than unpublished matter and the rapidly increasing volume of English translation[5] diminished the need for quotation. The strongest argument for his policy is that most of the Spanish books available referred to the first half of the century, for much of the best contemporary Spanish descriptive writing, including that by López de Velasco,[6] was not published until the nineteenth century.

The problem Hakluyt faced in respect of New Spain was to obtain current information. The best of the commercial reports – that by Henry Hawks written at the elder Hakluyt's request – was already assuming the aspect of history in 1589, when one of the marginal notes read: 'This is to be vnderstood of the time when this discourse was written. anno 1572.' Robert Tomson's observations, though evidently written in the 1580s, referred to an even earlier period, the 1550s. Hakluyt did well to supplement these with John Chilton's wide-ranging if uneven travelogue coming down to 1585 and Miles Philips' informative as well as exciting story ending in 1582. In 1600 all these and Bodenham's item were reprinted with a few amendments indicating no important second thoughts. Hakluyt's own research produced a small but significant extra piece of historical information – the item about Thomas Tison – but he was unable to match the older

[1] *The discoueries of the world, from their first originall vnto the yeere of our lord 1555 . . . by Antonie Galuano* (1601).
[2] Alonso de Ercilla y Zuñiga, *La Araucana* (Madrid, 1569, 1578, 1590).
[3] Ulrich Schmidel, *Viaje al rio de la Plata* (Madrid, 1555).
[4] Jean de Léry, *Histoire d'un voyage fait en la terre du Brésil* (La Rochelle, 1578).
[5] J. G. Underhill, *Spanish literature in the England of the Tudors* (New York, 1899); J. Parker, *Books to build an empire* (Amsterdam, 1965).
[6] Juan López de Velasco, *Geografía y descripción universal de las Indias* (Madrid, 1894).

with more recent matter. Job Hortop's now supplemented the other accounts of Mexico, but dated back to 1568–70. The only recent addition was the anonymous 'relation of the Hauen of Tecuanapa', evidently a captured document. Although no longer of much importance for modern knowledge of sixteenth-century New Spain, those records still constitute the main source on English activity there.[1]

In 1589 the Caribbean was not well represented. Both the style and the content of the report on Hawkins' first slaving voyage suggest that it was written by Hakluyt himself, long after the event, on the basis of a more circumstantial account, which he was allowed to use, but not to reproduce. The highly condensed and discreet product indicates radical editorial processing of a kind Hakluyt did not often undertake, but could carry out with great skill when required to do so. John Sparke gave a much more detailed and interesting description of the second voyage, but Hakluyt obtained nothing on John Lovell's venture, while the reports of the third voyage said little about the Caribbean. More recent and more detailed was Chilton's information on Spanish activity. For the Panama Isthmus raids of Drake and Oxenham Hakluyt was driven to adopt what was for him the unusual procedure of presenting the Spanish version of events, as recorded by Lópes Vas, without any English evidence. The account or accounts on which *Sir Francis Drake revived* was to be based[2] were probably already pre-empted by the intending editor of 'all the seruices of that worthie Knight' in 1589, when Hakluyt referred to the project in his address to the reader, and they remained beyond his reach in 1600. The only other specifically Caribbean item in 1589 was his own rendering of the *Black Dog* incident of the same year – another piece of thorough editorial processing, the raw material being private letters and the object

[1] But Hakluyt did have a hand in one major contribution to knowledge of this area – the illustrated native history of Mexico, which he acquired in France and passed on to Purchas, having had it translated from the Spanish into English by Michael Lok: Purchas, *Pilgrimes*, III (1625), 1065–117.

[2] Published in London, 1626, by Drake's nephew, Sir Francis Drake, with a dedication by Drake himself dated 1 January 1592 (whether Old Style or New is not known).

anti-Spanish propaganda.[1] Most of the known gaps in the 1589 Caribbean record relate to piratical raids by captains who had no desire for publicity, but whose activities might be known to the High Court of Admiralty. Hakluyt made surprisingly little use of his contact there with the judge of the Admiralty, Dr Julius Caesar. The story of Andrew Barker's expedition, which did in 1600 fill one of the gaps, showed what could be done with legal materials, but was apparently derived from the papers of Hakluyt the lawyer, who died in 1591. The largest gap was also filled in 1600 by the reproduction of Bigges' narrative of Drake's 1585–6 voyage, which had been published just before the 1589 edition.[2] The French description of the West Indies, which Hakluyt had included in his so-called 'Discourse of Western Planting', was not used, presumably because it had no direct connection with English enterprise, though in 1589 some general information on the area, even at this crude level, was perhaps desirable when English knowledge of those waters was still poor.

The 1600 volume contained a fine collection of Caribbean privateering narratives. Many more such voyages in fact occurred, as Admiralty Court and Spanish records have revealed, but surviving narratives comparable to those preserved by Hakluyt are very rare. The two on Cumberland's Puerto Rico expedition published by Purchas presumably came too late for inclusion. For the most important venture since 1589 – Drake's last voyage – Hakluyt secured the best of the many reports now known, though he probably had no choice in view of the controversial character of the chief alternatives.[3] To this anonymous journal he added Henry Savile's pamphlet, originally published in 1596.[4] He

[1] *English privateering voyages to the West Indies 1588–1595*, ed. K. R. Andrews (1959), pp. 50–8.

[2] Walter Bigges, *A summarie and true discourse of Sir Frances Drakes West Indian voyage* (1589); on other (including earlier) editions see *The Roanoke voyages*, ed. D. B. Quinn, I (1955), 294.

[3] Thomas Maynarde's 'Sir Francis Drake his voyage 1595' and John Troughton's journal. See K. R. Andrews, ed., *The last voyage of Drake and Hawkins* (1972), which also includes Savile and Antoneli, with further comment on Hakluyt's handling thereof.

[4] *A libell of Spanish lies: found at the sacke of Cales . . . by Henry Sauile esquire* (1596).

corrected Savile's translation of the Spanish text in various places, but left it still faulty, and otherwise made minor amendments to Savile's own commentary. Modern knowledge of this, as of nearly all Elizabethan West Indies voyages, has been greatly amplified by Spanish material, and Hakluyt's own inclusion of captured Spanish documents gave a new dimension to the 1600 volume. The letters intercepted in 1590 dovetail well with the English record, for their emphasis is on Spanish reactions to English attacks. Antoneli's report is more important still, being a survey of the defences of the Panama Isthmus, Cartagena and Santa Marta. This report is otherwise unknown and it is a pity that Hakluyt failed to mention how and when he came by it. The same regret must be felt about the two West Indian rutters, 'excellent' though they are. The first closely resembles the version in Sloane MS 2292, ff. 16–33, with slight changes of wording, usually helpful, and the addition of marginal notes. The second appears to be one of several widely varying versions known in England in the 1590s.[1] Neither would have been a startling revelation to privateering commanders in 1600, but their publication helped to disseminate information the Spanish authorities were still trying to conceal.

Hakluyt provides nearly all of what little is known about English voyages to Brazil in the reign of Henry VIII. In 1600 he improved his presentation of the 1589 material and added a small but precious item – another example of his diligence as a historian. He also now extracted from its context the reference in Thorne's 'book' to Cabot's River Plate voyage, setting it alongside other River Plate materials. Roger Barlow's fuller account would have been in place here, but Hakluyt presumably did not know of its existence.[2] The same may be true of the papers relating to Grenville's southward project, secret in their time and well buried by 1589. Hakluyt's record of contemporary English voyages to the southerly coasts of South America thus began

[1] Compare B.M., Sloane MS 2292, ff. 34–40, and the note at the end of this MS.

[2] Roger Barlow, *A briefe summe of geographie*, ed. E. G. R. Taylor (Hakluyt Society, 1932).

with Drake's circumnavigation.[1] Having agreed under pressure not to publish an account of this voyage, he evidently received permission to do so after the 1589 edition was completed. The narrative then sent out with most of the copies of the book was probably written by himself. It appears to be based mainly on two original reports, but contains material from at least one other primary source, the product being a heavily edited amalgam, the components of which are nevertheless for the most part clearly recognizable. Censorship was obviously responsible for the whole exercise, particularly for the elimination of substantial portions of John Cooke's report relating to Doughty, and for the studied presentation of Doughty's trial and death. 'The famous voyage' was retained in 1600. At one point four unimportant lines were omitted and at another an equally unimportant paragraph was inserted. More interesting was the substitution of 43 for 42 in the text and margin of the passage referring to the latitude reached on the north-west coast of America. Hakluyt clearly did not submit this account to the systematic revision that can be observed in some other cases, and the frequency of changes in numerical figures elsewhere suggests that he may have been merely correcting a misprint. The whole passage about California was repeated elsewhere in the 1600 volume, but with an introductory paragraph which inadvertently alters the main text's account of the immediately preceding events. The 1600 volume also contains Edward Cliffe's account of Winter's voyage and Nuño da Silva's 'relation', which is presented without explanation of how it was acquired. Comparison with the Spanish text has shown that Hakluyt made a number of small omissions and at one point misunderstood the Spanish.[2] He probably lacked the supplementary notes attached to the Seville copy. The inadequacy of the documentation of this voyage in *Principal navigations* was not Hakluyt's fault. He was probably denied access to, or at least permission to print, important documents that have (or have not, as in the case of Drake's journal) come to light since his time.

[1] H. R. Wagner, *Sir Francis Drake's voyage around the world* (San Francisco, 1925) analyses the sources.

[2] *New light on Drake*, ed. Zelia Nuttall (Hakluyt Society, 1914), pp. 256–71.

One consequence was that the geographical significance of the voyage remained obscure. Nor has the wealth of evidence since unearthed, particularly in Spain, done much to clarify it.

The small group of documents on the Brazil trade was well worth printing, but Griggs' account of the *Minion*'s voyage discreetly withholds much information made known to the Admiralty Court and Hakluyt failed to follow the story beyond 1581, though he must have known of subsequent trading ventures.[1] In 1600 he added a captured Portuguese letter on the Rio de Janeiro–Peru trade. Fenton's voyage presented problems akin to those of Drake's. The plans and proceedings were shrouded in secrecy and bedevilled with controversy.[2] Most of what was written about the voyage was unprintable and the only complete reports were those by Fenton and Luke Ward. Fenton's was probably thought unfit for general consumption, but in any case Ward's, which Hakluyt published, was the more detached and clearer narrative. Even this, however, referred to quarrels, and most of these passages were judiciously excised, along with a good deal of navigational detail, in 1600. Apart from Fenton's instructions, the only other relevant item Hakluyt gave in 1589 was the extract from Lopes Vas about the voyage of Diego Flores. This he repeated in 1600 (as he did the extracts on Drake and Oxenham), but also produced a different translation of the whole discourse. This procedure wasted space and demonstrated the variations obtainable from two free renderings of the same text. Oxenham's ship, for example, was of 140 tons in the one, and of 120 tons in the other. But Lopes Vas' survey of South America with special reference to Anglo-Iberian rivalry was recent and well-informed, and Hakluyt would have done well to publish it in full in 1589, though he probably felt it was not directly enough concerned as a whole with English activity. He evidently missed the notes on Brazil trade prepared for Fenton,[3] but did obtain the interesting instructions by Edward Cotton for commercial reconnaissance of the River Plate.

[1] T. S. Willan, *Studies in Elizabethan foreign trade* (Manchester, 1959), pp. 5–10.
[2] *The troublesome voyage of Captain Edward Fenton, 1582–1583*, ed. E. G. R. Taylor (1959).　　　　[3] P.R.O., S.P. Dom. Eliz., S.P. 12/153, 43.

Hakluyt's version of the Withrington and Lister voyage, included with no significant variations in both editions, appears, by comparison with a signed copy of the original in the Lans' downe MSS,[1] to have been thoroughly edited, chiefly in order to suppress Sarocould's trenchant criticism of Withrington, but also to reduce the length. Much of the detail thus eliminated was perhaps inessential, but some significant information was lost in the process. The two rutters which follow this in 1589 were probably obtained from Lopes Vas. These were replaced in 1600 by three others, a change for the better. Comparison of the first two 1600 rutters with MS copies shows that the editing was care' fully and helpfully performed, combining moderate respect for the text with improvements by expansion, unobtrusive correction and plentiful marginal comment.[2] The last voyage relevant to South America to be included in 1589 was Cavendish's cir' cumnavigation, on which Hakluyt was able to present fuller and better material in 1600. If the 1600 documentation of subsequent enterprise south of Guiana appears scrappy, this is a reflection of the character of the enterprise. Nevertheless Hakluyt's record was incomplete. The account of Chidley's expedition provokes ele' mentary factual questions the answers to which some of Hakluyt's acquaintances must have known.[3] He printed Janes' report of Cavendish's last venture, but not Cavendish's own, different story, though it is not clear when he acquired (as he sooner or later did) the latter. There are one or two references in Hakluyt's pages to the obscure activities of Abraham Cocke in and around the River Plate, but most of what little is known came to light after 1600. On Lancaster's Pernambuco raid Henry Roberts had already published a pamphlet, but Hakluyt did well to prefer the original account on which it was apparently based.[4] In com' pensation for this poor collection on more southerly voyages, Hakluyt had easy access to the first'rate Guiana material already

[1] B.M., Lansdowne MS 100, ff. 23–51.
[2] B.M., Sloane MS 2292, ff. 2–15.
[3] Andrews, *English privateering voyages*, pp. 59–85.
[4] *The voyages of Sir James Lancaster to Brazil and the East Indies, 1591–1603*, ed. Sir William Foster (Hakluyt Society, 1940).

published, and to these accounts by Ralegh and Keymis he added Thomas Masham's. Beside these, his extracts from Enciso and Acosta give vaguely relevant background – an unusual procedure for Hakluyt and not in this case notably successful. The more recent reports of Berrío, to which he inevitably lacked access, would have placed Ralegh's efforts in an altogether different light, as their modern publication has in fact done.[1] If there were, as is likely, further Guiana ventures directly following that of the *Watte*, Hakluyt would hardly have found time to include them in his second edition, but he continued to collect material on Guiana in his later years, handing it on to Purchas.

Hakluyt's own writings – notably his treatise advocating the capture of the Strait of Magellan, his socalled 'Discourse of Western Planting' and his 1598 notes on the possessions of Spain and Portugal in America[2] – show that he had a serious interest in the region and shared the aggressive ambitions of some of his countrymen with respect to it. The English here were belated intruders, whose original contribution to knowledge of the area was relatively small, but Hakluyt for the most part did what justice he could to their efforts, given the limits imposed on publication by prevailing political conditions. The cases in which he seriously doctored original material on his own initiative seem to be comparatively few. On the other hand he evidently withheld, presumably without conscious deliberation, a good deal of what he knew, both about the voyages themselves and about the documents he printed. To contemporaries his success in revealing the Spanish 'secrets of the West Indies' must have appeared impressive, though the Spaniards themselves had far greater general knowledge of the area. Although modern scholarship has revealed a great wealth of documentation unknown to Hakluyt, *Principal navigations* contains most of the best narrative material on English voyages to the region and in fact constitutes a lasting core of the record of English enterprise there.

[1] Sir Walter Ralegh, *The discoverie of the large and bewtiful empire of Guiana*, ed. V. T. Harlow (1928).

[2] Taylor, *Hakluyts*, I, 139–46; II, 211–326, 420–5.

21

North America

D. B. QUINN

Richard Hakluyt was the outstanding advocate of English exploration of and settlement in North America between 1580 and 1600, and he continued to take an influential part in North American occasions in the later years of his life. He had excep/ tional opportunities for collecting material on the colonizing voyages and in the two editions of his voyage-collection, *The principall navigations* (1589) and the third volume of *The principal navigations* (1600), he put together much the greater part of what is now known of the colonizing enterprises.

For the early English voyages to America he was able to draw on the materials on John and Sebastian Cabot (including the manuscript Cabot patent of 1496) which he had collected and printed in *Divers voyages* (1582)[1] and was able to add appreciably to them, mainly from published sources, but with the addition of a document on Cabot's second licence,[2] though he failed to discover the later Bristol grants of 1501 and 1502 in the Rolls Office. This was almost all that could be put together on these ventures before the nineteenth century, even if it left many pro/ blems unsolved and, in particular, left the respective roles of John and Sebastian Cabot unclarified. For the reign of Henry VIII Hakluyt had Robert Thorne's very general treatise of 1527 which he had already published in 1582.[3] He obtained some additional material on the 1527 voyage but assimilated it to some vague hints of a voyage in 1516, while his attempt to combine two defective accounts on the 1536 voyage was only partly successful.[4] It is

[1] *DV*, sigs. A1–4; Quinn, *Richard Hakluyt editor*, I, 10; II, 13–19.
[2] *PN* (1589), pp. 509–14; Quinn and Skelton, edd., *PN (1589)*, I (1965), xxviii; II, 507–14.
[3] *DV*, sigs. B1–D4; Quinn, *Richard Hakluyt editor*, I, 10–11; II, 21–43; *PN* (1589), pp. 250–8.
[4] *PN* (1589), pp. 515–19.

hard, however, to see what more he could have done, though he missed John Rastell's *A new interlude and a mery of the nature of the iiii elements* [1519], which would have given him some insights on English knowledge of North America before 1520.

Having eschewed in his first edition all accounts of non-English voyages, Hakluyt had very little indeed to use between 1536 and 1578. He gives one short extract from Laudonnière's *History* (which he had published separately in translation in 1587),[1] and a vivid impression of Florida, with an account of John Hawkins' brief call in 1565, from John Sparke.[2] He also had a letter on Drake's visit to California in 1579.[3] It is with the grant of a colonizing patent to Sir Humphrey Gilbert on 11 June 1578[4] that he gets into his stride. He was able to reprint from *Divers voyages* (which he had compiled as propaganda for Gilbert's venture) his cousin's notes on colonization in North America in 1578.[5] He adds also a valuable letter on Newfoundland to his cousin by Anthony Parkhurst,[6] but he gives us nothing on the first abortive voyage of Gilbert in 1578–9, which he could well have obtained and which would have resolved some problems of interpretation.[7] For the second colonizing project of 1580–3, however, he obtained a very good narrative by Edward Hayes,[8] and a short addendum to it by Richard Clarke,[9] and printed them together with a Latin letter from Stephen Parmenius to himself[10] and a note from Thomas Aldworth to Walsingham.[11] He also reprinted three tracts with whose original publication he had had something to do, those by David Ingram, Christopher Carleill and Sir George Peckham.[12] There was very little else he could hope to obtain on the 1583 voyage itself, though he does

[1] *Ibid.*, pp. 543–5. [2] *Ibid.*, pp. 538–43.

[3] *Ibid.*, Drake leaves; Quinn and Skelton, edd., *PN* (*1589*), II (1965), 643G–643I.

[4] *PN* (1589), pp. 671–9.

[5] *DV*, sigs. K1–3v; Quinn, *Richard Hakluyt editor*, I, 12–13, 113–18; *PN* (1589), pp. 636–8.

[6] *PN* (1589), pp. 674–7. [7] Cf. Quinn, *Gilbert*, I, 37–46.

[8] *PN* (1589), pp. 679–97. [9] *Ibid.*, pp. 700–1.

[10] *Ibid.*, pp. 697–9. [11] *Ibid.*, p. 718.

[12] *Ibid.*, 557–62, 718–25, 701–18; Quinn and Skelton, edd., *PN* (*1589*), I (1965), xxxii; II, 557–62, 718–25, 701–18.

not waste much space on the extensive preparations for it during the years 1580–3 of which his own propaganda compilation, the *Divers voyages*, comprised only a very small part.

In the years from 1584 onwards Hakluyt was deeply involved in the Roanoke voyages as adviser to Sir Walter Ralegh (even though he spent the greater part of the time in France) and, in return, he was able to get from Ralegh, Thomas Harriot and John White materials with which he could put together a very full documentation on the voyages from 1584 to 1588.[1] Ralegh's patent[2] was followed by Arthur Barlowe's discourse of the 1584 voyage.[3] Somewhat censored and prettied up, this version is more likely to have been Ralegh's than Hakluyt's. For 1585 he had the *Tiger* journal,[4] somewhat cut it seems, and a list of colonists.[5] He gives one letter from Lane to his cousin, the elder Richard Hakluyt,[6] but Sir Francis Walsingham had others,[7] which he evidently did not pass on to Hakluyt. For the Roanoke colony of 1585–6 he relied mainly on Lane's discourse[8] whose coverage was incomplete, since it concentrated on a few episodes only, and on a reprint of Thomas Harriot's *A briefe and true report* (1588). He did not obtain Harriot's narrative of the voyages and his detailed observations, 1584–7, which have disappeared,[9] though it is possible that some of the documents he prints may have come from the documentary collection on which Thomas Harriot based his own chronicle, and which would have been in Ralegh's possession. He was not able, either, to reprint Walter Bigges [*et al.*], *A summarie and true discourse* (1589), which had something on Drake's removal of the Roanoke colonists in 1586. Hakluyt was very conscious that these sources still left the picture of the colony incomplete. Consequently, he was working to enlarge its scope by getting Harriot to write notes for John White's Indian

---

[1] Quinn, *Roanoke voyages*, I, 3–76, is largely a critique of these materials and of Hakluyt's handling of them; Quinn and Skelton, edd., *PN* (1589), I (1965), xlii–xliii.

[2] *PN* (1589), pp. 725–8. [3] *Ibid.*, pp. 728–33.

[4] *Ibid.*, pp. 733–6. [5] *Ibid.*, pp. 736–7.

[6] *Ibid.*, p. 793.

[7] See Quinn, *Roanoke voyages*, I, nos. 25–7, 29, 30 (a map), 34.

[8] *PN* (1589), pp. 737–47. [9] See Quinn, *Roanoke voyages*, I, p. 387.

drawings which, with a further reprint of the Harriot tract, Theodor de Bry brought out as *America*, part i, at Frankfurt in 1590. Nevertheless, information collected on Chesapeake Bay during the winter of 1585–6 was held back, evidently for security reasons. For the 1586 voyage, Hakluyt failed to pick up from its participants any coherent narrative at all and was forced to com-pile one himself from obviously imperfect materials:[1] if he had tried harder he might have had better success. In the case of John White's colony of 1587, he obtained the very full narrative written by White himself,[2] quite adequate for Hakluyt's purpose, but a little one-sided in its judgements for ours. White's abortive attempt to bring aid to the colonists in the Armada year was also narrated by him for the benefit of Hakluyt's readers.[3] To keep them involved with the ventures he was even able to slip in later in the volume a document assigning rights in 'Virginia', dated as late as 7 March 1589.[4]

In the decade between the appearance of *The principall naviga-tions* (1589) and the publication of volume III of *The principal navigations* in 1600, Hakluyt was less closely concerned in North American voyaging, if only because there were very few expedi-tions in which to be involved. His original contributions to the material on North America in 1600 were therefore much fewer than in 1589 – his coverage, in any event, having been very full for the ventures of 1578–88. He was, however, able at this time to expand somewhat his earlier programme through the decision to include foreign sources where no English voyage narrative adequately covered the ground. He was thus able to give some-thing like a complete coverage to eastern North America and to bring in something about the west.

Hakluyt obtained nothing new to add to his scattered informa-tion on the English voyages of the reigns of Henry VII and Henry VIII though he managed to clarify somewhat his account of the 1527 voyage,[5] but he was able to fill out the picture of the early discovery of the eastern seaboard and the river valleys by

---

[1] *PN* (1589), pp. 747–8. [2] *Ibid.*, pp. 764–70.
[3] *Ibid.*, pp. 771–3. [4] *Ibid.*, pp. 815–17.
[5] *PN*, III (1600), 1–10, 129–31.

resuscitating Verrazzano from *Divers voyages*, and also the accounts of the Cartier voyages already published in 1580.[1] To them he was able to add incomplete accounts of the Cartier voyage of 1541–2 and the Roberval expedition of 1542–3, together with some material from the *Cosmographie* of Jean Alfonse de Saintonge.[2] The main novelty for the first half of the century came with the addition of a reasonable selection of the Spanish materials for the exploration of western America. He was able to proceed from Fray Marcos de Niza to Coronado and thence to Ulloa and Alarcón, the texts taken from Ramusio and from Gómara, the latter having been published in English in 1596.[3] He continued into the second half of the century with a new English translation of the Espejo material which he had published in Spanish and French in 1586.[4] There is a mention in May 1590 of a further new expedition to Cíbola being planned[5] under Rodrigo del Río.

Hakluyt was, similarly, able to fill out the picture of the eastern coastline. He brought in the whole of Laudonnière's *Notable history*, which he had already published, to give a full picture of French Florida, 1562–8, along with two depositions taken in 1586,[6] though he had nothing to balance it with on the Spanish side. Indeed, the whole scale and nature of Spanish enterprise in eastern North America remained under-represented. This may have been partly due at least to the need to play down the role of Spain for propaganda purposes, so that eastern North America should appear to be much more an exclusive preserve of the

[1] Taylor, *Hakluyts*, II, 226. [2] *PN*, III (1600), 301–42.

[3] *Ibid.*, pp. 362–82, 397–439; Francisco López de Gómera, *The pleasant historie of the conquest of Weast India, now called New Spaine* (1596).

[4] See pp. 468–9, 534–5, below.

[5] *PN*, III (1600), 397. Rodrigo del Río de Loza was an important official in the northern frontier district of Mexico, and governor of Nueva Viscaya. It does not seem that he himself planned an expedition into New Mexico in 1590 but he was concerned about this time in trying to stop the slave-hunting raid by Gaspar Castañade Sosa directed into this area (cf. P. W. Powell, *Soldiers, Indians and silver* (1952), pp. 186–9, 197, 217–18, 280–2, and G. P. Hammond and A. Rey, *The rediscovery of New Mexico, 1580–94* (1966), p. 302).

[6] *PN*, III (1600), 361–2.

French and English than it was in practice: it may also have been partly due to lack of suitable sources, though Hakluyt had at least a copy of the detailed narrative published by the Gentleman of Elvas[1] of Hernando de Soto's expedition, which he was to publish in translation in 1609 as *Virginia richly valued*. He does not seem to have had at hand anything on the Spanish Florida colony from 1565 onwards or on the attempt to establish a Spanish mission on Chesapeake Bay 1570–2, though Drake's destruction of the fort at San Agustín in 1586 appears briefly.[2]

Hakluyt's investigation of surviving Cartier–Roberval materials during his stay in France had thrown up a few items on subsequent French activities in the early 1580s, but he made no reference to the fact that he had obtained Jacques Noël's map of the St Lawrence valley which for the first time showed Lake Ontario, though he had this information incorporated in the general map included in volume II.[3] He did not publish 'The relation of Mr Stephen Bellanger', a copy of which he had sent to Dr Julius Caesar, judge of the High Court of Admiralty, in 1584,[4] nor the other scraps of information on French activities in Canada which he had used, along with a summary of Bellenger, in his 'A particuler discourse' in the same year.[5]

The largest body of materials on North America surviving from the 1589 edition related to the English ventures of 1578–88. Consequently, for this period, Hakluyt had no striking novelties to offer. He contented himself with going over the existing materials carefully and in detail so as to present his material in a form which satisfied him more adequately, the 1589 edition having been rushed through the press with consequent blemishes in the text. He also both culled and added a few items to make the coverage more effectively complete. From the documents on the

---

[1] Fidalgo de Elvas, *Relaçam* (Evors, 1557); see John Brereton, *A briefe and true relation of the discouerie of the north part of Virginia* (1602), p. 46, for information from this book, probably by Hakluyt.

[2] *PN*, III (1600), 235–6.

[3] See above, p. 68.

[4] First printed in D. B. Quinn, 'The voyage of Étienne Bellenger to the Maritimes in 1583; a new document', *Canadian Historical Review*, XLIII (1962), 328–43.

[5] Taylor, *Hakluyts*, II, 233, 278–9.

Gilbert ventures he cut out David Ingram's narrative as being unreliable, and added the Latin poem by Stephen Parmenius, *De nauigatione Humfredi Gilberti . . . carmen*, as revised by the Hungarian poet shortly before he sailed to his death on Gilbert's 1583 expedition.[1] Hakluyt had been largely responsible for the first appearance of the poem in print in 1582 as propaganda for Gilbert's voyage, and it was included now more as a memorial to Parmenius than as a document of evidential value.[2] Two small items on Bristol's involvement in Christopher Carleill's share of the venture were also inserted for the first time.[3] Similarly, in regard to the Roanoke voyages, Hakluyt eliminated the account of the abortive 1588 voyage as being no longer of interest, and also the 1589 assignment of rights in Virginia which had ceased to operate. This time he put in the Bigges account of Drake's expedition of 1585–6 which contained something on San Agustín and the aiding of the Roanoke settlement.[4] He was also able to round off the series with John White's account of his last attempt to find the Lost Colonists in 1590, adding also the letter of 1593 (or 1594) which enclosed the narrative.[5] There was more to the voyage than was contained in the narrative, but Hakluyt did not elucidate its context. We hear nothing of further voyages to the Roanoke–Chesapeake Bay area, though there is a possibility that a visit was contemplated in 1591,[6] and we are told later that Samuel Mace's expedition of 1602 marked the fifth attempt to find them, which, since we know only of those of 1588 and 1590, leaves three voyages, some of them possibly carried out before 1600, unaccounted for.

Hakluyt did include one group of new English documents concerning relatively recent voyages to the Maritimes, the Magdalen Islands, Anticosti, and parts of western and southern Newfoundland, with which he had, himself, some association,

---

[1] *PN*, III (1600), 138–46.

[2] Edited by D. B. Quinn and N. M. Cheshire in *The new found land of Stephen Parmenius* (Toronto, 1972).

[3] *PN*, III (1600), 181–2.   [4] *Ibid.*, pp. 546–8.

[5] *Ibid.*, pp. 288–95, 287–8.

[6] K. R. Andrews, *Elizabethan privateering* (1964), pp. 165–6; *English privateering voyages, 1588–95* (1959), pp. 102, 110.

and which covered areas not hitherto represented by English narratives. The St Lawrence voyages of 1591–7[1] are reasonably well represented in the chosen narratives but Hakluyt did not reveal the name of the Basque pilot employed by the English or admit that the 1597 voyage was planned to create a settlement of radical nonconformists in the Gulf of St Lawrence.[2] Hakluyt did not include anything at all on the English fishery in south-eastern Newfoundland between 1583 and 1600 during which time it had proliferated at the expense of the Portuguese and Basques. This was scarcely because he could not obtain adequate information, but either because he did not consider the area sufficiently dramatic for inclusion or else because he preferred to keep activities there, which included a good deal of fighting and pillaging, to some extent under a security blanket. Hakluyt's frankness about the recent St Lawrence voyages is, when we recollect there was a war on, somewhat surprising. It may be that by 1600 it had already been decided to concede that area wholly to the French, so that English activities there, as recently as 1597, were only of geographical and historical interest.

In general, with the exceptions mentioned, Hakluyt presented in 1600 a very adequate coverage of the voyages which had revealed North America to Europeans. There is not to our knowledge very much on English expeditions that he could easily have obtained. Nor, judging by what Purchas later printed from his collections, was he able during the last stage of his collecting activity between 1600 and about 1613 to add more than a small number of documents on English ventures prior to 1600. He had a good deal more on Spanish activities in North America than he published, but not enough, except in the case of the Soto and Cabeza de Vaca material, to make much difference to the general picture he presented. We are therefore indebted to him for what

[1] *PN*, III (1600), 189–200.

[2] See D. B. Quinn, 'England and the St Lawrence, 1577–1602', in J. Parker, ed., *Merchants and scholars* (1965), pp. 117–44; 'The first Pilgrims', *William and Mary Quarterly*, 3rd ser., XXIII (1966), 59–90; and J. Rousseau, 'Les toponymes Amérindiens du Canada chez les anciens voyageurs anglais, 1591–1602', *Cahiers de Géographie de Québec*, X (1966), 263–77.

can only be regarded as an exceptionally detailed and comprehensive coverage of an area in which he had a unique personal interest.

During the years between 1580 and 1590 Hakluyt's main official sponsor and mentor was Sir Francis Walsingham and it was largely while he was under his influence or in his service that Hakluyt found and assembled the North American material included in his 1589 collection. In the 1590s his patrons were the Cecils, first Lord Burghley and later Sir Robert Cecil. It was with Burghley's encouragement that Hakluyt interested himself in the St Lawrence ventures. Sir Robert Cecil had called him in to advise on the further conduct of the Guiana question in 1596 and it was to him that Hakluyt dedicated volumes II and III of the enlarged edition. He made no secret, in his dedicatory epistles, of his desire to involve Cecil in support for further North American ventures, and he also drew attention to his own part in making North America and its prospects known in England through the publication of narratives about it. In 1600 he claimed,[1] and was largely justified in doing so:

> Of this New world and euery speciall part thereof in this my third volume I haue brought to light the best & most perfect relations of such as were chiefe actours in the particular discoueries and serches of the same, giuing vnto euery man his right, and leauing euery one to mainteine his owne credit.

He concluded with his famous statement to Cecil: 'Thus Sir I haue portrayed out in rude lineaments my Westerne Atlantis or America.'

He had indeed done his best to find effective narrators and to give them their heads in telling their own story. He did not object to tampering in detail with the texts they put before him.[2] He suppressed from time to time material it might be impolitic to print, but was, nonetheless, willing to allow his narrators at

[1] *PN*, III (1600), sigs. A2v, A3v.
[2] See Quinn and Skelton, edd., *PN* (1589), I (1965), li–lii; Quinn, *Roanoke voyages*, I, 82–8; *Richard Hakluyt editor*, I, 38–40. Other detailed analyses require to be done before a definitive picture emerges.

times to be surprisingly frank about recent events and controversial issues. (It should be remembered, too, that his text was
censored before publication, in 1589 by Dr John James and in
1598–1600 by Sir Robert Cecil himself.) It is notable, too, that
he preferred, when he could get them, straightforward accounts
of what had happened by participants in the North American
voyages to propaganda tracts on what might be found there by
future searchers. He re-used an appreciable amount of the promotion material for the Gilbert ventures, but none, except Harriot
(and that had independent merit), for the Roanoke voyages.
Because he was himself involved in most of the ventures between
1580 and 1597 he took special trouble to obtain narratives on
them, and, precisely because he knew the people concerned, he
was, in the great majority of cases, able to obtain them. His
success can be judged in the end by the very high proportion of
the materials on North America for the period 1578–97 which
have survived only because he evoked and conserved them.

22

The Arctic

T. E. ARMSTRONG

It may be said at once that Hakluyt served his readers well in bringing to their notice the achievements of English navigators in Arctic exploration. He was living at just the right time, when exciting ideas of routes to Cathay by the north-east and by the north-west were being put to the test. Almost the whole of what he tells us is concerned with these two projects, and relates to the second half of the sixteenth century.

Full cover is given to the attempts on the North-east Passage. For this, Hakluyt was able to use not only published accounts (as Clement Adams' narrative of Chancellor's voyage of 1553, or, in the 1598–1600 edition, excerpts from Giles Fletcher's *Of the Russe common wealth* (published in 1591)), but much unpublished material received, one way or another, from the records of the Muscovy Company. Hakluyt's contacts in this area of activity were good, and either his cousin Richard Hakluyt, or William Borough – both good friends – may have helped him get hold of any material which he could not obtain directly from the Company itself. The result is the inclusion of a number of reports, letters, and items of miscellaneous information, which combine to throw light on the working of the Company as well as on the journeys undertaken. Examples of these are Stephen Borough's own accounts of his 1556 and 1557 voyages, instructions to Pet and Jackman for their 1580 voyage, directions for killing a whale, and, in the second edition, Richard Johnson's notes on the Samoyeds he saw in 1556.[1]

On voyages to the north-east, then, Hakluyt did well by his public. The suspicion is that he may have done too well. His purpose in writing the *Principall navigations*, he tells us, was to

---

[1] For detailed description of the sources of the first edition, see Quinn and Skelton's introduction to *PN* (*1589*), 1 (1965).

publicize English voyages. His presentation of the voyages of Willoughby and Chancellor leaves a clear impression that England was first in this field. In the preface to the second edition he writes of the English nation as 'the first discouerers of a Sea beyond the North cape (neuer certainly knowen before) and of a conuenient passage into the huge Empire of Russia by the bay of S. Nicolas and the riuer of Duina'. But the English were not the first to make use of the waterway round northern Scandi-navia, and furthermore, it is highly probable that Hakluyt was aware of this. Sigismund von Herberstein was ambassador of the Holy Roman Empire to Moscow in 1516–18 and again in 1526. He published his *Rerum Moscouiticarum commentarii*, a most inter-esting account of Russia at that time, in 1549, and there were many later editions, in Latin, Italian and German, before the end of the century. Hakluyt, in his second edition, quotes an excerpt on the region of 'the Pechora, Yugria and the Ob'.[1] Yet not many pages later in von Herberstein's book[2] there is an account of a sea voyage from the Dvina round the north of Scandinavia in 1496. This voyage was made by Grigoriy Istoma (von Herber-stein's source), who, as interpreter to Ivan III of Moscow, had made the voyage with David, the returning Danish ambassador (and also an acquaintance of von Herberstein). Nor was such a voyage extraordinary at that time. Russian chronicles make it clear that David arrived from Denmark in 1494 by the same route, and a Soviet historian has produced evidence to show that Russian ships went to north Norway by this route on many occasions in the previous century.[3] So the route was by no means unknown, even outside Russia, and it seems quite unlikely that the well-informed Hakluyt should have been ignorant of this. He might possibly have doubted the veracity of von Herberstein's

[1] Hakluyt, PN (1598–1600), I, 492–4. The passage quoted may be found in R. H. Major's edition of von Herberstein's book, entitled *Notes upon Russia*, 2 vols. (1851–2), II, 37–44.

[2] *Ibid.*, II, 105–12.

[3] I. P. Shaskol'skiy, 'Ob odnom plavanii drevnerusskikh morekhodov vokrug Skandinavii', in *Puteshestviya i geograficheskiye otkrytiya v xv–xix vv.* (Moscow, Leningrad, 1965), pp. 26–8.

second-hand account, but no one else has done so since (except in points of detail). Admittedly, with his emphasis on English achievements, he had no obligation to include any mention of these voyages; but he should have moderated his claim for English priority.

Russian scholars, it may be added, have long been aware of this discrepancy. Hamel referred to it,[1] and Zamyslovskiy was well aware of the earlier Russian voyages.[2] Others have joined them since.[3] Hamel suggested[4] that von Herberstein's account of Istoma's 1496 voyage might have given the idea to Sebastian Cabot to initiate the 1553 voyage of Willoughby and Chancellor, for an Italian edition of von Herberstein's book was published in 1550 in Venice – Cabot's place of birth and the home, no doubt, of many of his friends. This seems a very reasonable possibility. A little less plausible, perhaps, is the suggestion[5] that Willoughby and Chancellor's agreement to meet, if separated, at Wardhouse (Vardø) shows that they knew the book too, since the place is prominently mentioned in von Herberstein's account. This particular reason seems unconvincing, for Wardhouse was evidently known to Scots before 1553. Chancellor himself mentions meeting Scots there,[6] and it may not be coincidence that Ambassador David was by birth a Scot.[7] Least plausible of all is the claim[8] for Russian priority of discovery of this water-

[1] J. Hamel, *Tradescant der Ältere 1618 in Russland* ... (St Petersburg and Leipzig, 1847), pp. 79–83. There were later editions in English (J. Hamel, *England and Russia*, 1854) and Russian (I. Kh. Gamel', 'Anglichane v Rossii v xvi i xvii stoletiyakh', Appendices to *Zapiski Imperatorskoy Akademii Nauk*, VIII, no. 1 (1865), and xv, no. 2 (1869)).

[2] Ye. Zamyslovskiy, *Gerbershteyn i yego istoriko-geograficheskiye izvestiya o Rossii* (St Petersburg, 1884), pp. 93–115.

[3] M. I. Belov, *Istoriya otkrytiya i osvoyeniya Severnogo morskogo puti. Tom 1. Arkticheskoye moreplavaniye s drevneyshikh vremen do serediny xix veka* (Moscow, 1956), pp. 74–5. I. P. Shaskol'skiy, 'Ob odnom plavanii' (1965), pp. 7–30.

[4] Hamel, *Tradescant* (1847), pp. 82–3.

[5] Belov, *Istoriya* (1956), p. 75. Shaskol'skiy, 'Ob odnom plavanii' (1965), p. 30. Hamel, *Tradescant* (1847), p. 114, hints at this too.

[6] *PN* (1589), p. 283.

[7] von Herberstein, *Notes*, II (1852), 105.

[8] Belov, *Istoriya* (1956), p. 75.

way. Russians undoubtedly preceded the English; but it is very probable that Norsemen preceded the Russians.[1]

Apart from the apparent playing-down of foreign achievement, there are no major gaps, as far as we know, in the cover Hakluyt provided. Many voyages were made to the White Sea and Hakluyt is silent about their details, but these were not exploratory voyages. The Dutch voyages to Novaya Zemlya in 1594-6 might possibly be expected to have found a place in the second edition. Nay, Barents, and their companions complemented the work of English predecessors and made spectacular advances. But the first published account – de Veer's – came out only in 1598, and it would have been difficult, if not impossible, to incorporate a summary in time (Purchas, of course, has it). There is a minor point on which one might have wished him to comment. Purchas quotes[2] a report made in 1584 by Anthony Marsh, chief factor of the Muscovy Company. Marsh puts in the mouth of some unnamed Russian contact of his the statement: 'Heretofore your people haue bin at the said Riuer of Obs mouth with a Ship, and there was made shipwracke, and your people were slaine by the Samoeds, which thought that they came to rob and subdue them.' There is no evidence anywhere else of an English voyage to the Ob before 1584, and it would be fascinating to know more of this. But Hakluyt might have been unable to ascertain more; indeed, from the date one might guess that Hakluyt had Marsh's report in his possession, but preferred for some reason not to use it. So he can hardly be blamed for the omission.[3]

The changes that Hakluyt made between his two editions were in the direction of clarifying or simplifying. There were sixteen separate items relevant to north-eastern voyages in the first edition. For the second, he added five, and trimmed or cut three. The cuts included, for instance, the Latin version of Clement Adams' account of Chancellor's voyage of 1553 (the English translation

---

[1] F. Nansen, *In northern mists* (1911), II, 135-40.
[2] Purchas, *Pilgrimes*, III (1625), 805.
[3] Hamel, *Tradescant* (1847), p. 238, thought the shipwrecked party might have been that of Jackman, who disappeared in this region in 1581.

being retained), while the additions were a new narrative of the same voyage by Chancellor himself, and background notes from Fletcher's *Of the Russe common wealth* and from von Herberstein's *Rerum Moscouiticarum commentarii.*[1]

On the voyages to the north-west, Hakluyt provides a no less full story; in some ways, perhaps, fuller, for it is reasonably certain that there were only six English voyages and he deals well with all of them. The first three (1576–8) were led by Frobisher, and Hakluyt gives us an unpublished account of the first, by Christo-pher Hall, the captain of the *Gabriel*, and published accounts of the others: Dionyse Settle's of the second and Thomas Ellis' of the third – the latter supplemented by an unpublished note by Thomas Wiars. In the second edition he adds (with certain cuts) the fullest published account of all, that by George Best and covering all three voyages. It is not clear why he did not use this earlier, for it was published a decade before his first edition; one must assume he could not obtain permission. He prefaces the voyage accounts with excerpts from works by Sir Humphrey Gilbert and Richard Willes arguing the existence of a North-west Passage. In contrast to the north-east voyages, however, Hakluyt does not complement his narratives with official letters or reports. There is no parallel to his access to the Muscovy Company papers. It seems likely that he could have obtained such access if he had wished; but possibly the row about Fro-bisher's 'gold', and the heavy debts incurred by the backers, made the subject a rather unsavoury one even in 1589. Such part of the inside story as has survived is given in the Hakluyt Society's edition[2] and in Stefansson's more recent and more fully annotated account.[3]

The remaining three voyages were John Davis' (1585–7). Hakluyt gives us unpublished accounts of each. In the second edition he adds the narrative of all three meanwhile included by

---

[1] The possibly rather curious editorial cuts are examined in detail by R. O. Lind-say, 'Richard Hakluyt and *Of the Russe common wealth*', BSA, *Papers*, LVII (1963), 312–27.

[2] *The three voyages of Martin Frobisher*, ed. R. Collinson (Hakluyt Society, 1867).

[3] *The three voyages of Martin Frobisher*, ed. V. Stefansson and E. McCaskill (1938).

Davis himself in his *The worlds hydrographicall description* (1595). Hakluyt in this way deals so fully with the subject that the editor of the Hakluyt Society's volume on Davis[1] could not only not add any more material three centuries later, but would have been very short of material if Hakluyt had not collected and published what he did.

A final item relevant to the north-western voyages was added by Hakluyt in his second edition. This was a summary of the alleged discoveries of the brothers Zeno at the end of the four-teenth century. The map which accompanied the original account (published by a descendant at Venice in 1558) caused confusion to later voyagers, Frobisher and Davis among them, by its fanciful distribution of land in the North Atlantic. But this map was not reproduced by Hakluyt. The account of the Zeni has been called a hoax and a sixteenth-century forgery. This charge was rebutted by the Hakluyt Society's editor,[2] who argues that the author was honestly mistaken, and argument continues today.[3] In any case, there was no reason why Hakluyt should not have included this summary, for the cartographic puzzle that it presented was not elucidated until much later, and the conflict between the Zeno map and the experience of Frobisher and Davis was not yet suffi-ciently well-defined in his time.

Apart from the north-east and north-west, Hakluyt mentions very briefly a few much earlier voyages. One of these is potentially interesting: the voyage, or voyages, of Nicholas of Lynn to the north in 1360 and later. Hakluyt collects his information from Mercator's world map of 1569 and from John Dee. The interest here is in how little he tells. Mercator apparently knew Nicholas' own account, called *Inventio fortunatae* (or *fortunae*), but this is now lost. Hakluyt writes as if he had not seen it. More's the pity,

[1] *The voyages and works of John Davis the navigator*, ed. A. H. Markham (Hakluyt Society, 1880).

[2] *The voyages of the Venetian brothers Nicolò and Antonio Zeno*, ed. R. H. Major (Hakluyt Society, 1873).

[3] See E. G. R. Taylor, 'A fourteenth century riddle – and its solution', *Geo-graphical Review*, LIV (1964), 573–6; and R. A. Skelton, T. E. Marston and G. D. Painter, *The Vinland map and the Tartar relation* (New Haven and London, 1965), pp. 197–9.

for a longer summary of its contents could scarcely have failed to add something to the accounts of the four authors by whose quoted extracts the existence of the work is known.[1]

In respect of his two chief Arctic interests, Hakluyt unquestionably made a major contribution to our knowledge. His accounts of the explorations of the second half of the sixteenth century were full and fair. No important source has subsequently come to light, and many would surely have been lost if Hakluyt had not recorded them. The worst one can accuse him of is of ignoring the earlier achievements of foreigners. This is misleading only in the case of the White Sea, for elsewhere the English, as it happened, had the field to themselves. But this is not a shortcoming that Hakluyt himself would have taken very seriously, for his stated intention was to 'recommend to the world the industrious labours and painefull trauels of our countrey men'.

[1] See R. A. Skelton, 'Mercator and English geography in the 16th century', *Duisburger Forschungen*, VI (1962), 161–2. The fullest extract is in E. G. R. Taylor, 'A letter dated 1577 from Mercator to John Dee', *Imago Mundi*, XIII (1956), 56–68.

PART THREE

FROM 1552 TO 1616

23

A Hakluyt Chronology

D. B. and A. M. QUINN

The materials for Hakluyt's life, as distinct from his works, are somewhat exiguous. Professor G. B. Parks, *Hakluyt*, pp. 242–62, gave a full chronology and list of his manuscripts as they were known in 1928, while E. G. R. Taylor made many of his miscellaneous writings and a somewhat limited correspondence available in her *Hakluyts* in 1935. R. A. Skelton had made a beginning on a revised chronology for the Handbook very shortly before his death but had not made any appreciable progress with it. We have in what follows revised the 1928 chronology and have attempted to relocate the documents which have moved or have been renumbered since then, a task in which Professor Parks, himself, has given valuable assistance. It has also been possible to elaborate the earlier picture in detail. Information from the London Company records, Christ Church, Bristol Cathedral and Westminster Abbey, fill out to some appreciable extent the tale of what he did and when, while a few additional manuscripts have come to light. We still lack any extensive personal data which would throw an intimate light on his personality, and we have no portrait. It is possible that further research on his City background and connections would throw more light on the circumstances under which he collected so much of his materials in London. Study of his Oxford associations, especially within the small circle of contemporaries and near-contemporaries at Christ Church, could also prove valuable, while his place in the group of scholars which includes Camden, the Saviles, Garth, Cope, Mercator, Ortelius and van Meteren, and which finds only some small representation in the learned correspondence of the period as at present known, needs clarification. His Bristol links by way of the cathedral chapter and the mercantile community may also be worth further study. His activities at Westminster

Abbey made him one of the key figures in a group of intellectual clerics as well as an active administrator of the internal economy of the Abbey. Though his Westminster activities help to fill out the record of his later years they are still rather lightly documented and further searches in the materials on Jacobean London may prove fruitful. Whether, without the discovery of some personal correspondence – which is not very likely – it will ever be possible to draw a convincing personal portrait of him remains problematical. A full list of data may, we hope, provoke further attempts at this desirable result.

The Dean and Chapter and Archivist of Westminster Abbey have put us in their debt. Mr N. H. MacMichael has been especially helpful; so were the Librarian of Christ Church, Dr J. F. A. Mason, Neil M. Cheshire and the Rev. George Malcolm, Wetheringsett. We are indebted also to the Dean and Chapter of Bristol Cathedral and to Miss Elizabeth Ralph, formerly City Archivist in Bristol; the Court, Clerk and Archivist of the Clothworkers' Company in London; the Librarian of the Inner Temple; the Librarian, Norwich Cathedral; the Keeper of Manuscripts, National Library of Wales; Librarians of the Norsk Polarinstituut and Universitetsbiblioteket, Oslo; the Museum 'Prins Hendrik', Rotterdam and the New York Public Library; the Curator of Manuscripts and Librarian of the Henry E. Huntington Library; Archivists of the Ipswich and East Suffolk Record Office, Norwich and Norfolk Record Office, Lincolnshire Record Office, besides officials of the British Museum, Bodleian Library and Public Record Office.

When Hakluyt was in France between 1583 and 1588 he was inclined to use New Style dating for the day and month, and may occasionally have done so later. He also adopted calendar dating for the year but he was not entirely consistent in this practice after he returned to England in 1588, so that it is sometimes difficult and occasionally impossible to know whether English style, with the year beginning on 25 March, or calendar dating, beginning with 1 January, is being employed. Where we have doubts about the method of dating for day and month we have added an asterisk and where the year is not clear we have added a dagger.

1552

Hakluyt was born in London, before 30 March since his application for a marriage licence, 30 March 1604, gave his age as 'about 52', which should mean he was born between 1 January and 29 March 1552. He was the second son of Richard Hakluyt, skinner, of London and Margery, his wife (his elder brother was Thomas; his younger brothers Oliver and Edmond followed him; his two sisters, Katherine and another, came at the end of the family). (Parks, *Hakluyt*, pp. 242–5; G. J. Armytage, ed., *Allegations for marriage licenses*, I (Harleian Society, XXV, 1887), 286. He is described on 19 July 1612 (below under date) as 60 years of age, which confirms his year of birth as 1552.)

1564

He was elected a Queen's Scholar at Westminster School during the head-mastership of Thomas Browne. (G. F. R. Barker and A. H. Stenning, *The Record of Old Westminsters*, I (1928), 411. No record of his earlier schooling appears to have survived.)

1568

Richard Hakluyt, visiting his elder cousin and namesake, Richard Hakluyt, lawyer, in the Inner Temple, was inspired by him to study geographical literature. (Dedication to *PN* (1589), *2r; letter to van Meteren, 1594; cf. Taylor, *Hakluyts*, II, 396–7, 419.)

September–December 1569

Richard Hakluyt is mentioned in the records of Westminster School:

(a) 'The bill for the money paid the scolers for xj weekes in ye plage that is betwene michaelmas and Chrystmas 1569'.

'More to master Alveye [prebendary of Westminster Abbey] for Rabbett viij^s vj^d more ij^s vj^d–xj^s. for meredyth viij^s vj^d more ij^s vj^d–xj^s. for hacklett viij^s vj^d more ij^s vj^d–xj^s.'

(Extracts, Westminster Abbey Muniments 38789.)

(b) 'leyd out as appereth of ye ether syde, to ye scholars at ye dissolution of ye which I have of master Burser 24 Septembris.'

'Master poryes bill for iij^{li} xij^s vj^d being money payd to the scollers at their departure at Michaelmas.'

'a. meredith ij^s vj^d: a. hackluit ij^s vi^d: [below] a: rabbet ij^s vj^d Telotson.'

(Extracts, Westminster Abbey Muniments 38790.)

Scholars of Westminster School, in time of plague in London, were sent to the country property of the Abbey, Chiswick Manor. The entry refers to Richard Hakluyt, as his brother Oliver, who was also a Queen's Scholar, would have been referred to as 'Hakluyt Minor'.

1570

Hakluyt was elected, as one of the two Queen's Scholars from Westminster School, to Christ Church, Oxford. He presumably entered during the Christmas term, but the list of students which was made up every Christmas and enrolled in the Chapter Book is lacking for 1570. (*PN* (1589), sig. *2r; Joseph Welch, *A list of scholars* (1788), p. 16; John Sergeaunt, *Annals of Westminster School* (1898), p. 70; Joseph Foster, *Alumni Oxonienses*, II (1894), 627; information from Dr J. F. A. Mason, Librarian of Christ Church.)

1571

For the weeks beginning 8 January 1571 to 13 June following Hakluyt appears in the Weekly Battel Books of Christ Church. (Christ Church Archives, x(1).c.17. He is also in the book x(1).c.16 (where the date of Christmas 1570 on f. 21v marks the end of the Christmas term), from f. 31v following.)

24 December 1571. Hakluyt appears in the register of admissions and elections amongst the 'Discipuli primi vicenarii'. (Christ Church Archives, Chapter Book, 1549–1619, f. 32; see H. L. Thompson, *Christ Church* (1900), pp. 34–7, for an explanation of ranks and duties.) In 1571 Hakluyt's tutor was 'Master Broune' (his fellow pupils being Stransome and Winshurst). (*Ibid.*, f. 57.)

1573–4

Michaelmas 1573–25 March 1574. Payment by the Skinners' Company, 'Item. Richard Hackelet of Christchurch in Oxford towards his exhibition for one half year at 13s. 4d. quarterly, ending at our Lady Day 26s. 8d.' (Skinners' Hall, London, Receipts and Payments, 1500–1607, printed in John James Lambert, *Records of the Skinners of London* (1933), pp. 373–4.) Hakluyt takes his degree of Bachelor of Arts (supplicated 16 January 1574, admitted 19 February 1574, determined in the academic year 1573–4). (*Register of the University of Oxford*, ed. Andrew Clark, II, iii (1888), 39.) He was entered amongst the twenty 'Philosophi secundi vicenarii' of Christ Church on 20 December 1574, as '*Dominus* Haclet', indicating that he had taken his bachelor's degree. (Christ Church Archives, Chapter Book, f. 35v. He appears again on 20 December 1575 (f. 37) and on 18 December 1577 (f. 38v) in the same grade.)

1574-5

Michaelmas 1574–Michaelmas 1575. Payment by the Skinners' Company 'To Richard Hackelett, a student in Oxon, by year 53s 4d.' (Lambert, *op. cit.*, p. 375.)

1575

Disbursement by the executors of the will of Robert Nowell (d. 1569), at the hands of Dr Laurence Humfrey, President of Magdalen College, Oxford. 'To one Mr Hakeluite Bachelor of Arts of Christe College in Oxforde the xiith of May [1575]. by Dr Humfrey.' (Book of Payments, Towneley MSS, f. 87, H.M.C., *Fourth Report* (1874), p. 614, and see pp. 407, 411–12. The payment a little later 'To one Mr Hackeluett the iiijth of June 1575 of Christe Church in Oxforde ij^s vj^d', may have been, if not to him, to his brother Oliver who was also, at this time, at Christ Church.)

18 May 1575 and 7 October 1575, Hakluyt has leave to be absent from Christ Church. (Christ Church Archives, Sub-Dean's Book (liii.b.1), ff. 4v., 5.)

1575-6

'D. Hacluit' appears in the Daily Battels Book. (Christ Church Archives x.c.l.)

1576-7

'D. Hacluit' appears in the Daily Battels Book; and from f. 20v, 'Mr Hacluit', indicating that he had become an M.A. (Christ Church Archives, x.c.3.)

1577

Hakluyt supplicated as a Master of Arts on 14 May 1577, was licensed on 27 June and incorporated in the same year. (*Register of the University of Oxford*, ed. Andrew Clark, II, iii (1888), 39.)

From this time onwards Hakluyt was a senior member of the University of Oxford and eligible to retain his Studentship at Christ Church indefinitely, subject to residence and until he married. There is no record that he became a Tutor after he became B.A., but there are no lists of Tutors for the appropriate period in the Christ Church Archives, though there is no real doubt that he was one (see also under 10 May 1580).

Hakluyt stated (*PN* (1589), dedication, *2r) that after wide reading in geography 'in my publike lectures [I] was the first, that produced and shewed both the olde imperfectly composed, and the new lately reformed Mappes, Globes, Spheares, and other instrumentes of this Art for demonstration in the common schooles, to the singular pleasure, and generall contentment of my auditory'. Both E. G. R. Taylor (*Hakluyts*, II, 397n.) and Mark H. Curtis (*Oxford and Cambridge in transition* (1959), p. 234) assume that these were lectures under the auspices of the University. This is denied by J. N. L. Baker (*The history of geography* (1963), pp. 119–21), who says that 'at some date after taking his Bachelor's degree in 1574 he gave some public lectures . . . It is probable . . . that the lectures were given to members of his own Society, Christ Church'.

May 1577

24 May, Hakluyt gets leave of absence from Christ Church: he returns on '19°' [June?]. (Christ Church Archives, Sub-Dean's Book (liii.b.1), f. 6v.)

August 1577

13 August, at the meeting of the Court of the Clothworkers' Company: 'This daie also was graunted to Richard Hacklytt beinge a scoller in christes- churche in Oxforde who as he saith is alredie *proceded* maister of Arte and is entred into the studie of dyui*ni*tie / Vpon the Condic*i*on that he be *proceded* maister of Arte as aforesaid & do studie diui*ni*tie & so continue the same studie the next avoidaunce of the penc*i*on of vj^{li} xiij^s iiij^d by yere graunted by this Companie to *Master* Wilson Scoller and which he nowe enioyeth / When the same shal become voide by Death Resignac*i*on or otherwise / He To enioye the same duringe ye Companies pleasure'. (Cloth- workers' Hall, Acts and Orders of the Court of the Clothworkers' Com- pany, 1558–81, f. 210; see T. Girtin, 'Mr. Hakluyt scholar at Oxford', *GJ*, CXIX (1953), 208; *The golden ram* (1958), pp. 53–4.)

1577

Hakluyt discussed plans for North-west Passage ventures, contemplated in the Netherlands, with Abraham Ortelius in London. (Taylor, *Hakluyts*, II, 279.)

1577–9

Hakluyt appears in the Daily Battels. (Christ Church Archives, Daily Battels Book, x.c.4.)

January 1578

21 January 1578, the Clothworkers' Company resolves to continue Mr Wilson's exhibition at Oxford for a further two years (thus postponing the effect of the grant to Richard Hakluyt on 13 August 1577, though the delay was in fact only five months). (Acts and Orders of the Court of the Cloth- workers' Company, 1558–81, f. 214.)

June 1578

June 1578, Richard Hakluyt's pension from the Clothworkers' Company took effect, and he received his payment for the year ending midsummer 1579: 'Item paid to Richarde Hackluyt Scholler of Oxford of the beneuo⁄lence of this howse towardes his exhibic*io*n and is paiable q*ua*rterlie vj^{li} xiij^s iiij^d.' (Clothworkers' Hall, Renter Warden's Accounts, 1578–9, f. 5v (from rents of properties in Mincing (Minchin) Lane).)

December 1578

December 1578, Hakluyt is again among the Philosophi secundi vicenarii of Christ Church but as 'Magister' (i.e. M.A.), instead of 'Dominus' (B.A.) previously. (Christ Church Archives, Chapter Book, 1549–1619, f. 41.)

Late 1577 or early 1578

Daniel Rogers, a nephew of Ortelius and well⁄known for many years to the elder Richard Hakluyt (Taylor, *Hakluyts*, 1, 6–7, 78n., 80), must also have been known to the younger Hakluyt while the latter was still at Oxford. Rogers went to the Netherlands with Elizabeth's envoy to the Prince of Orange, Philip Sidney, in March 1577, but took over himself as envoy in June, when Sidney left on a mission to central Europe (J. A. van Dorsten, *Poets, patrons and professors* (1962), pp. 19–22, 32). Either in September–October 1577 or, more probably, in December 1577–January 1578, he wrote Latin verses addressed 'Ad Iuvenem Hacklitum', to the younger Hakluyt. In them he mentioned that at the Queen's orders he has been at the camp of the Prince of Orange for some six months ('six months have passed and the moon has come back for a seventh time, summer has gone and bleak winter is upon us'): he feels deprived of Hakluyt's presence and urges him to visit him since he cannot visit Hakluyt, concluding 'For I can do without homeland and ancestral hearth, but not any longer without your company, my friend.'

Rogers, at a somewhat later date – he was in England for parts of 1578 and 1579 and then not until 1584 (Van Dorsten, pp. 62, 68) – addressed another short verse 'Ad Iuvenem Hacklitum'. In this he said that Hakluyt had asked why he should have shrunk from marrying a rich wife, but he was determined, himself, not to sell his independence for a dowry.

The poems are to be found in the collection 'Danielis Rogersij, Albimonti Angli, Infantia', ff. 183v and 233, respectively. This manuscript was formerly in the possession of the marquess of Hertford and was purchased at Sothebys on 23 June 1969 (lot 169) by Maggs Brothers for the Henry

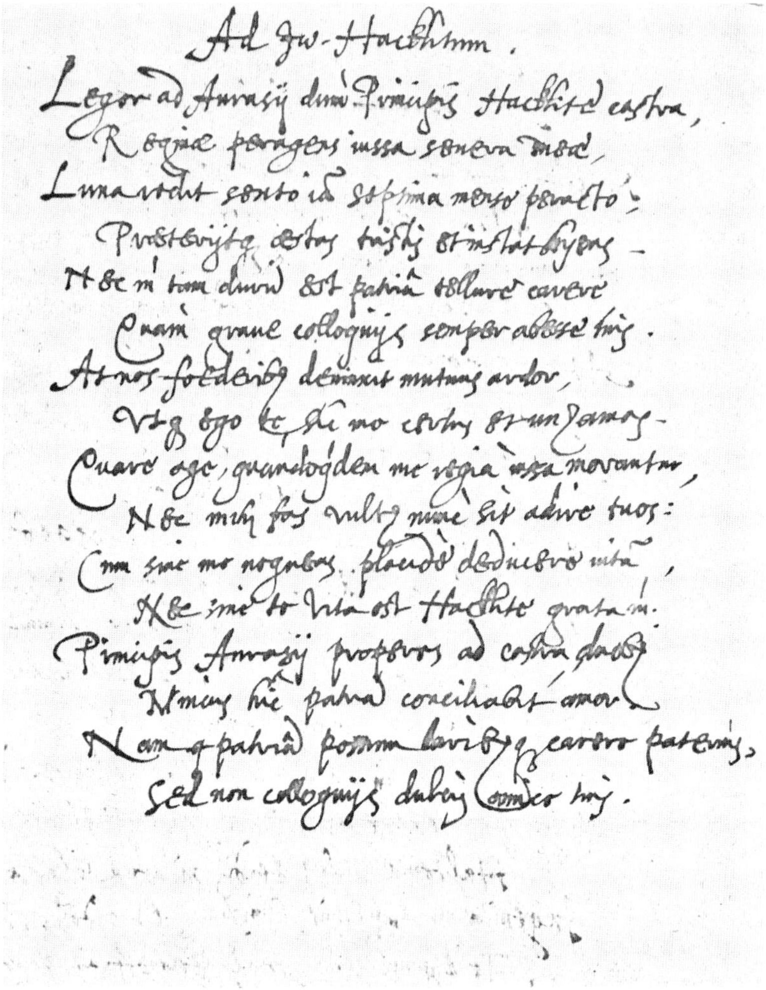

Fig. 7 Latin poem by Daniel Rogers addressed to the Younger Hakluyt, c. 1577–8.

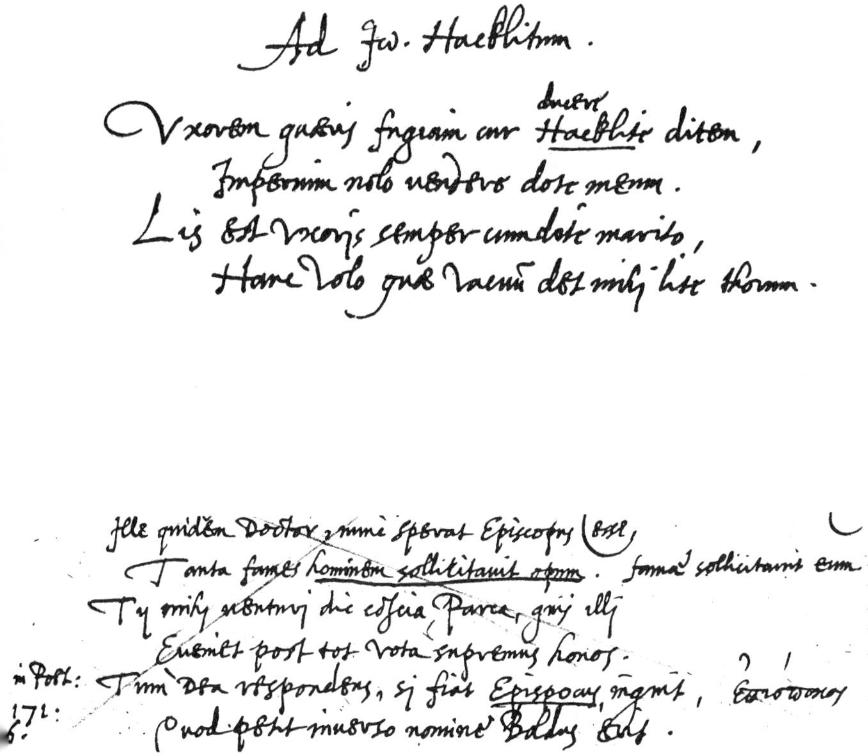

Fig. 8   Latin poem by Daniel Rogers addressed to the Younger Hakluyt, n.d.

E. Huntington Library where it is now MS H.M. 31188. (We are indebted to Mr John Maggs and to Miss Jean E. Preston, Curator of Manuscripts, Henry E. Huntington Library, for help in locating the verses, and to Mr Neil M. Cheshire for his invaluable help in transcribing and translating them. They are reproduced by permission of Mr Robert O. Dougan, Librarian of the Henry E. Huntington Library.)

1578

Poem by R.H. ('R.H. Gent, in commendation of the Authours well imployed tyme'), prefixed by John Florio, *Florio his first fruites* (1578) [sig. **4], which may be by Richard Hakluyt, in view of his association with Florio's translations from Ramusio in 1580 (or earlier).

271

1580 (or earlier)

Hakluyt lent John Florio his copy of G. B. Ramusio, *Navigationi et viaggi*, vol. III; and helped to finance as well as inspire translations of Cartier narratives in *A short and briefe narration*, which was entered 7 June 1580 in the Stationers' Register (Arber, *Transcript*, II, 169), the dedication being dated 25 June 1580: it was probably published in the summer. (Quinn, *Richard Hakluyt editor*, pp. 3–7, 34–8, 46–7.) Hakluyt appears to have intended the volume as publicity for the St Lawrence area, in support of an expedition, subsidiary to Sir Humphrey Gilbert's ventures, by Edward Cotton to the Gulf of St Lawrence in 1580.

May 1580

10 May 1580. The Court of the Clothworkers' Company, in granting to Gabriel Bowman an exhibition of £6 a year towards his maintenance at Oxford, adds 'And m*aste*r Hackluyt to be his Tutor yf may be, Or else his Tutor to be appointed by m*aste*r Waddington'. (Acts and Orders of the Court of the Clothworkers' Company, 1558–81, f. 240v; Girtin, *GJ*, CXIX, 209; *Golden ram*, p. 55.)

1580

28 July 1580. Gerard Mercator wrote from Duisburg to Hakluyt at Oxford on the supposed North-east Passage, in reply to a letter of Hakluyt's no longer extant. (*PN* (1589), pp. 483–5 (Latin and English); Taylor, *Hakluyts*, I, 159–62 (English); M. van Durme, *Correspondance Mercatorienne* (Antwerp, 1959), pp. 157–61 (French translation). As a result Hakluyt held discussions with Rumold Mercator in London. *DV* (1582), ¶2ʳ.)

1580

'A discourse of the commodity of the taking of the Straight of Magellanus.' This was probably prepared by Hakluyt for Sir Francis Walsingham shortly after the news reached England of the death of King Henry of Portugal on 30 January 1580. (P.R.O., S.P. Domestic, Elizabeth, S.P.12/229, 97; printed Taylor, *Hakluyts*, I, 139–56.)

December 1580

21 December, Hakluyt was admitted one of the twenty Theologi in Christ Church, a rank intended for those in Priest's Orders (so that before this date we may assume he had been ordained Priest). (Christ Church Archives, Chapter Book 1549–1619, f. 42; see H. L. Thompson, *Christ Church* (1900), p. 35.) He was later (see under 19 July 1612) said to have been ordained deacon and priest by John Piers, bishop of Salisbury.

March 1581

25 March 1581. Richard Hakluyt preached the quarterly Lambe Sermon in the Lambe Chapel of St James-in-the-Wall, before the Court of the Clothworkers' Company, and received payment: 'Item paid to Richard Hackluyt our scholler for his chardges vpp and downe from Oxenforde at master Lambes sermon at his Chappell at our ladye daye ouer and besides his stipende of vj^s viij^d for the said Sermon xxvj^s viij^d.' (Renter Warden's Account, 1580–1, f. 8.)

July 1581

3 July 1581. Hakluyt has leave of absence from Christ Church: he returns 1 August. (Christ Church Archives, Sub-Dean's Book (liii.b.1), ff. 13, 13v.)

1581

[c. July 1581]. Richard Hakluyt wrote to Jean Hotman from Oxford (in Latin), mentioning the fall of Breda to the Spaniards on 29 June 1581, and referring to mutual friends, Gentili, Paulet and others. (Jean and François Hotman, *Epistolae* (1700), p. 292.)

August 1581

The statement, made by Mr Tom Girtin (*GJ*, CXIX, 209; *Golden ram*, p. 55) that Hakluyt preached to the Clothworkers on election day (1 August) has not proved to be verifiable from the Clothworkers' records.

September 1581

2 September 1581. At a meeting of the Court of the Clothworkers' Company, 'This daie it was ordered and agreed that master Hakluytt our scholler at Oxforde shall haue our bookes of St Augustines workes out of this howse for the furtherannce of his studye putting in sufficient suerties for the safe delivery of the same vppon demaunde.' (Acts and Orders of the Court of the Clothworkers' Company, 1581–1605, f. 2v; Girtin, *GJ*, CXIX, 210; *Golden ram*, p. 55 (providing evidence that Hakluyt returned the books).)

October 1581

29 October, Hakluyt has leave of absence from Christ Church: he returns 5 November. (Christ Church Archives, Sub-Dean's Book (liii.b.1), f. 13v.)

1581

Late in the year, Stephanus Parmenius Budaeus (Stephen Parmenius of Buda), joined Hakluyt at Christ Church and is referred to by him in 1584 as 'lately my bedfelowe in Oxforde'. (Taylor, *Hakluyts*, II, 231; Quinn and Cheshire, *Parmenius*, pp. 8–9.)

December 1581

21 December 1581, Hakluyt was elected one of the four Cancionators (with preaching duties ?) of Christ Church. (Christ Church Archives, Chapter Book, 1549–1619, f. 44.)

Late 1581–early 1582

Hakluyt had discussions with Sir Francis Walsingham, Sir Francis Drake, and Alderman George Barne of the Muscovy Company about the endow⁄ment of a lectureship in navigation in London. He referred to it, and to a promise of Drake's support, in his dedication of *Divers voyages* to Sir Philip Sidney. (Taylor, *Hakluyts*, I, 208; *DV* (1582), sig. ¶3–3v.)

1581–2

Late 1581–spring 1582, Hakluyt was compiling material for *Divers voyages*, apparently assisted by Parmenius. He introduced the latter to Sir Humphrey Gilbert, to whom he presented the manuscript of his poem 'De nauigatione Humfredi Gilberti . . . carmen'. (Quinn and Cheshire, *Parmenius*, pp. 22, 26–7.)

1582

[*c.* March 1582]. Hakluyt dedicated *Divers voyages* to Sir Philip Sidney, attempting to enlist his aid for the American enterprises with which Sir Humphrey Gilbert was associated. The purpose of the book was to make available what was known about eastern North America in order to assist more direct propaganda in support of the Gilbert ventures, several expedi⁄tions under, or associated with whom, were expected to set out in the summer.

March 1582

19 March 1582. Hakluyt has leave of absence from Christ Church. (Christ Church Archives, Sub⁄Dean's Book (liii.b.1), f. 14v.)

1582

Hakluyt praised Michael Lok who made the map of the North⁄west Passage for *Divers voyages* (sig. ¶4r).

1582

[Before 25 March 1582]. Dr Antonio de Castillo (or Castilho), Portuguese ambassador in London, told Hakluyt of a Portuguese voyage to the

North-west Passage in 1574, on which he wrote a note in *Divers voyages* (sig. 2v, referred to by him in 1584, see Taylor, *Hakluyts*, II, 286). It could just possibly have been through him that he had had an opportunity to see cartographic materials on North America by Alonso de Chaves and Hieronimo de Chaves. (*DV* (1582), sig. ¶3; see p. 50, above.) In 1587 he referred to him as 'by his office keeper of all the records and monuments of their discoveries' (*A notable historie*, sig. 4; *PN*, III (1600), 303, the latter giving the date as 1581).

April 1582

[Early April]. William Camden wrote to an unnamed correspondent, who is most likely to be Richard Hakluyt, from London (in Latin) to say 'I will look after Master Parmenius of Buda since you have commended him to me', and also sent him news about Netherlands affairs. (Draft in B.M., Additional MS 36294, f. 2, see Quinn and Cheshire, *Parmenius* (1971), pp. 12–13, 211–19.)

May 1582

21 May. *Divers voyages* entered in the Stationers' Register. (Arber, *Transcript*, II, 411, licensed to Thomas Woodcock under the hands of John Aylmer, bishop of London, and both wardens of the Stationers' Company.)

22 May, a copy was already in the hands of Sir Edmund Brudenell who inscribed and dated it. (Elkins Collection, Philadelphia Free Library; Quinn, *Richard Hakluyt editor*, I, 32–3, pl. 2a.)

June 1582

27 June [1582]. Thomas Savile wrote to William Camden reporting a rumour in Oxford that there was something of Hakluyt's in the press (probably having belated news of the appearance of *Divers voyages* in May). (Thomas Smith, *V.cl. Camdeni et illustrium virorum . . . epistolae* (1691), p. 18: 'rumor est apud nos Hackluiti nonnulla jamdudum praelo subjecta; nec apparet quicquam, ut timor me ceperit iniquiùs pressa excessisse è vivis. Ergo non crediderunt se Deo & Patriæ? quàm sint haec nova obstinata! sed Musæ meliora . . . Raptim è collegio Mertonensi a.d. vi. Kal. Junii' [1582]. He had written earlier (pp. 4–5): 'Neque vel à te vel ab Hackluito, vel ab alio quopiam literula saltem unica delata est. Sed enim ignosco tibi, Camdene, V.Cl. tibi, inquam, quem multis nominibus occupatissimum scio; Hackluito non item, quem sola novitatis cupido Londinum pretraxit . . . Raptim è musæo a.d. ii Kal. Jun.' (1582, or possibly earlier, Smith placing it with letters of 1580).)

[June, before 21 June]. Parmenius published his poem, *De nauigatione*

Humfredi Gilberti ... carmen, influenced by Hakluyt, though we do not know precisely what part Hakluyt played in the actual production process. (Quinn and Cheshire, *Parmenius,* pp. 27–9.)

July 1582

22 July. Hakluyt has leave of absence from Christ Church. (Christ Church Archives, Sub-Dean's Book (liii.b.1), f. 15.)

December 1582

21 December 1582. Hakluyt was elected one of the two Censors (repre-sentatives of the Tutors?) of Christ Church. (Christ Church Archives, Chapter Book, 1549–1619, f. 44v.)

1582

December 1582. Jean Hotman wrote, from the Court at Windsor, to Hakluyt, commending to him Cevallius, citizen of Geneva. (Jean and François Hotman, *Epistolae* (1700), pp. 305–6.)

c. 1582–3

William Camden drafted a letter to an unnamed correspondent in which he referred to attempts by friends ('Mr Deane, and D. Lewes') to obtain for him an academic position (apparently the headmastership of Westminster School) which would involve him in entering into 'scole degrees': 'But this is strange to me that I had no inckling therof but by Mr. Hackluyttes letters, and yours': he would not accept. (B.M., Additional MS 36294, f. 10 (a name below, 'M^r [   ] Sandall[es]' may be that of the addressee): it could well be 1582–3: Camden asked grace for M.A. only in 1588. Another draft on f. 11 indicates that the headmastership of the school may be what is in question: he was already second master.)

1583

January or February 1583. John Newbery consulted Hakluyt, and obtained from him a letter of Thomas Stevens from Goa and other notes. (Taylor, *Hakluyts,* I, 29; *PN* (1589), pp. 207–8.)

1583 or earlier

Hakluyt acquired, possibly from his elder cousin, a short account of the East Indies by Francisco Fernandes which he gave to Newbery at his departure. (*PN,* II (1599), i, 246.) It is represented, as 'The Relacion of

Francisco Fernandes', in B.M., Additional MS 48151, ff. 159–60v. Curiously, Hakluyt did not print it in his second edition of *Principal navigations*.

March 1583

11 March 1583. Sir Francis Walsingham wrote to Thomas Aldworth, mayor of Bristol, commending Richard Hakluyt and Thomas Steventon, the bearers of the letter, who were discussing with him Bristol contributions to Sir Humphrey Gilbert's voyage.

11 March 1583. Sir Francis Walsingham wrote to Richard Hakluyt, wishing him to continue his study on and aid for the western discoveries. (*PN*, III (1600), 181–2; Quinn, *Gilbert*, II, 346–7; Taylor, *Hakluyts*, I, 196–7.)

27 March 1583. Thomas Aldworth wrote to Sir Francis Walsingham, reporting on Richard Hakluyt's visit to Bristol. (*PN*, III (1600), 182; Quinn, *Gilbert*, II, 350–1.)

Probably at this time Hakluyt picked up information on the coasting of Florida by a Spanish fleet (in 1582) from 'Master Ienynges and Master Smithe the *Master* and *Masters* mate of the shippe called the Toby belonginge to Bristowe'. ('Discourse of Western Planting', Taylor, *Hakluyts*, II, 240.)

On this, or another, occasion he collected 'certaine notes and examinations' on the voyages of Andrew Barker (1574–6), probably from 'M. John Barker of Bristol, brother vnto our Captaine M. Andrew Barker'. (*PN*, III (1600), 528–30.)

March–April 1583

31 March 1583. Parmenius signed the dedication of a revised version of 'De nauigatione Humfredi Gilberto ... carmen', which he probably presented to Hakluyt early in April, after his return from Bristol. (Quinn and Cheshire, *Parmenius*, p. 43.)

1583

[Early in 1583]. David Ingram's *A true discourse of the aduentures & trauailes of David Ingram* (1583), appeared (no copy now surviving), in the revelations of whom, August–September 1582, Richard Hakluyt had been associated and whose account he may have prepared for press. (Cf. Quinn, *Roanoke voyages*, I, 4; *Gilbert*, II, 281–310; *PN* (1589), pp. 557–62.)

May 1583

Late in May or in June Christopher Carleill published *A breef and sommarie discourse vpon the intended voyage to the hethermoste partes of America* (another edition entitled *A discourse vpon the entended voyage to the hethermoste partes of*

America also appeared), which may have been influenced and prepared for press by Hakluyt. (Parker, *Books to build an empire* (1965), pp. 113–15, 249.)

May 1583

28 May 1583. John Newbery wrote to Richard Hakluyt from Aleppo on his intended journey to India, recalling Hakluyt's earlier assistance. (*PN* (1589), p. 208; *PN*, II (1599), 245–6; Taylor, *Hakluyts*, I, 197–8.)

June 1583

June 1583. Hakluyt was said by Parmenius in August (see under 6 August) to have contemplated following Sir Humphrey Gilbert across the Atlantic in a subsequent vessel.

23 June 1583. Hakluyt has leave of absence from Christ Church. (Christ Church Archives, Sub-Dean's Book (liii.b.1), f. 17.)

August 1583

6 August. Stephen Parmenius wrote to Richard Hakluyt from St John's Harbour, Newfoundland (in Latin). He told him he had already written to Laurence Humfrey, President of Magdalen College, a mutual friend, and asked Hakluyt to communicate with his patron, Henry Unton, of Wadley, Berkshire, who also appears to have been known to Hakluyt. (*PN* (1589), 697–9; *PN*, III (1600), 161–3 (both Latin and English); Taylor, *Hakluyts*, I, 199–202, and Quinn, *Gilbert*, II, 379–83 (English only); Quinn and Cheshire, *Parmenius*, pp. 55–7, 167–85 (Latin and English, with a new translation).)

August–October 1583

August 1583. Richard Hakluyt was appointed chaplain and secretary to Sir Edward Stafford, who was leaving to act as resident ambassador in France. He left London about 20 September, reached Boulogne with Stafford after a rough voyage on 28 September, and arrived in Paris on 7 October. (*Cal. S.P. For. 1583–4*, pp. 117, 128.)

August 1583

Queen Elizabeth, through the earl of Leicester, Chancellor of the University of Oxford, requested leave for Hakluyt from Christ Church, which was granted from 30 August. (Below under 14 December.)

ANALYSIS, SEV

refolutio perpetua in oc-
to libros Politicorum. A-
riſtotelis,

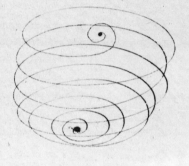

Fig. 9   Title-page of Hakluyt's autograph *Analysis* of Aristotle's *Politics*, 1583.

September 1583

1 September 1583. Richard Hakluyt signed at Christ Church, Oxford ('Ex aede Christi Oxoniae. Calendis Septembris') his dedication of his analysis of Aristotle's *Politics* (*Analysis seu resolutio perpetua in octo libros Politicorum Aristotelis*) to Queen Elizabeth. (B.M., Royal MS 12 G. XIII, ff. 1–47 (Latin, in Hakluyt's italic hand throughout). Taylor, *Hakluyts*, I, 203 (dedication only; Latin).)

3 September. The Court of the Clothworkers' Company, at Lord Burghley's request, continued Hakluyt's pension while he was in France. (Acts, 1581–1605, f. 28.)

September 1583

26 September 1583. Hakluyt was the subject of a brief, commendatory verse in Latin by William Gager (printed in Parks, *Hakluyt*, p. 8), while Oliver his brother earned a long poem. Gager entered Christ Church as a Queen's Scholar from Westminster School in 1574, and composed in 1583 a series of verses addressed to senior members of Christ Church which is now B.M., Additional MS 22583. (Verse to Richard, f. 62, to Oliver, f. 63; for Gager's entry to Christ Church see Welch, *A list of scholars* (1788), p. 17.)

1583–4

Hakluyt's name appears in the Daily Battels in Christ Church, but with a payment only of ten pence on his behalf in the second week. (Christ Church Archives, Daily Battels, 1583–4, f. lv.)

1583

[Between October and December 1583]. Hakluyt saw in Paris many furs from Canada in the possession of Valeron Perosse and Mathieu Grainer, furriers to Henry III. (Taylor, *Hakluyts*, I, 205, 207, 211, 233.)

1583–4

[Between October 1583 and the beginning of January 1584]. Hakluyt twice held discussions with Dom António, claimant to the throne of Portugal, and a number of his captains and pilots. (Letter of 7 January 1584, Taylor, *Hakluyts*, 206–7.)

Hakluyt met in Paris Pierre Pena, the French botanist, and through him expected to meet a Savoyard who had been in Japan. (*Ibid.*)

December 1583

14 December 1583, the Dean and Chapter of Christ Church grant Hakluyt leave of absence while he is in France. The entry (Christ Church Archives, Chapter Book 1549–1645) reads:

Master Rychard Hackluit	14. December 1583. Leaue was graunted by the deane & chapter to master Rychard Hackluit (vpon certificat from the right honorable therle of Leycester by his Lordships lettres in her Maiesties name, signifieng that it was her highnes pleasure that the sayd master Hackluit being chosen preacher to Master Edward Stafforde her maiesties Embassadour into France shovld inioye his full allowance of this howse in suche & so ample manner, as Master Lawrence Bodley had in the lyke ser[uice] during his abode [in the lyke seruice: crossed out] with Sir Amyas Powlet her maiesties Ambassadour there) that it should be Lawfull to him to be so absent, & so benefited, obseruatis obseruandis: his sayd leaue to begine Augusto Vltimo. 1583. Tobie Mathew Decanus

c. December 1583–January 1584

Hakluyt visited Rouen, and through a friend of his, André Mayer, instrument maker, was introduced to Étienne Bellenger ('Stephen Bellanger' to Hakluyt), who told him of his 1583 voyage to the Maritimes and Maine and of his proposed voyage in 1584. (Taylor, *Hakluyts*, II, 227, 266; *Canadian Historical Review*, XLII (1962), 328–39.)

September 1583–July 1584

Hakluyt made the acquaintance of André Thevet, cosmographer royal, obtaining from him information on the fur trade to Canada. (Taylor, *Hakluyts*, I, 207.)

January 1584

7 January 1584.* Richard Hakluyt wrote to Sir Francis Walsingham from the ambassador's house in Paris on his activities in France. (P.R.O., State Papers, Domestic, Elizabeth S.P. 12/167, 7; Taylor, *Hakluyts*, I, 205–7; calendared in *Cal. S.P. For., July 1583–July 1584*, p. 298, and *Cal. S.P. Dom., 1581–90*, p. 150.)

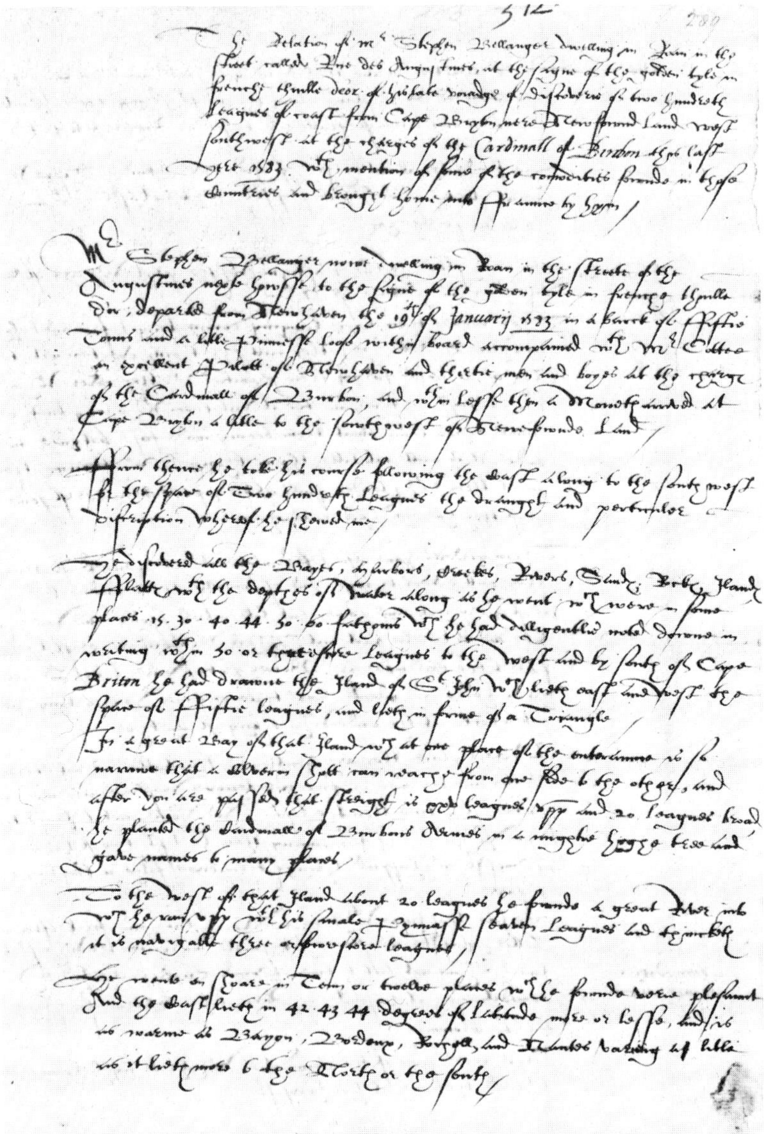

Fig. 10 First page of Hakluyt's autograph manuscript of 'The Relation of Mr Stephen Bellanger ... of his late voiadge of discoverie ... 1583' (1584).

January 1584

Hakluyt declared himself willing to embark on a North American venture (apparently with Christopher Carleill). (Letter of 7 January 1584, Taylor, *Hakluyts*, I, 206.)

c. February 1584

About February (and before 1 March) Hakluyt wrote 'The Relation of *Master* Stephen Bellanger dwelling in Roan in the street called Rue de Augustines at the sine of the golden tyle in french thuille deor of his late voiadge of discoverie of two hundreth leagues of coast from Cape Bryton nere Newfound Land West southwest at the charges of the Cardinall of Burbon this last yere 1583. With mention of some of the comodities fownde in those Cunntries and brought home into Fraunce by hym.' (Autograph MS in papers of Dr Julius Caesar, judge of the admiralty, B.M., Additional MS 14027, ff. 289–90v; first printed by D. B. Quinn, 'The voyage of Étienne Bellenger to the Maritimes in 1583: a new document', *Canadian Historical Review*, XLIII (1962), 339–43. See also T. N. Marsh, 'An unpublished Hakluyt manuscript', *New England Quarterly*, XXV (1962), 247–52.) It is highly probable that Hakluyt sent another version (perhaps more extensive but not now extant) to Walsingham as well.

1584

[Spring 1584]. Hakluyt discussed the St Lawrence valley with M. de Leau of Morlaix in the presence of certain Englishmen in Paris. (Taylor, *Hakluyts*, II, 288.)

April 1584

1 April 1584.* Richard Hakluyt wrote to Sir Francis Walsingham, advocating the creation of a lectureship in navigation, and sending news from France. (P.R.O., S.P. Dom., Eliz., S.P. 12/170, 1; Taylor *Hakluyts*, I, 208–10; calendared in *Cal. S.P. For., July 1583–July 1584*, pp. 445–6, and *Cal. S.P. Dom., 1581–90*, p. 169.) Before 1 April Hakluyt had made the acquaintance of Nicolas Bergeron, the executor of Peter Ramus. (*Ibid.*)

1583–4

Between his arrival in France in October 1583 and his departure about July 1584 Hakluyt visited the French Royal Library in the Abbey of St Martin, where he saw a Cartier MS. (Taylor, *Hakluyts*, II, 285.)

1584

Hakluyt met a Captain Muffett (or Moffet), in Paris, who had been a prisoner in Spain, and considered the Spaniards feared foreign settlement north of Florida. ('Particuler discourse', Taylor, *Hakluyts*, II, 241–2; Moffet is referred to by Sir Edward Stafford, 2 April 1584, S.P. 78/11, 69, *C.S.P. For.*, *1583–4*, p. 446.)

1584

Summer 1584 [before July ?]. Hakluyt was shown in Paris by Dom António a world map, on which was depicted a North-west Passage. (Taylor, *Hakluyts*, II, 287.)

July 1584

21 July 1584. Sir Philip Sidney related how Hakluyt had urged him to follow up the North American enterprise of Sir Humphrey Gilbert (Carleill having now retired from the more northerly enterprise and Ralegh con-centrating on the more southerly). (Sidney, *Complete works*, ed. A. Feuillerat, III (1923), 145; Quinn, *Roanoke voyages*, I, 90.) This would seem to indicate that Hakluyt had arrived in London some little time before.

1584

During his visit to England Hakluyt went once to Christ Church, where a payment by him of six shillings and eight pence is recorded in the Daily Battels. Later, a nominal payment of ten pence was made on his behalf. (Christ Church Archives, Daily Battels, 1584–5, ff. 16v, 23v.)

1584

July to September. Hakluyt was in London, engaged on the preparation for Walter Ralegh of a long memorandum on colonization prospects for pre-sentation to the Queen. The manuscript was completed very shortly after the return of Amadas and Barlowe with news about the first English exploration of the North Carolina–Virginia coast 'about the middest of September' (*PN* (1589), p. 733). It was not intended to be published either in 1584 or in Hakluyt's lifetime, as it was regarded as a confidential study of English external relations so far as the non-European world was concerned and as Hakluyt was himself in the Queen's service in the diplomatic sphere.

One manuscript only survives (written after the beginning of 1585 as it refers to the knighting of Ralegh) which is entitled 'A particuler discourse concerninge the greate necessitie and manifolde comodyties that are like to growe to this Realme of Englande by the Westerne discoueries lately

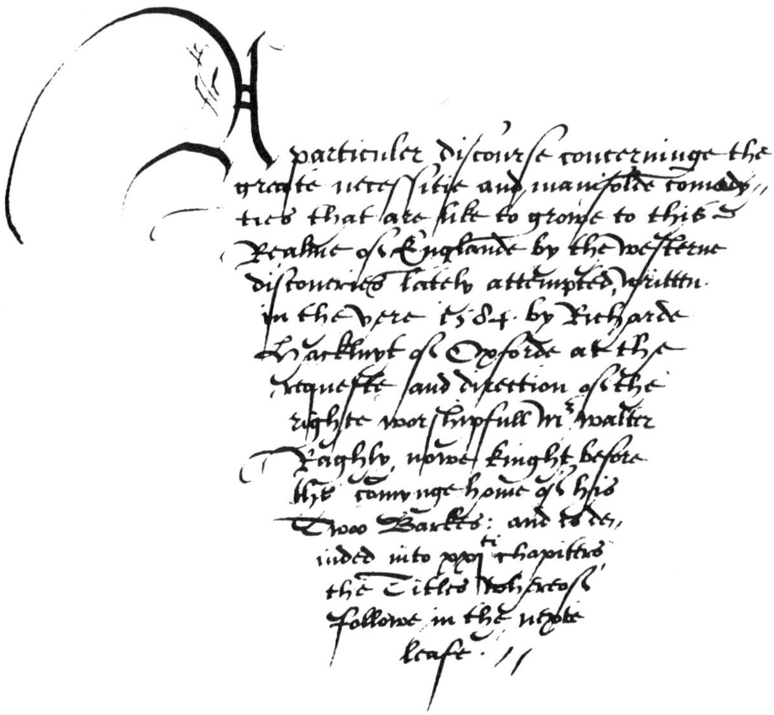

Fig. 11 Title-page of the only surviving manuscript of 'A particuler discourse'
(*Discourse of western planting*) (1584).

attempted'. It was first published, with the title *A discourse on western planting*, with an introduction by Leonard Woods, edited by Charles Deane (Cambridge, Mass., 1877) and simultaneously as *Documentary history of the state of Maine*, vol. II (Collections of the Maine Historical Society, Second Series, 1877). A second edition, this time with the title 'Discourse of western planting' appeared in E. G. R. Taylor's *Hakluyts*, II (1935), 213–326. The manuscript descended from (1) Sir Peter Thomson, d. 1770 (its early history being unknown) to (2) his son Peter Thomson, (3) to Viscount Valentia, (4) to Sir Thomas Phillipps (May 1854), who gave it the number Phillipps 14097, and allowed it to be used for the 1877 edition, (5) to Sothebys sale, 19 May 1913 (Phillipps Catalogue, pt. xvi, lot 43), (6) to Henry Stevens and Son (for £215), (7) to Dodd, Livingston, New York (October 1915 for £270) (8) to I. N. Phelps Stokes, (9) through Edward S. Harkness to New York Public Library, where it remains, and which gave permission for its re-publication in 1935.

September 1584

[September 1584]. Hakluyt discussed a recent Breton voyage to Canada with Mr Pryhouse [Prideaux?] of Jersey at the Stone House in Philpot Lane, London, and also with John de la Marche. (Taylor, *Hakluyts*, II, 278.)

October 1584

5 October 1584. Hakluyt was received in audience by Queen Elizabeth ('two days before my despatch') to whom he presented 'A particuler discourse' (the royal copy being lost and the surviving copy presented to another, possibly Walsingham). He also gave the Queen his autograph copy of his 'Analysis' of Aristotle's Politics. He was granted in recompense the next reversion to a vacant prebend in Bristol Cathedral, the warrant being dated 5 October. (P.R.O., Patent Roll, 26 Eliz., pt. 13, m. 4. C.66/1249; *Cal. S.P. For.*, 1584–5, p. 713; Taylor, *Hakluyts*, II, 333–4; Parks, *Hakluyt*, p. 248.)

1584

It was probably during his stay in England in 1584 that Hakluyt 'exhorted', as he said, Marco Antonio Pigafetta of Vicenza to publish his *Itinerario* (1585), the record (in Italian) of a journey from Vienna to Constantinople in 1567 (dedication to the earl of Hertford, declaring Hakluyt to be *amantissimo delle cose di Geografia*). (Sig. A2v–3.)

He was a brother of the Philippo Pigafetta of Vicenza (see below, p. 312) introduced by Henry Cobham from Paris to Walsingham on 17 September

1582, saying 'He has written a book of his "voyage" passed in Turkey and Judea, which he desires her Majesty may see'. (*Cal. S.P. For.*, *May–Dec. 1582*, pp. 262, 329.)

October 1584

7 October.* Hakluyt left for Paris where he had arrived by 15 October.* (Taylor, *Hakluyts*, II, 333–4; S.P. For., France, S.P. 78/12, 90; *Cal. S.P. For.*, *1584–5*, p. 106.)

16 October.* Stafford writing to Walsingham from Paris, says, 'On arriving here yesterday I found Mr. Hacklitt with a packet from you.' He says, 'I find from Mr. Haklitt that Drake's journey is kept very secret in England, but here it is in everyone's mouth.' (S.P. For., France, S.P. 78/12, 92; *Cal. S.P. For.*, *1584–5*, p. 108.)

1585

Hakluyt sent to an unknown correspondent the chapter headings (enclosed) of 'A particuler discourse'. He says he has sent the first copy to Sir Francis Walsingham; he will provide the second copy to the recipient of his note (not identified) if he desires it. (P.R.O., S.P. Dom., Eliz., S.P. 12/195, 127; Taylor, *Hakluyts*, II, 346 (omitting the chapter headings); *Cal. S.P. Dom.*, *1581–90*, p. 377.) He also sends some particulars of the embassy of the 'king' of Japan to Pope Gregory XIII, with the oration of the ambassador and the reply of the pontiff.

1585?

About 1585 Charles Thynne commended Hakluyt ('whom I know to be faithfull and secret') to Walsingham. (S.P. For., France, S.P. 78/14, 120.)

April 1585

7 April 1585.* Richard Hakluyt wrote to Sir Francis Walsingham from Paris mentioning his interview with the Queen before leaving England. He stressed the help he had given Sir Walter Ralegh with the preparation of the 1585 Virginia voyage and sent news from France. (P.R.O., S.P. Dom., Eliz., Add., S.P. 15/29, 9; *Cal. S.P. Dom.*, *Add. 1580–1625*, p. 141; *Cal. S.P. For.*, *1584–5*, p. 713; Taylor, *Hakluyts*, II, 343–5.)

May 1585

May 1585. Hakluyt left Paris with letters dated 4 May from Stafford for the Queen, Burghley and Walsingham. (P.R.O., S.P. For., Eliz., S.P. 78/13, 119; *Cal. S.P. For.*, *1584–5*, pp. 461–2.)

1585

24 May 1585. Hakluyt, described as master of arts and professor of theology, exhibited his mandate of 5 October 1584 to the Dean and Chapter of Bristol Cathedral for the next vacancy in the first prebendal stall (the precise date of his admission is unknown, but his stipend dated from 29 September 1586). (J. Le Neve, *Fasti ecclesiae Anglicanae*, I (1854), 226–7; Bristol Cathedral, Treasurer's Accounts, as pp. 290–1, below.)

1585

Late in 1585 Richard Hakluyt again visited André Thevet and was lent by him 'in good faith' the manuscript of René de Laudonnière's 'L'histoire notable de la Floride'. This was 'four months or thereabouts', Thevet tells us, before the book was printed in Paris by Hakluyt (see p. 292, below).

After 1585

At some time after 1585 Hakluyt obtained the report on the measures which Álvaro de Bazán, marquess of Santa Cruz, on 26 October 1585 at Lisbon, recommended should be taken to counter Drake's raid (the original being in Biblioteca Nacional, Madrid, MS 9372, lacking folios 133–8). He printed it in *Principal navigations*, III, 530–4, in Spanish and in translation. Earlier he had made a few notes in English from it, beginning 'That the castles of this citie, riuer, and territorie bee victuayled' and signed 'Richard Hakluyt preacher'. These came into the hands of Henry Stevens of Vermont who sold them to Sir Thomas Phillipps. They were offered for sale in 1951 by Messrs William H. Robinson Ltd. (Robinson, *Catalogue*, no. 81, Item 55, with facsimile; J. Winter Jones, ed., *Divers voyages* (1850), pp. cx–cxi, had already drawn attention to them and had printed a facsimile. They are now in the collection of Paul Mellon.)

1586

[January–February 1586]. Richard Hakluyt supplied a Latin verse in honour of Sir Walter Ralegh to Laudonnière's *L'histoire notable de la Floride* (Paris, 1586). (Reprinted Taylor, *Hakluyts*, II, 349 (with literal translation).)

March 1586

1/11 March 1586. Hakluyt was on his way to England, a letter having been sent this morning 'by Mr. Hetley [*sic*] my lord ambassador's minister'. (P.R.O., S.P. For., France, S.P. 78/15, 42; *Cal. S.P. For.*, 1585–6, pp. 406–7.)

March 1586

1 March 1586.* Martin Basanier dedicated his edition of Laudonnière, *L'histoire notable de la Floride*, to Sir Walter Ralegh, mentioning Hakluyt's part in making the publication possible. (Reprinted, Taylor, *Hakluyts*, II, 350–2.)

1586

24 April 1586. Sir Edward Stafford wrote to Walsingham from Paris, saying, 'I am sending by this bearer for my son and desire that both he and "Hacklytt" should come with him.' (S.P. For., France, S.P. 78/15, 107; *Cal. S.P. For., 1585–6*, p. 574.)

May 1586

6 May 1586. Stafford wrote again to Walsingham 'I despatch the bearer the sooner that he may come with my son and Mr. Hacklytt.' (P.R.O., S.P. 78/15, 123; *Cal. S.P. For., 1585–6*, p. 606.)

June 1586

24 June 1586. Oliver Hakluyt appeared before the sub-dean of Christ Church on behalf of Richard Hakluyt and signified that the latter had been installed in and received possession of a canonry in the diocese of Bristol. (Christ Church Archives, Sub-Dean's Book, 1555–1629 (liii. b.1), f. 17.)

July 1586

15 July. Stafford wrote to Walsingham from Paris 'I desire to have . . . Hacklytt.' (P.R.O., S.P. For., France, S.P. 78/16, 38; *Cal. S.P. For., 1586–8*, p. 53.)

1586

Sometime shortly after 28 July 1586 Hakluyt took down, orally, 'The relation of Pedro Morales a Spaniard', brought to England by Sir Francis Drake. (*PN*, III (1600), 361; Quinn, *Roanoke voyages*, II, 761–6.)

He also, with Thomas Harriot, was present when 'The relation of Nicholas Burgoignon, aliâs Holy', was taken down, probably at the same time. (*PN*, III (1600), 361–2; Quinn, *Roanoke voyages*, II, 763–6.)

September 1586

29 September 1586. Hakluyt's stipend of £20 a year as a prebendary of Bristol Cathedral begins and continues to 29 September 1616 (so that he received in all £620, less deductions for subsidies and other charges). He

is known to have been present at the meeting of the chapter early in October, when the accounts were signed, only in 1590, 1591, 1592, 1593, 1595: he may have held an exemption from attending chapter meetings later in his life. (Bristol Cathedral, Treasurers' Accounts, Computa, 1572–93 (fair copies with copied signatures); Original Accounts, 1590, 1592, 1595 (with signatures); Computa, 1602–19; Original Accounts, 1603–4, 1608, 1611, 1613, 1614, 1615, his signature, or copied signature, being absent from all accounts, 1602–16.)

October 1586

Hakluyt vacated his Studentship at Christ Church. Dr J. F. A. Mason. Librarian of Christ Church, writes 'He last appears in the Daily Battels for the second week of Christmas Term 1586, and has disappeared by the next week (Archives, x.c.7). By this time he was, very briefly, the senior Student on the list. The voidance must be connected with his installation as a pre-bendary of Bristol: in the Sub-Dean's Book (liii.b.1) is an entry for his notification of his installation on 24 June 1586 (above, p. 289), and he seems to have vacated his Studentship some three months later. The terms were dated by the feasts at their conclusion, so he vacated his Studentship in October 1586.' (In the Daily Battels Book, 1585–7 (x.c.7), Hakluyt appears paying nothing in the list until f. 21v when he pays twelve pence, and next on f. 29v when he pays ten pence, the final payment on f. 53v being 'm^r Hackluit 1^d ob q^a q^a – iij^d [*sic*]', his name then disappearing from the list.)

1586

12 November 1586.* Martin Basanier dedicated his translation of A. de Espejo, *Histoire des terres nouuellement descouuertes* (Paris, 1586), to Hakluyt.

December 1586

30 December 1586.* Hakluyt wrote to Sir Walter Ralegh from Paris, sending news of France and making inquiries on American matters. (Bodleian Library, Clarendon MS 36, ff. 2r–3v; O. Ogle and W. H. Bliss, edd., *Calendar of the Clarendon State Papers*, I (1872), 500; printed, Taylor, *Hakluyts*, II, 353–6; extract, Quinn, *Roanoke voyages*, I, 493–4.)

Between 1586 and 1589

Hakluyt failed to obtain a narrative of the 1586 Virginia voyage after Sir Richard Grenville's return so he composed his own from such information as he could obtain: 'The third voyage made by a ship sent in the yeere 1586, to the reliefe of the Colony planted in Virginia, at the sole charges of Sir

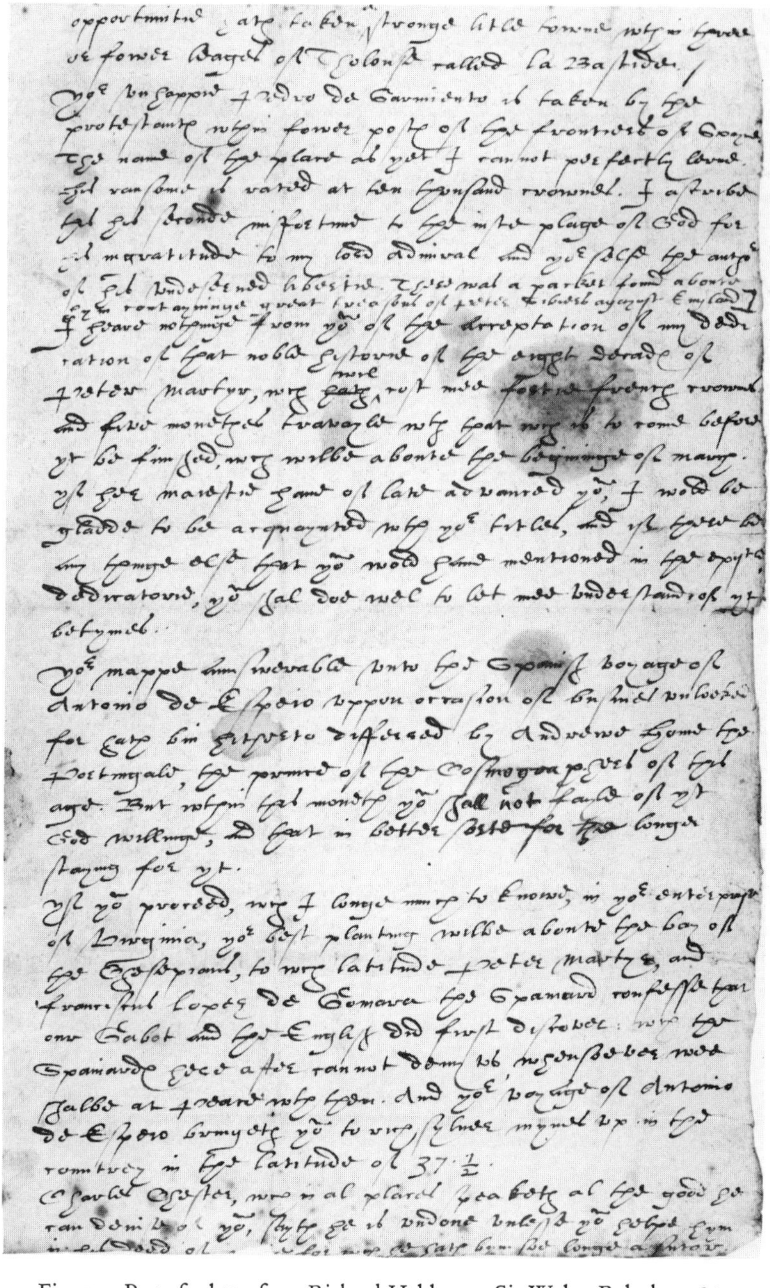

Fig. 12   Part of a letter from Richard Hakluyt to Sir Walter Ralegh, 1586.

Walter Ralegh.' (*PN* (1589), pp. 747–8; see Quinn, *Roanoke voyages*, I, 477–80.)

1587

Richard Hakluyt and Martin Basanier visited André Thevet in Paris and presented him with a copy of the printed version of René de Laudonnière's *L'Histoire notable de la Floride* (1586), the manuscript of which Hakluyt had earlier borrowed from Thevet and now returned. Thevet afterwards complained he had put it into print under Basanier's name without his permission (it had on its title-page 'Mise en lumiere par M. Basanier' and he also signed the dedication). Thevet regarded this as plagiarism, but it would not seem that Hakluyt did so nor did it prevent him publishing his English translation of it. Presumably there was some misunderstanding about the terms under which it was borrowed, as Hakluyt and Basanier would scarcely have presented themselves in a friendly way to Thevet if the situation had been precisely as he indicated. At the same time he may well have had grounds for feeling strongly aggrieved. The passage appears as a rough draft (written in 1587) in Thevet's 'La grande insulaire', Bibliothèque Nationale, MS Fonds français 15452, f. 177v:

Il y en a vne petite histoire imprimée l'année passée laquelle fidelement i'auois prestée suz bonne foy à vn certain Anglois, nommé Richard Hakluit escrite a la main l'ayant communiquée à ieune homme Parisien la feirent imprimer touz deuz a Paris soubs nommé M. Basanier – me la tindre quatre mois ou enuiron, au bout duquel temps la firent imprimée A Paris. I'ay icy a me condoloir auec mes amis contre ces plagaires et imposteurs lesquels ne pouuans gainger aucune chose sur moy par leurs sinistres entreprises, qu'ils auoient couués en lour ame ont pensé qu'ils osteroient le credit et authorite que mes peregrinations auoient acquis aux rapports que i'ay fait en ma Cosmographie et liure de mes singularités. Ayant commis ces deux personnages telle vilanie en mon endroit tous deux m'apporterent l'vn des liuures qu'ils firent imprimer pensans me gratifier auec ma coppie bien escrite – lequel liure ils dedierent a vn Chevalier milord d'Angleterre nommé Walter Ralegh.

Relations do not seem to have been broken off between Hakluyt and Thevet as it would appear that he acquired the Codex Mendoza from him in 1587, possibly on this occasion (see pp. 294–5, below).

January 1587

24 January, the Court of the Clothworkers' Company recorded 'a mocion was made towchinge the pencion of vj^{li} xiij^s iiij^d paide to master Hakluyt

(and by hym to be surrendered and geven vpp at the annunciation of our ladye nexte)'. (Acts and Orders of the Court of the Clothworkers' Company, 1581–1605, f. 75; cf. Girtin, *GJ*, CXIX, 212; *Golden ram*, p. 56.) Hakluyt had received his pension in the years 1578–9 (as above), in 1579–80 (Renter Warden's Account, 1579–80, f. 6v), in 1580–1 (*ibid.*, 1580–1, f. 8), 1581–2 (*ibid.*, 1581–2, f. 7v), 1582–3 (*ibid.*, 1582–3, f. 7v), 1583–4 (*ibid.*, 1583–4, f. 7v), 1584–5 (*ibid.*, 1584–5, f. 8v), 1585–6 (*ibid.*, 1585–6, f. 8v), making a total of £53 6s 8d over eight years. His pension does not appear in the accounts for 1586–7 though he was entitled to demand its payment up to 25 March 1587. It seems probable that he ceased to ask for it (or it was intimated that he should not do so) whenever he became assured of institution at Bristol Cathedral.

February 1587

22 February 1587.* Hakluyt dedicated, in Latin, his edition of Peter Martyr, *De orbe nouo . . . decades*, to Sir Walter Ralegh (sig. a3–a5). (Reprinted, with English translation, Taylor, *Hakluyts*, II, 356–69; extracts, Quinn, *Roanoke voyages*, II, 513–15.) On the title-page he stressed the considerable value to the reader of the index he had supplied.

February 1586 or February 1587

In 1600 Hakluyt printed 'Examen de los maestros y Pilotos, que navegan en las flotas de Espanna . . . Written by me Pedro Dias . . . vpon the request and gratification of M. *Richard Hakluyt*, in February 1586'.† (*PN*, III (1600), 864–8, Spanish and English.) Pedro Diaz had been brought to England by Sir Richard Grenville in October 1585 and escaped in 1588 (Quinn, *Roanoke voyages*, II, 785–95): as Hakluyt is not known to have been in England either in February 1586 or February 1587, it may be that his request was conveyed to Diaz by letter.

May 1587

1 May 1587. F[ilips] G[alle] S[culptor ?] dedicated to Hakluyt (*Doctiss. et ornatiss. Rich. Hakluyto*) the map of America he prepared for Hakluyt's edition of Peter Martyr's *De orbe nouo* (1587). (See Quinn and Skelton, edd., *PN* (1589), I (1965), xlviii.)

May (or November) 1587

1 May 1587, at London, Hakluyt dated his reprint of his dedication of the English Laudonnière to Ralegh in *Principal navigations*, III (1600), 303.

There is no date in *A notable historie* (1587), and the dedication contains in any case matter not available before October 1587, namely a reference to Captain Stafford's return from Virginia. (A problem arises as to whether Captain Edward Stafford, said to have returned before the dedication was written, came in the *Lion* on 18 October or the fly boat on 8 November or, if he did not leave the pinnace behind, which seems less likely, at some slightly earlier date than 18 October.) (Cf. Taylor, *Hakluyts*, II, 372–3; Quinn, *Roanoke voyages*, II, 505, 532, 547–8, 615.) The date may none the less be evidence that Hakluyt was in England by 1 May and completed then an earlier draft of the dedication.

September 1587

13 September 1587. Richard Hakluyt, lawyer, in his will names Richard Hakluyt, in succession to his brothers, Oliver and Edmond, as eventual heir to Burropps farm, Eyton, and lands in Luston, Herefordshire. (National Library of Wales, Aberystwyth, Hereford Probates, Pre-1660, Bundle Ha-3; printed Taylor, *Hakluyts*, II, 370–1: will proved 4 March 1590–1.)

September 1587

There is a small piece of indecisive evidence which could indicate that Hakluyt in fact reached London only on 7 September. In the Codex Mendoza (verso of a preliminary leaf) is written 'O: yourselfe in gold rydinge to London ye 7th of September 1587 / V'' (Owe yourself in gold, riding to London the 7th of September 1587, £5). Though it does not appear to be in Hakluyt's normal hand, this may be because it was a rough note in a secretary hand not so easily identifiable as his italic, but it could well be that of a messenger who brought the manuscript to England, rather than Hakluyt himself.

c. 1587

Hakluyt acquired from André Thevet the 'Codex Mendoza', a major Aztec MS. Purchas says that while Hakluyt was in Paris in Stafford's service, he bought it 'for 20. French crownes' after Thevet's death. But Hakluyt was in France only from 1583 to 1588; the inscription in English (see under 7 September) indicates it was in English hands in 1587, while Thevet did not die until 1592. Purchas says that Hakluyt 'procured Master Michael Locke in Sir Walter Raleighs name to translate it. It seemes that none were willing to be at the cost of cutting the Pictures, and so it remained among his papers till his death.' (The MS descended through Purchas and Selden to the Bodleian Library as Arch. Selden A 1; many times re-edited, the edition by James Cooper Clark (London, 3 vols., 1938) has both facsimiles and useful editorial matter: the Purchas reference is *Pilgrimes*, IV (1625), 1065–6, see also his *Pilgrimage* (1617), p. 983; A. Adhémar, *André Thevet* (Paris, 1947), p. 82, accepts the view that Hakluyt bought it after 1592. Purchas printed it in *Pilgrimes*, III, 1066–117.)

October 1587

Hakluyt completed his dedication to Sir Walter Ralegh of his translation of Laudonnière's book (see under 1 May, above). It was published as *A notable historie* before the end of the year. (Facsimile edited by Thomas R. Adams (Farnham, Surrey, 1964); reprinted in *PN*, III, 301–60; for the dedication see Taylor, *Hakluyts*, II, 372–8; Quinn, *Roanoke voyages*, II, 545–52.)

1587

Theodor de Bry visited England, met Hakluyt and was introduced to the existence of the North American drawings of both John White and Jacques le Moyne de Morgues. (See Quinn, *Roanoke voyages*, I, 39; II, 547; Hulton and Quinn, *The American drawings of John White*, I, 25–6.)

After 1587

Hakluyt acquired and put his name on a collection of ordinances (etc.) by Duarte de Meneses, relating to the government of Portuguese colonies in Africa and Asia, *c.* 1534–87 (incipit 'Foral dos vzos e custumes dos Canaris lauradores desta Ilha de Goa'). (B.M., Additional MS 28433; abbreviated in translation in Purchas, *Pilgrimes*, II (1625), 1506–33.) A translation, with which Hakluyt may have had something to do, was amongst the manuscripts of the marquess of Hertford in 1874 ('A register or collection of the uses, lawes, and customes of the Canaries or inhabitants of the island of Goa and of the landes thereunto belonging': with other items paralleling the original). (H.M.C., *Fourth report* (1874), appendix, p. 252. Its present whereabouts are not known. It appears probable that the original can be equated with 'The notable intercepted register or Matricola, of the whole gouernemente of the Easte India' taken in the *Madre de Deus* in 1592, p. 305, below.)

1588

January 1588. Hakluyt delivered to Lord Burghley in London a letter from Sir Edward Stafford, dated 8 January at Paris. (P.R.O., S.P. For., France, S.P. 78/18, 7, 19; *Cal. S.P. For.*, *1586–8*, p. 486.)

10 February. Stafford mentions to Walsingham a letter sent by 'Mr. Hacklytt'. (S.P. 78/18, 19; *Cal. S.P. For.*, *1586–8*, p. 510.)

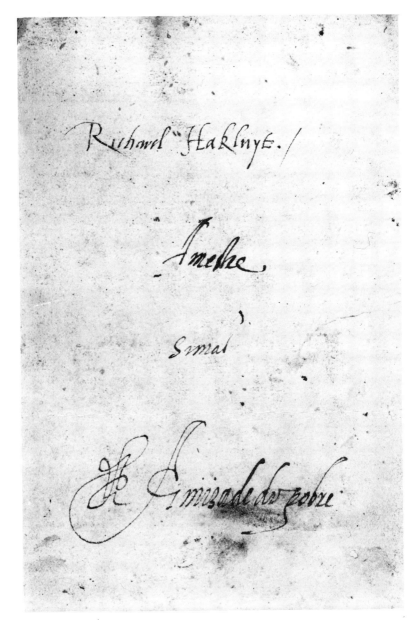

Fig. 13   Fly-leaf and title-page of Duarte de Meneses' collection of

[manuscript in 16th-century Portuguese cursive]

foral dos vsos E custumes dos canaris Lauradores desta
Jlha de goa e destas suas anexas

Dom Joaõ pergraca de deos Rei de purtugal e dos algarues daqui e dalem mar, &
a primera Sõr de guine e da conquista nauegacaõ comercio de tiopia arabia persia E da
India &c a quoantos esta nosa carta de foral virẽ dada aos gacares E lauradores E
pouoadores das aldeas E Jlhas da nosa cidade de goa fasemos saber q[ue] p[e]llo que das diligẽ
cias E Jsames q mãdamos fazer per Juisti ficasaõ E declaracaõ dignos & erã obriga
dos a pagar E pagauaõ aos Reis E Sõres dantes de ser nosa de Suas erancas,
foros E obrigacões E outros em ca Rages E assios dereitos vsos E custumes en q e[s]
tauaõ E lhe deuiamos Mãdar goardar achamos per q[ue] das ditas diligẽcias q[ue] elles nos
Saõ obrigados a pagar o q nesto outro foral da pagua dos ditos dereitos p[or]te E outro se[r]
a q[ue] hamos q ouuerã destes vsos de vsar dereitos E custumes na Maneira & forma seguinte

A haouse q cada hũa aldea das ditas Jlhas te certos gacares dellas mais dellas menos Se
gũdo o Seu custume E as ditas Jlhas E aldeas saõ E q o dito nome gacar quer diser gouer
nador ministrador E p[o]r ser isto ordenouse daqui e tempo an tigo foraõ q[ua]tro homes a
proueitar hũa Jlha E outra mar inhada e aprouejtada a que al aprouejtaraõ E forte fiserã
em tal maneira E tambẽ q per espaco de tempo foi em tanto crecimento q se fes nella grande
pouoasaõ E aqueles principiadores p[e]llo Seu bom gouerno E ministramento E grangeam[en]to
foraõ chamados p[e]llo gacares E despois vierã Sores E Sogerigadores Sobrelles aos quaes
obrigaraõ dar Renda E foros p[or] deixarẽ e suas racas E custumes E nas podesa
ber o como Sodesto

Vesta Jlha de tisoare onde esta cercada a cidade de goa
ha trinta e hũa aldeas E Saõ as Seguintes

Neuraogrãde	goarecha
gancim	cogir
nella	duguari
aJosim	murrena
caraolim	mora hinopequens
batim	Siumbel
taleigaõ	panelim

documents on the government of the Portuguese colonies.

1588

By 21 March Hakluyt had returned to Paris. (P.R.O., S.P. For., France, S.P. 78/18, 42, 47; *Cal. S.P. For., 1586–8*, pp. 550, 564.)

April 1588

11 April.* Hakluyt wrote from Paris to Lord Burghley, transmitting the petition of the earl of Westmorland, and asking a favour for his cousin Wigmore. (P.R.O., S.P. 15/30, 96; *Cal. S.P. Dom., Add., 1580–1625*, pp. 248–9. This was followed on 25 April by a letter from Stafford to Walsingham on Westmorland. B.M., Harleian MS 288, f. 187.)

27 April.* 7 May. João de Castro brought a letter to Stafford to despatch to Walsingham by 'Mr. Haquin [*sic*] the minister and secretary of her Majesty's ambassador'. (S.P. For., France, S.P. 78/18, 78; *Cal. S.P. For., 1586–8*, p. 603.)

c. 1587–8

At some time after renouncing his Studentship at Christ Church, and probably during one of his visits to England in 1587 or 1588, Hakluyt married Douglas Cavendish. Davy says Hakluyt's wife was daughter of Richard Cavendish of Hornsey, uncle of Thomas Cavendish, but as he did not know her Christian name his authority is not so firm as one would wish. (David Elisha Davy's 'Suffolk Collections', vol. xlvii, B.M., Additional MS 19122, f. 350; no parish registers of Hornsey are extant for this period.)

1588

In 1588 Theodor de Bry made a further visit to England, collecting material, through Hakluyt, for his proposed American volumes from Thomas Harriot, John White, and the widow of Jacques le Moyne. The precise dates and details of his relations with Hakluyt on this visit are not known. (Quinn, *Roanoke voyages*, I, 39; II, 547; Hulton and Quinn, *American drawings of John White*, I, 25–6.)

May 1588

6–7 May 1588. Hakluyt set out from Paris, carrying Stafford's letters, including one from João de Castro, a Portuguese, dated 27 April,* to Walsingham. (P.R.O., S.P. For., France, S.P. 78/18, 78; *Cal. S.P. For., 1586–8*, pp. 601–3; Parks, *Hakluyt*, p. 250.)

29 May 1588. Hakluyt was sent by Stafford to Burghley on confidential French business ('I am fain to send Haklit'). (P.R.O., S.P. For., France, S.P. 78/18, 100–1; *Cal. S.P. For., 1586–8*, pp. 627–30.)

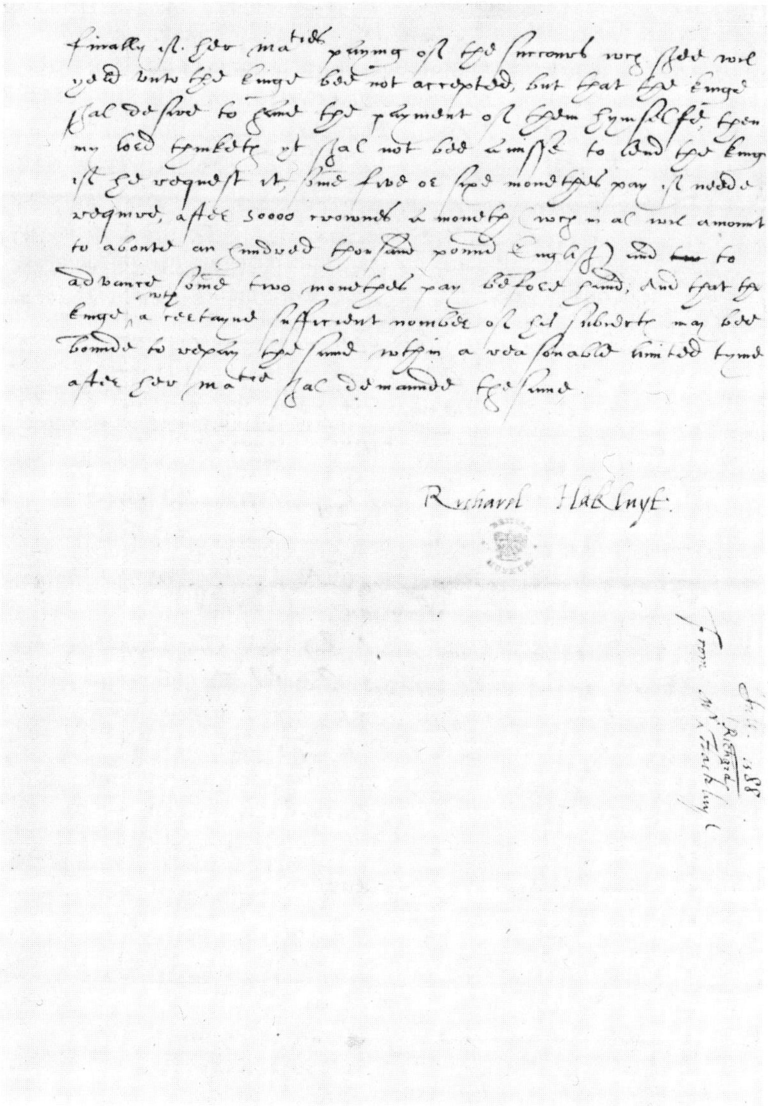
finally if her matie payinge of the souldiours wch shee will
yeeld unto the kinge bee not accepted, but that the kinge
shal desire to have the payment of them himselfe, then
my lord thinketh yt shal not bee amisse to lend the kinge
if he request it, some fiue or sixe monethes pay if neede
require, after 50000 crownes a monethe wch in al will amount
to aboute an hundred thousand poundes Englishe and to
advance some two monethes pay before hand, And that the
kinge a reteyninge sufficient nombre of his subiectes may bee
bounde to repay the same within a reasonable limited tyme
after her matie shal demande the same.

Richard Hakluyt.

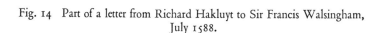

Fig. 14 Part of a letter from Richard Hakluyt to Sir Francis Walsingham, July 1588.

July 1588

July 1588. Hakluyt wrote down for Walsingham the text of a verbal message he had earlier delivered to Burghley (B.M., Harleian MS 288, ff. 212–13v), dated 27 April,* from the Portuguese, João de Castro. (P.R.O., S.P. For., France, S.P. 78/18, 78; *Cal. S.P. For.*, *1586–8*, pp. 601–3; Parks, *Hakluyt*, p. 250.)

July 1588

27 July. Hakluyt reached Paris on his return, bringing first, incomplete, news of the Armada action. (P.R.O., S.P. For., France, S.P. 78/18, 135; *Cal. S.P. For., July–December 1588*, p. 85.)

August 1588

1 August 1588. A letter attributed to Richard Hakluyt was written from Paris to Sir Thomas Heneage and other members of the privy council on French and Spanish matters. (H.M.C., *Rutland*, I, 256–8 (ser. 24) – a copy but with every indication that it bears his name; Parks, *Hakluyt*, pp. 250–1.) This certainly does not read as if it was by Hakluyt. On 15 June, while Hakluyt was still in England, an 'R.H.' wrote to 'Mr. Jacquelin' from Paris giving French news. (B.M., Harleian MS 288, ff. 202–3v.) It would thus appear that there was another man there in the English service with the same initials, and it is probably to him that the August letter should be attributed.)

1588

Hakluyt returned to London during the winter, escorting the Countess of Sheffield (Lady Douglas Stafford) from Paris to London. (*PN* (1589), *2v, but with no conclusive evidence that this was before 31 December.)

1588

Hakluyt made a copy of his 'Analysis siue Resolutio Methodica in octo Libros Politicorum Aristotelis', signing it 'Authore Richardo Hackluito Oxoniense. 1588'. (Sloane MS 1982, ff. 1–60.)

November 1588

25 November 1588. Abraham Ortelius wrote to William Camden that he had heard from Emanuel van Meteren that Hakluyt was hopeful of producing an edition of Abulfeda's geography. (Thomas Smith, *V. cl. Camdeni et epistolae* (1691), p. 33.) This might suggest that Van Meteren had been able to talk to Hakluyt in London about the middle of November, though he could, of course, have obtained his information indirectly.

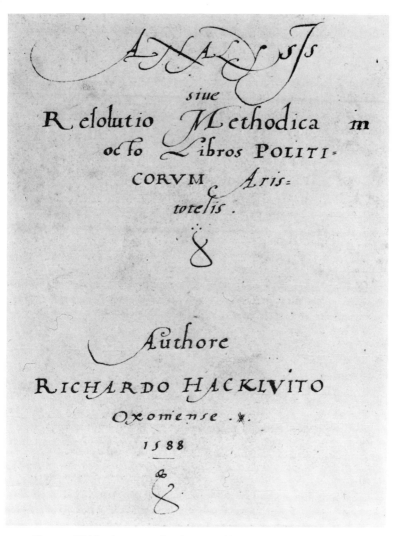

Fig. 15   Hakluyt's autograph title-page of his copy of his *Analysis* of
Aristotle's *Politics*, 1588.

1589 or earlier

Hakluyt picked up some garbled references to the 1527 North American voyages from Martin Frobisher and from Richard Allen. (*PN* (1589), p. 517.)

He received from Antony Garrard, merchant of London, some informa‑ tion on English voyages to Brazil, *c.* 1540. (*PN* (1589), p. 521.)

He received from Anthony Jenkinson the safe conduct from Suleiman the Great, given to him in 1553, written in Turkish and French. (*PN* (1589), p. 83.)

1589 or earlier

After his return (or conceivably on an earlier visit to England) Hakluyt rode to Thomas Butts, Great Ryburgh (Ryburgh Magna), Norfolk, to obtain such information as Butts could recall of his part in Richard Hore's expedition to North America in 1536. (*PN* (1589), p. 517. Butts died in 1593, part of his tomb chest being still in Great Ryburgh Church.)

January 1589

1 January 1589. Robert Parke, in his dedication to Thomas Cavendish of his translation of J. González de Mendoza, *The historie of the great and mightie kingdome of China* (1588), acknowledged that the work was prepared 'at the earnest request and encouragement of my worshipfull friend Master Richard Hakluit, late of Oxforde, a gentleman, besides his other manifolde learning and languages, of singular and deepe insight in all histories of discouerie and partes of Cosmographie'. (Sig. ¶3v.)

January 1589

24 January 1589. In his dedication to Sir Francis Drake of his translation of A. Meierus, *Certaine briefe, and speciall instructions* (1589), Philip Jones referred to 'M. Richard Hakluit, a man of incredible deuotion towarde your selfe, and of speciall carefulnesse for the good of our Nation: as the world inioying the benefit of some of his trauels can giue testimonie, & is possible to giue better, if that rare & excellent worke which he now plyeth [*PN* (1589)], once come to publike view. In the meane time I record his diligence.' (Sig. A3v; for the date see Quinn and Skelton, edd., *PN* (1589), I (1965), xix–xx.)

March 1589

7 March 1589. Hakluyt was named twelfth of nineteen grantees from Sir Walter Ralegh of rights under the City of Ralegh assignment of 7 January

1587, which they undertook to support. (*PN* (1589), pp. 815–17, added out of order; see Quinn, *Roanoke voyages*, II, 569–76.)

May 1589

15 May 1589. Abraham Ortelius wrote from Antwerp to Jacob Cool or Cole (Ortelianus) noting that he has seen advertised in the Frankfurt book fair catalogue Hakluyt's edition of Peter Martyr's *Decades* (Paris, 1587). He inquired if Hakluyt added anything, or else why did he publish this edition. He is interested to learn that Cool has been discussing fossils with Hakluyt. (*Abrahami Ortelii . . . epistulae*, ed. J. H. Hessels (1887), pp. 393–5 (in Latin).)

September 1589

1 September 1589, 'the voiages and Discoueries of the Englishe nation', under warrant from Sir Francis Walsingham, was entered in the Stationers' Register. (Arber, *Transcript*, II, 529.)

November 1589

17 November 1589. Hakluyt completed his dedication of *Principall navigations* to Sir Francis Walsingham; it is largely autobiographical. (Sig. *2–3; reprinted, Taylor, *Hakluyts*, II, 396–401.)

In his preface to the reader, Hakluyt made acknowledgements to Edward Dyer, Richard Staper (with whom he had early contacts through the Clothworkers' Company), William Borough, Anthony Jenkinson, Sir John Hawkins, Sir Walter Ralegh, Richard Hakluyt, lawyer, his cousin, Richard Garth, Walter Cope, Emery Molyneux, and William Sanderson, besides giving a general account of the layout of the work. (Sig. *3v–4v; reprinted Taylor, *Hakluyts*, II, 401–9; discussed, Quinn and Skelton, edd., *PN* (1589), I (1965), xxxiii–xlvii.)

Complimentary verses were contributed by the Rev. Hugh Broughton (in Greek); Marco Antonio Pigafetta (in Italian), William Camden and Philip Jones (both in Latin).

April 1590

20 April 1590. Hakluyt was instituted rector of Wetheringsett with Blockford, Suffolk, diocese of Norwich (which he was to hold for 26 years). The patron was the Countess of Sheffield (Lady Douglas Stafford): by 1603 the patronage had passed to Sir Stephen Soames. (Norfolk Diocesan Records, Norfolk and Norwich Record Office, R/14, f. 188r; Anthony à Wood, *Athenae Oxonienses*, ed. Philip Bliss, II (1815), cols. 186–7; Archbishop of Canterbury's return, 1603, B.M., Harleian MS 595, printed in Suffolk

Institute of Archaeology and Natural History, *Proceedings*, XI (1901–3), 26; assembled in Parks, *Hakluyt*, p. 252.)

Above the entries in the Wetheringsett Register, 1556–1779, for the year beginning 25 March 1590, Hakluyt entered his name in his own hand and the clerk then added three further words so that it reads, 'Mʳ Richard Hakluit entered person'. (Norwich Diocesan Records, Ipswich and East Suffolk Record Office, FB 151/D1.)

1590

April–May 1590. Theodor de Bry published at Frankfurt editions in four languages of his *America*, part i. In his epistle to the reader in the English-language edition (his dedication to Ralegh was dated 30 April), he stated that he was offering the true pictures of the North American Indians which 'by the helfe of Maister Richard Hakluyt of Oxford Minister of Gods Word, who first Incouraged me to publish the Worke, I creaued out of the verye original of Maister Ihon White'. (*America*, pt. i, ***3v.) The Latin captions supplied by Thomas Harriot for the White plates were translated into English by Hakluyt (title-page: 'Translated out of Latin into English by Richard Hackluit').

The French edition of *America*, pt. i, 'Au Lecteur', mistakenly said that Hakluyt had been in Virginia: 'qui a esté audit pays, & est cause de l'ad-uancement de ce present Traicté'. (See Parks, *Hakluyt*, p. 252.)

c. 1590

Henry Lane wrote to Hakluyt, with information on Muscovy Company expeditions. (*PN*, I (1598), 374–5; reprinted in Taylor, *Hakluyts*, II, 409–13.)

August 1590

25 August 1590. Ortelius wrote to Jacob Cool from Antwerp to salute Hakluyt for him; he had already heard of the work on Florida (possibly the material by Le Moyne which Theodor de Bry was to publish in 1591). Hakluyt had asked (apparently through Cool) that Ortelius should make a map of the area from Mexico City northwards. Ortelius is willing to do so, and make due acknowledgement, if Hakluyt will supply the material ('si ipse copiam mihi fecerit, lubens edam, non sine honorifica Domini Haccluti mentione, in ea'). (Ortelius, *Epistulae*, ed. Hessells, pp. 442–3.)

1591

Theodor de Bry made no specific reference to Hakluyt for the Le Moyne material which he published in Latin and German as *America*, part ii, 1591.

1591–2

Hakluyt wrote 'A briefe note of the Morsse and the vse thereof'. He was shown by his old friend Dr Alexander Woodson of Bristol a walrus ('morse') tooth brought from the Magdalen Islands, Gulf of St Lawrence, and set out incentives which he thought should attract Bristol seamen and merchants into exploiting a walrus fishery.

June 1592

20 June 1592. Hakluyt was appointed executor in his brother's, Edmond's, will, being left 'my free land in Eaton [Eyton, Herefordshire] and elsewhere'. (P.R.O., Prob. 12, formerly P.C.C. 18 Nevill; printed in Taylor, *Hakluyts*, II, 413–14; probate granted to Richard Hakluyt, 1 February 1593.)

1592

John Williamson, cooper and citizen of London, gave Hakluyt some impressions of voyages to the Mediterranean in 1534–5 on which he served. (*PN*, II (1599), i, 98.)

1592

The Portuguese East Indian carrack, the *Madre de Deus* (known in England in its Spanish form as the *Madre de Dios*) was captured at sea on 3 August 1592 and brought to Dartmouth on 7 September. Hakluyt was the beneficiary in so far that he received a treatise by Duarte Sande [p. 220, above] 'printed in Latine in Macao a citie of China, in China-paper, in the yeere a thousand fiue hundred and ninetie, and was intercepted in the great Carack called Madre de Dios two yeeres after, inclosed in a case of sweete Cedar wood, and lapped vp almost an hundred fold in fine calicut-cloth, as though it had beene some incomparable iewell' (*PN*, II (1599), sig. *4). He returned later to this capture when he noted as sources for the East Indies '*Duarte Sande* printed in *Macao*. 1590. The notable intercepted register or *Matroclia* [or 'Matricola'], of the whole governemente of the *Easte India* in the *Madre de Dios* 1592. [see p. 211, above] with divers other bookes, and letters written from *Iapan, China*, and yᵉ *Indies*. which haue bin intercepted.' (Henry E. Huntington Library, Ellesmere MS 2360; cf. Taylor, *Hakluyts*, II, 467. Professor Taylor (*ibid.*, I, 59) says that 'All the geographical materials (including maps) obtained from this prize were handed over to Hakluyt'. There does not seem to be direct evidence that maps were acquired by him in this way, though she assumes that the 'large Italian intercepted map of the *Malucos*', of which he made copies and notes, came from the *Madre de Deus*

(Bodleian Library, MS Selden Arch. B. 8, f. 85r; Taylor, *Hakluyts*, II, 482). There is, likewise, no direct evidence that '*all* the geographical materials' from this prize came to him, though it is clear many did so.)

January 1593

3 January 1593. Hakluyt's son, Edmond, was christened at Wetheringsett. ('Edmond sonne of Richard Hackluytt and Duglas his wife baptized ye fourth day of Iune'.) (Wetheringsett Register, 1556–1779, as above; Taylor, *Hakluyts*, I, 53.)

February 1593 (*or February 1594*)

4 February 1593† (or 1594). John White wrote to Hakluyt, from Newtown in Kilmore, Co. Cork, on the ill-success of his Virginia voyage of 1590, of which he has sent a narrative. (*PN*, III (1600), 287–8; reprinted Taylor, *Hakluyts*, II, 415–17, and Quinn, *Roanoke voyages*, II, 712–16.)

1593

Hakluyt's *Principall navigations* was commended as 'a worke of importance' by Gabriel Harvey. (*Pierces supererogation* (1593), p. 49.) Harvey included 'Hacluit' amongst those Englishmen of his time, with Digges and Blundeville, most worthy of commendation in past and present. (Note in copy of his Quintilian (1542), G. C. Moore-Smith, *Gabriel Harvey's marginalia* (1913), p. 122.) He also noted in his 1598 Chaucer 'I looke for muche as well in verse, as in prose, from mie two Oxford Friends, Doctor Gager, & M. Hackluit: both rarely furnished for the purpose' (*ibid.*, p. 233). It was possibly this edition which Hakluyt used for his quotations from Chaucer. (Lumley 1008 has been identified as B.M., Royal MS 18. c. II.)

c. 1593

Hakluyt wrote 'A briefe note concerning the voyage of M. George Drake of Apsham to the Isle of Ramea in the aforesayd yere 1593'. (*PN*, III (1600), 193; reprinted Taylor, *Hakluyts*, II, 483–4.) Hakluyt was promised a narrative by George Drake but when it did not appear had to write the voyage up himself.

c. 1594

Hakluyt took the story of James Lancaster's 1591–4 voyages 'from the mouth of Edmund Barker of Ipswich'. (*PN*, II (1599), ii, 102.)

1594-5

On the initiative of Jacob Walcke (or Valcke), treasurer of Zeeland, who wrote to him on 25 November 1594, Emanuel van Meteren, then in London, enlisted Hakluyt's advice for the projected Barents voyage in search of the North-east Passage. Walcke then wrote directly to Hakluyt (the letter is not extant), who replied on 6 December, from Wetheringsett by Ipswich. This letter, translated into Dutch by Van Meteren (the form in which it exists), was sent on by Van Meteren to Walcke who added further details (December 15/25). Walcke authorized Van Meteren to obtain Hakluyt's professional opinion which he completed in February, and was paid for it by Van Meteren. His report has not survived, though a translation of the Pet–Jackman narrative, which he included, has. (Algemeen Rijksarchief 's-Gravenhage, Archief van de Staten van Holland en West-Friesland Inv. No. 2687, Recueil Commercie 1455–1646, ff. 63–8; edited by S. L. L'Honoré Naber, *Reizen van Willem Barents*, II (1917), xv, 201–10 (Linschoten-Vereeniging Werken xv); Taylor, *Hakluyts*, II, 417–20 (translation of Hakluyt–Van Meteren letter of 6 December 1594); Parks, *Hakluyt*, p. 253.)

February 1595

In letters of 8/18 February and 14/24 February 1595 Van Meteren urged Hakluyt to send him Francis Pretty's account of Cavendish's circumnavigation and also the rutter (by Thomas Fuller) which had been made on the same voyage. (Algemeen Rijksarchief, Recueil Commercie (as above), see P. A. Tiele, *Mémoire bibliographique sur les journaux des navigateurs néerlandais* (Amsterdam, 1867); Rubens Borba de Moraes, *Bibliographia brasiliana*, I (Amsterdam, 1958), 149.)

After July 1595

The Reverend Hugh Branham of the parish of All Saints, Harwich, passed to Hakluyt a letter he had received from Gudbrander Thorláksson, bishop of Hólar, on antiquities of Greenland and Iceland. See p. 402 below.

c. 1595-6

Robert Dudley wrote an account of his West Indies voyage (1595) 'at the request of M. Richard Hakluyt'. (*PN*, III (1600), 574.)

Barents took with him on his last North-east Passage voyage a Dutch translation of Hugh Smith's narrative of the Pet–Jackman voyage of 1580, which Hakluyt had published in *Principall navigations* in 1589. On 17 August 1875 it was found on Novaya Zemlya by Captain Marten Gundersen of the Norwegian sloop *Regina* under the ruins of Barents' winter quarters (*Behouden Huys*), 56 pages of clear handwriting still surviving, along with two charts, said to be of 'Germania inferior', now lost. After a long period of obscurity in Norway (during which a copy was made which is now Norsk Polarinstituut, Oslo, MS 91 (08)) the manuscript was brought to Holland in 1929 by H. H. Dresselhuys and was acquired by D. G. van Beuningen, who presented it to the Maritiem Museum 'Prins Hendrik', Rotterdam, where it remains. G. B. Parks, who printed a facsimile page (but gave its provenance by mistake as 'the Norwegian National Library'), considered that Hakluyt supplied the English version for Barents' use as part of his dealings with Walcke and van Meteren (*Hakluyt*, p. 253), while van Nouhoys, curator of the Rotterdam museum at the time of the acquisition of the manuscript, maintained that Barents had more probably had a Dutch version made (from the 1589 printed version) well before 1595 and that Hakluyt had nothing to do with making it available for translation or for its going on the 1596 voyage ('The ship's council on the expedition of Pet and Jackman', *The Mariner's Mirror*, XVI (1930), 411–14), though there does not appear to be conclusive evidence either way. (We are grateful for the assistance of Dr K. A. Z. Lundquist, deputy director, Norsk Polarinstituut, Oslo, and Dr Vibeke Eeg-Henriksen, librarian, and to Dr E. A. de Vries, librarian, Maritiem Museum 'Prins Hendrik', Rotterdam.)

1596

Charles Fitz-Geffrey, *Sir Francis Drake his honorable lifes commendation* (Oxford, 1596; S.T.C. 10943), used *Principall navigations* (1589) freely and without acknowledgement.

1596

Thomas Harriot dated 1596 a note which included the references, 'M. Hakluyt of Canada some mappes of it. A rutter of the riuer of Plate. / A Plot of the Caspian sea.' (B.M., Sloane MS 2292, f. 41; see Quinn, 'England and the St Lawrence', in J. Parker, ed., *Merchants and scholars* (1965), p. 139.)

c. 1596

About 1596 Hakluyt translated from Joseph de Acosta, *Historia natural y moral de las Indias* (Seville, 1590; published in English in 1604), 'Certaine Briefe Testimonies Concerning the mightie River of Amazones ... together with some mention of the rich and stately empire of Dorado, called by Sir Walter Ralegh and the natural inhabitants Guiana ...' (*PN*, III (1600), 698–9; represented in S.P. 12/25, 43, *Cal. S.P. Dom., 1581–90*, p. 710.)

c. 1595-8

'The true Limites of all the Countries and Prouinces at this present actually possessed by ye Spaniard and Portugales in the West Indies.' In style and content attributable to Hakluyt. (Refers to the latest ('last') edition of Ortelius for the facts that the most northerly Spanish possession in Mexico is San Miguel (St Michael, Culiacán, New Galicia); that in Guastacan (on the Gulf coast), Tampico, Panuco and Santiago de los Valles are so distinguished; also that beyond Trinidad south to Pernambuco there are no Christians inhabiting (P.R.O., S.P. Col., C.O. 1/1, 32; printed in Taylor, *Hakluyts*, II, 420-5 (assigned to 1598); this note would fit either the 1592 or 1598 editions of *Theatrum orbis terrarum*, ff. 8-9).

c. 1596-7

Hakluyt was admitted to the library of Lord Lumley after an introduction by his friend Anthony Watson, bishop of Chichester (consecrated 15 August 1596), the Queen's high almoner. (*PN*, I (1598), sig. **1v; Taylor, *Hakluyts*, II, 437-8, 446.)

c. 1597

Hakluyt copied the MSS of the Rubruquis, Carpini and Odoric expeditions from versions in Lord Lumley's library. (They are now B.M., Royal MS 13, A. XIV, ff. 198-213 (Carpini) and MS 14. C. XIII, ff. 216-24 (Odoric), ff. 225-35 (Rubruquis). See C. R. Beazley, ed., *The texts and versions of John de Plano Carpini and William de Rubruquis* (1903), pp. xvi-xviii. Hakluyt's versions are in *PN*, I (1598), 21-117.)

1597

Summer 1597. Sir Robert Cecil consulted Hakluyt 'touching the state of the Country of Guiana, and whether it were fit to be planted by the English': Hakluyt was impressed by his knowledge of western voyages and navigation and by his judicious balancing of the issues involved in further Guiana ventures. (Dedication to *PN*, II (1599), *4r-4v; Taylor, *Hakluyts*, II, 462.)

August 1597

August 1597. Hakluyt's wife, Douglas (*née* Cavendish) died at Wethering‐sett: 'Duglasse Hackluytt ye wieff of mr. Richard Hackluytt parson of Wethering*sett* was buryed ye viij day of August.' (Wetheringsett Register, 1556-1779, see p. 304, above; Parks, *Hakluyt*, p. 253; Taylor, *Hakluyts*, I, 53.)

Before 1598

Thomas Tilney of Hadleigh, Suffolk, allowed Hakluyt to use a manu/
script on the Tilney family of Shelley, Suffolk. (*PN*, II (1599), i, 29.)

Hakluyt took extracts from ledgers once belonging to Sir William
Locke (Lok), mercer, Sir William Bowyer, John Gresham and other
merchants on English voyages to the Mediterranean, 1511–34. (*PN*, II
(1599), i, 96–7.)

Hakluyt took down from Edmund Barker an account of Lancaster's
voyage, 1591–4. (*PN*, II (1599), ii, 102–10.)

Hakluyt took notes from a ledger once owned by Nicholas Thorne of
Bristol. (*PN*, II (1599), ii, 3.)

January 1598

1 January 1597–8. Abraham Hartwell dated from Lambeth Palace, where
he was secretary to George Abbot, archbishop of Canterbury, the dedication
to Abbot of his translation of Duarte Lopes, *A reporte of the kingdome of
Congo* (1597). In his address to the reader he tells that as he was returning
from Norfolk and lay at the house of a learned prelate in Suffolk ['*Master*
H[ugh] Castelton', or Casselton, prebendary of Norwich Cathedral, rector
of Thornton, Suffolk], there came to him (probably from Wetheringsett)
'a curious and diligent searcher and obseruer of Forreine aduentures and
aduenturers [*Master* R[ichard] Hackluyt], as by his good paines appeareth...
[who] presently presented me with this Portingall Pilgrime lately come to
him out of the Kingdome of Congo, and apparrelled in an Italian vesture:
intreating me very earnestly, that I would take him with me, and make him
English'. (Sig. *1r: the book was entered in the Stationers' Register on 25
August 1595 (Arber, *Transcript*, III, 47), indicating that the encounter
between Hartwell and Hakluyt in Suffolk had taken place before that date.
Lumley 1439.)

January 1598

16 January 1597–8. William Phillip, the translator of *The description of a
voyage made by certaine ships of Holland into the East Indies* (1598), refers to the
Fitch-Newbery documents and others in *Principall navigations* (1589), as
appearing 'in a booke written by M. Richard Haclute, a Gentleman very
studious therein, entitled the English voyages'. (Sig. A1r.)

January 1598

21 January 1598. John Wolfe the printer, in his dedication to Dr Julius
Caesar of *Iohn Huighen van Linschoten. his discours of voyages into y* Easte &*

West Indies (1598), wrote (sig. A1v), 'About a Tweluemonth agoe, a learned Gentleman brought vnto mee the Voyages and Nauigation of Iohn Huyghen van Linschoten into the Indies written in the Dutche Tongue, which he wished might be translated into our Language, because hee thought it would be not onely delightfull, but also very commodious for our English Nation.' The translator, William Phillip, in his address to the reader, says, 'Which Booke being commended, by Maister Richard Hackluyt, a man that laboureth greatly to aduance our English Name and Nation, the Printer thought good to cause the same to bee translated into the English Tongue'. (Sig. A3v. The book was entered in the Stationers' Register on 21 June 1597 (Arber, *Transcript*, III, 85–6).)

May 1598

1 May 1598. Emmanuel van Meteren dated at the Hague his preface to *Beschryvinge van de overtreffelijcke ende wijdt-vermaerde Zee-vaerdt van Edelen Heer ende Meester Thomas Candish* (Amsterdam, Cornelis Claesz, 1598), a copy of which is in the John Carter Brown Library, in which he published translations of the Francis Pretty narrative and Thomas Fullers' rutter of Cavendish's circumnavigation for which he had asked Hakluyt in February 1595. (Theodor de Bry, *America*, part VIII (1599), contained a Latin translation by Artus of the Dutch version of Pretty, antedating Hakluyt's printing of it in English in 1600.)

June 1598

13 June 1598. William Phillip's translation of Gerrit de Veer's narratives of the three Dutch voyages to the north-east was entered in the Stationers' Register (Arber, *Transcript*, III, 118). If it was published, no copy is known to have survived, while the 1609 edition makes no reference to an earlier appearance. The entry, at least, was probably inspired by Hakluyt, who had been intimately associated with the preparations for the Barents voyage of 1596.

October 1598

7 October 1598. Hakluyt signed his dedication to Charles Howard, earl of Nottingham, lord high admiral, of *Principal navigations*, I, concerning himself mainly with sea power. (Sig. *2–3v; reprinted Taylor, *Hakluyts*, II, 426–32.) In the preface to the reader he set out the main topics covered in the volume but made no acknowledgements, except to thank Lord Lumley for the use of his library and the bishop of Chichester for getting him admitted to it. (Sig. *4–6, **1–2v; reprinted Taylor, *Hakluyts*, II, 433–51.)

December 1598 or early 1599

Principal navigations, I, was published with commendatory verses by Hugh Broughton (in Greek), Richard Mulcaster (two, in Latin), William Camden (Latin), Marco Antonio Pigafeta (Italian). (Sig. **3–3v; Foster Watson, 'Hakluyt and Mulcaster', *GJ*, XLIX (1917), 48–53: it was not entered in the Stationers' Register.) The volume was withdrawn about September 1599 when exception was taken to the appearance of an account of the Cadiz expedition, 1597: it was reissued with an excision of the offending item and with a new titlepage later in 1599 along with the second volume and the map (see pp. 491, 494–6, below).

August 1599

23 August 1599. Edward Wright, in his dedication to Charles Howard, earl of Nottingham of *The hauenfinding art* (1599) (sig. A2r), stated he was informed 'by my learned friend and most earnest and effectuall furtherer of Nauigation for the common good of his Countrey, M. Richard Hackluit, vpon the dedication of his first volume of discoueries vnto your Lor[dship] about a yeere since' of the affection Nottingham had to the advancement of knowledge and skill among seamen and of his approaches to Queen Elizabeth 'for the establishing of an ordinary Lecture to be read for their instruction'.

October 1599

16 October 1599. Hakluyt was present at a meeting of the committee (which included Richard Staper) set up on 24 September to act as directors of the East India voyage. The activities of the Dutch were discussed and Hakluyt was probably called in to tell what he knew of their voyages. (Henry Stevens, *The dawn of British trade to the East Indies as recorded in the Court Minutes of the East India Company, 1599–1603* (1886), p. 10.)

October 1599

24 October 1599. Hakluyt signed his dedication to Sir Robert Cecil of *Principal navigations*, II (1599), discussing the contents, paying tribute to Sir Edward Osborne, Richard Staper and William Harborne, mentioning material in the hands of Thomas Harriot and referring to the opinions of Caesar Frederick – Cesare Federici (though perhaps only as expressed in his book *The voyage and trauaile of M. C. Frederick into the East Indies* (editions of 1588 and 1591). (Sig. *2–4v; reprinted Taylor, *Hakluyts*, II, 453–64.)

1599

Principal navigations, II, probably appeared before the end of the year, and was issued with the modified volume I, the two being normally found bound together. (See p. 491, below.)

November 1599

23 November 1599. Hakluyt was promised, at the request of Sir Robert Cecil, the next reversion to a chaplaincy at the Hospital of the Savoy, London. (William Mount, master of the Savoy, to Sir Robert Cecil, 23 November 1599. Cecil MS 74/97; H.M.C., *Cecil*, IX (1897), 397–8.)

1600

Edward Wright, in his 'laudatory address' to William Gilbert, prefaced to *De magnete* (1600), commends 'our very learned fellow-countryman Richard Hakluyt' ('doctissimi nostri Richardi Hackluit') for the material he assembled on the Portuguese voyages. (Sig. *4r; the book was entered in the Stationers' Register on 7 December 1599 (Arber, *Transcript*, III, 546), so that he may represent an almost immediate reaction to the appearance of the second volume; English translation by P. F. Mottelay (1893), p. xxxviii.)

c. March 1600

Hakluyt appears to have drawn up, on behalf of the East India merchants, notes on 'The places in the East Indies where the subjects of the King of Spayne haue any Fortes and settled Residence'. (Copy of *c.* 1625 in B.M. Sloane MS 25, ff. 13–13v, printed in Taylor, *Hakluyts*, II, 487–8. Sir William Foster, *English quest of eastern trade* (1933), p. 148, regarded them, and the letter of Fulke Greville to Cecil, 10 March 1599–1600 (cited Taylor, *Hakluyts*, II, 468n.), as part of the preparations for the diplomatic talks with Spain which were planned to take place in the early summer of 1600 (and did so at Boulogne in June).)

May 1600

18 May. Hakluyt was recommended by the Privy Council (Cecil and Nottingham being amongst those present) to George Abbot, archbishop of Canterbury, for the vacancy expected in the benefice of Great All Hallows, Thames Street, London (which he did not get). (*A.P.C.*, *1599–1600*, pp. 330–1; Parks, *Hakluyt*, pp. 201, 254.)

September 1600

1 September 1600. Hakluyt signed his dedication to Sir Robert Cecil at London of *Principal navigations*, III (1600), emphasizing the prospects of North American settlement, referring to 'my worshipfull friend M. doctor Gilbert' (William Gilbert), and acknowledging help from John Pory. (Sig. A2–3v; reprinted, Taylor, *Hakluyts*, II, 469–74.)

1600

Principal navigations, III, was published before the end of the year.

1600

Thomas Windebank, reporting to Sir Robert Cecil his dealings with the Queen, stated that 'I attempted the signing of the bill for Mr. Hackluit, recommended by my Lord Admiral [the earl of Nottingham] and yourself, but had the repulse with answer that she would not grant any prebend in Westminster till they fell void'. (Without date, Cecil MS 83/48, calendared in H.M.C., *Cecil MSS*, X, 436–7.)

c. February 1601

15 January 1601. John Pory, in his dedication to Sir Robert Cecil of his translation of Johannes Leo Africanus, *A geographical historie of Africa* (1600), commended Hakluyt as 'the onely man that mooued me to translate it'. Hakluyt added a prefatory piece (the only time he did this), 'An appro⁄bation of the historie'. (Sig. e 5r; reprinted, Taylor, *Hakluyts*, II, 475–6; entered in the Stationers' Register, 1 September 1600 (Arber, *Transcript*, III, 64).)

January 1601

29 January 1601. Hakluyt attended the meeting of the governor and com⁄mittee of the East India Company ('Mr Hacklett the historiographer of the viages of the East Indies, beinge here before the Comitties and having read vnto them out of his notes and bookes divers instruccions for provisions of Jewelles. was required to sett downe in wryting a note of the principall places in the East Indies wher Trade is to be had to thend the same may be vsed for the better instruccion of our factors in the said voyage'). (Stevens, *Dawn of British trade*, pp. 123–4.)

February 1601

Hakluyt wrote notes for the East India Company on 'The chiefe places where sondry sortes of Spices do growe in the East Indies . . . A remem⁄

Fig. 16   Hakluyt's autograph Notes on East Indian commodities, 1601.

brance of what is good to bring from the Indyas into Spayne . . . Notes of certayne comodities in good request in the East Indies, the Malucoes, and China . . .' (Bodleian Library, Arch. Selden B. 8, ff. 84–96 (ff. 93–6 being in Hakluyt's hand); printed *Divers voyages*, ed. J. W. Jones, pp. 151–71; partly printed, Taylor, *Hakluyts*, II, 476–82; see Stevens, *Dawn of British trade*, p. 124.)

c. February 1601

'Noates of remembrances for yᵉ Right Honorable yᵉ Lordes of her Maiestes moste Honorable Privie Councell presented by yᵉ Merchannts entendinge a voiage to yᵉ Easte Indies', were drawn up, most probably on the basis of a draft by Hakluyt, after his report on 29 January and his subsequent com/ mentaries. (Henry E. Huntington Library, Ellesmere MS 2360 (so far un/ published); another manuscript, entitled 'Certaiyne Reesons why the English Mercants may trade into the East Indies', is in P.R.O., S.P. Col., C.O. 1/1, 17 (from which, probably at second hand, Taylor, *Hakluyts*, II, 465–8, is derived); see Stevens, *Dawn of British trade in the East Indies*, p. 124.)

February 1601

16 February 1601, reward of £10 by the governor and committee of the East India Company to Hakluyt 'for his travailes taken in instruccíons and advyses touching the preparing of the voiage and for his former advyses in setting the voyage in hand the Last yere', with 30s 'for 3 mappes by him provided'. (Stevens, *Dawn of British trade*, p. 141.)

October 1601

29 October 1601. Hakluyt, dedicating at London his translation of Antonio Galvano (Galvão), *The discoueries of the world*, to Sir Robert Cecil, reported that Walter Cope, 'a gentleman of rare and excellent partes', had urged him when preparing his *Principal navigations*, 'to draw them into a short sum, adding that in his opinion that course woulde prooue most acceptable to the world, especially to men of great action and employment', but that he then decided 'I could not conueniently alter my course'. (Sig. A2r; reprinted Taylor, *Hakluyts*, II, 483–6.) In the dedication Hakluyt described himself as 'Your Honors Chaplein' (sig. A4r), no other authority having been found for this appointment.

c. December 1601

The discoueries of the world probably appeared before the end of the year. (Entered in Stationers' Register, 30 September 1601, Arber, *Transcript*, II, 192.)

1601 or later

Hakluyt bought a discourse of Brazil by Fernão Cardim from Francis Cooke. Purchas (*Pilgrimage* (1614), p. 842) refers to it as 'a discourse of Brasil ... taken from a Portugall Frier, and by Francis Cooke sold to Master Hakluit', but in his *Pilgrimes* (IV (1625), 1289) says it was 'taken by one Frances Cooke of Dartmouth in a Voyage outward bound for Brasil, An. 1601. who sold the same to Master Hacket [a misprint for Hakluyt] for twenty shillings; by whose procurement it was translated out of Portugall into English'. (See pp. 82–3, above.)

1602

January 1602. Thomas Harriot recommended that the 'Booke of Voyages', namely *Principal navigations*, be carried by Samuel Mace on his forthcoming North American voyage. (B.M., Additional MS 4788, f. 417v; Quinn, 'Thomas Hariot and the Virginia Voyages of 1602', *William and Mary Quarterly*, 3rd series, XXVII (1970), 273.)

1601–2

William Walker, in his dedication to Sir Thomas Smith of Jacob van Neck, *The iournall ... of the voyage ... by eight shippes ... from Amsterdam the first day of March, 1598* (1601), described the translation as 'seconded by the perswasion of M. Richard Hakluyt, a man for his matchles industrie in collecting the English Voyages most incomparably wel deseruing of this state'. Walker, like Hakluyt, told Smith that he was concerned to provide material for the guidance of 'your East Indie voyage', the Dutch having gained their knowledge from English accounts of voyages to the East: 'All these Voyages, and sundrie other important discourses of the East Indies, Pegu, China, the Malucos, Philippinas and Iapan, are to be found in the second and third volumes of M. Hakluyts English Voyages.' (Sig. ¶2v; the book was entered in the Stationers' Register on 16 January 1601 (Arber, *Transcript*, III, 178).)

May 1602–November 1616

The records of Westminster Abbey contain a uniquely detailed record of Hakluyt's activities during the last fourteen years of his life. The Chapter Act Books (volumes for 1542–1609, and 1609–42) contain a signed and dated record of his presence at Chapter meetings. These comprise 4 May 1602 (Act Book, 1542–1609, f. 268), 3 December 1602 (f. 269), 23 May 1603 (f. 270), 27 July 1603 (f. 270v), 3 December 1603 (ff. 274v, 275v, two signatures), 10 May 1604 (f. 276v), 4 December 1604 (f. 284v), 30 April

1605 (f. 285v), 3 December 1605 (f. 286v), 4 December 1605 (f. 287), 4 December 1606 (f. 292), 4 May 1607 (f. 293), 3–4 December 1607 (f. 294v), 15 February 1608 (f. 295), 3 May 1608 (f. 296, two signatures), 7 December 1608 (f. 297v), 15 May 1609 (f. 298): 5 December 1609 (Act Book, 1609–42, f. 1v), 25 January 1610 (f. 2), 2 March 1610 (f. 2), 6 March 1610 (f. 2), 7 May 1610 (ff. 3, 3v, two signatures), 27, 30 June 1610 (f. 4v, two signatures), 3–5 December 1610 (f. 6), 24 April 1611 (f. 7), 4 December 1611 (f. 8), 11 May 1612 (f. 9), 5 December 1612 (f. 10, two signatures), 5 May 1613 (f. 11), 6 December 1613 (f. 12v), 25 May 1614 (f. 13), 6 December 1614 (f. 13v), 11 May 1615 (f. 14v), 15 May 1615 (f. 15), 6 December 1615 (f. 15v, 16v, two signatures), 3 May 1616 (f. 17v). He was absent from the meeting of 19 May 1606 (Act Book, 1542–1609, f. 289v), and was dead by the time of the meeting of 7 December 1616 (Act Book, 1609–42, f. 19).

September 1602–November 1616

Richard Hakluyt signs, with other members of the Chapter of Westminster Abbey, the annual accounts of the receiver general, the steward and treasurer, of which almost continuous series remain amongst the muniments of Westminster Abbey, though the dates of the signatures are not recorded. The stewards' accounts usually record his payment for commons. The treasurers' accounts are of more interest: they record both his payment for commons, ranging from £8 to £10 a year, and also his stipend of £28 or £28 5s as prebendary. During the years 1603–5, when he acted as arch-deacon, 1608–9 as steward, and 1614–15 as treasurer, he receives the additional fee of £4 per annum. He last signed the account for 1614–15, but the account for 1615–16 made provision for his commons and his fee. (Westminster Muniments, 1602–3 (33656); 1603–4 (his name is omitted from the list of prebendaries but the total remains the same for the twelve (£334), and as he signed the account he presumably received payment) (33657); 1604–5 (33658); 1605–6 (the duplicate only, not signed) (33659); 1606–7 (33660); 1607–8 (33661); 1609–10 (33662); 1610–11 (33663); 1611–12 (33664); 1612–13 (both copies, one with the signatures copied) (33665, 33666); 1612–13 (both copies, one unsigned) (33667, 33668); 1613–14 (33669); 1614–15 when he was treasurer (33670); 1615–16, not signed by him (33671); 1616–17, without mention of him (33672).)

May 1602

4 May 1602. Hakluyt was installed as a prebendary (fourth stall) of West-minster Abbey. (J. Le Neve, *Fasti ecclesiae anglicane*, III (1854), 353.)

4 May 1602. Hakluyt first attended the meeting of the Chapter. (Chapter Book, 1542–1609, f. 268.)

1602

John Brereton, *A briefe and true relation of the discouerie of the north part of Virginia* (1602), appeared late in 1602 and went into an enlarged edition of the same date (but possibly appearing early in 1603). It is highly probable that Hakluyt supplied some materials, ancillary to the narrative, for it, but the internal evidence suggests that it was put together by Edward Hayes and, probably, John Brereton himself.

3 December 1603

Richard Hakluyt appointed archdeacon of Westminster Abbey. ('Item it is decided yᵗ master Hakluyt shall be Archdeacon', Chapter Book, 1542–1609, f. 275v.) His fee was £4.

c. January to March 1603

Hakluyt helped to induce merchants at Bristol, after various meetings, to finance an expedition to North America, under Martin Pring. He went to London with John Angel and Robert Salterne to obtain a licence from Sir Walter Ralegh which was granted. *Speedwell*, 50 tons, and *Discoverer*, 26 tons, left the King Road of Bristol on 20 March and returned after a visit to Maine and Massachusetts, *Discoverer* in midSeptember and *Speedwell* on 2 October. Hakluyt, clearly, revised the narrative, which is assigned to Pring but in fact was written by another. (Purchas, *Pilgrimes*, IV (1625), 1654–5, the narrative reaching Purchas from Hakluyt.)

After 1603

Sir Walter Ralegh somehow obtained after 1603 João de Castro's 'Roteiro de dom Ioham de Castro da viagee que fizeram os Portugueses defaindia Goa ate Soez', an illustrated rutter written by Gaspar Aloisius, 1543, which, Ralegh said, 'I haue giuen Mʳ· Richard Hakluit to publish'. (The rutter is B.M., Cotton MS, Tiberius D. IX, ff. 1–92 (it is not known how it got into Sir Robert Cotton's hands); Ralegh, *Historie of the world* (1614), bk. 2, ch. 3, sect. 8; Purchas, *Pilgrimes*, I (1625), 1122; R. A. Skelton, 'Ralegh as a geographer', *Virginia Magazine*, LXXI (1963), 148.)

March 1604

18 March 1604. Hakluyt (and a number of Portuguese resident in London) learnt from a Portuguese pilot, Simão Fernandes of Lisbon, that he heard

in Peru in 1600 an expedition had been sent to the Philippines which met with islands near the Solomon Islands. (Purchas, *Pilgrimes*, IV (1625), 1432; printed, Taylor, *Hakluyts*, II, 489. He does not seem to have been the pilot of this name who was active in England, *c.* 1573–89.)

March 1604

30 March 1604. Giving his age as 'about 52 years' and stating he had been a widower for 'about 7 years', Hakluyt, described as one of the chaplains of the Savoy, applied for a licence to marry Frances Smithe, now of St Lawrence in the Jewry, widow of William Smith, formerly of St Botolph without Bishopsgate, the marriage to be celebrated at St Michael Wood St. (G. J. Armytage and J. L. Chester, edd., *Allegations for marriage licences issued by the bishop of London, 1530–1610* (1887), p. 286 (Harleian Society Publications, XXV); Parks, *Hakluyt*, p. 255 (noting that the marriage is not recorded at St Michael's).)

4 December 1604

Richard Hakluyt was re-appointed archdeacon of Westminster Abbey. ('It is decided that master Hakluyt shalbe Archdeacon for this next yeare', Chapter Book, 1542–1609, f. 284v.)

Late 1604 or early 1605

Hakluyt had conversations on Pacific voyages, as he related some two years later, with Luis Tribaldos de Toledo, Latin secretary to Juan de Tassis, Conde de Villamediana, Spanish ambassador in London. (Purchas, *Pilgrimes*, IV (1625), 1432, 1565; Taylor, *Hakluyts*, II, 489.)

1605

William Camden, *Remaines concerning Britain* (1605), p. 170, discussing John Oxenham's exploits, refers the reader to 'the Discoueries [*PN* (1598–1600)] of the learned and industrious M. Rich. Hakluit'.

1605

That *Principal navigations* was in use is shown from [Nathaniel Butter?], *Sir Thomas Smithes voiage and entertainment in Rushia* (1605), where it is said the Volga is known through 'the worthy labors of Master Richard Hakluyte', and Sir Jerome Horsey's activities there are cited from 'M. Hackluyts workes'. (Sig. D3v, Ii.)

July 1605

7 July 1605. Luis Tribaldos de Toledo wrote to Hakluyt from Valladolid on Oñate's expedition of 1599, and of work which a mutual friend, Andrés García Cespedes, was doing on Pacific voyages. (Purchas, *Pilgrimes*, IV, 1565–7, apparently translated by Hakluyt from the Latin; Taylor, *Hakluyts*, II, 490–1.)

October 1605

31 October. Hakluyt ('Mr. Hackelett') and Spero Pettingarre dined at the Mitre (Sir William Monson was there, and a number of persons implicated or possibly implicated in the Gunpowder Plot). They afterwards went to Pettingarre's chamber to peruse a rutter of Sir Francis Drake's works of navigation and so parted. (H.M.C., *Cecil*, XVIII (1938), 522, from Cecil MS 112/160.)

c. 1605

Joseph Hall, *Mundus alter et idem* [1605 ?], bk. 3, cp. 5, in the English version, *The discouery of a new world*, translated by J. Healey [1609 ?], p. 161, makes a possible reference to Hakluyt and Ralegh: it reads 'Hacksters, who are ministers both to his [that of the 'Duke of Cholerikoye'] furie and gluttony' (though Duke Swash-buckliero, duke of Cholericoye, is 'the model & Embleme of all tyranny' and the Hacksters make up his guard of 10,000 men !).

April 1606

10 April 1606. Hakluyt (as 'Richard Hackluit Clarke prebendarie of Westminster') is third among the grantees in the Virginia Company charter. (P.R.O., Patent Roll 4 James I, part 15, C. 66/1709 (printed accurately in P. L. Barbour, *The Jamestown voyages*, I (1969), 24–44); the Chancery Warrant, C. 82/1729, no. 1, in which his name also appeared was dated 5 April.)

1606

William Warner, *A continuance of Albions England* (1606), commended his readers to Hakluyt. In the complete *Albions England* (1612) we have (in the celebration of Anthony Jenkinson and other Muscovy Company worthies), 'For, sauing of discouerers we purpose not to dwell, / Els would we here reuiue, but that through Hakluits pen they liue, / (To him, your fames sweet Trumpeter, yee English Garlands giue).' (Bk. 11, cp. 68, p. 288.) Also 'Omitted men and named Men, and Lands (not here, indeede, / So written of as they deserue) at large in Hakluit reede.' (Bk. 12, cp. 70, p. 295.) Warner may have been the earliest to identify the book with the man.

1606

Michael Drayton's *Poemes lyrick and pastorall* (entered in Stationers' Register, 19 April 1606 (Arber, *Transcript*, III, 320)) contained 'the Virginian voyage' (ode II, sig. C5r), in which we have: 'thy Voyages attend / Indus-trious *Hakluit* / whose Reading shall inflame / men to seeke fame; / and much commend / to aftertimes thy wit.' (See Michael Drayton, *Poems*, ed. J. Buxton (1953), p. 125.)

November 1606

24 November 1606. Licence for five years to Richard Hakluyt (with Robert Hunt) to go to Virginia while retaining canonries at Westminster and Bristol, his rectory at Wetheringsett and his chaplaincy at the Savoy. (P.R.O., Patent Roll, 4 James I, part 14, C. 66/1708 (Latin): partly translated in P. L. Barbour, ed., *The Jamestown voyages*, I (1969), 62–4.)

December 1606

5 December 1606. Richard Hakluyt witnesses an act of the Chapter of Westminster Abbey in favour of Richard Neile, bishop of Rochester, and his wife Dorothy. (Westminster Abbey Muniments 9382.)

5 December 1606. Hakluyt also witnesses an indenture between Richard Neile, bishop of Rochester, and dean of Westminster, and the Chapter, granting Robert Knowlys lodgings over the east cloister, 'Whereof some parte was some tyme employed for a library'. (Westminster Abbey Muniments 18093.)

May 1607

4 May 1607. Richard Hakluyt witnesses an indenture between the dean of Westminster and the Chapter, leasing the rectory of St Botolph-without-Aldersgate to Thomas Mountforde, doctor of physic and prebendary. (Westminster Abbey Muniments 13511.)

July 1607

30 July 1607. William Keeling, bound for the East Indies in the *Dragon*, says: 'We had some speech of Sierra Leona. I hauing formerly read well of the place, sent for the Booke [*PN* (1598–1600)], and shewed it my Master, who as my self, tooke good liking to the place.' (Purchas, *Pilgrimes*, I, iii, 188.)

1608

Hudson's voyage up the east Greenland coast to Spitsbergen led him, according to Purchas, to call a point close to 80° N. lat., 'Hakluyts Head-land' (now Amsterdam Island). (Purchas, *Pilgrimes*, III (1625), 464; it was sighted by Robert Fotherby in 1615, *ibid.*, III, 728.)

1608

In the 'subsidy of Armour' in Suffolk, 1608, 'Mr. Richard Hakluyt' is rated under those assigned to supply 'Petronelles'. (Anthony Harison, *The Registrum Vagum*, II, 256 (Norfolk Record Society, 1964).)

September 1608

29 September 1608. Hakluyt entered as a free tenant of the manor of Stoke, lordship of Leominster, Herefordshire: 'Eaton – Richard Hackluyt pro messuagio ijs. viijd.' (P.R.O., Exchequer, Land Revenue, Miscellaneous Books, L.R. 2/217, f. 183; Parks, *Hakluyt*, p. 257.)

29 September 1608–28 September 1609

Richard Hakluyt served as steward of Westminster Abbey. (The minutes of the meeting of the Chapter on 7 December 1608 (Chapter Book, 1542–1609, f. 297v) neglected to record the offices allotted for the year 1608-9.) His account as steward (Westminster Abbey Muniments 33927) was signed by him and he added to it in his own hand a 10-line memorandum on dealings in wheat.

3 December 1608

Richard Hakluyt was appointed with other members of the Chapter of Westminster Abbey to negotiate with William Smith, the Abbey's tenant of the manor of Chiswick, for a new lease which would give the Abbey 'part of the mansion house . . . to the vse of the College . . . suche composition' to be made by 'master Deane and Doctor Mountford and master Hackluit' (Chapter Book, 1542–1609, f. 296).

April 1609

15 April 1609. Hakluyt signed his dedication to the council and adventurers of the Virginia Company, 'From my lodging in the Colledge of Westminster', of his translation of The Gentleman of Elvas, *Virginia richly valued*. (Reprinted, Taylor, *Hakluyts*, II, 499–503.) He saw this narrative of the expedition of Hernando de Soto as providing justification for the Virginia settlement.

1609

In his dedication to Sir Thomas Smith of G. de Veer, *The true and perfect description of three voyages* (1609), the translator, William Phillip, began:

'Being intreated by some of my Friends, and principally by M. Richard Hakluyt (a diligent obseruer of all Proceedings in this nature) to Translate and publish these three yeares Trauelles and Discoueries, of the Hollanders to the North-east . . .' (Sig. A2r: translation had already been entered on 13 June 1598, but may not have been proceeded with; see p. 311, above.)

P. Erondelle (*Noua Francia* (1609), sig. ¶¶ 2v.) thanks Hakluyt 'for the first procuring of this translation'.

May 1609

23 May 1609. Hakluyt was named in the second Virginia Company charter. (P.R.O., C. 66/1796, m. 5; Alexander Brown, *The genesis of the United States*, II (1890), 215.)

1609–16

Hakluyt held two shares of £12 10s each, rated at £21, in the Virginia Company, which came to his son Edmond at his death and which were transferred by him to John Moore in 1621. (S. M. Kingsbury, ed., *Records of the Virginia Company of London*, III (1933), 84, 326.)

1609 or later

Hakluyt translated Grotius' *Mare Liberum* (Amsterdam, 1608). The MS was originally bound in parchment, entitled 'Mare liberum / The free Sea' (now in modern binding with patch of vellum preserved), 26 leaves; f. 2 has, in seventeenth-century hand 'Translated into English by Mr Richard Hackluyt &c.' The heading on f. 3 is 'The free sea / or / A disputation concerning the right wch ye Hollanders ought to haue, to the Indian Marchandize for trading'. (Text runs ff. 3–24v. In Hakluyt's hand throughout, a fair copy. Inner Temple MS 529. See H.M.C., *11th report*, app., pt. VII, p. 234; Parks, *Hakluyt*, p. 257; extracts printed in Taylor, *Hakluyts*, II, 497–9.) It is possible that Hakluyt made the translation for the East India Company.

March 1611

14 March 1611. The widow of George Bishop entered his stock and rights. 'His parte of Englishe voyages 3 vol.' (i.e. *PN* (1598–1600)) in the Stationers' Register. (Arber, *Transcript*, III, 454.)

April 1611

4 April 1611. East India Company's commission to Captain John Saris: 'Item for the better comforte and recreation of such of our Factors as are recidinge in the Indies: Wee haue sent . . . Master Hackluites Voyadges to

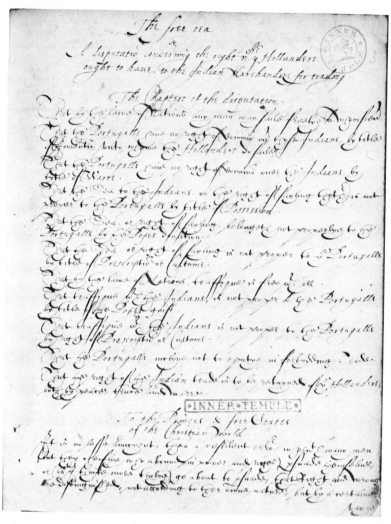

Fig. 17   First page of Hakluyt's autograph manuscript of his translation of Grotius'
Mare liberum, 'The free sea'.

recreate their spirittes with varietie of historie.' (*The first letter book of the East India Company, 1600–19*, ed. G. Birdwood and W. Foster (1893), p. 419.)

1611

Edmond (or Edmund) Hakluit, Richard's son, matriculated pensioner at Trinity College, Cambridge, 1611; Queen's scholar from Westminster School, 1612; B.A. 1615–16; fellow 1618; M.A. 1619. (Welch, *A list*, p. 26; *Admissions to Trinity College, Cambridge*, ed. W. W. Rouse Ball and J. A. Venn, II (1913), 251; Parks, *Hakluyt*, p. 258.)

July–August 1611

24 July and 16 August 1611. Josias Logan wrote to Hakluyt from Pechora, giving an account of the Samoyeds and of the prospects of contacts with Cathay. (Purchas, *Pilgrimes*, III (1625), 546–7, the Muscovy Company expedition having on 17 June named a river 'Hakluyts River', *ibid.*, 531, located on Kolguyev Ostrov (see Parks, *Hakluyt*, p. 258).)

July–September 1612

19 July 1612. Richard Hakluyt was presented to the rectory of Gedney, Lincolnshire, by his brother Oliver (patron for this turn by grant of Queen Anne, 1 August 1604). He was admitted at Buckden, Huntingdonshire (by William Barlow, bishop of Lincoln), and was to be inducted at Gedney on 24 September following. His age was given as 60 (confirming a birth date of 1552), and he was stated to have been ordained deacon and priest by John Piers, bishop of Salisbury [1577–89]. (Lincolnshire Record Office, Diocesan Records, Presentation Deed no. 34.)

July 1612

26 July 1612. Hakluyt was named in the charter to the North-west Passage Company. (P.R.O., S.P., Sign Manuals, S.P. 39/2, 30; *Cal. S.P. Col., East Indies, China and Japan, 1513–1616*, p. 240.)

August 1612

20 August 1612. Hakluyt's will conveyed most of his property to his son and heir Edmond Hakluit and to his wife Frances Hackluit (manor of Bridge Place, Suffolk, bought from John Scriven, late of Barbican, tene-ments in Leominster Ore; tenements in the north-west end of Tothill St., Westminster, near the White Hart Tavern, bought from Mr Line), with

legacies to his brother Oliver Hakluyt, Joan, Oliver's daughter, his sister Katherine Morer (or Moore), living in Holborn, John and Barbery Morer, her children, Mistress Longe, dwelling in the Tower, Thomas Peter and his wife, the Rev. Edward Riggs, Hakluyt's curate Mr Colman, his sister Bacon, his servant Thomas Button, Lionel Pearson, Mary Upson, the townsmen of Wetheringsett and Brockford for the poor, the College of Westminster (Westminster Abbey), furnishings in his chamber in the Savoy to the Savoy, and his lodgings and chamber at Bristol to the College (Chapter) there, Thomas Hakluyt his cousin, Oliver Cogram, Mistress Dorothe Patrickson, and John Davyes her son, Richard Ireland, Mr Wilson, and Michael Locke the younger. John Davyes to be supervisor of his will; his son Edmond sole executor; Edward Riggs, John Colman and David Allshais, witnesses; signed as parson of Wetheringsett, and apparently made there. (P.R.O., Prob. 12/12 (1616), 109 (formerly P.C.C. 109 Cope); printed in J. W. Jones, ed., *Divers voyages* (1850), pp. 145–50; reprinted in Taylor, *Hakluyts*, II, 506–9.)

October 1612

16 October 1612. At the manorial Court of the Manor of Bridge Place, Coddenham, Suffolk, Richard Hakluyt, described as professor of theology, and his son Edmond, were confirmed by the steward, John Lea, to be in possession of the manor. (Bridge Place Court Rolls, 1612, extracted (c.1926) by the Rev. V. Redstone, for Professor G. B. Parks (by whom the extract was given to me), when it was in the hands of Steward, Rouse, Vulliamy and Son (now Steward, Vulliamy and Watkins), solicitors, Ipswich; it has not been deposited with the later records of the manor in the Ipswich and East Suffolk Record Office.)

1612

Michael Lok, dedicating his translation of Peter Martyr's *De orbe nouo* (1612) to Sir Julius Caesar (in Latin), referred to the encouragement and exhortation to do so he had received from Richard Hakluyt (*idque suasu, & hortatu ornatissimi viri Richardi Hackluit, de Republica bene meriti*). (Sig. A3v.)

1613

Samuel Purchas in the first edition of his *Pilgrimage* (1613), pp. 625–6, expresses thanks for information by various people on Newfoundland 'all whose Discourses and experiments hereof, Master Hakluit hath collected and bestowed on the World'. (Repeated in 1614, p. 747; 1617, p. 930; 1626, p. 822.)

1614

At the visitation by the bishop of Lincoln (Richard Neile), Richard Hakluyt, rector of Gedney, was absent and was excused. (Lincolnshire Record Office, Lincoln Diocesan Records, Liber Cleri, 1614, f. 57.)

January 1614

Sir Julius Caesar compiling notes to refute the Dutch claim to priority in whaling at Greenland cites naming of Hakluyts Foreland. ('10. Ian. 1613[-14]. The question betweene th'Ambassadour of the States, & yᵉ marchants of Muscovy company touching yᵉ trade of Greenland . . . This land in a chronicle of Amsterdam is called Hacluits foreland. Pontanus. - 1611.' B.M., Lansdowne MS 142, f. 387.)

22 January 1614. Meeting of Court of East India Company. 'A book of dialogues, heretofore translated into Latin by the Hollanders, and printed with the Malayan tongue, Mr. Hakluyt having now turned the Latin into English, and supposed very fit for the factors to learn, ordered to be printed before the departure of the ships.' (*Cal. S.P. Col., E.I., China and Japan, 1513–1616*, p. 272.)

March 1614

Augustine Spalding's (or Spaulding's) revision of Hakluyt's translation of Gothard Arthus, *Dialogues in the English and Malaiane languages* (entered in Stationers' Register, Arber, *Transcript*, III, 249, 9 March 1614), published, with reference to Hakluyt in dedication to Sir Thomas Smith. (Sig. ¶2–2v; extracted in Taylor, *Hakluyts*, II, 510.) Spalding commends Smith for erecting the lecture in navigation and for employing skilful mathematicians and geographers: 'Lastly, you haue caused these Dialogues of the languages of the Isle of Madagascar and of the Malaian tongues, presented vnto you by Master Richard Hackluyt, a singular furtherer of all new discoueries and honest trades, to be set forth in our English tongue.'

1613 or 1614

Captain John Saris, commander of the East India Company's Eighth Voyage, acquired a map of China at Bantam late in 1612. He may have sent it home with the *Hector* and the *Thomas*, which returned in 1613, or brought it himself in 1614. Hakluyt acquired it and it passed to Purchas, who wrote (*Pilgrimes*, III, 401): 'The originall Map, whence this present was taken and contracted, was by Captain Saris (whose industrie and acts haue both heere and elsewhere enriched this worke) gotten at Bantam of a

Chinese, in taking a distresse for debts owing to the English Merchants ...
Master Hakluyt procured it of the Captaine, professing his intent to giue it
to Prince Henry of glorious memory, who being suddenly aduanced to a
higher view in Heauen, and Master Hakluyt following, this Map came to
my hand, who sought to expresse my loue to the publike in communicating
what I could thereof.' (Purchas is wool-gathering, since Prince Henry had
died in 1612, long before Hakluyt could have had the map.)

1614

Ralph Hanson (or Handson), who had been named in the 1612 charter of
the North-west Passage Company, declared that Hakluyt persuaded him to
publish his translation of Bartholomew Pitiscus, *Trigonometry* (1614). (Sig.
A2v; E. G. R. Taylor, *Mathematical practitioners of Tudor and Stuart England*
(1954), p. 203 (*sub* Handson); Taylor, *Hakluyts*, II, 510.) In his dedication
to Sir Thomas Smith and John Wolstenholme he thanks them for endowing
the lecture in navigation: he himself translated Pitiscus for 'some priuate
friends, at whose request, (and Mr. Richard Hakluit his earnest persuasion,
who hath deserued well of our Nation:) I was afterwards induced to perfect
and publish'.

1614

Samuel Purchas in the second edition of his *Pilgrimage* acknowledges a
number of documents and narrative sources made available to him by
Hakluyt since the appearance of the first edition. 'I acknowledge that
Ramusius and M. Hakluit, in their Books of Voyages, haue beene two
Libraries vnto me of many Nauigations and Discoueries heere mentioned:
and now in this Edition I haue beene much beholden to M. Hakluit for
many written Treatises in this kinde.' (Sig. A 5.) Again 'Master Hakluit
... hath beene as Admirall, holding out the light vnto me in these Seas, &
as diligent a guide by land ... And now his helpes in this second Edition,
haue much more obliged me (that I say not thee) vnto his laborious Collections; for which our English Nauigations, both for memoriall of passed,
incouragement of present, and instructions to the future, are ... indebted
beyond recompence: and your poore Pilgrime ... doth according to his
wit, without hacking, professe Hakluit (in this kinde) his greatest Benefactor' (pp. 782-3).

1614-15

6 December 1514. Hakluyt was elected treasurer of Westminster Abbey.
The minutes of the Chapter on 6 December include the item: 'Officers for
this year 1614 ... *Maste*r Hacluyt Threasurer', the election being nominally

for the year 29 September 1614–29 September 1615. (Chapter Book of Westminster Abbey, 1609–42, f. 13v.)

Account (in Latin) of Richard Hakluyt, prebendary, as treasurer of Westminster Abbey, 29 September 1614–29 September 1615. He pays in for commons, 'De Magistro Hakluyt – x^{li}' (f. 1r): he receives for his stipend as prebendary £32 5s, 'Et in Feodum Magistri Hakluyt Thesaurii ibidem ad iiij^{li}. per annum iiij^{li}.' (f. 2r). He signs with the other pre-bendaries, without date, on f. 8v. (Westminster Abbey Muniments 33670.)

Book of accounts, 1614–15, beginning with 'The receptes of Certaine Arrerages of rentes'. F. 110r is headed 'Liuere money / Hackluit. Money paid to master Treasurer of Westminster Colledge for one whole yeare vizt. from Michaelmas 1514 vntill Michaelmas 1615 as followeth vizt.' [actually 1 December 1614–30 November 1615]. Richard Hakluyt signs individually each item (64 signatures in all, exceptionally strong and consistent): 2, 19, 20, 24 December; 9 January; 20 February; 1 March; 3, 7, 9, April; 4, 9, 13, 19, 25, 27 May; 9, 22, 27, 29, 30 June; 4, 21, 22 July; 11, 14 August; 13, 23 September; 12, 20, 21, 22, 26, 27 October; 11, 13, 15, 16, 21, 23, 25, 28, 30 November; with from one to three signed items on each date. He signs at the end, without date (f. 117v), with other members of the Chapter. (Westminster Abbey Muniments 33636.)

July–August 1615

A Muscovy Company vessel under Robert Fotherby, exploring off the east Greenland coast, sighted land which was named 'Sir Thomas Smiths Iland' (now Jan Mayen), and at 71° N. saw a great mountain (Beeren-berg, 8,000 ft), to which the name 'Mount Hakluyt' was given. (Purchas, *Pilgrimes*, III (1625), 730; Parks, *Hakluyt*, pp. 210–11.)

1615

Before Hakluyt's death, annalists referring to the English voyages commonly indicate that further materials can be found in *The principal navigations*.

William Camden (*Annales* (1615), pt. i, p. 470) says of the voyages of Drake and Cavendish, 'Si particulares desideres, adeas Anglorum nauiga-tiones tribus voluminibus à Richardo Hakluito diligentissime descriptas.'

Edmond Howes, continuing John Stow (*Annales . . . continued by Edmond Howes* (1615), p. 942), says of the Virginia voyages 'And thus much at this time, & in this place, touching this plantation shall suffice, by reason Maister Hackluit, Captaine Smith, and others, haue written sundry discourses thereof.' (But for Howes he was not alone, but one among a number of authorities.)

July 1616

5 July 1616. William Baffin, exploring Baffin Bay, named 'Hakluits Ile' between 'Whale Sound' and 'Sir Thomas Smiths Sound' at 78° N. (Purchas, *Pilgrimes*, III, 847. It appears on the map of the Arctic published by Henry Hondius at Amsterdam in 1636, reproduced in Cumming, Skelton and Quinn, *Discovery of North America* (1971), p. 299.)

November 1616

23 November 1616. Hakluyt died. (William Camden, in his brief 'Annals, 1602–23', in Smith, *V. cl. Camdeni . . . epistolae* (1691), p. 24 (sig. 3H iv), gives 'Nov. 23. Richardus Hackluyt Praebendarius Monasteriensis obiit'. Surprisingly this is also the date of the grant of probate of his will (see pp. 326–7, above), so that one or other date might seem to be mistaken.)

23 November 1616. Probate of Hakluyt's will granted to his son, Edmond. (P.R.O., Prob. 12/12 (1616), 109, formerly P.C.C. 109 Cope; Taylor, *Hakluyts*, II, 509.)

26 November 1616. Hakluyt was buried in Westminster Abbey. (Westminster Abbey Register in a corrupt entry made after 1660 gives '1626 [*sic*] Nov. 26. Richard Hackler, Prebendary of this Church' [in the Abbey]. J. L. Chester, *Registers of Westminster Abbey* (1876), p. 113; H. P. Stanley, 'A note on Hakluyt's grave', *Notes and Queries*, 7th series, VIII (1889), 108, 215 (location unknown).)

1617

Richard Harvey wrote in his copy of Hakluyt's edition of Peter Martyr's *De orbe nouo* (1587) 'R^d. Hackluyt is deade, 1616. 1617.' (B.M., catalogue number C45 b. 10.)